BRIAN K. VAUGHAN
WRITER

STEVE SKROCE
ARTIST

MATT HOLLINGSWORTH
COLORIST

FONOGRAFIKS
LETTERING & DESIGN

RICHARD ISANOVE
COVER COLORIST CHAPTERS 4-6

MATHIEU CHALIFOUX
TRANSLATION ASSISTANCE

ERIC STEPHENSON
COORDINATOR

image

imagecomics.com

O Canada!

Our home and native land!

True patriot love in all thy sons command.

With glowing hearts we see thee rise,

The True North strong and free!

From far and wide,

O Canada, we stand on guard for thee.

God keep our land glorious and free!

O Canada, we stand on guard for thee.

O Canada,

WE STAND ON GUARD

for thee.

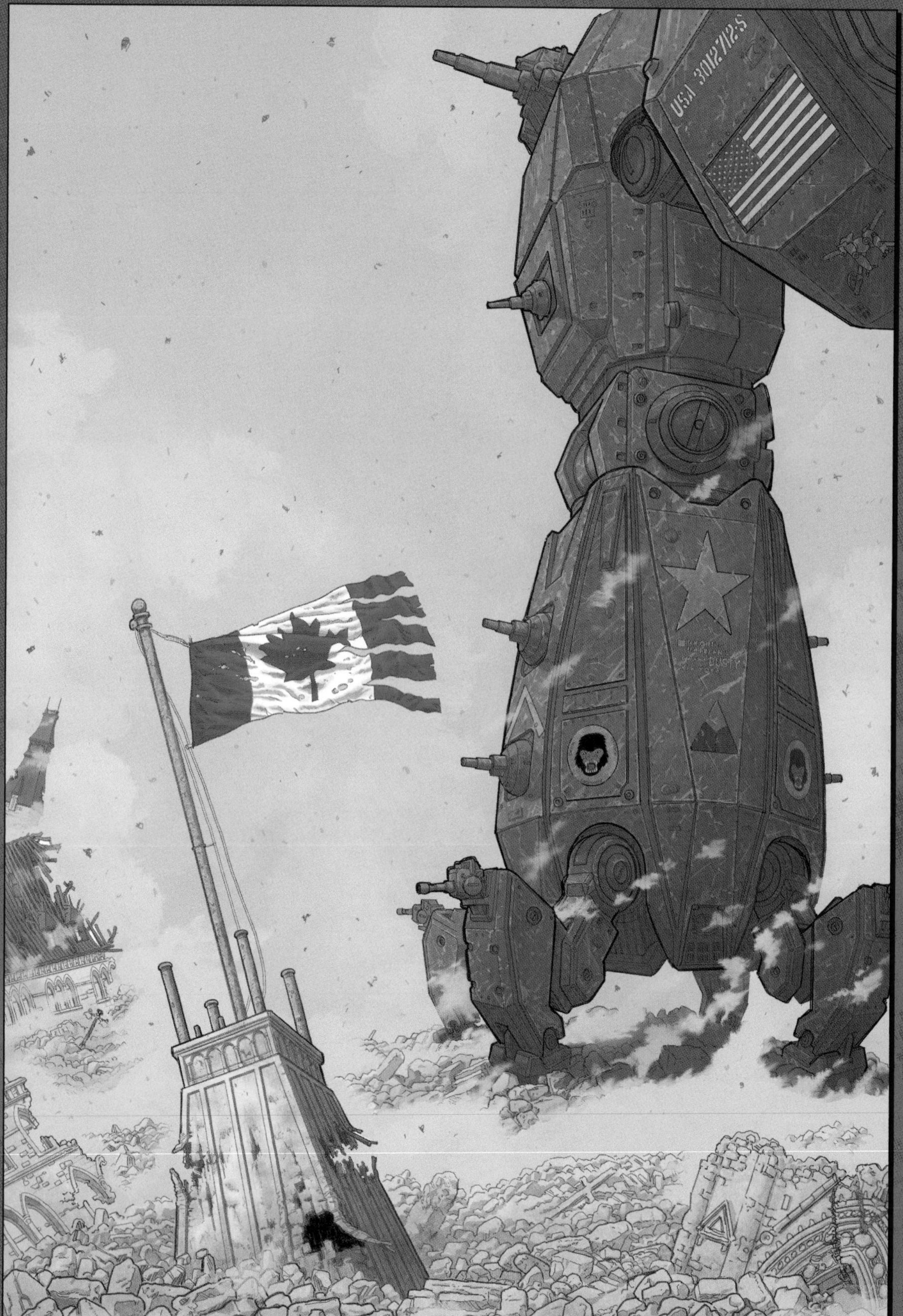
USA 3012712:S

CHAPTER ONE

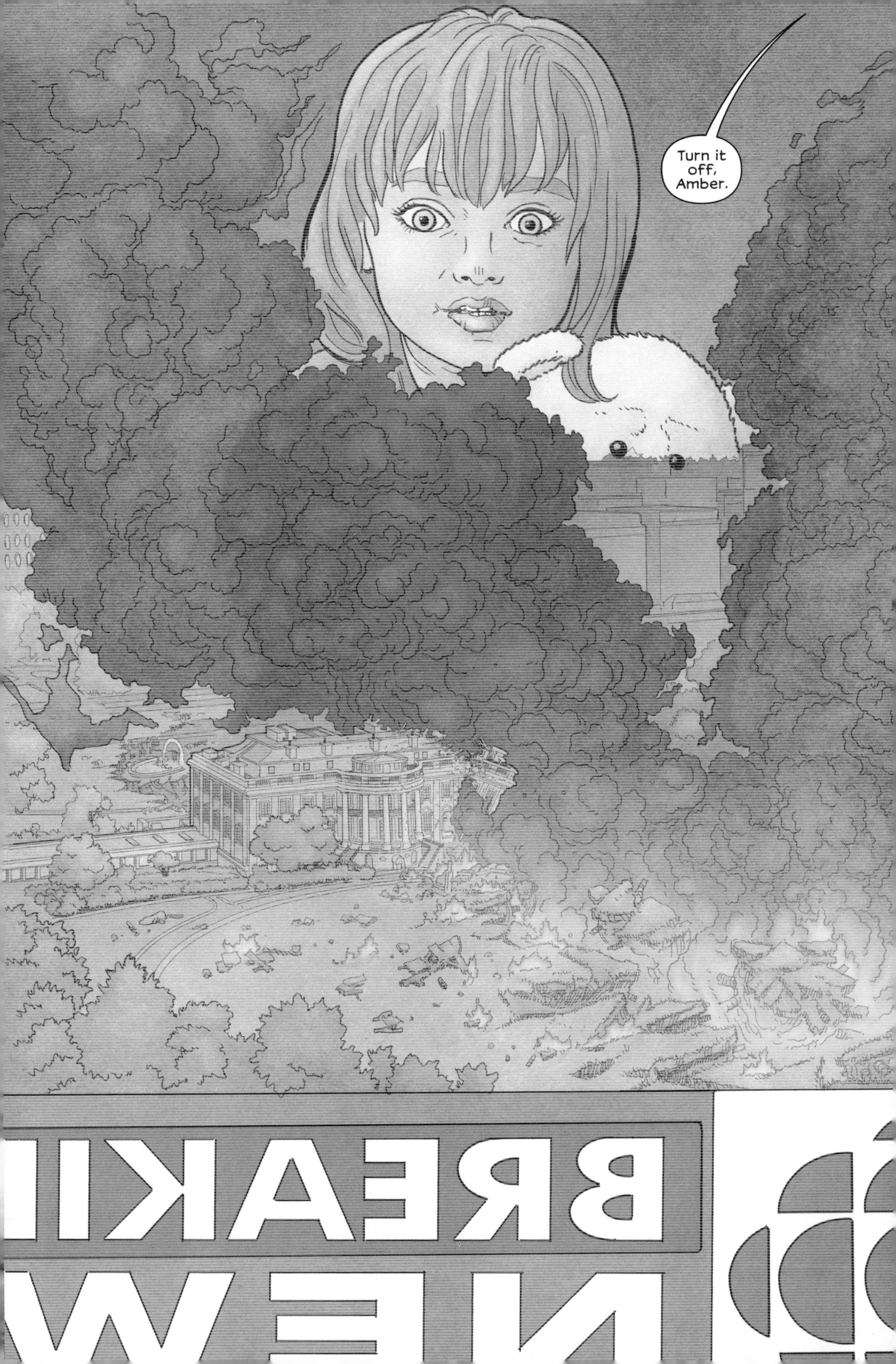
Turn it off, Amber.

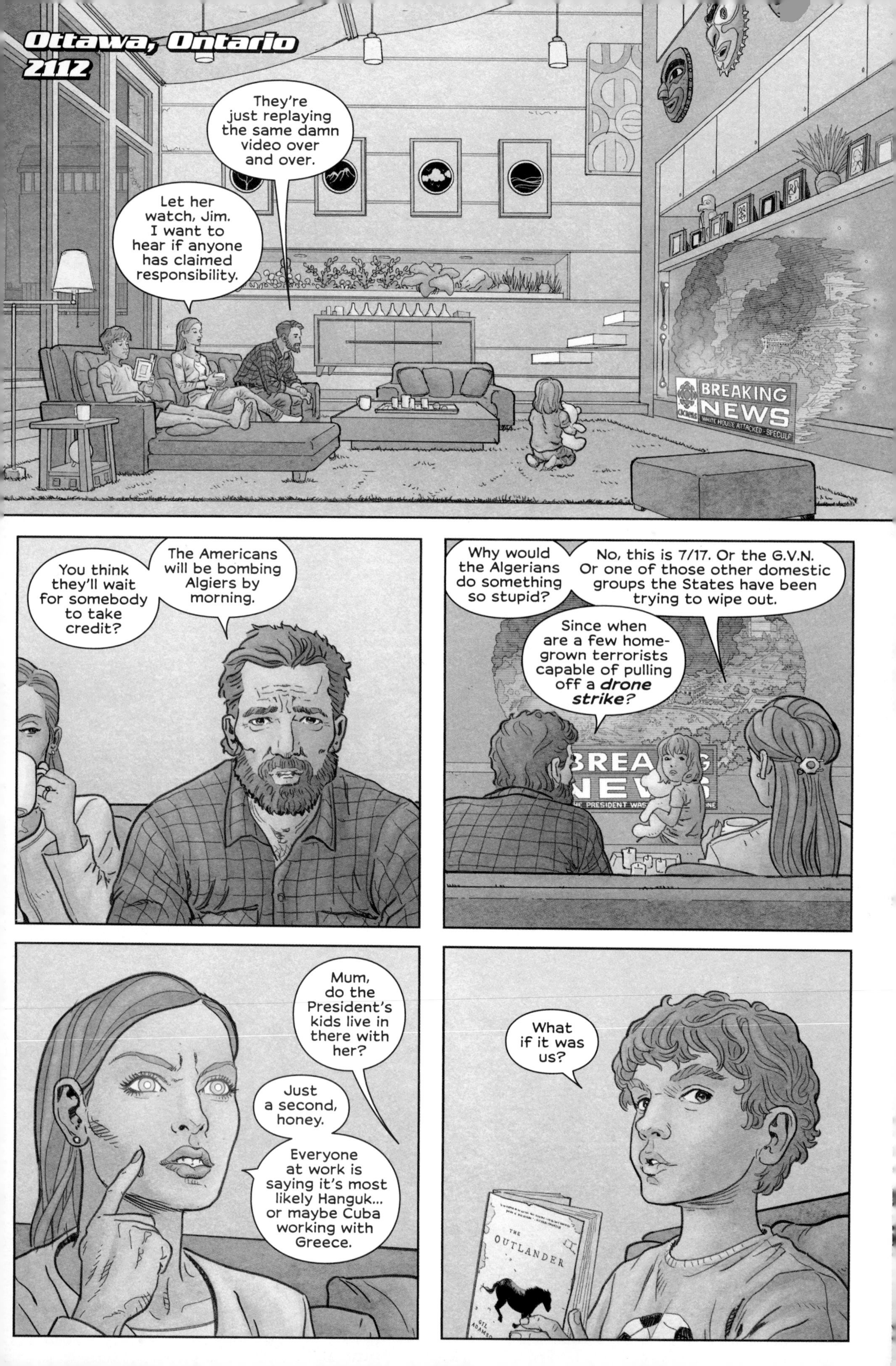

Ottawa, Ontario 2112
They're just replaying the same damn video over and over.
Let her watch, Jim. I want to hear if anyone has claimed responsibility.
BREAKING NEWS
You think they'll wait for somebody to take credit?
The Americans will be bombing Algiers by morning.
Why would the Algerians do something so stupid?
No, this is 7/17. Or the G.V.N. Or one of those other domestic groups the States have been trying to wipe out.
Since when are a few home-grown terrorists capable of pulling off a *drone strike?*
Mum, do the President's kids live in there with her?
Just a second, honey.
Everyone at work is saying it's most likely Hanguk... or maybe Cuba working with Greece.
What if it was us?
THE OUTLANDER

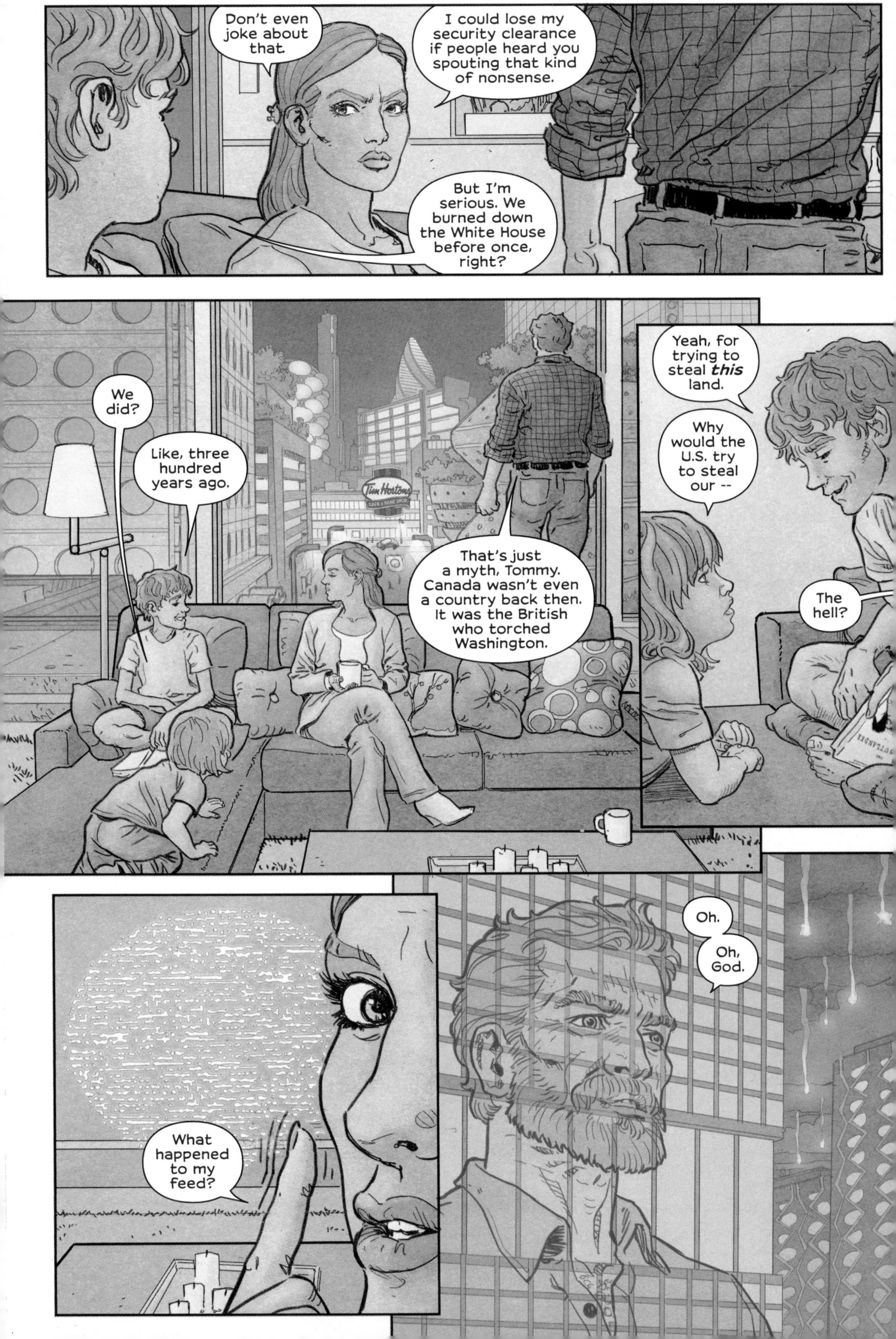
Don't even joke about that.
I could lose my security clearance if people heard you spouting that kind of nonsense.
But I'm serious. We burned down the White House before once, right?
We did?
Like, three hundred years ago.
Tim Hortons
That's just a myth, Tommy. Canada wasn't even a country back then. It was the British who torched Washington.
Yeah, for trying to steal **this** land.
Why would the U.S. try to steal our --
The hell?
What happened to my feed?
Oh.
Oh, God.

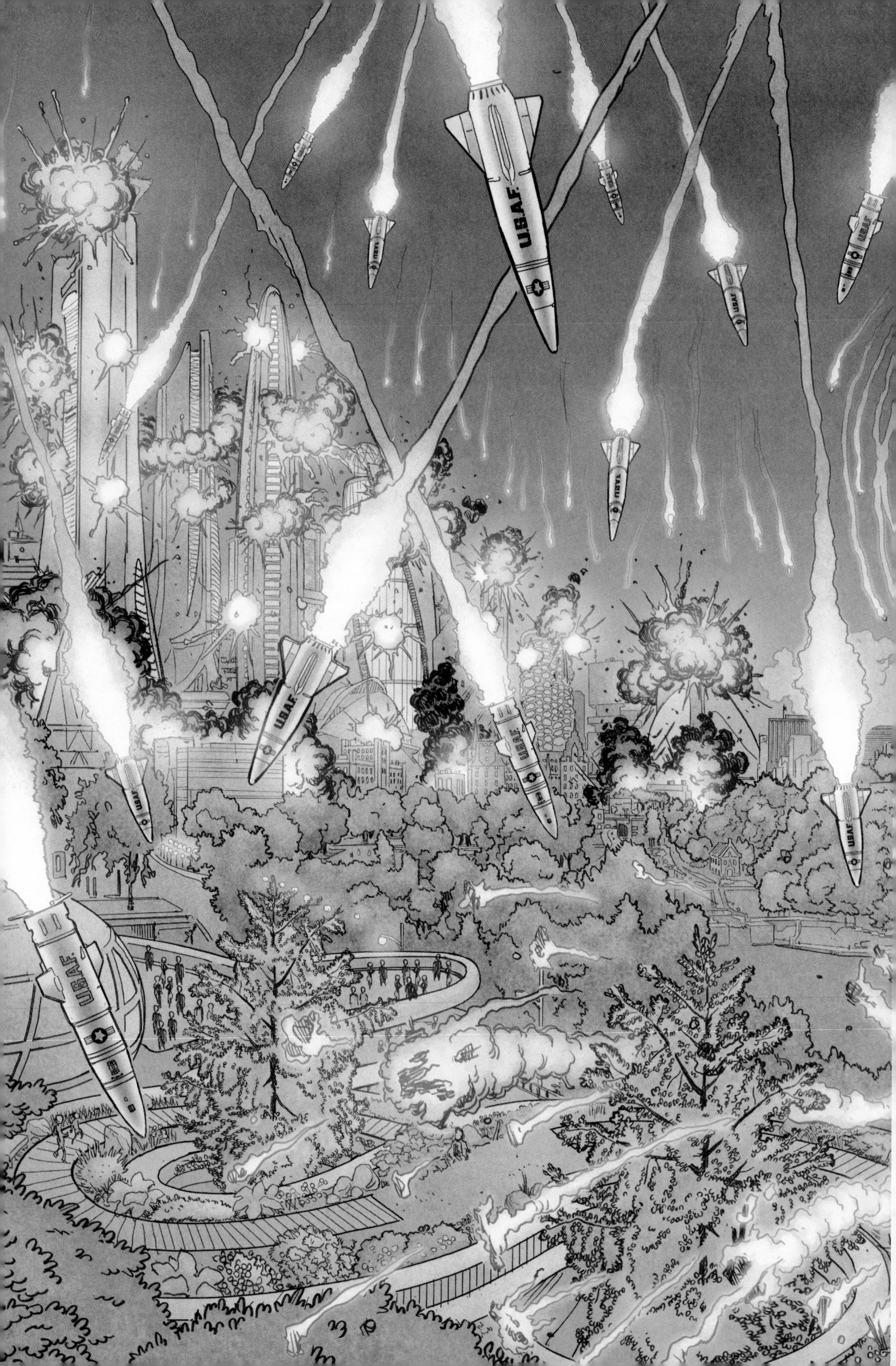
U.S.A.F.
U.S.A.F.
U.S.A.F.

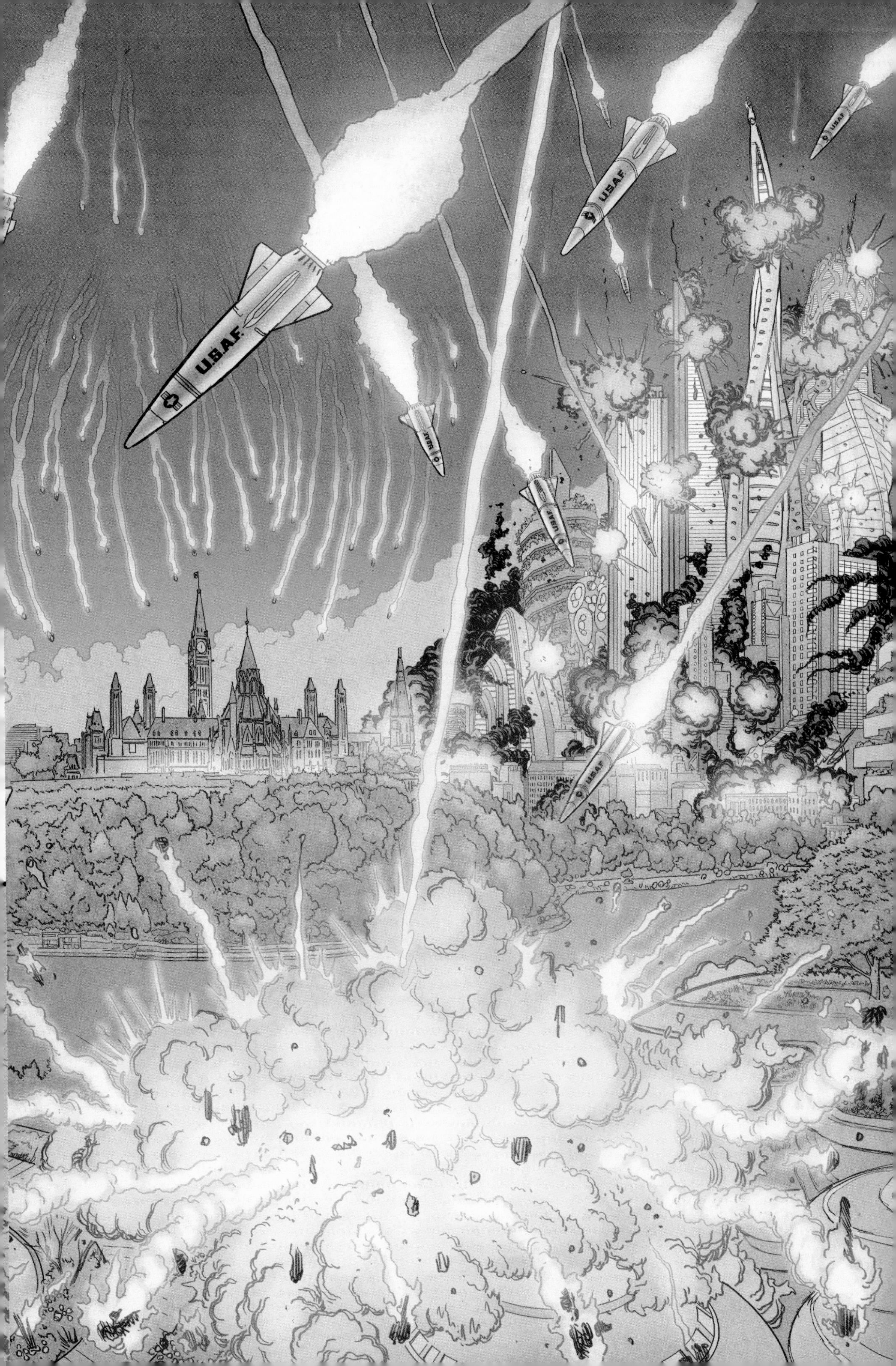
U.S.A.F.

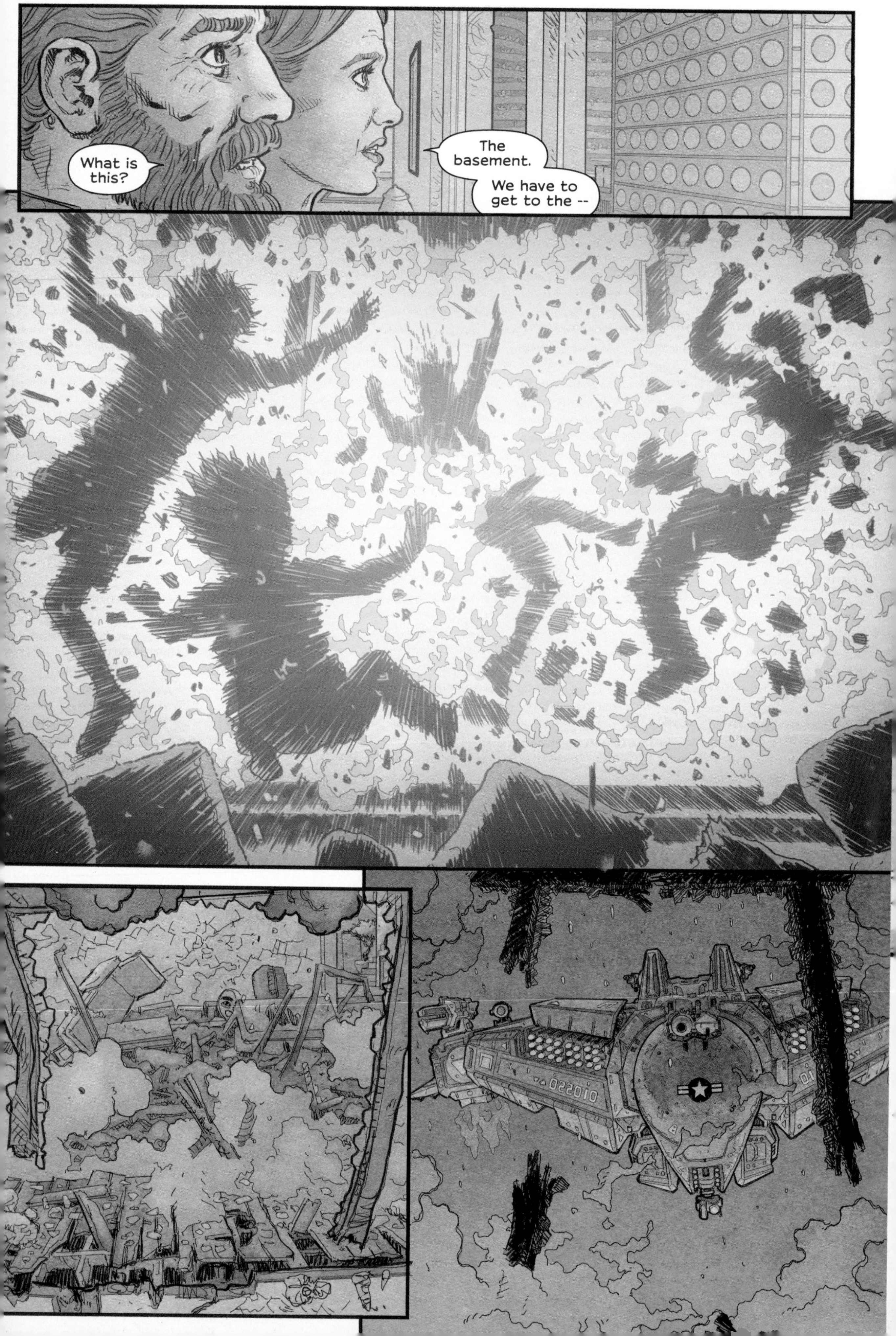
What is this?
The basement.
We have to get to the --
022010
010

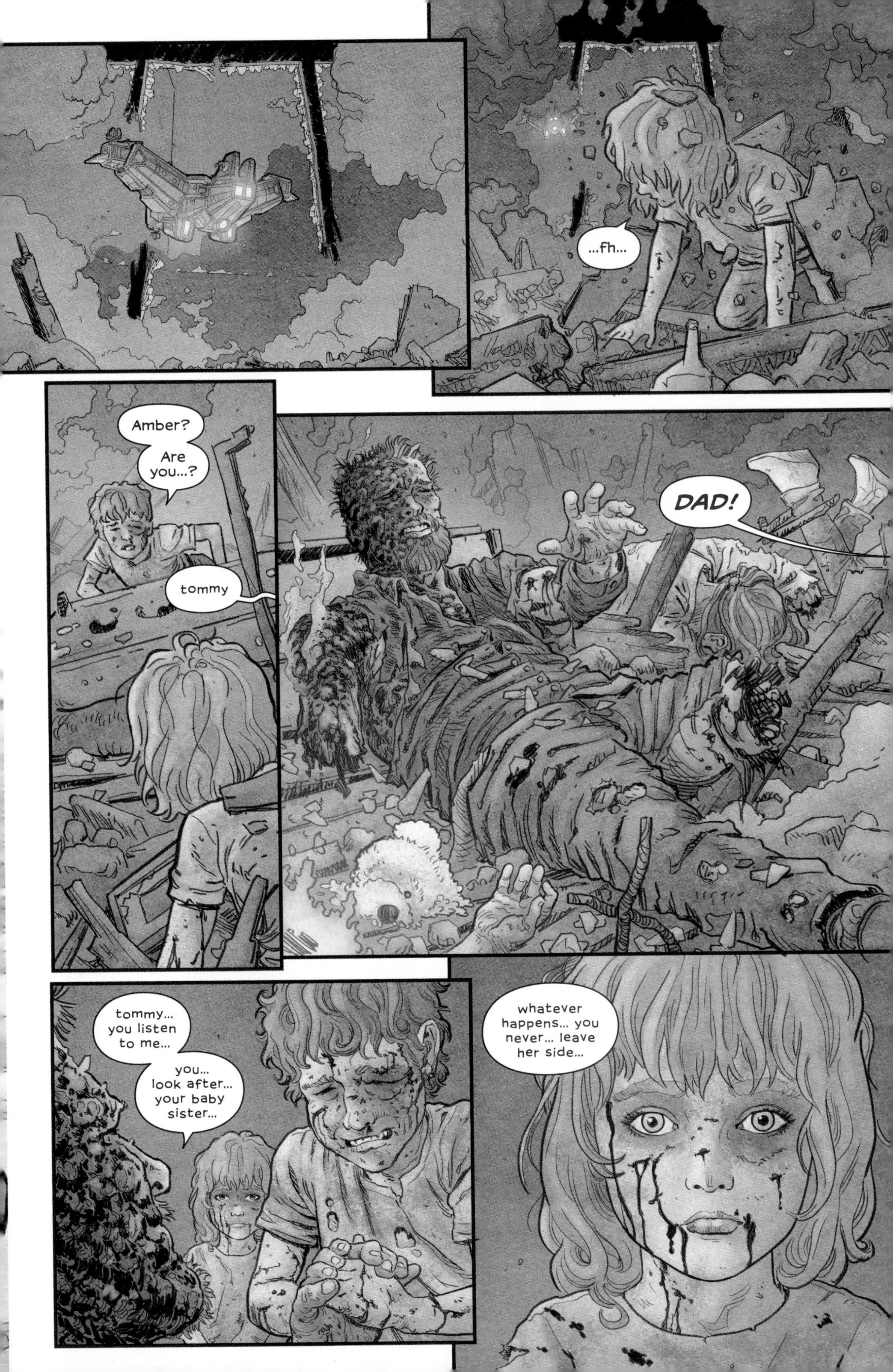
...fh...
Amber?
Are you...?
tommy
DAD!
tommy... you listen to me...
you... look after... your baby sister...
whatever happens... you never... leave her side...

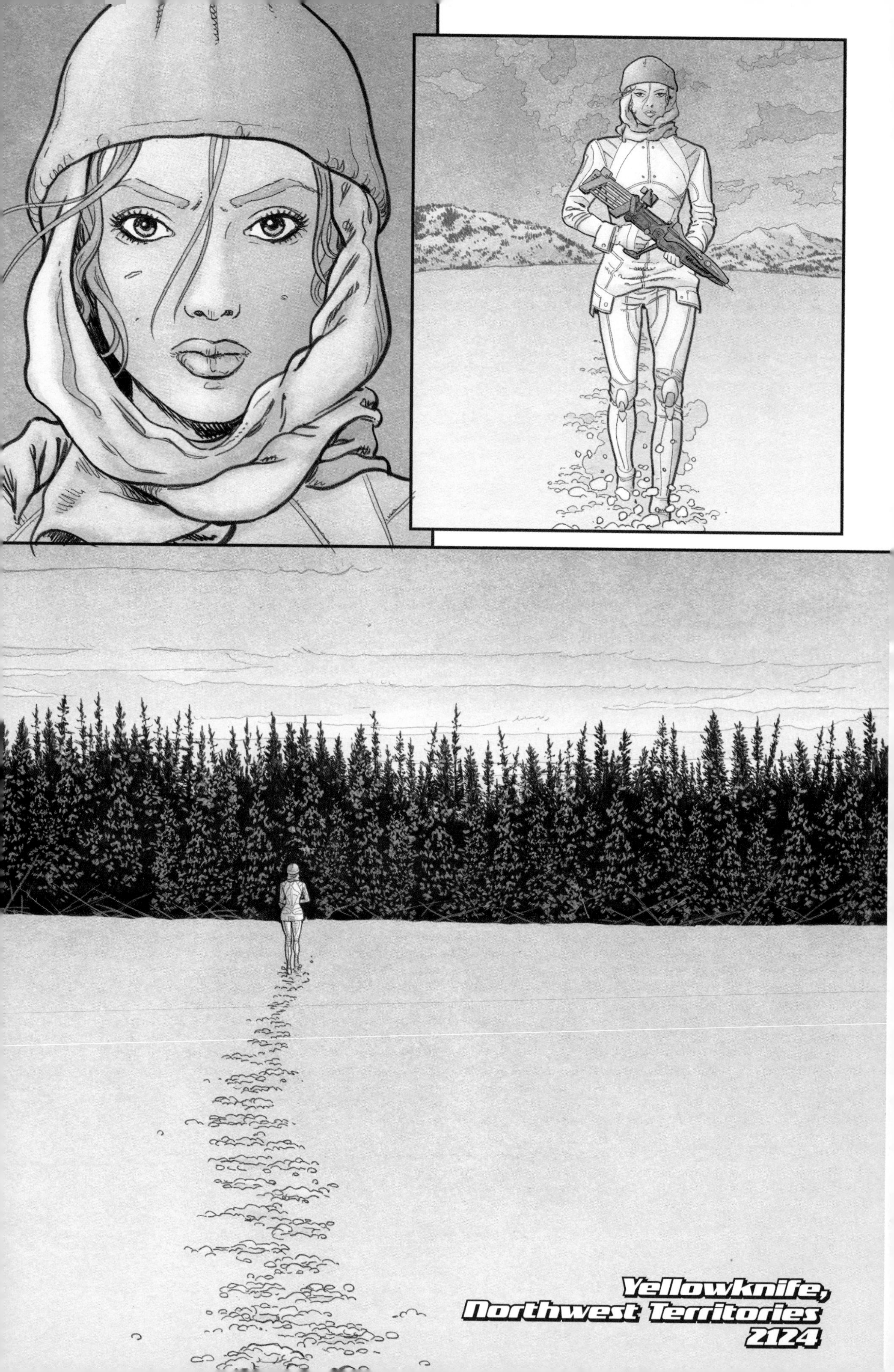
Yellowknife,
Northwest Territories
2124

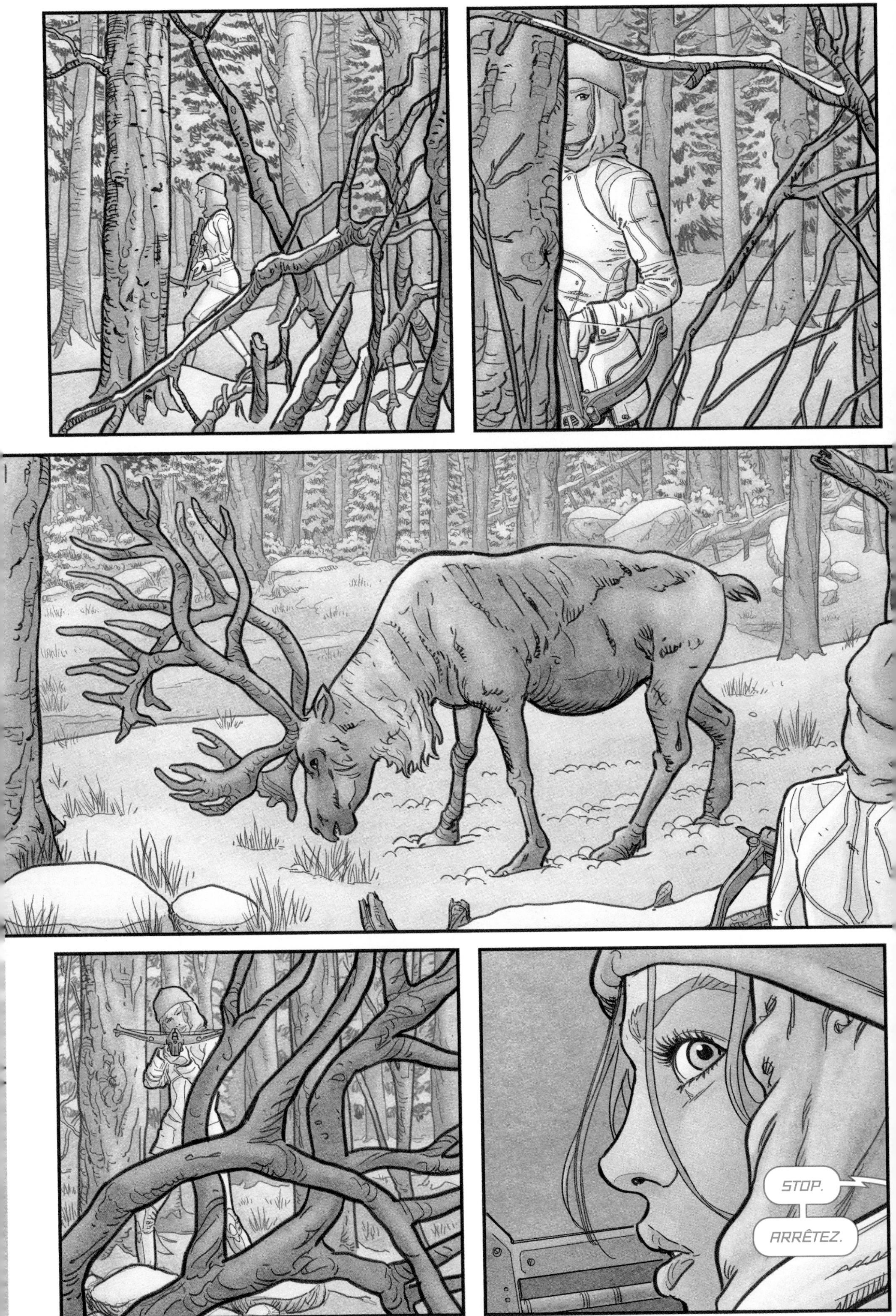
STOP.
ARRÊTEZ.

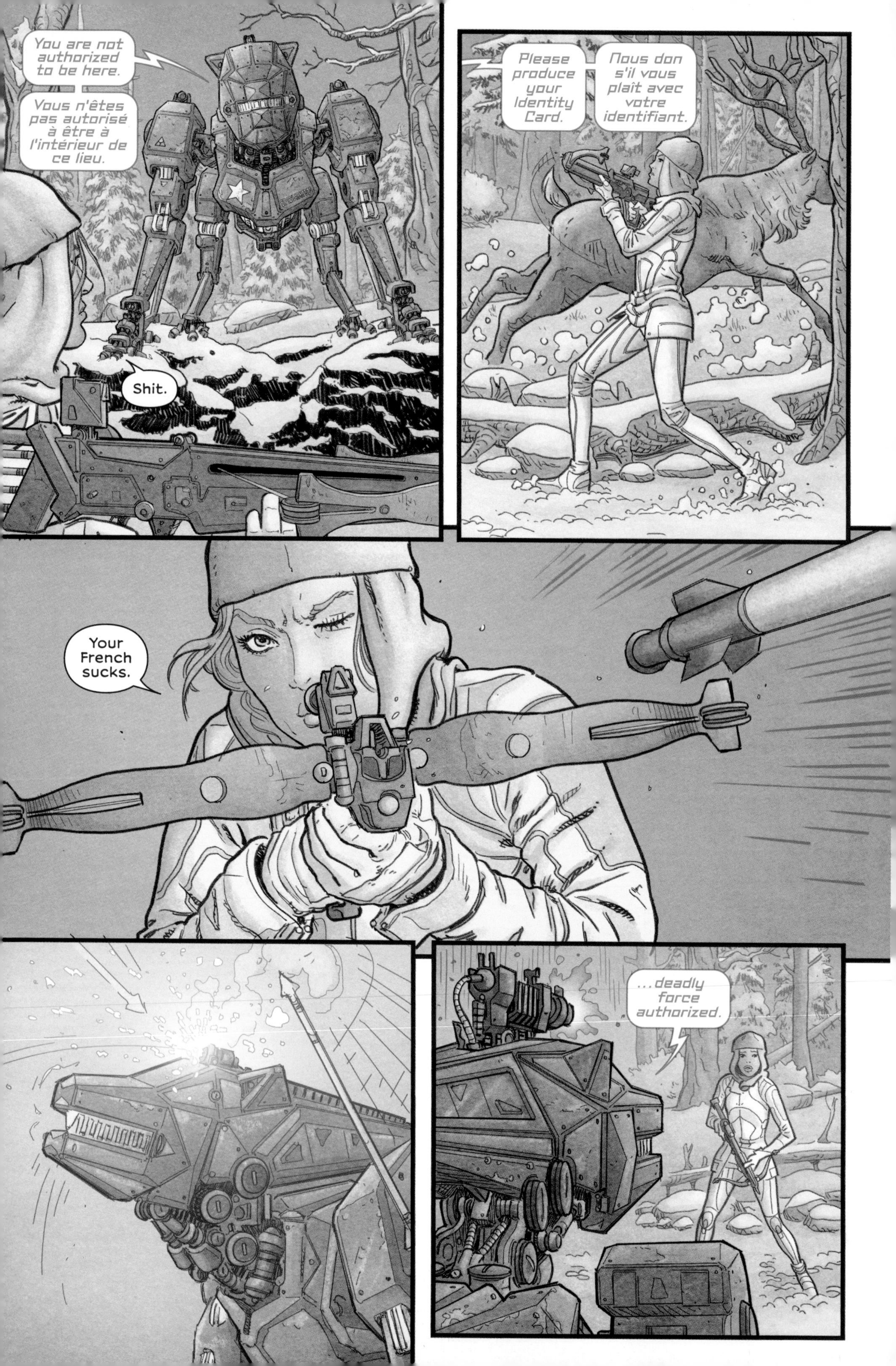
You are not authorized to be here.
Vous n'êtes pas autorisé à être à l'intérieur de ce lieu.
Shit.
Please produce your Identity Card.
Nous don s'il vous plaît avec votre identifiant.
Your French sucks.
...deadly force authorized.

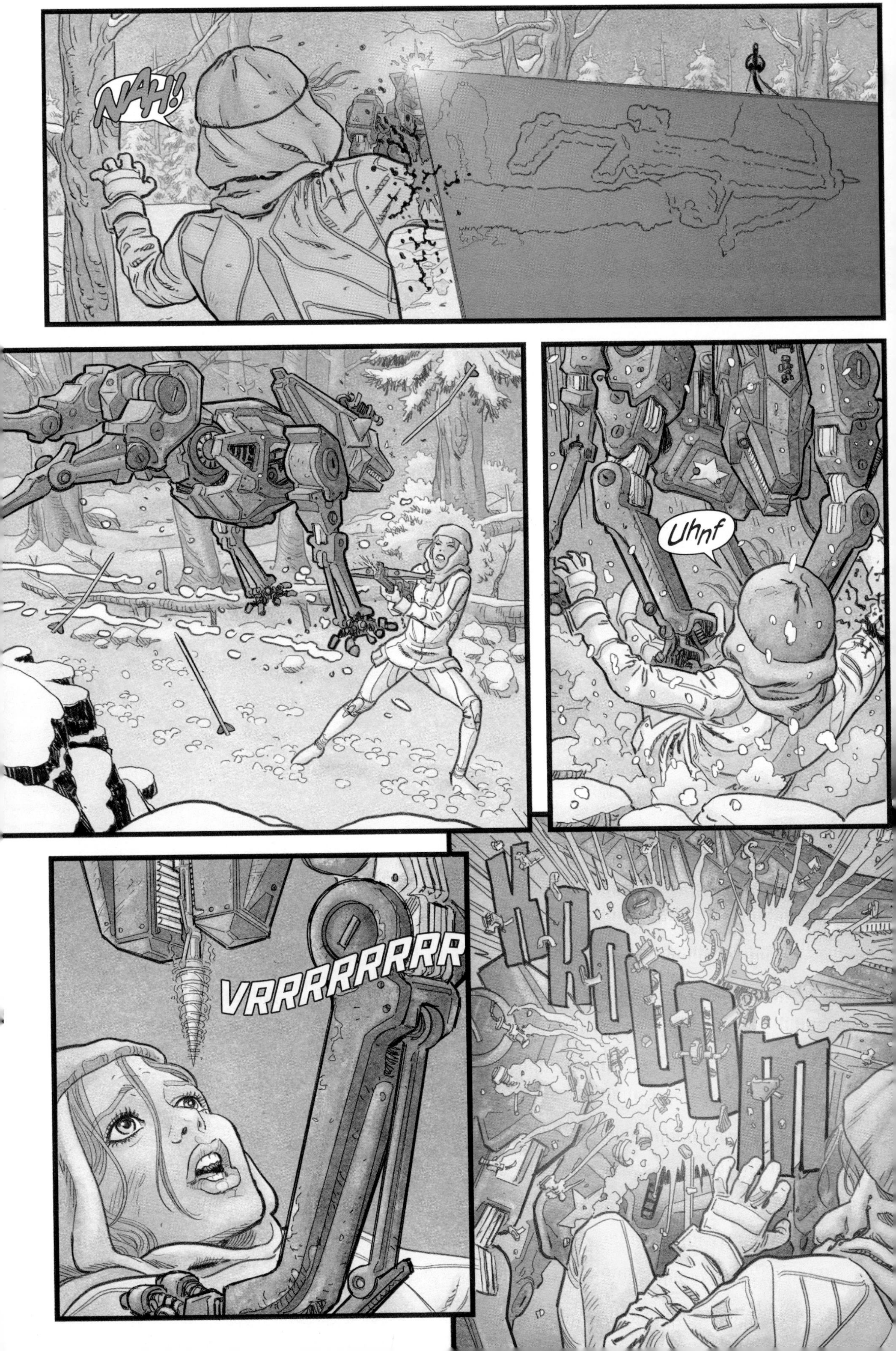
NAH!
Uhnf
VRRRRRRRRR
KROOOOM

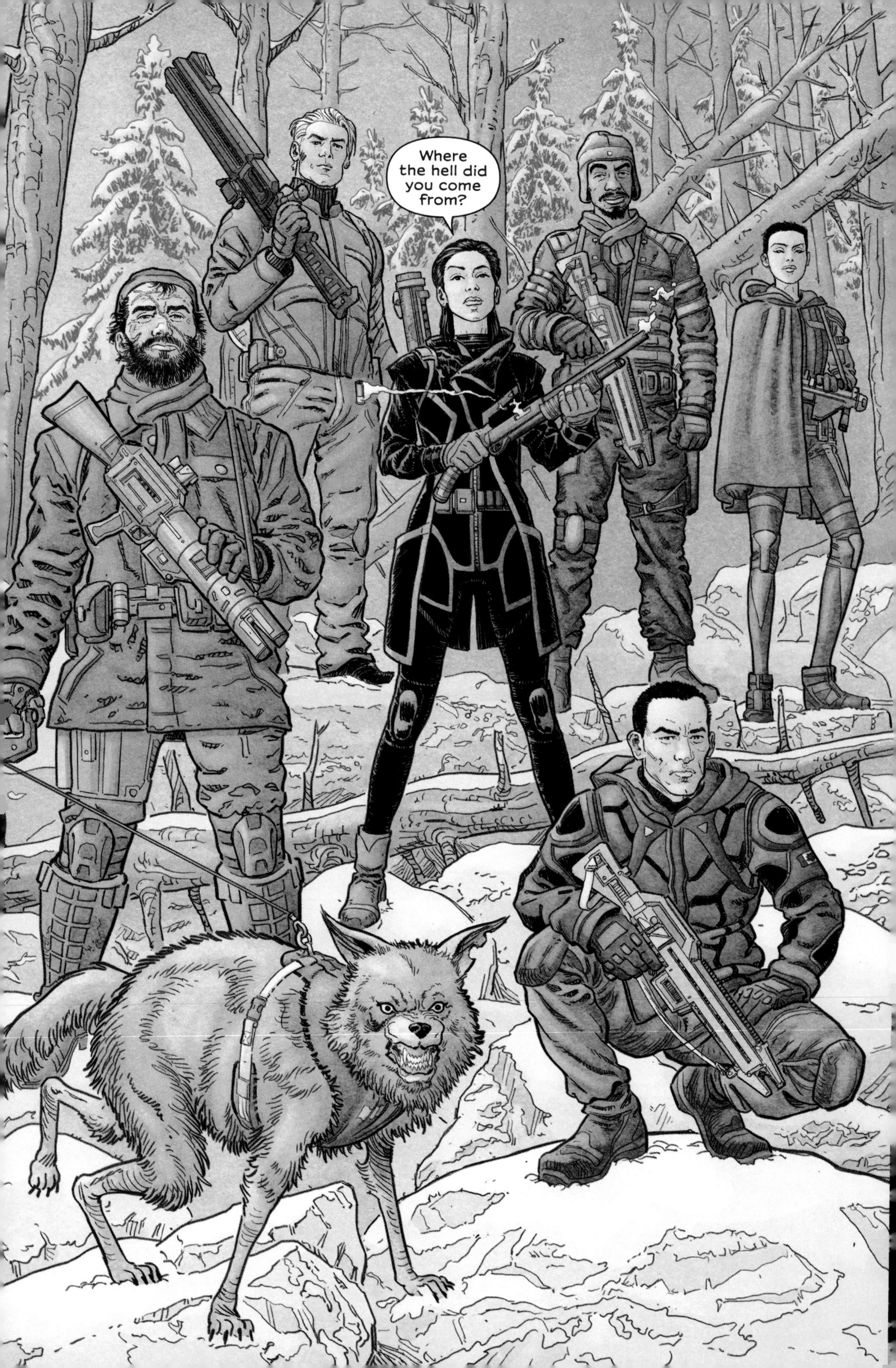
Where the hell did you come from?

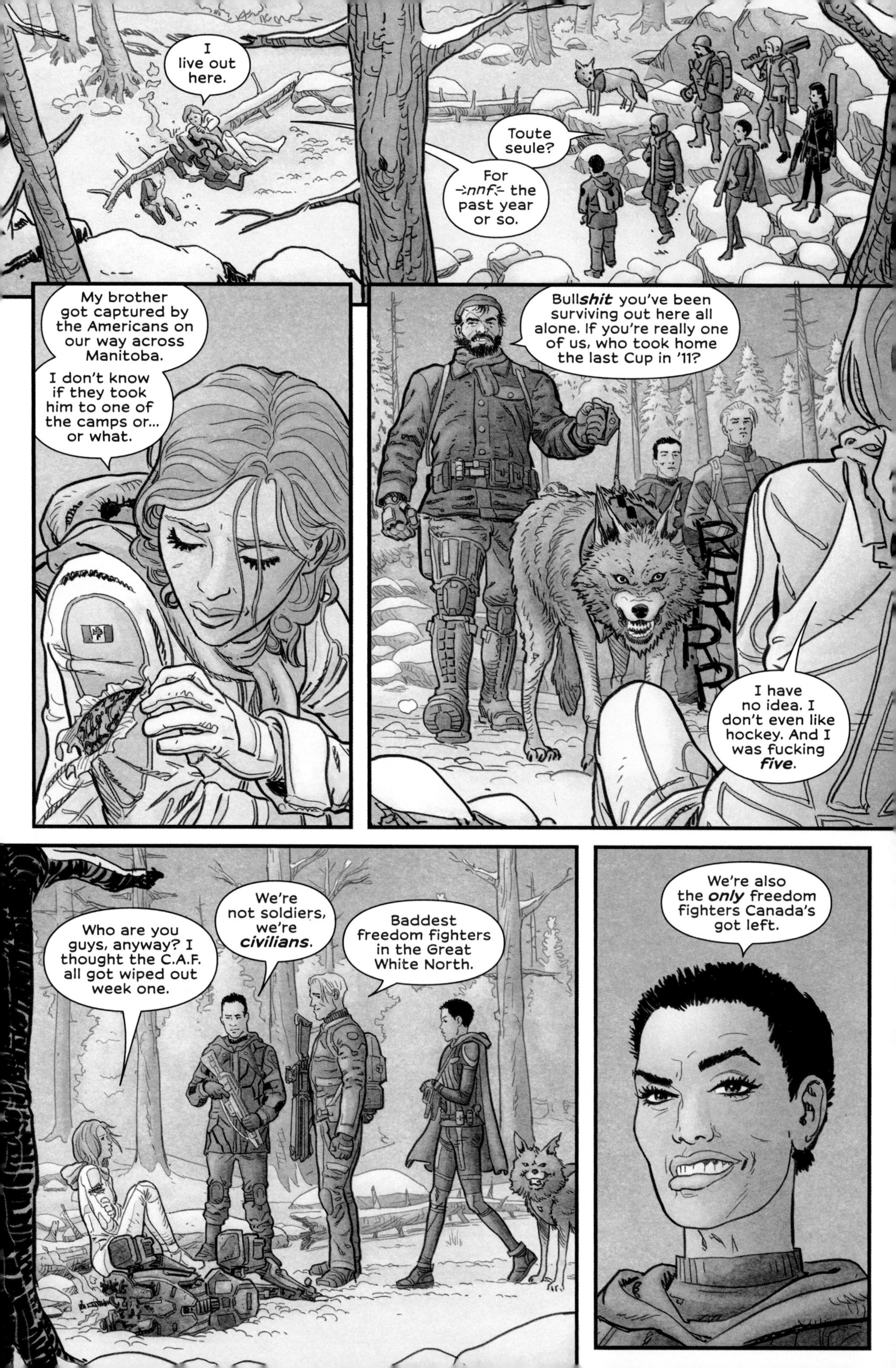

I live out here.
Toute seule?
For -nnf- the past year or so.
My brother got captured by the Americans on our way across Manitoba.
I don't know if they took him to one of the camps or... or what.
Bull*shit* you've been surviving out here all alone. If you're really one of us, who took home the last Cup in '11?
I have no idea. I don't even like hockey. And I was fucking *five*.
Who are you guys, anyway? I thought the C.A.F. all got wiped out week one.
We're not soldiers, we're *civilians*.
Baddest freedom fighters in the Great White North.
We're also the *only* freedom fighters Canada's got left.

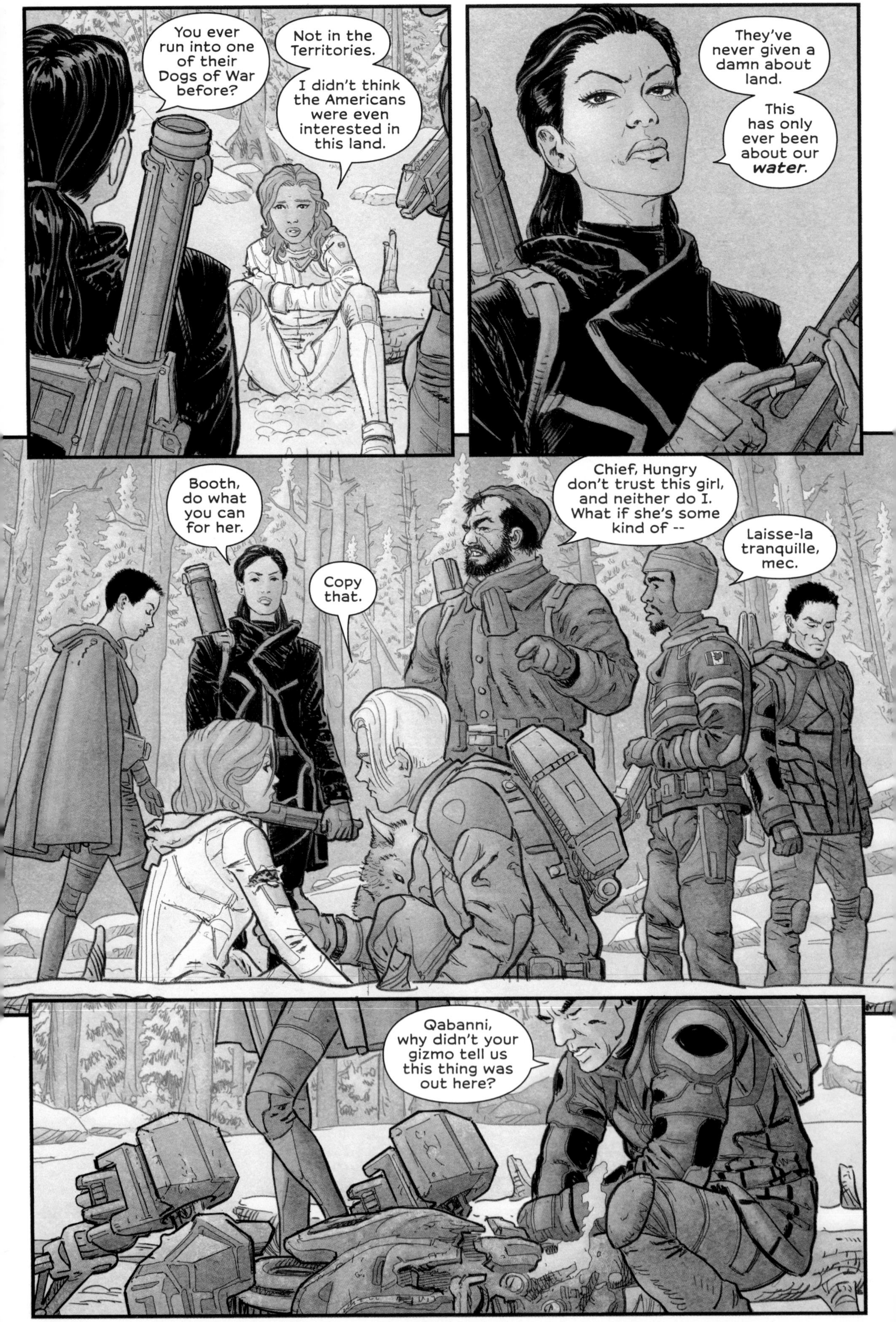
You ever run into one of their Dogs of War before?
Not in the Territories.
I didn't think the Americans were even interested in this land.
They've never given a damn about land.
This has only ever been about our ***water***.
Booth, do what you can for her.
Copy that.
Chief, Hungry don't trust this girl, and neither do I. What if she's some kind of --
Laisse-la tranquille, mec.
Qabanni, why didn't your gizmo tell us this thing was out here?

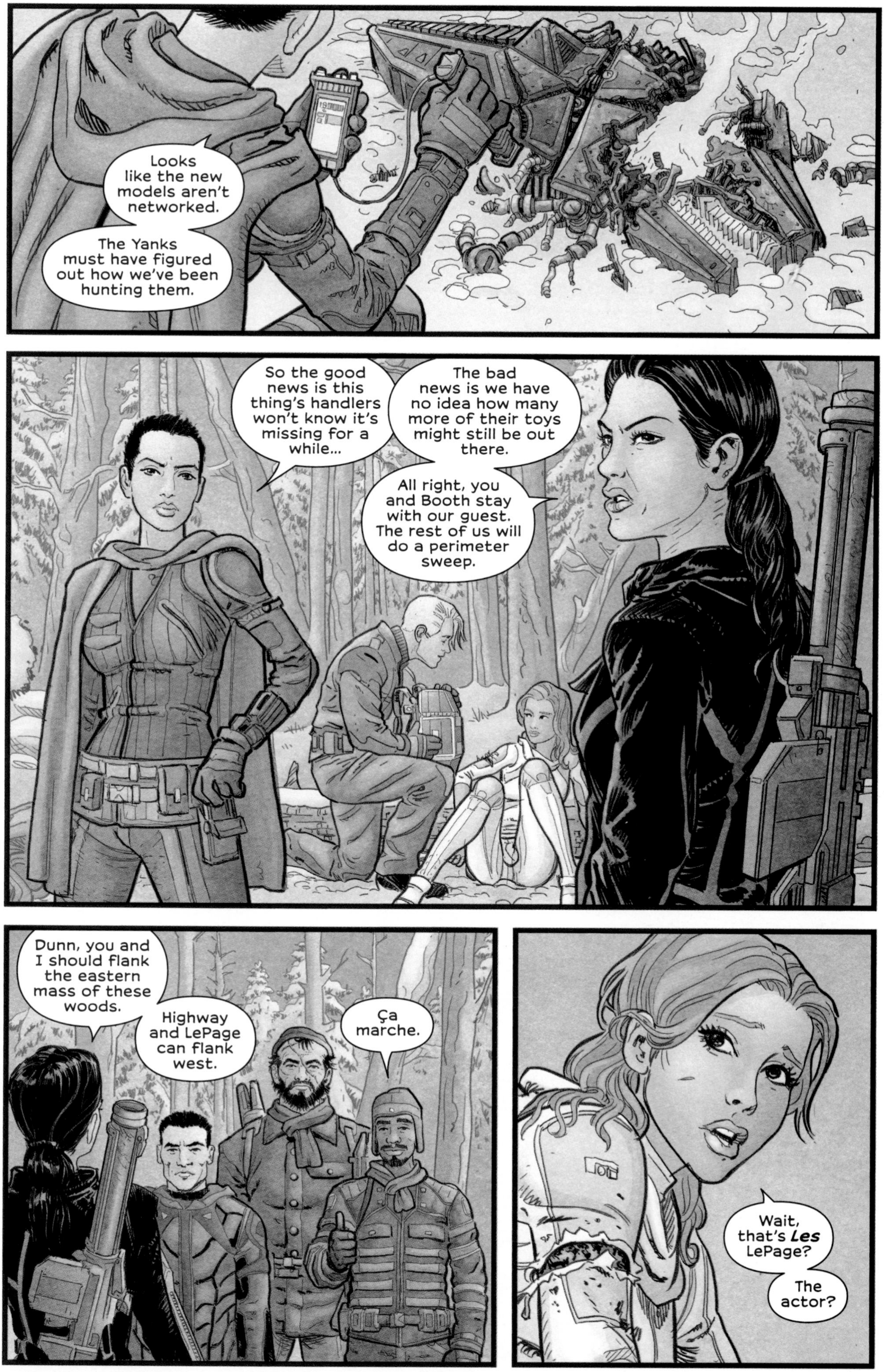
Looks like the new models aren't networked.
The Yanks must have figured out how we've been hunting them.
So the good news is this thing's handlers won't know it's missing for a while...
The bad news is we have no idea how many more of their toys might still be out there.
All right, you and Booth stay with our guest. The rest of us will do a perimeter sweep.
Dunn, you and I should flank the eastern mass of these woods.
Highway and LePage can flank west.
Ça marche.
Wait, that's *Les* LePage?
The actor?

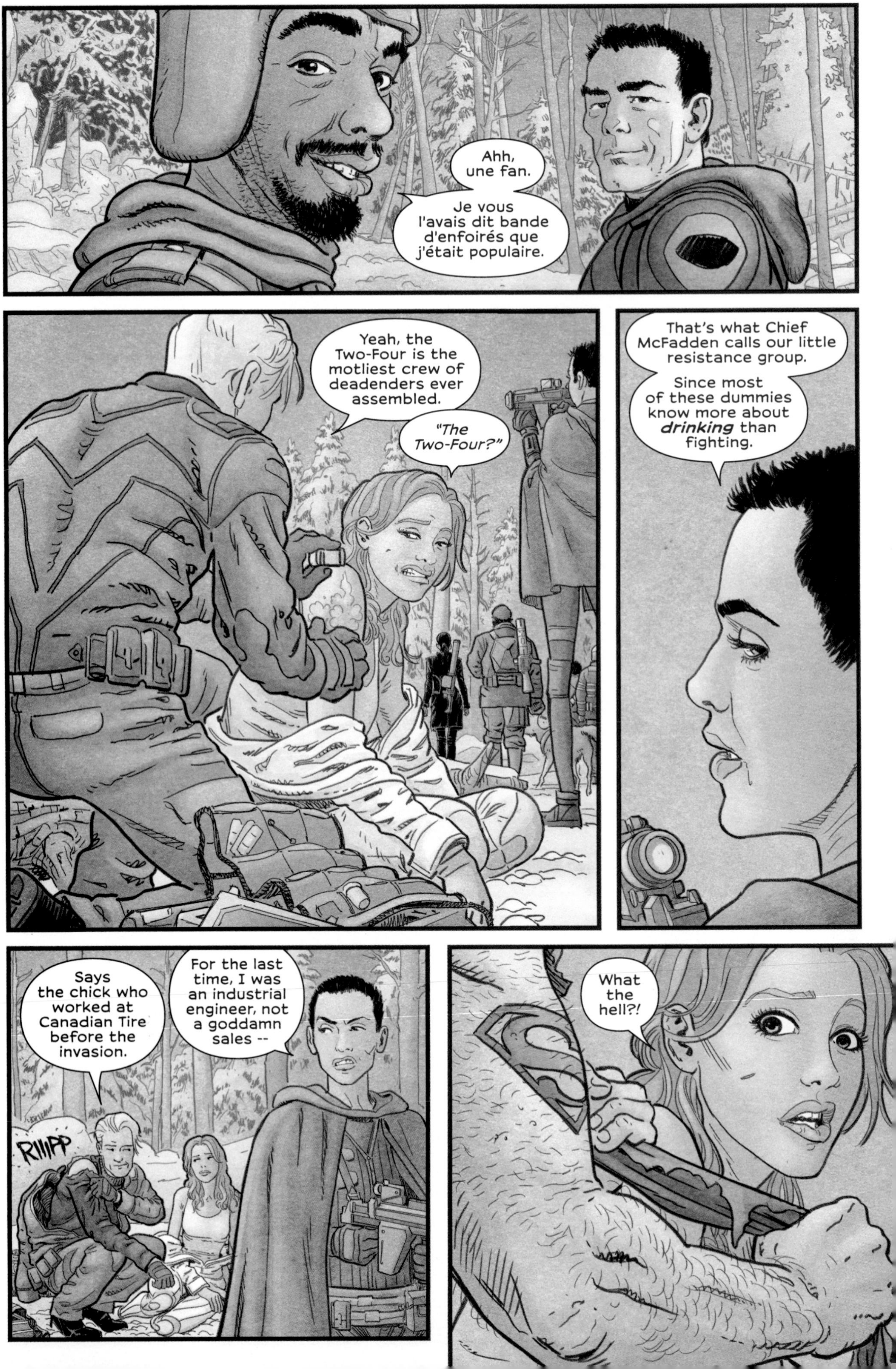
Ahh, une fan.
Je vous l'avais dit bande d'enfoirés que j'était populaire.
Yeah, the Two-Four is the motliest crew of deadenders ever assembled.
"The Two-Four?"
That's what Chief McFadden calls our little resistance group.
Since most of these dummies know more about *drinking* than fighting.
Says the chick who worked at Canadian Tire before the invasion.
For the last time, I was an industrial engineer, not a goddamn sales --
RIIIPP
What the hell?!

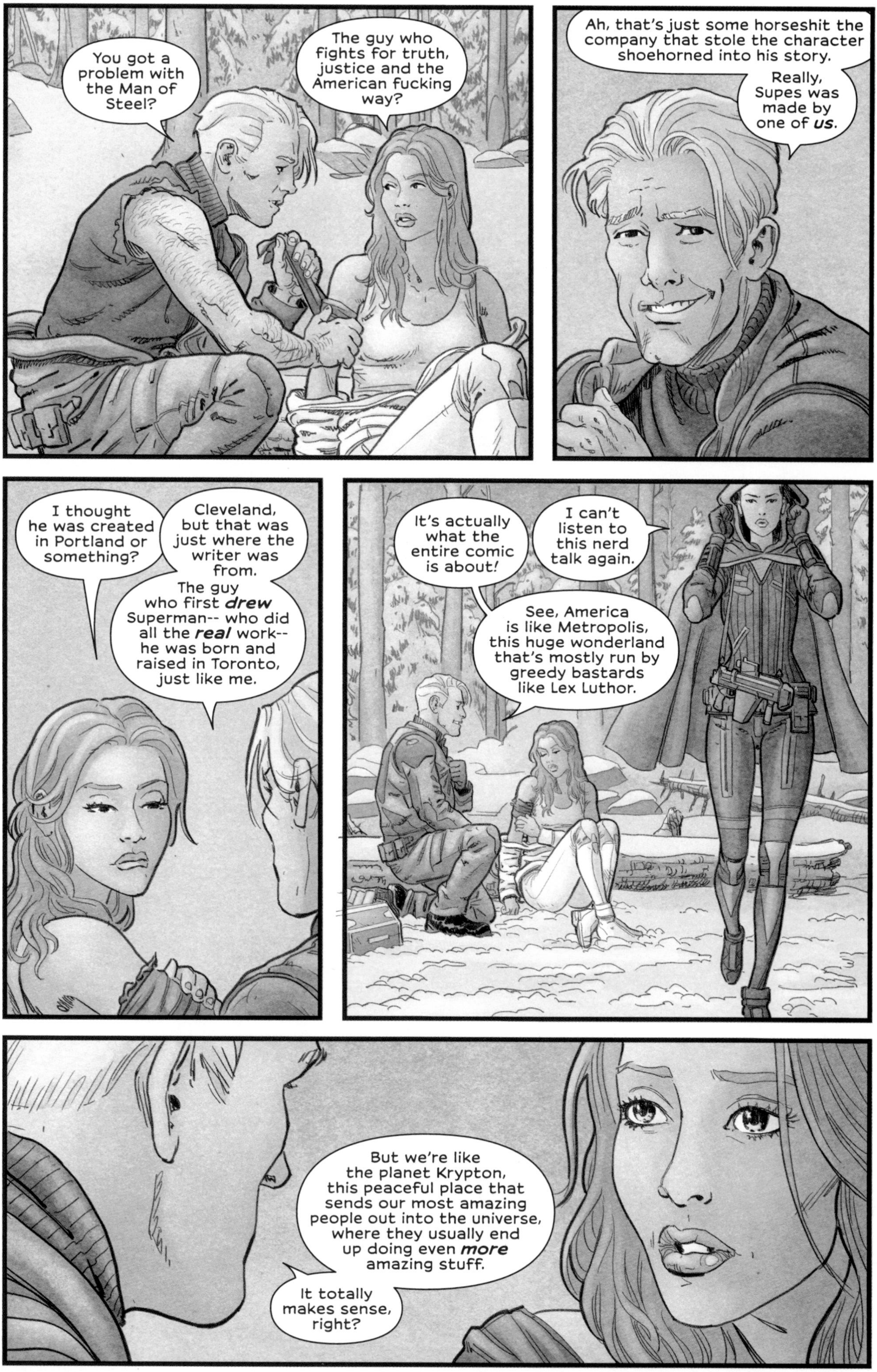
You got a problem with the Man of Steel?
The guy who fights for truth, justice and the American fucking way?
Ah, that's just some horseshit the company that stole the character shoehorned into his story.
Really, Supes was made by one of *us*.
I thought he was created in Portland or something?
Cleveland, but that was just where the writer was from.
The guy who first *drew* Superman-- who did all the *real* work-- he was born and raised in Toronto, just like me.
It's actually what the entire comic is about!
I can't listen to this nerd talk again.
See, America is like Metropolis, this huge wonderland that's mostly run by greedy bastards like Lex Luthor.
But we're like the planet Krypton, this peaceful place that sends our most amazing people out into the universe, where they usually end up doing even *more* amazing stuff.
It totally makes sense, right?

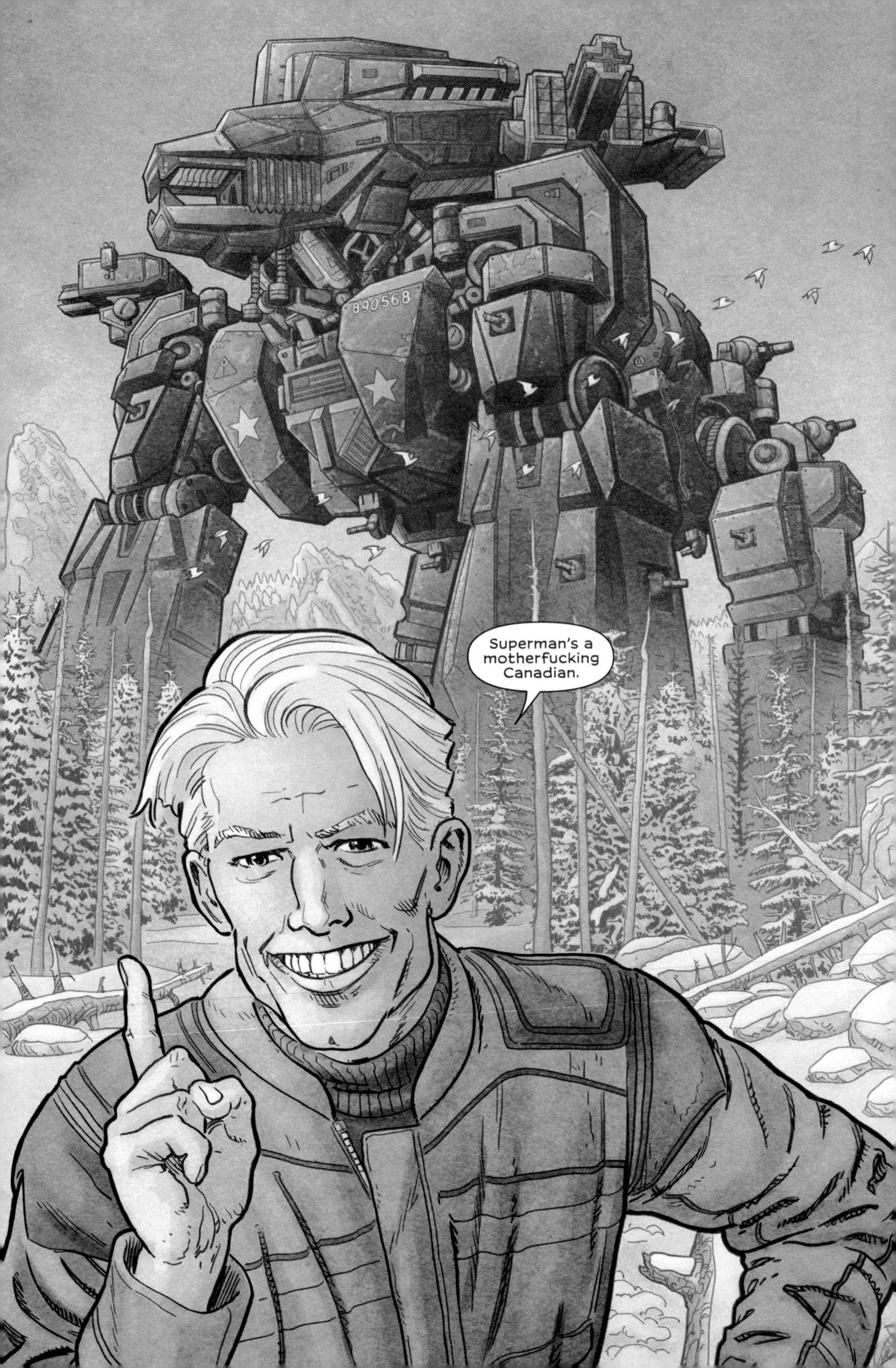
Superman's a motherfucking Canadian.
890568

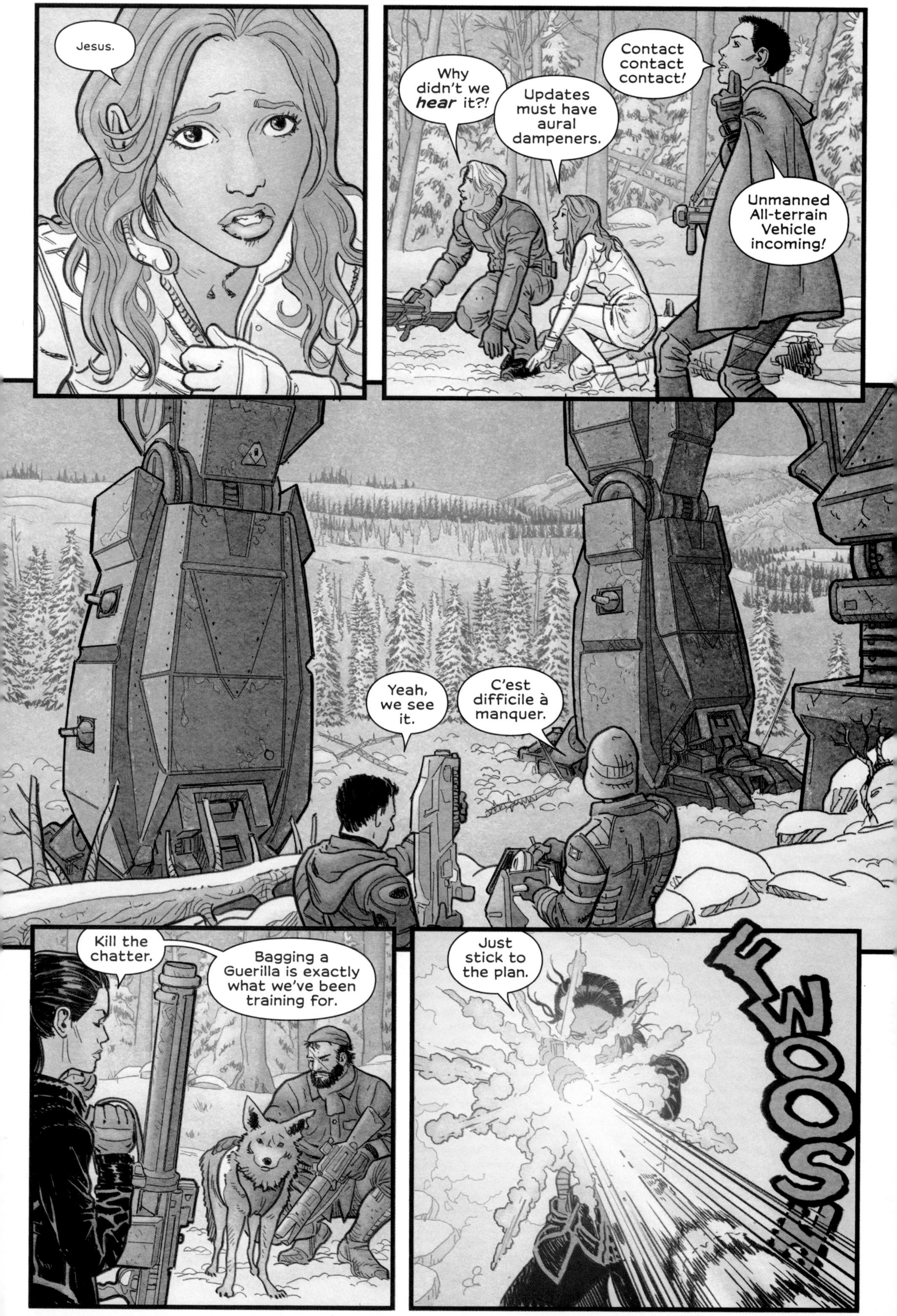
Jesus.
Why didn't we *hear* it?!
Updates must have aural dampeners.
Contact contact contact!
Unmanned All-terrain Vehicle incoming!
Yeah, we see it.
C'est difficile à manquer.
Kill the chatter.
Bagging a Guerilla is exactly what we've been training for.
Just stick to the plan.
FWOOSH!

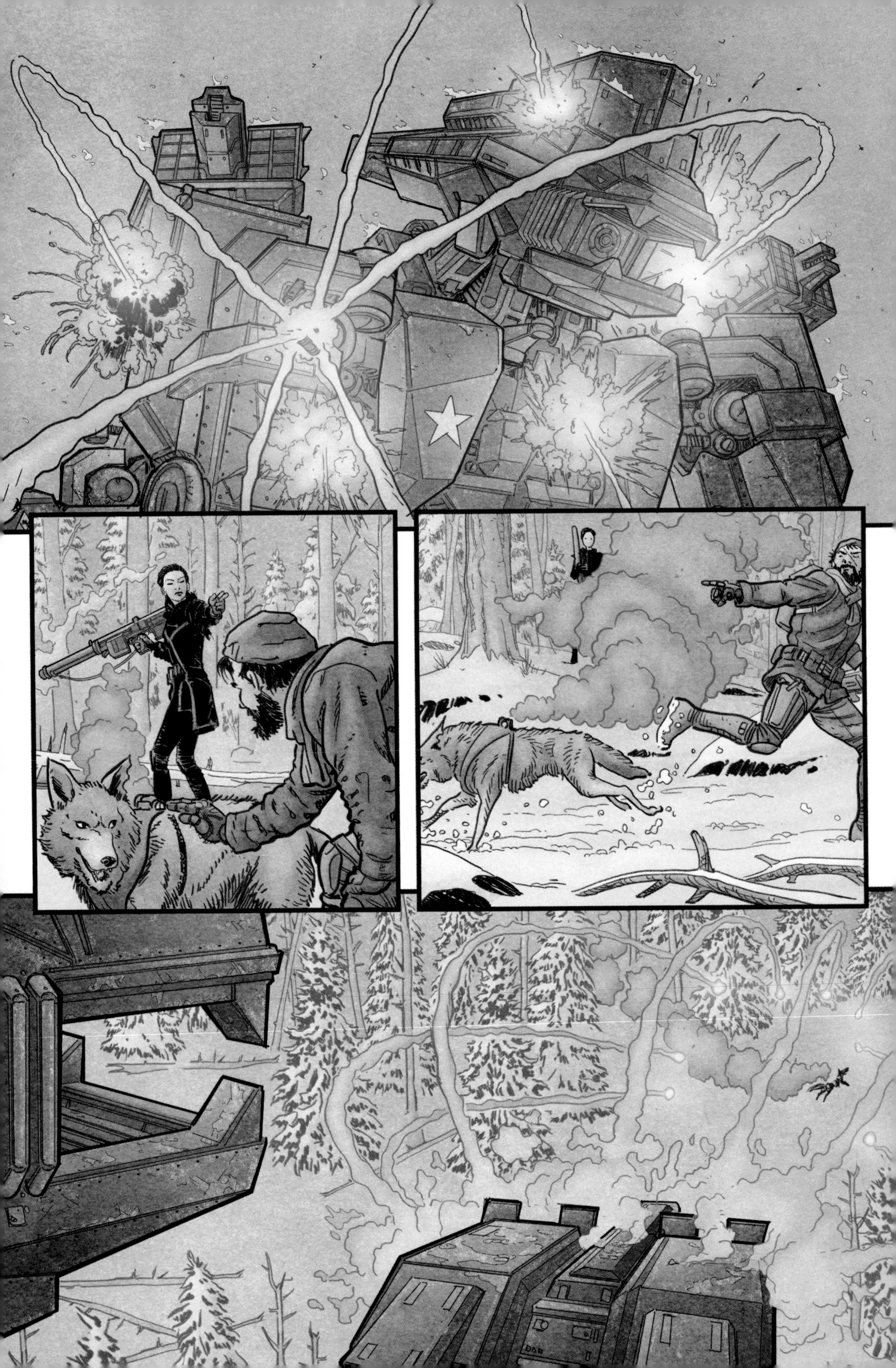

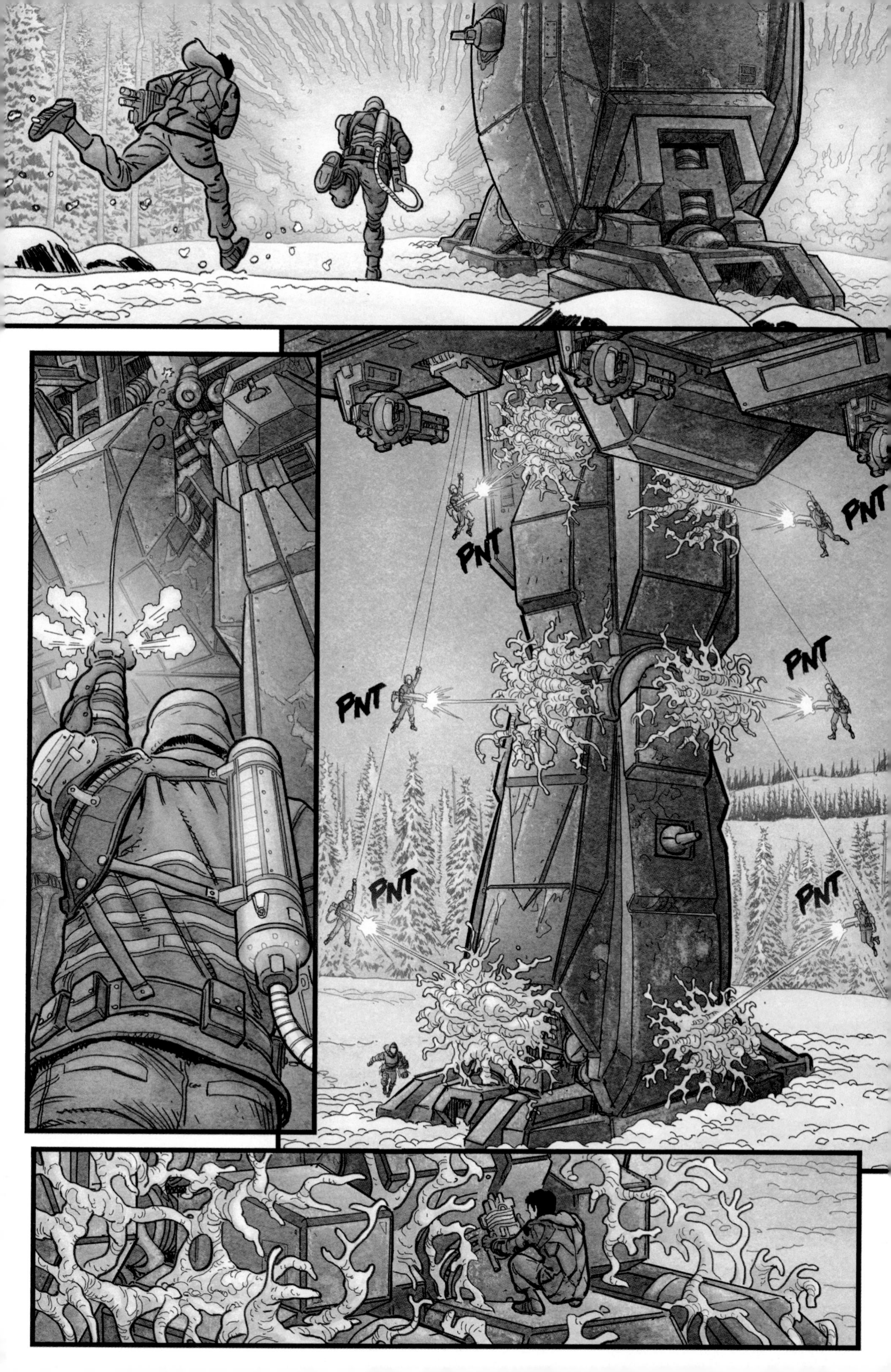
PNT
PNT
PNT
PNT
PNT
PNT

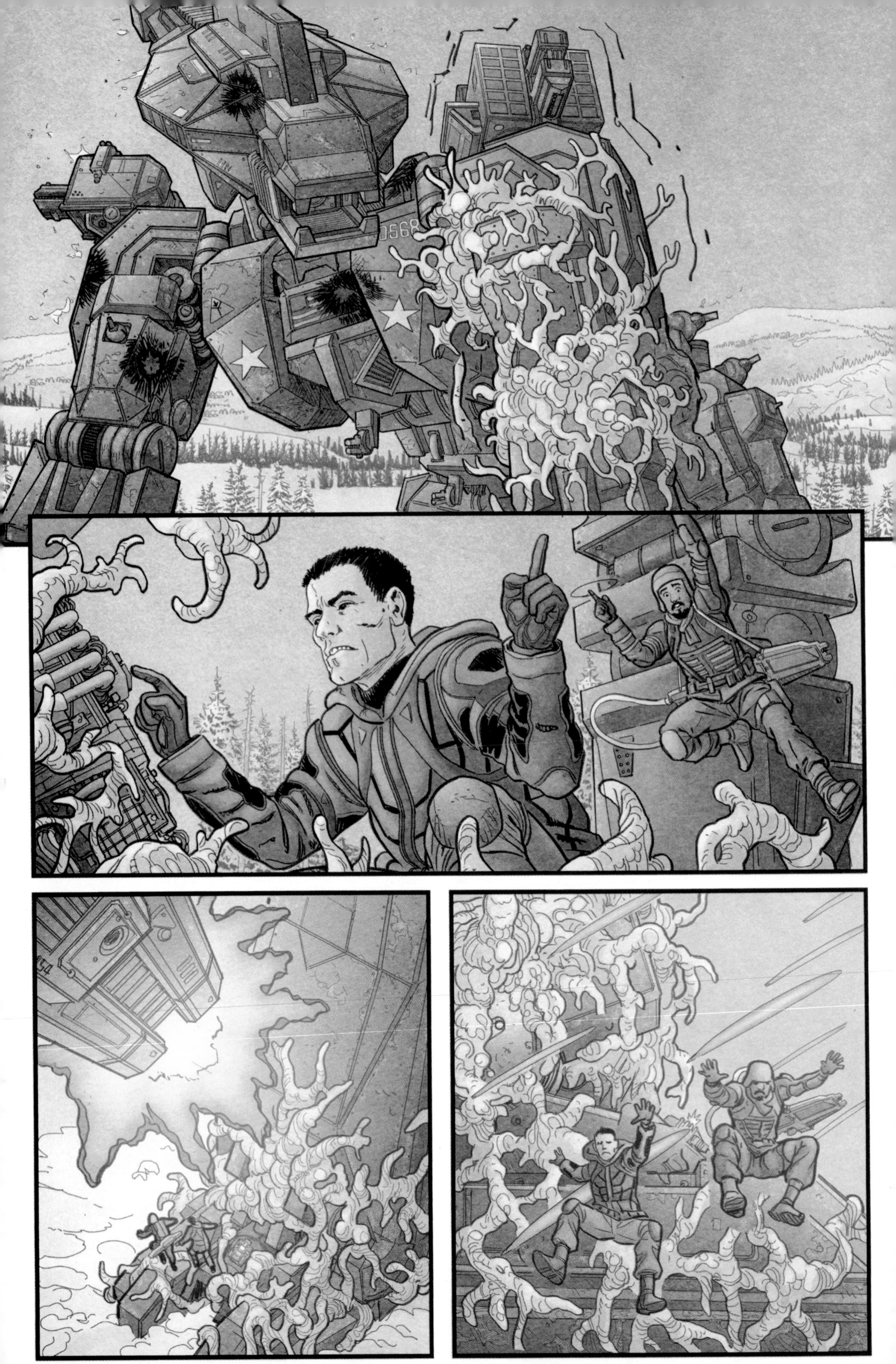
0568

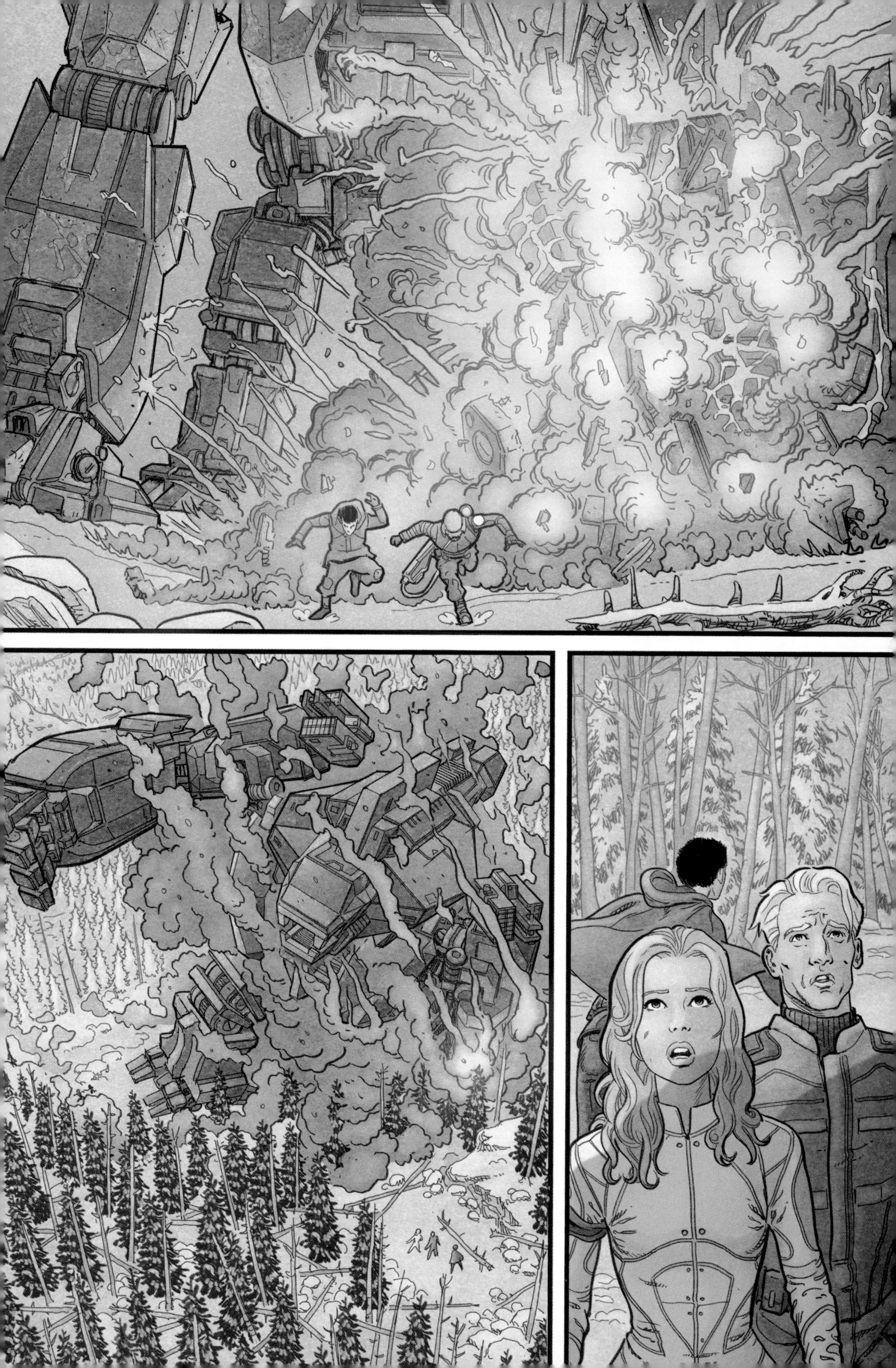

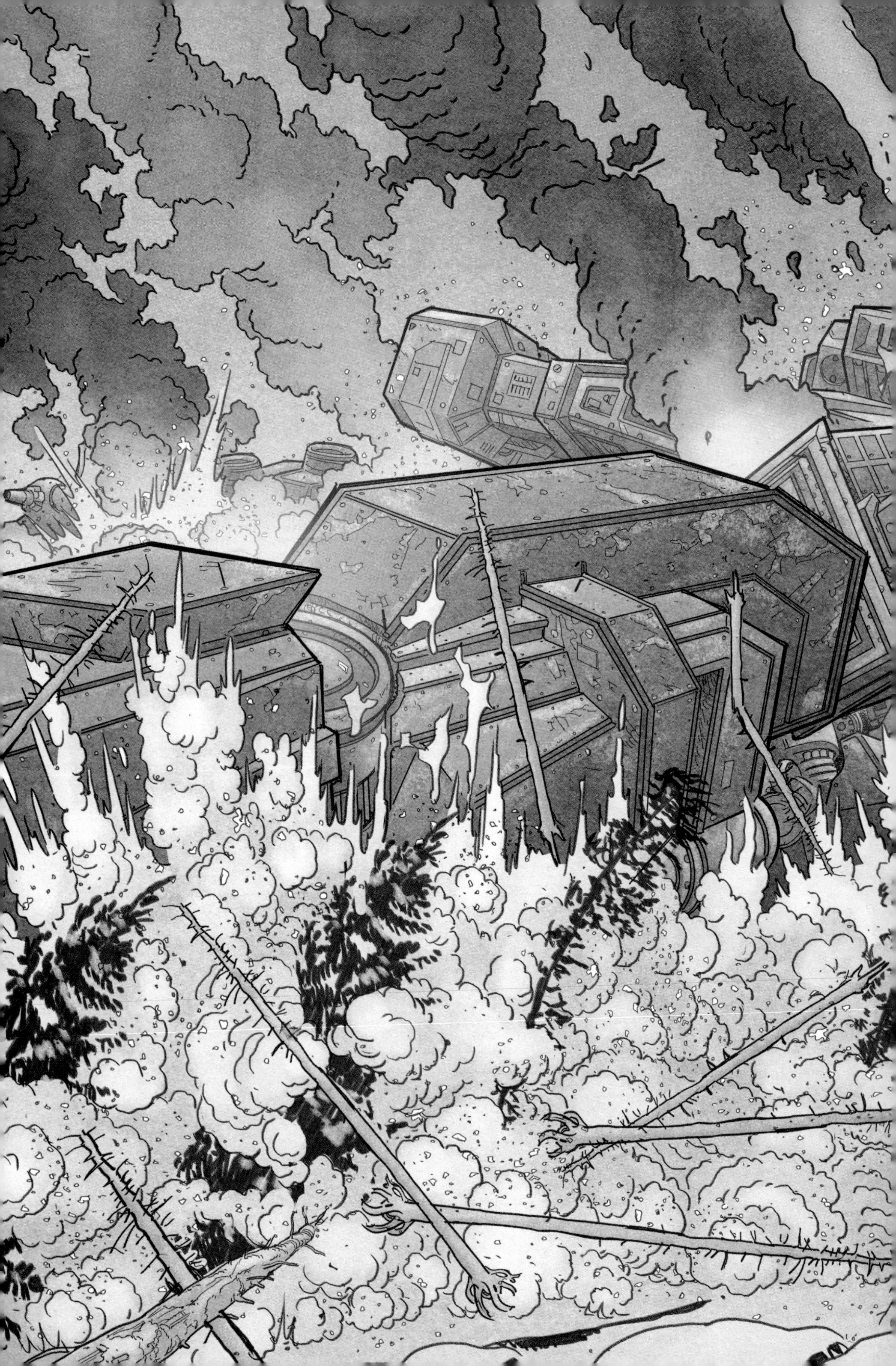

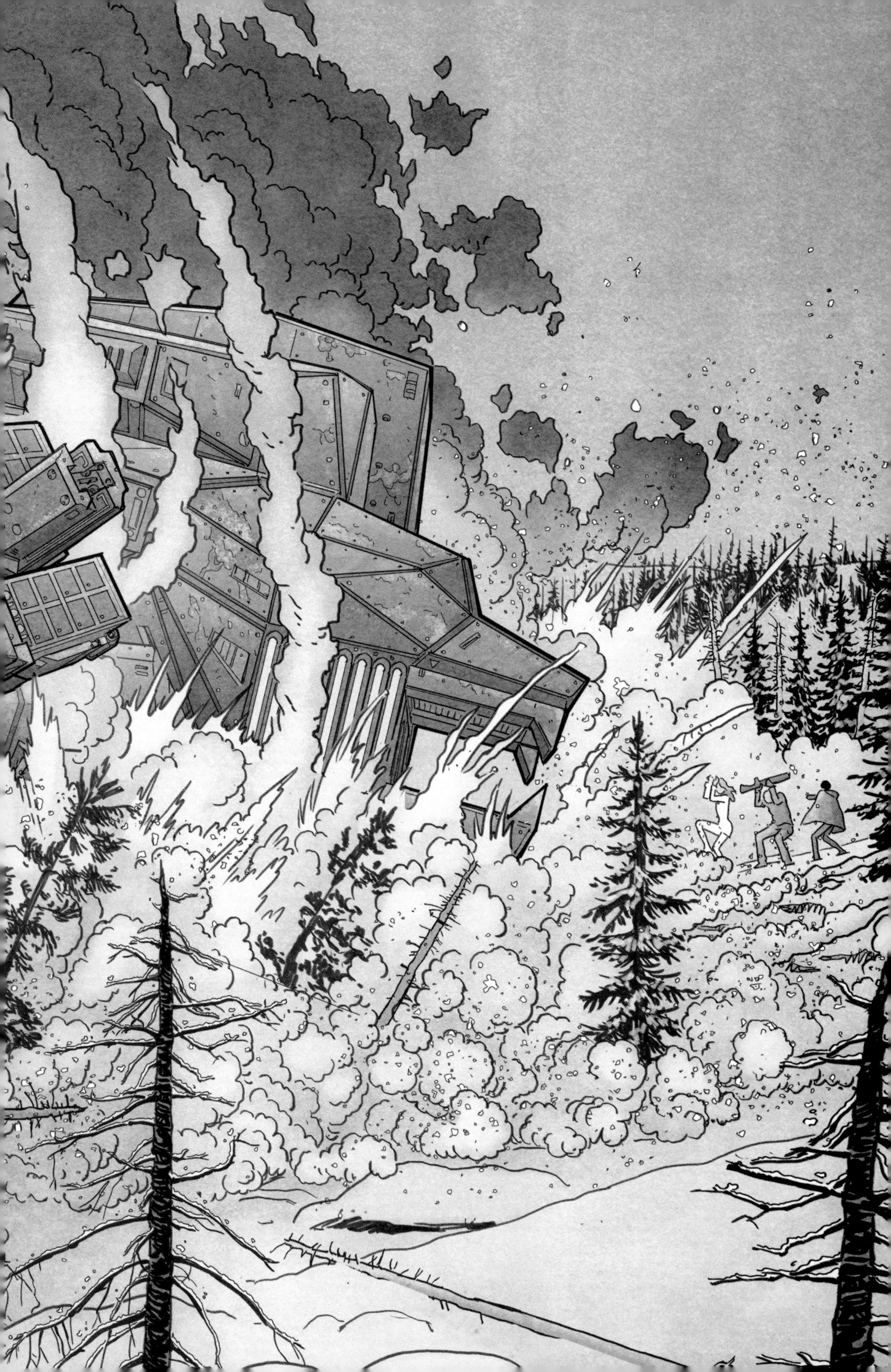

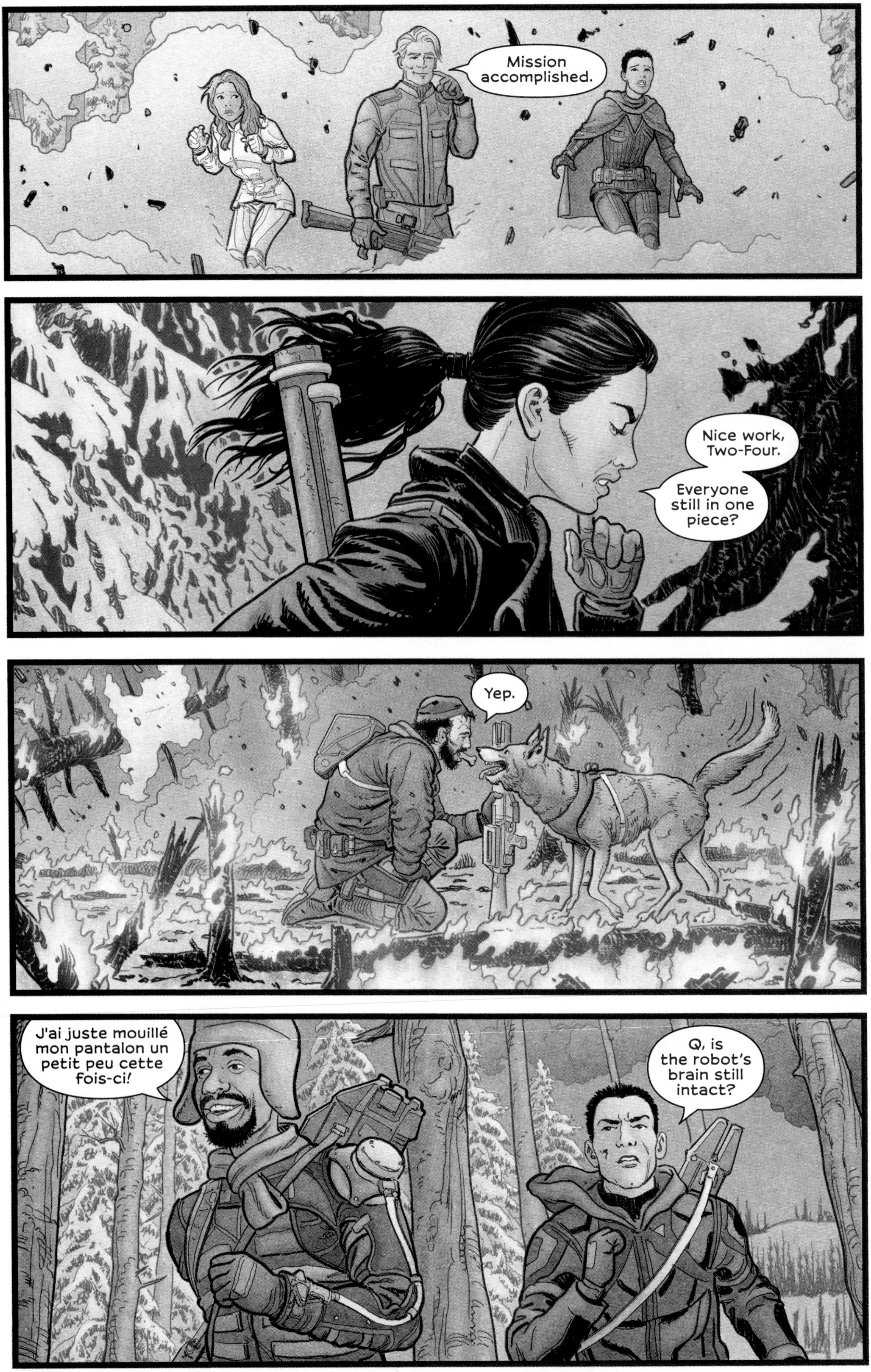

Mission accomplished.
Nice work, Two-Four.
Everyone still in one piece?
Yep.
J'ai juste mouillé mon pantalon un petit peu cette fois-ci!
Q, is the robot's brain still intact?

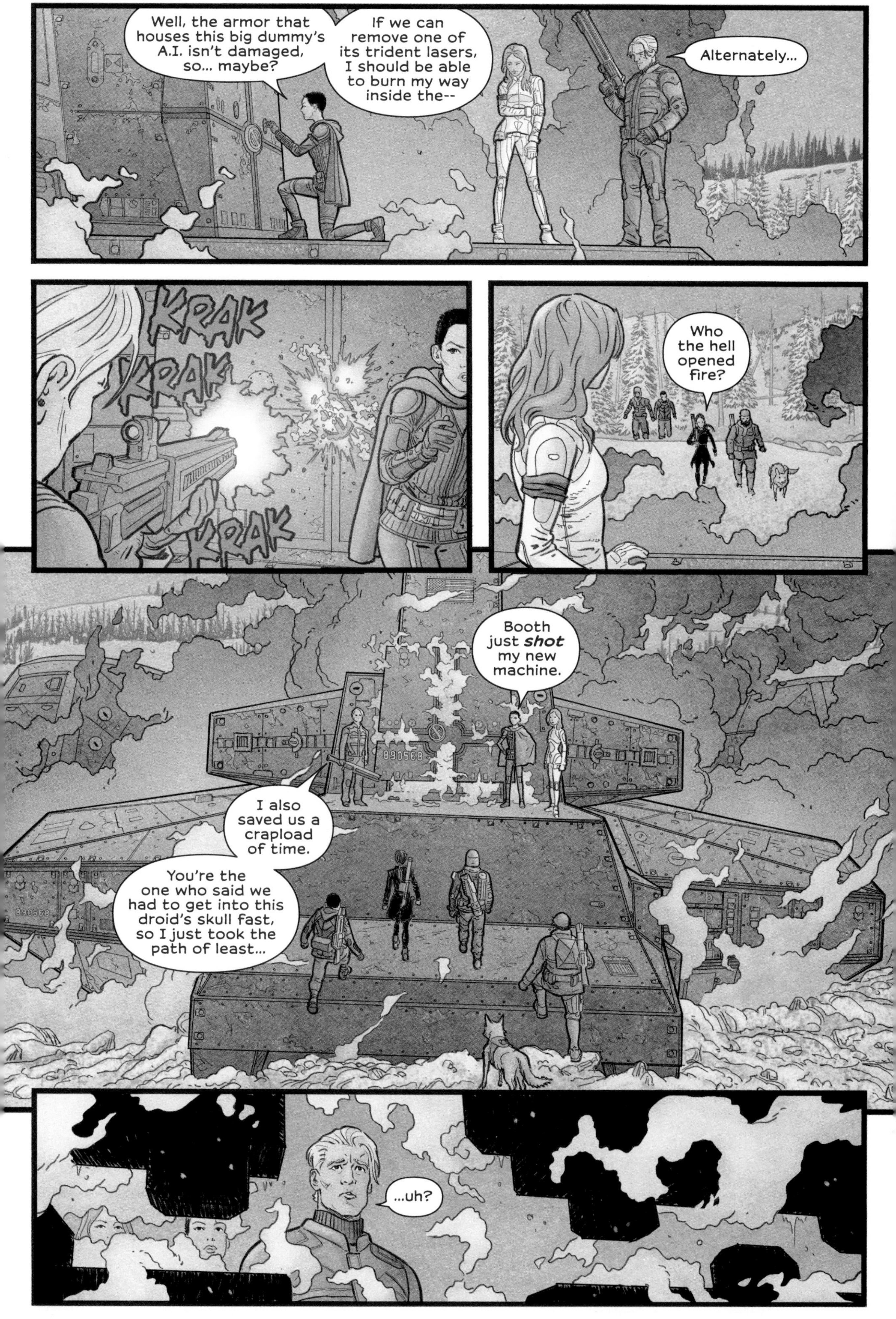
Well, the armor that houses this big dummy's A.I. isn't damaged, so... maybe?
If we can remove one of its trident lasers, I should be able to burn my way inside the--
Alternately...
KRAK
KRAK
KRAK
Who the hell opened fire?
Booth just ***shot*** my new machine.
890568
I also saved us a crapload of time.
You're the one who said we had to get into this droid's skull fast, so I just took the path of least...
890568
...uh?

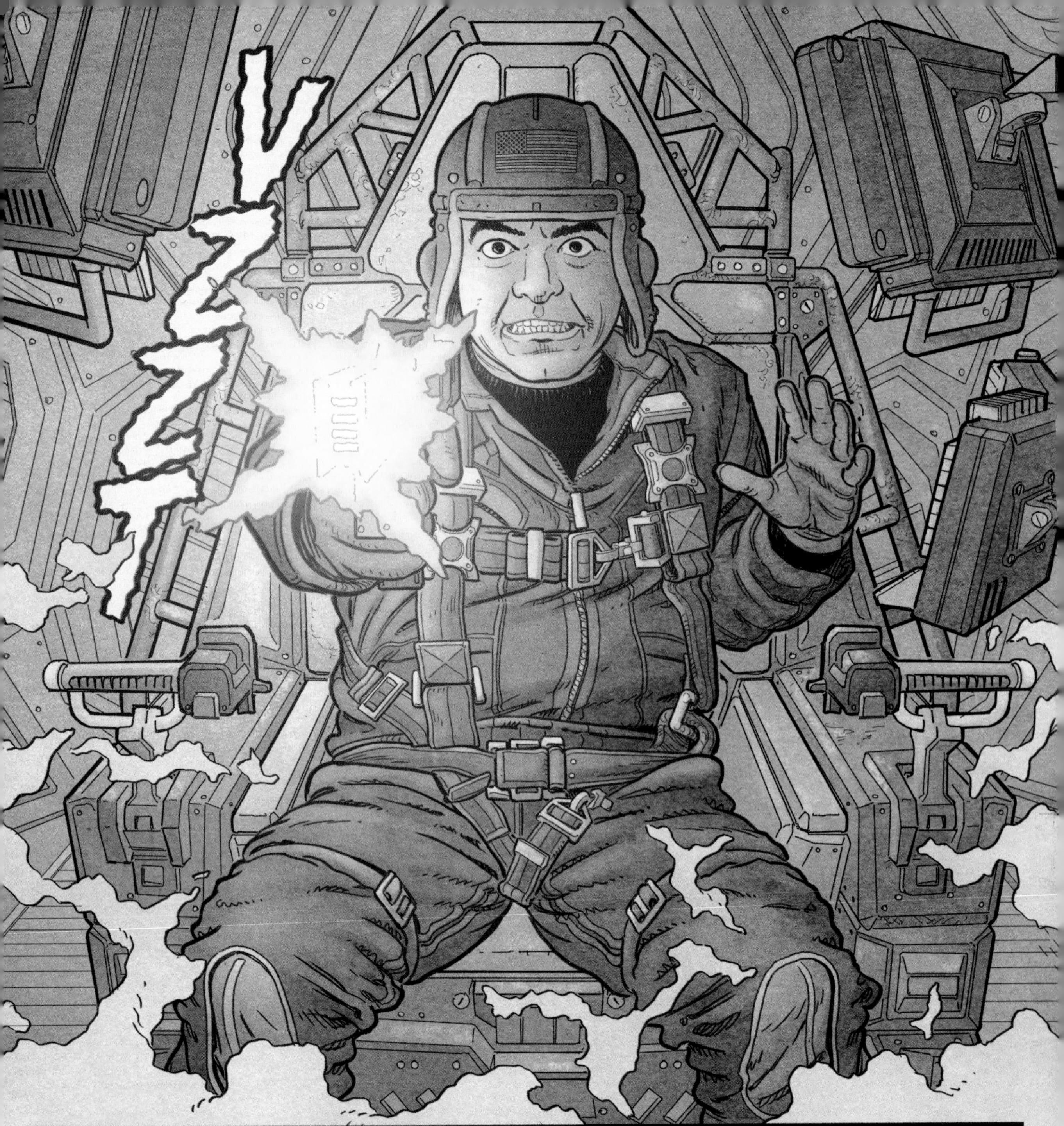
VZZT

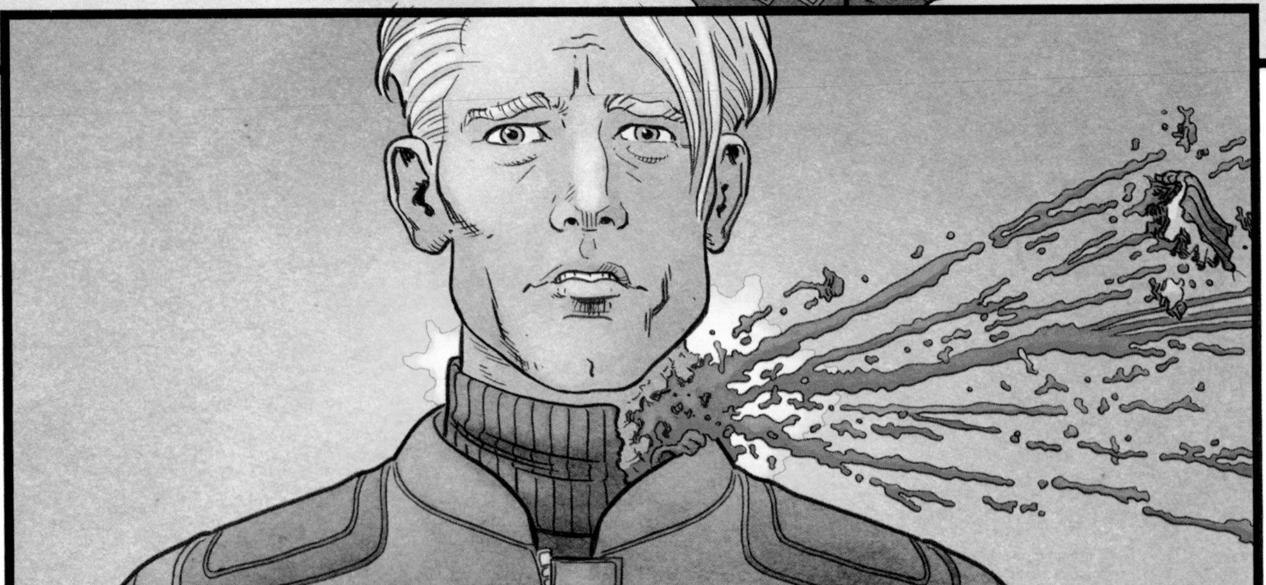

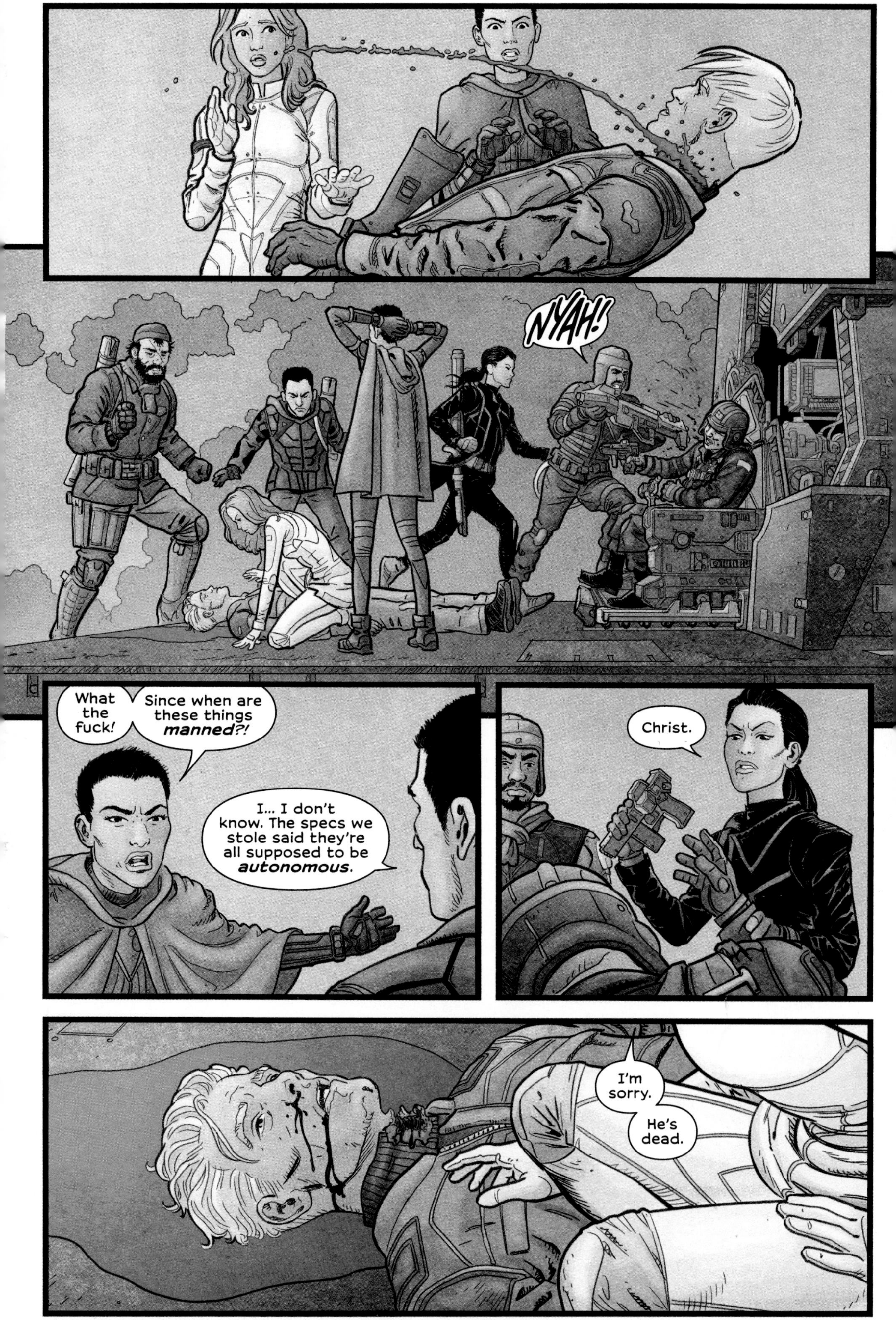
NYAH!
What the fuck!
Since when are these things *manned*?!
I... I don't know. The specs we stole said they're all supposed to be ***autonomous***.
Christ.
I'm sorry.
He's dead.

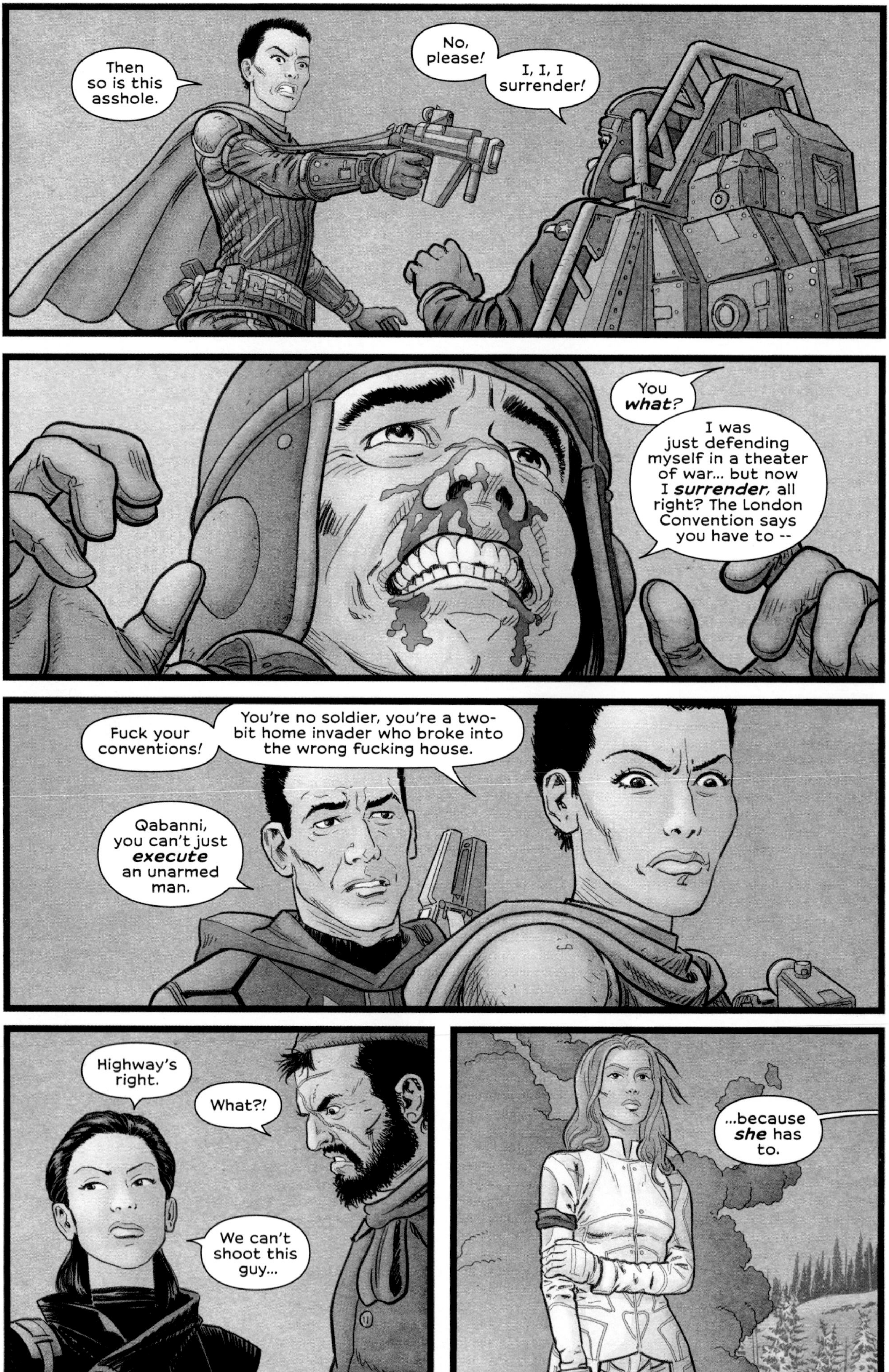
Then so is this asshole.
No, please!
I, I, I surrender!
You *what*?
I was just defending myself in a theater of war... but now I *surrender*, all right? The London Convention says you have to --
Fuck your conventions!
You're no soldier, you're a two-bit home invader who broke into the wrong fucking house.
Qabanni, you can't just *execute* an unarmed man.
Highway's right.
What?!
We can't shoot this guy...
...because *she* has to.

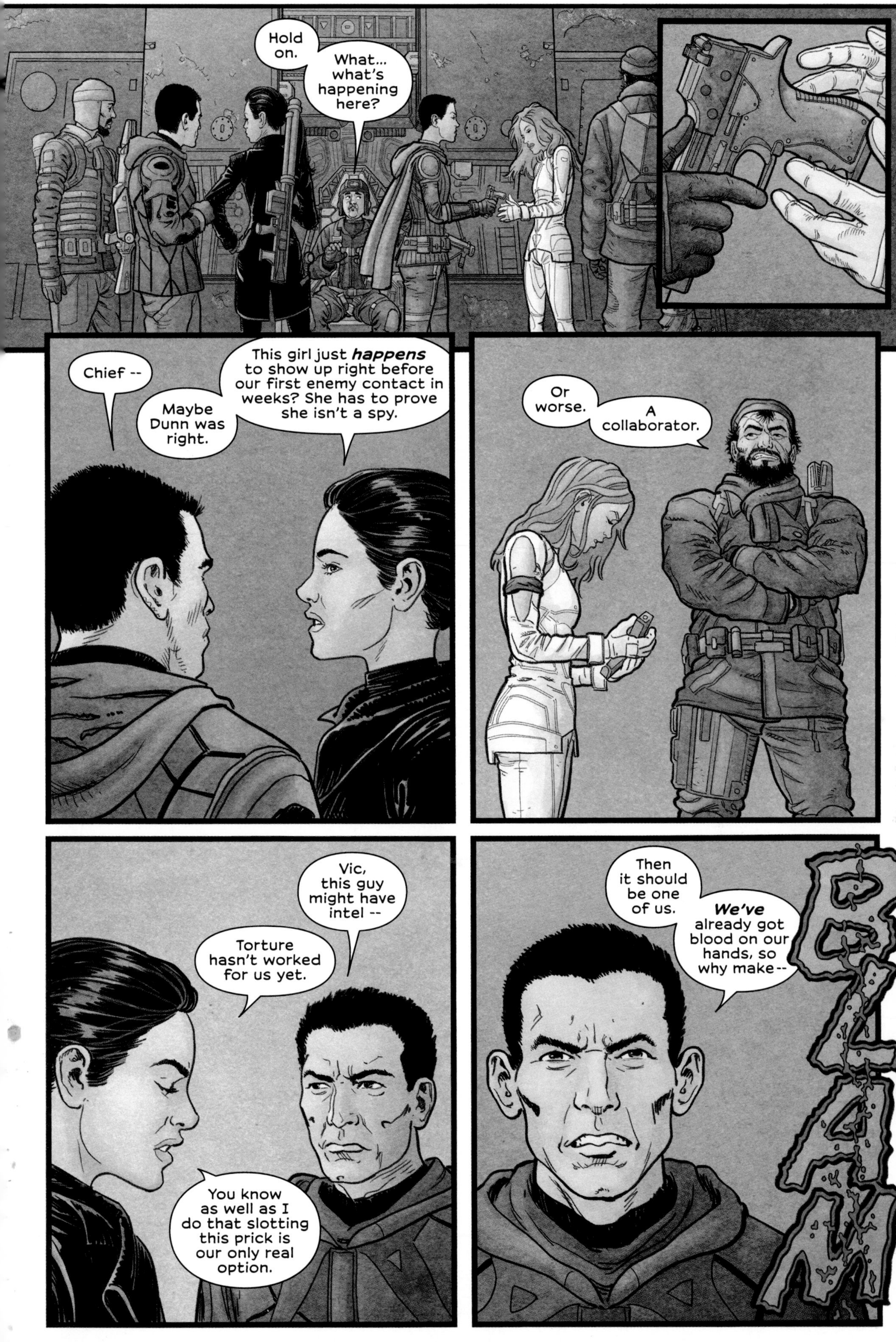

Hold on.
What... what's happening here?
Chief --
Maybe Dunn was right.
This girl just ***happens*** to show up right before our first enemy contact in weeks? She has to prove she isn't a spy.
Or worse.
A collaborator.
Vic, this guy might have intel --
Torture hasn't worked for us yet.
You know as well as I do that slotting this prick is our only real option.
Then it should be one of us.
We've already got blood on our hands, so why make --

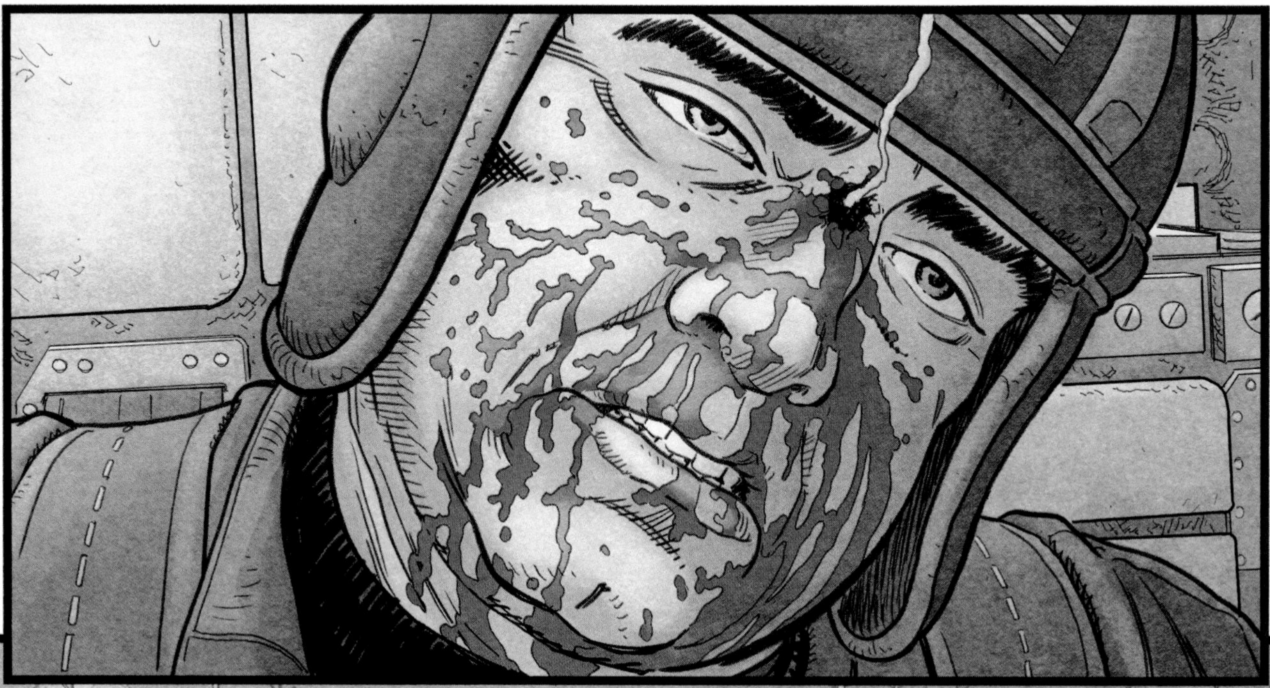

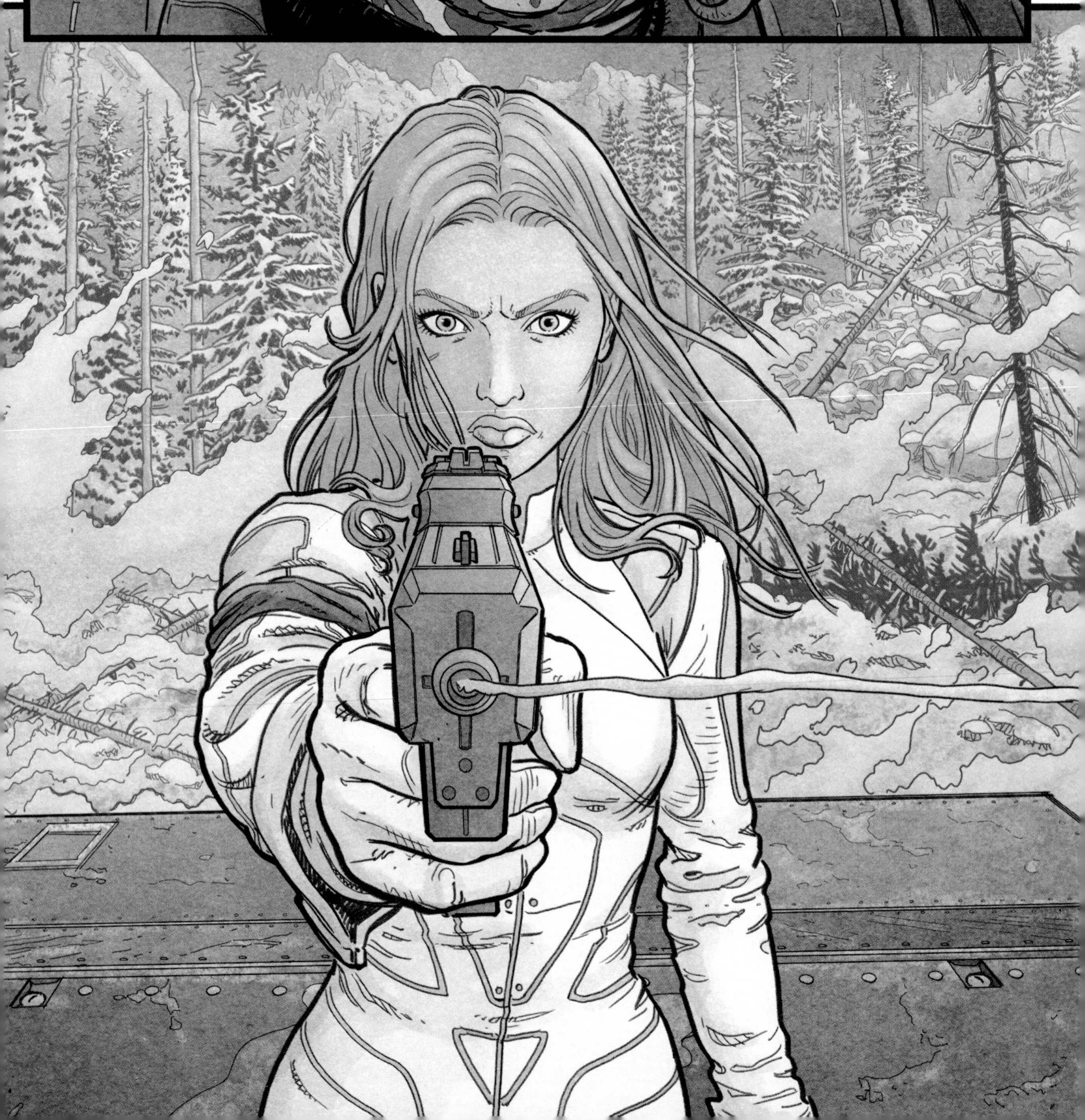

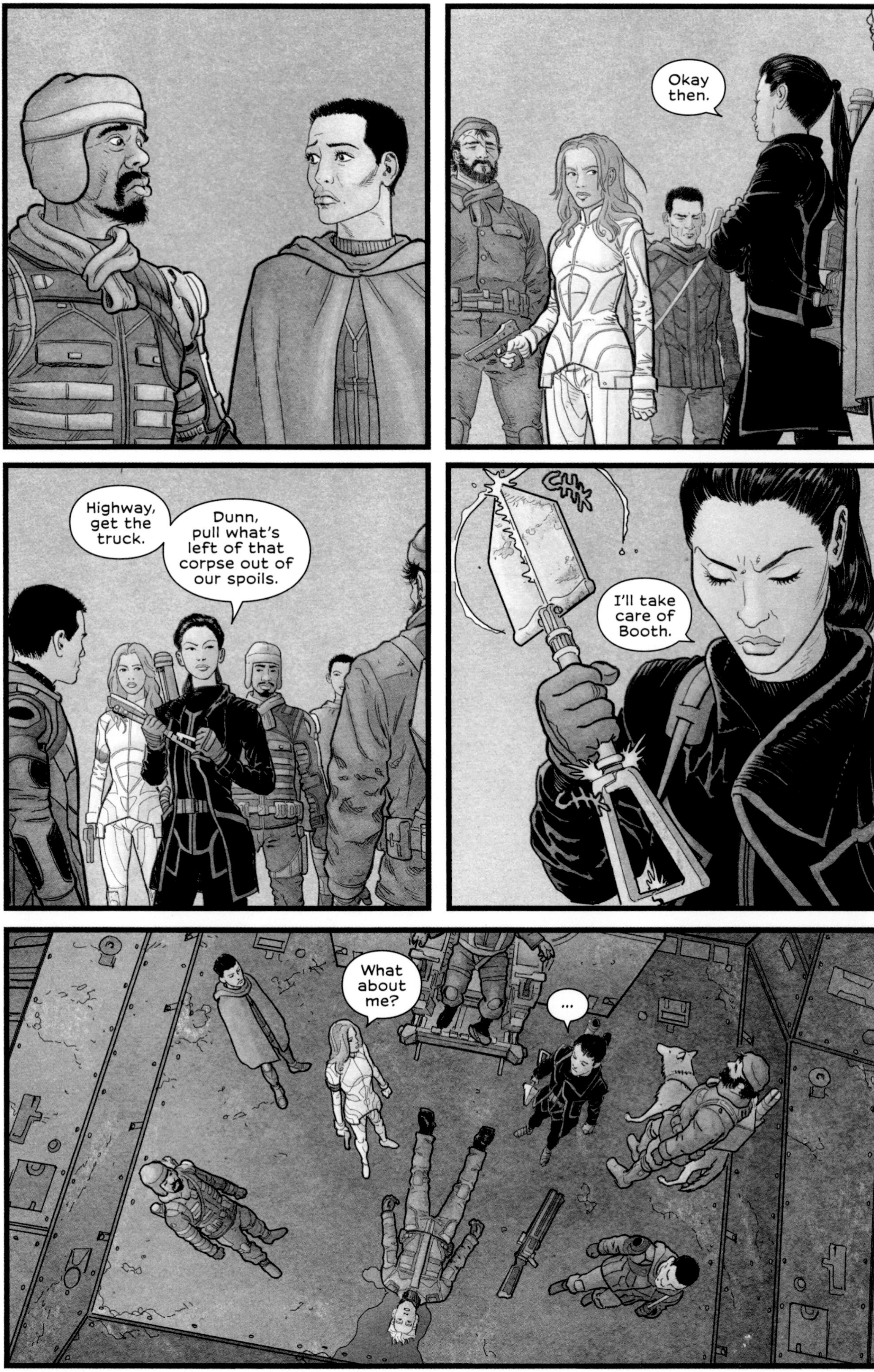
Okay then.
Highway, get the truck.
Dunn, pull what's left of that corpse out of our spoils.
CHK
I'll take care of Booth.
CHK
What about me?
...

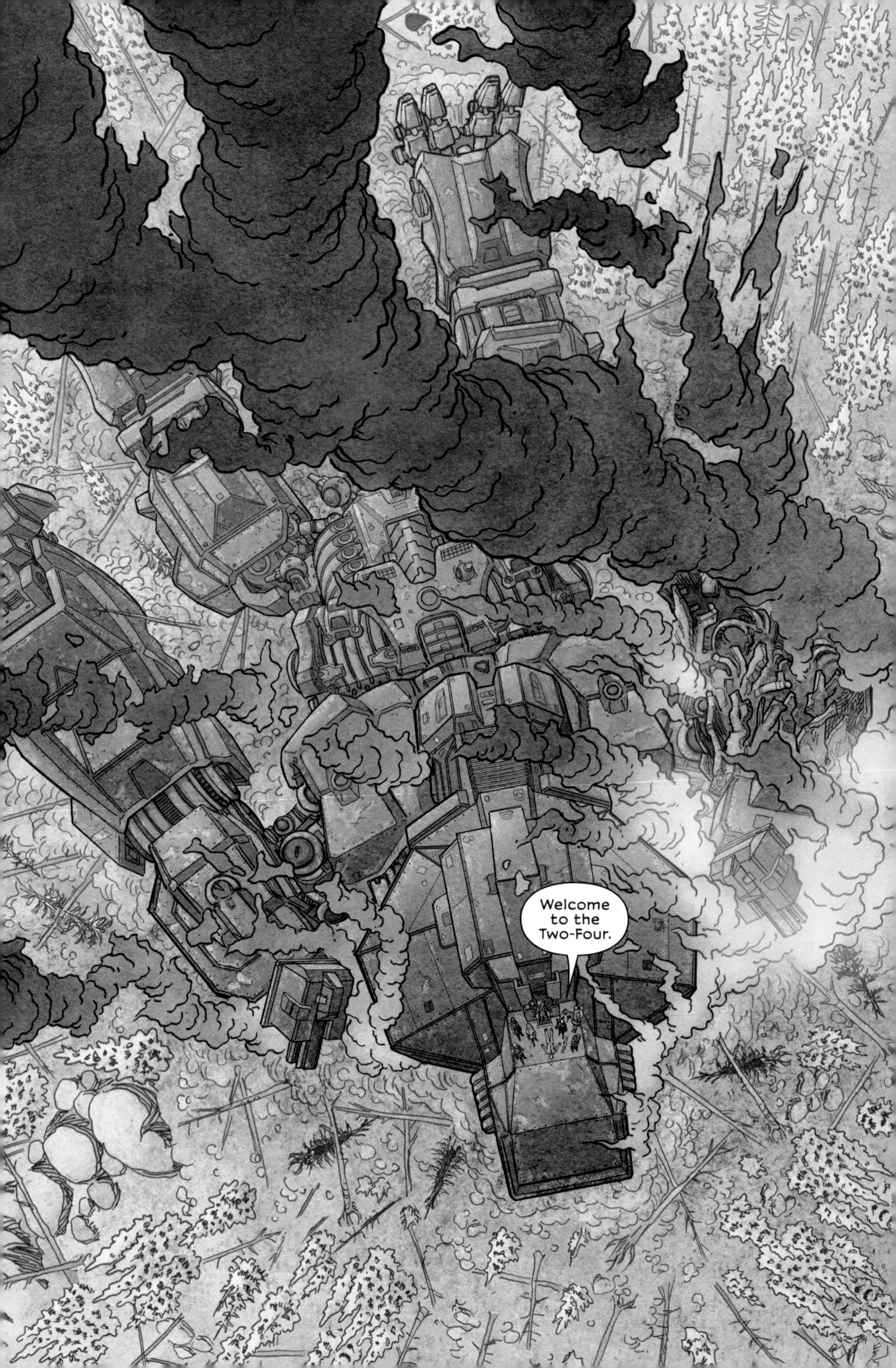
Welcome to the Two-Four.

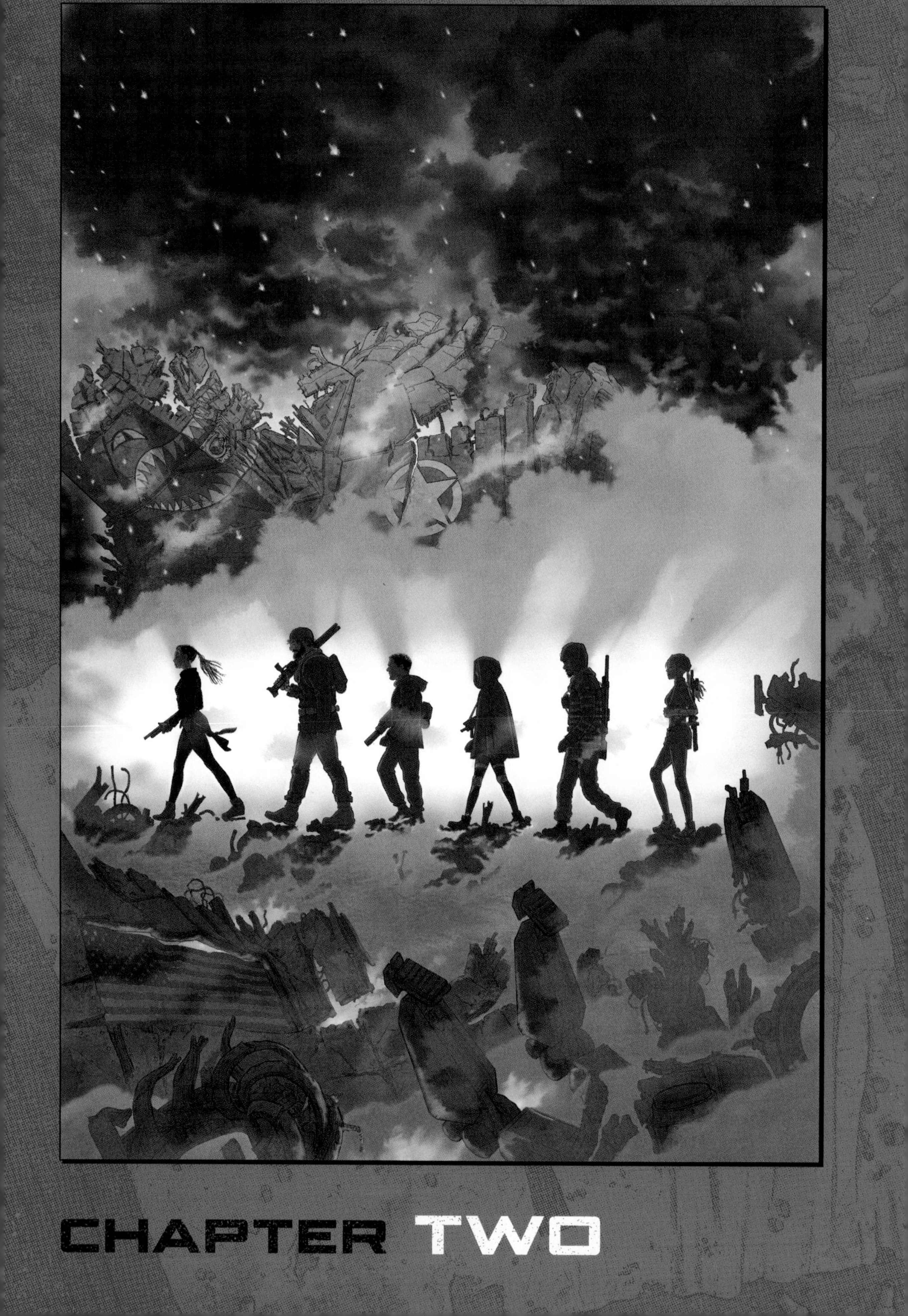

CHAPTER TWO

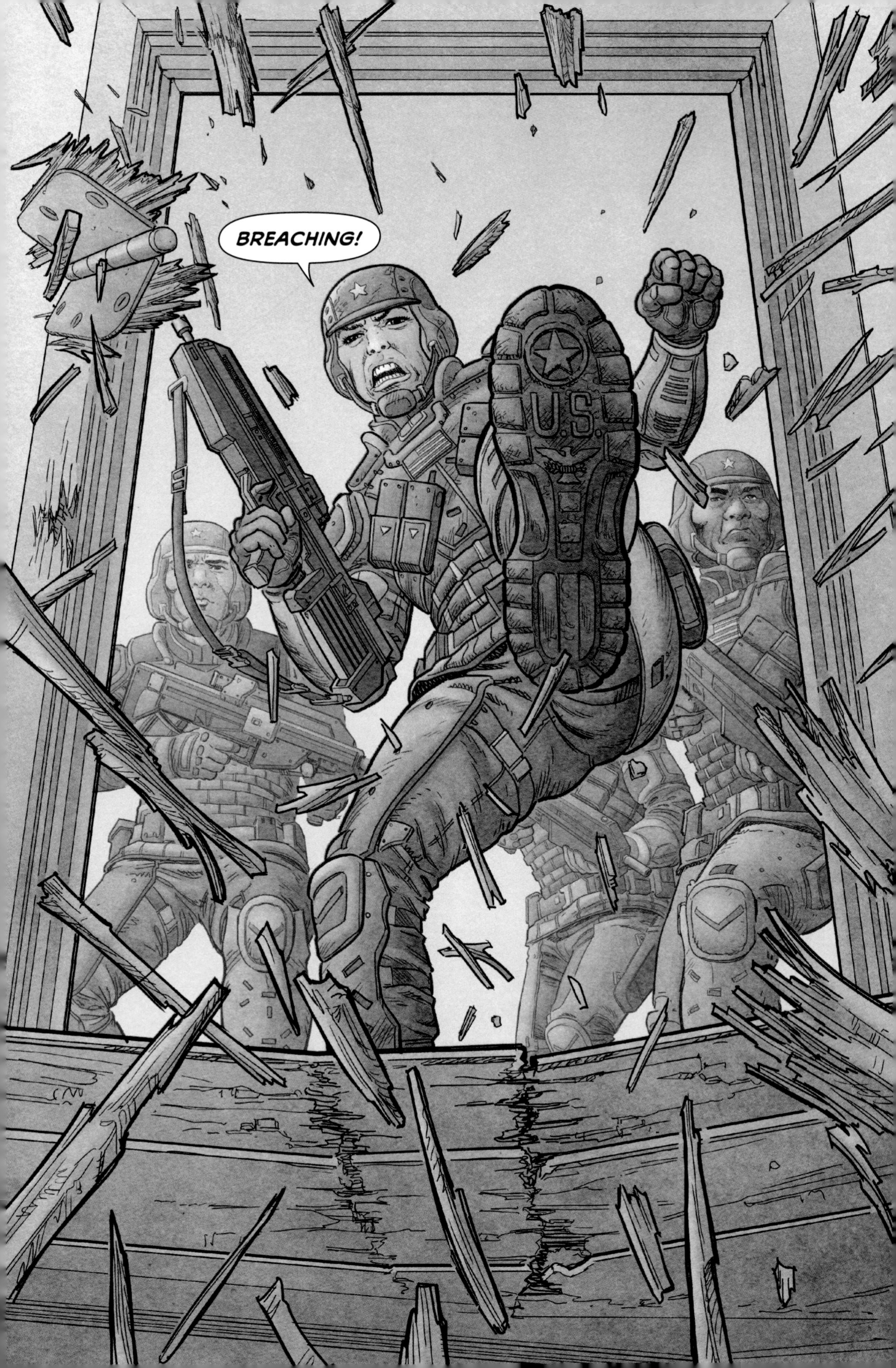
BREACHING!
U.S.

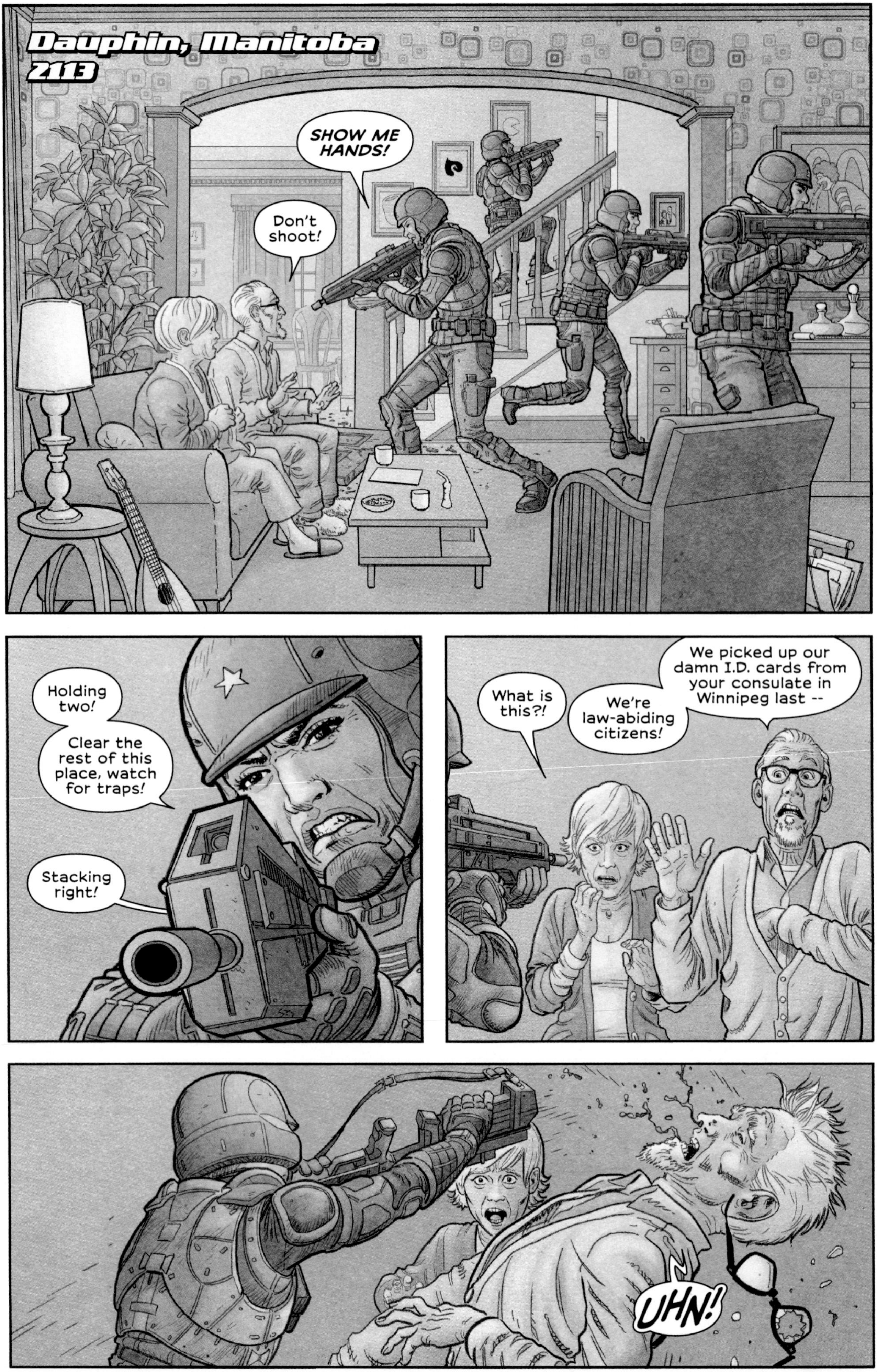
Dauphin, Manitoba
2113
SHOW ME HANDS!
Don't shoot!
Holding two!
Clear the rest of this place, watch for traps!
Stacking right!
What is this?!
We're law-abiding citizens!
We picked up our damn I.D. cards from your consulate in Winnipeg last --
UHN!

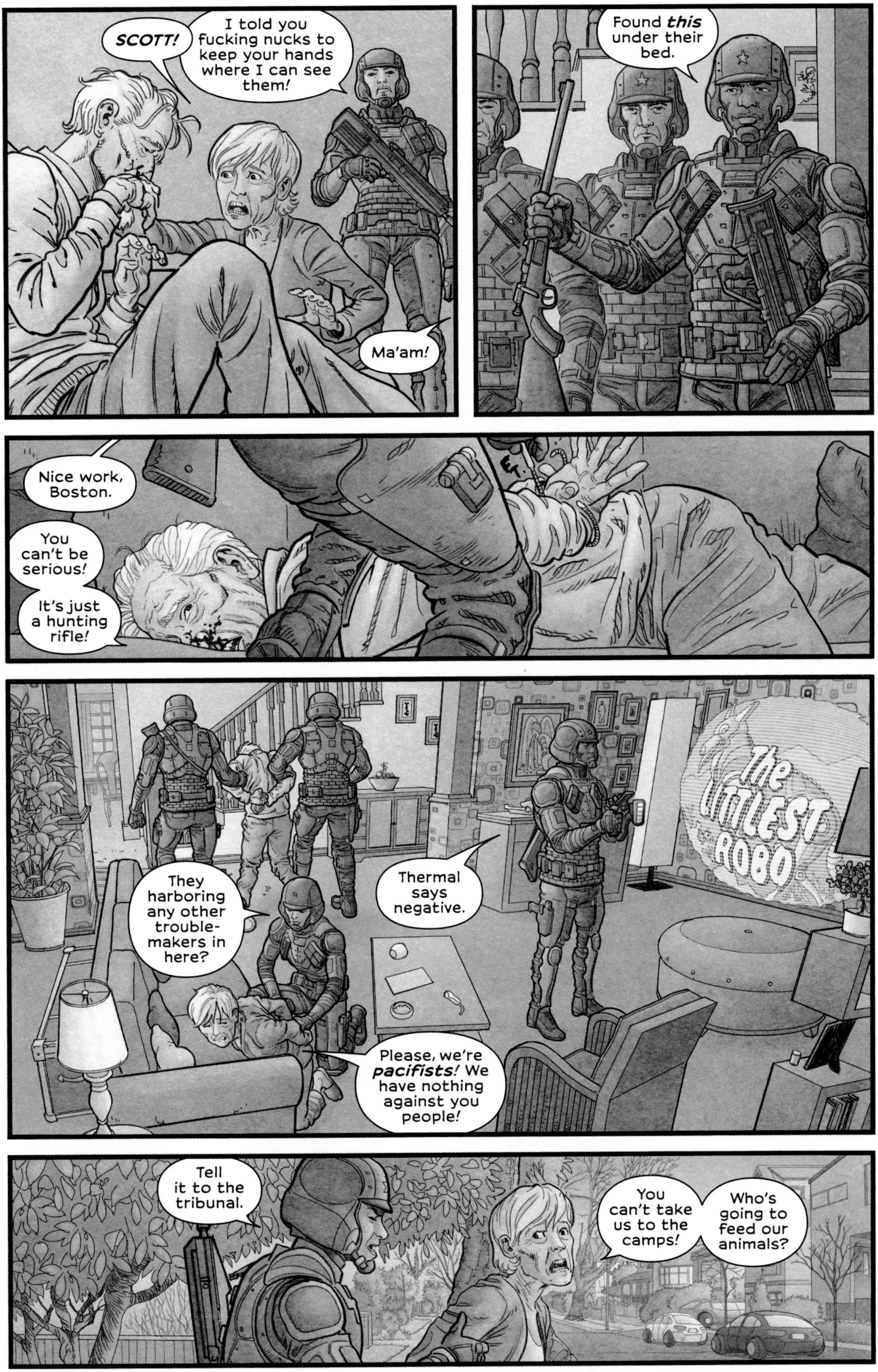
SCOTT!
I told you fucking nucks to keep your hands where I can see them!
Ma'am!
Found *this* under their bed.
Nice work, Boston.
You can't be serious!
It's just a hunting rifle!
The LITTLEST ROBO
They harboring any other trouble-makers in here?
Thermal says negative.
Please, we're *pacifists!* We have nothing against you people!
Tell it to the tribunal.
You can't take us to the camps!
Who's going to feed our animals?

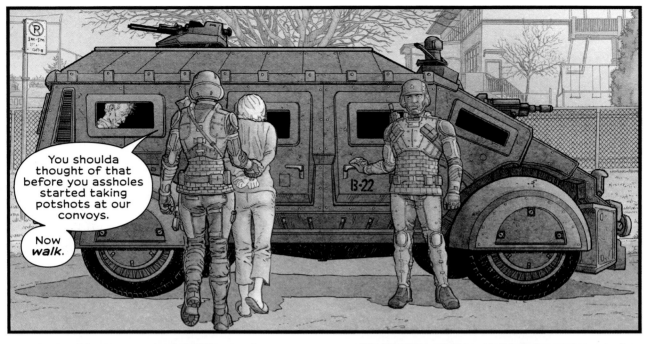

You shoulda thought of that before you assholes started taking potshots at our convoys.

Now *walk*.

RURF RURF RURF ARK ARK ARK

Amber?

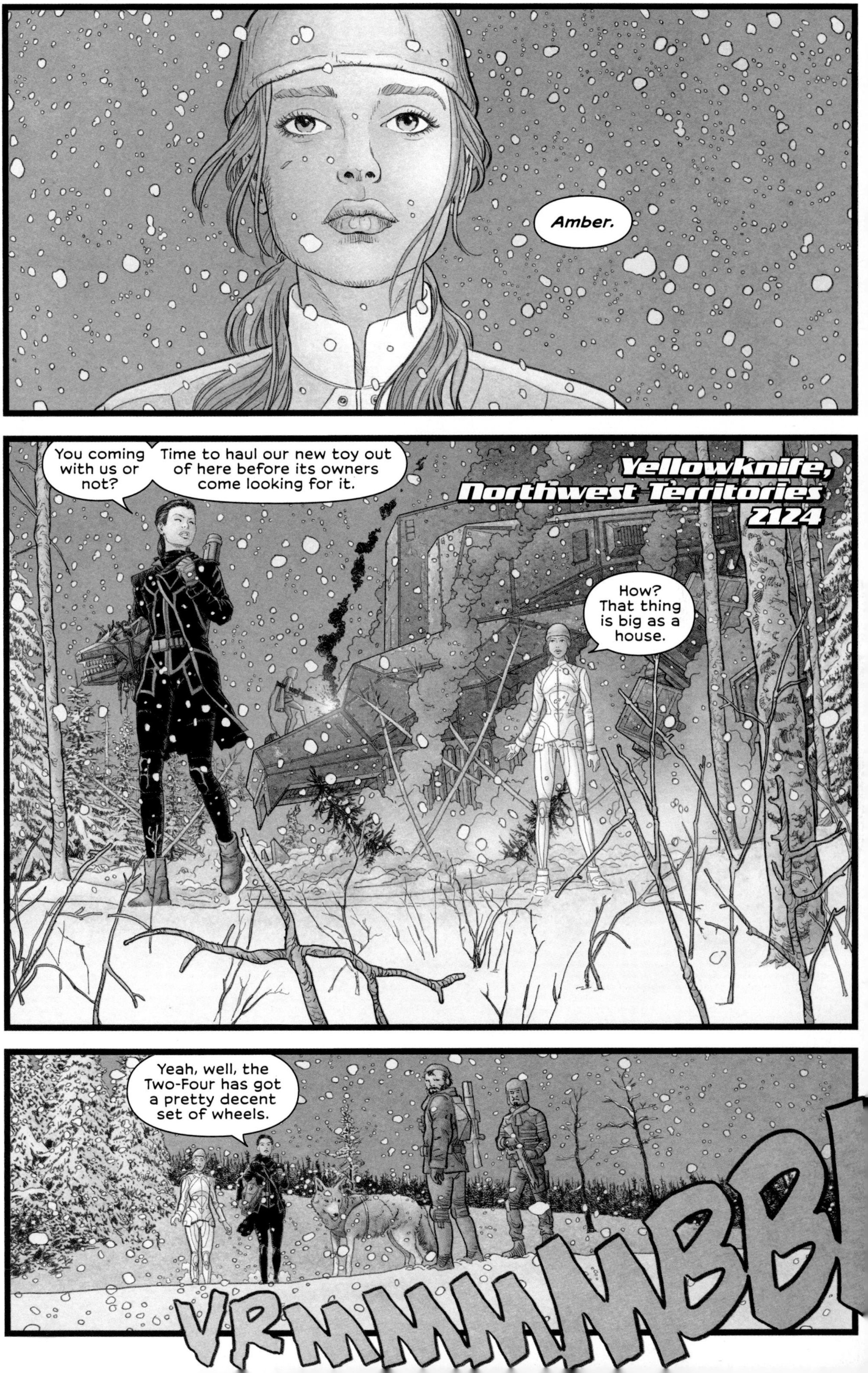
Amber.
You coming with us or not?
Time to haul our new toy out of here before its owners come looking for it.
Yellowknife, Northwest Territories 2124
How? That thing is big as a house.
Yeah, well, the Two-Four has got a pretty decent set of wheels.
VRMMMMBB

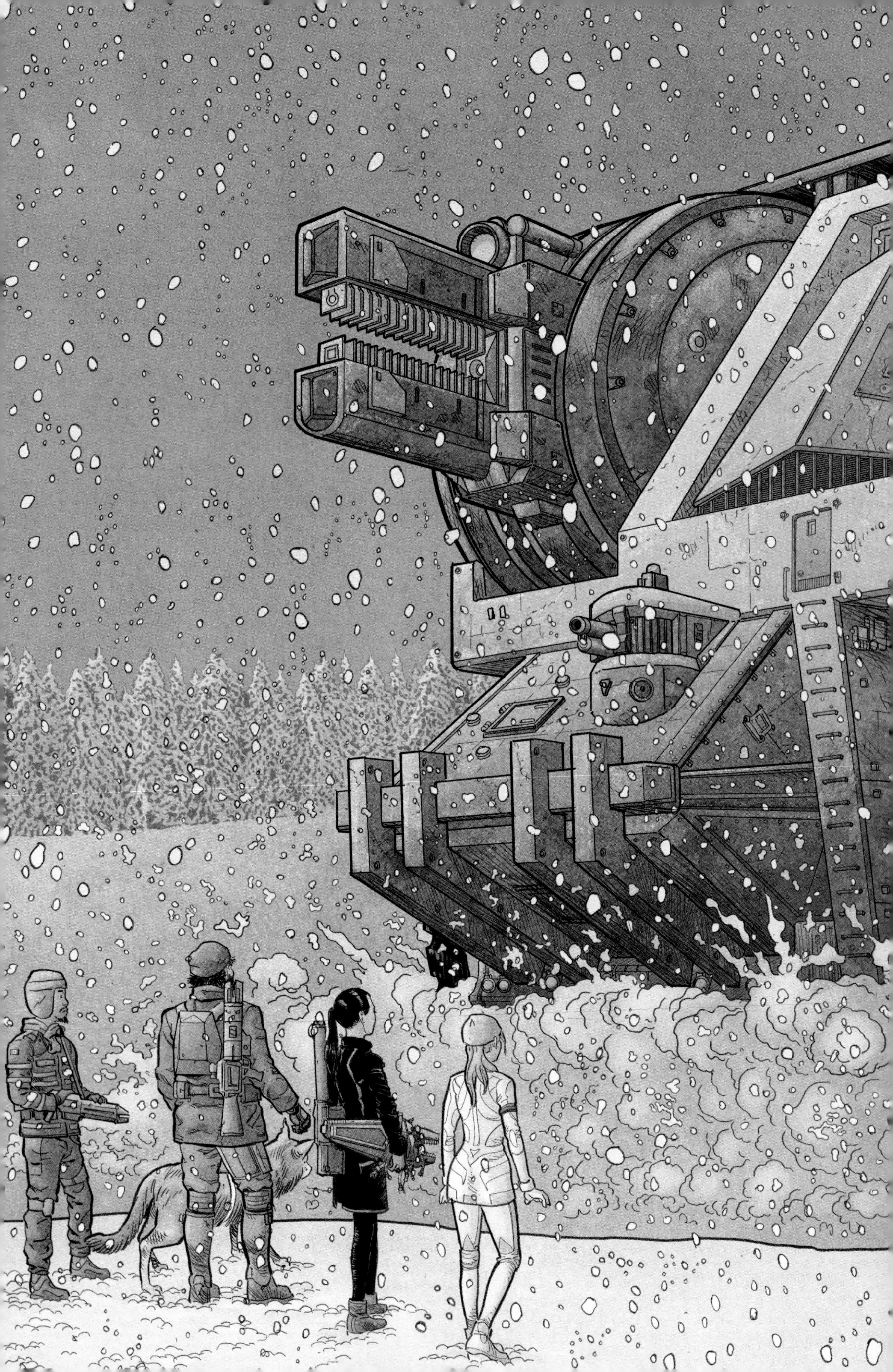

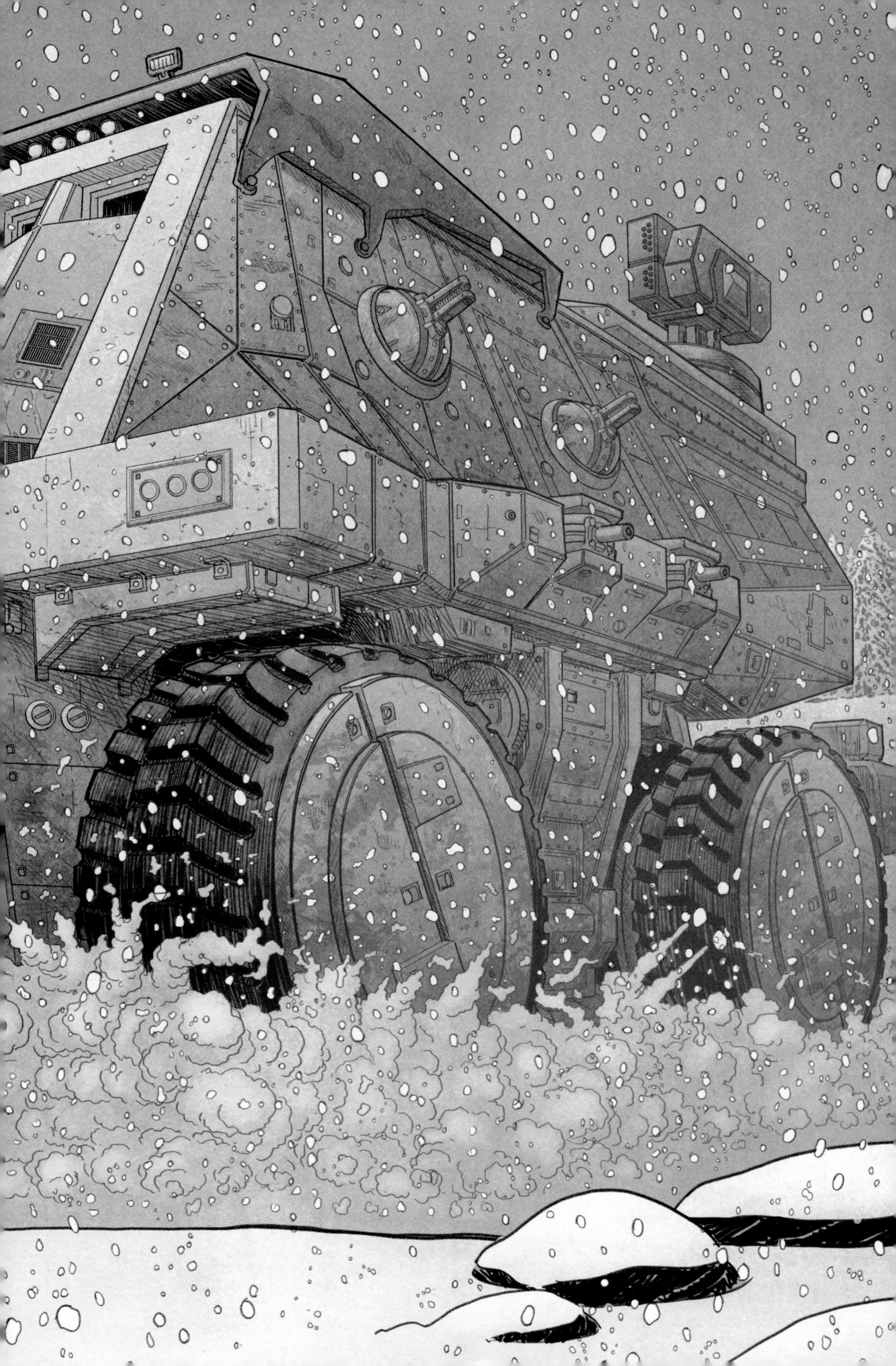

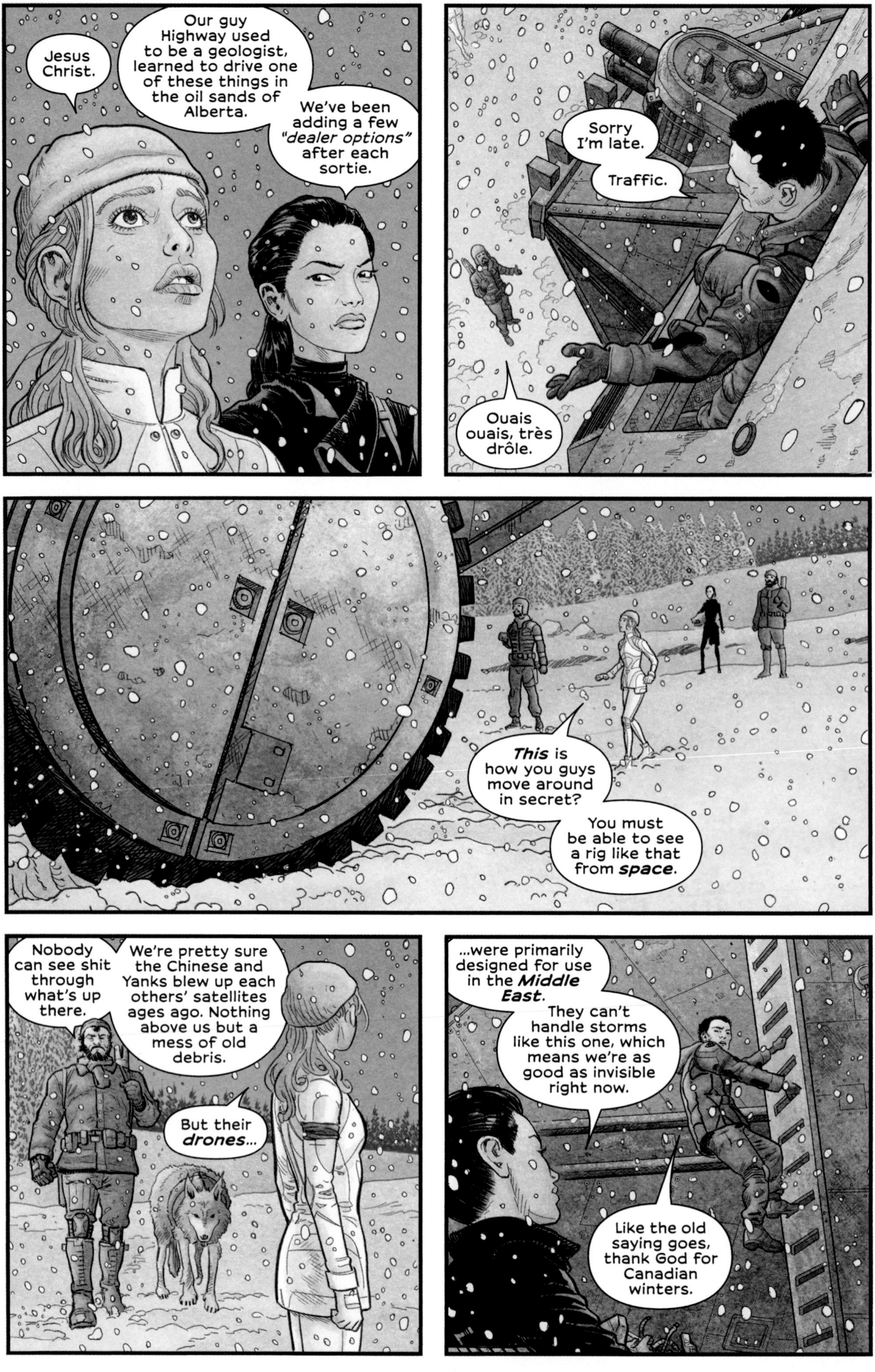
Jesus Christ.
Our guy Highway used to be a geologist, learned to drive one of these things in the oil sands of Alberta.
We've been adding a few *"dealer options"* after each sortie.
Sorry I'm late.
Traffic.
Ouais ouais, très drôle.
This is how you guys move around in secret?
You must be able to see a rig like that from *space*.
Nobody can see shit through what's up there.
We're pretty sure the Chinese and Yanks blew up each others' satellites ages ago. Nothing above us but a mess of old debris.
But their *drones*...
...were primarily designed for use in the *Middle East*.
They can't handle storms like this one, which means we're as good as invisible right now.
Like the old saying goes, thank God for Canadian winters.

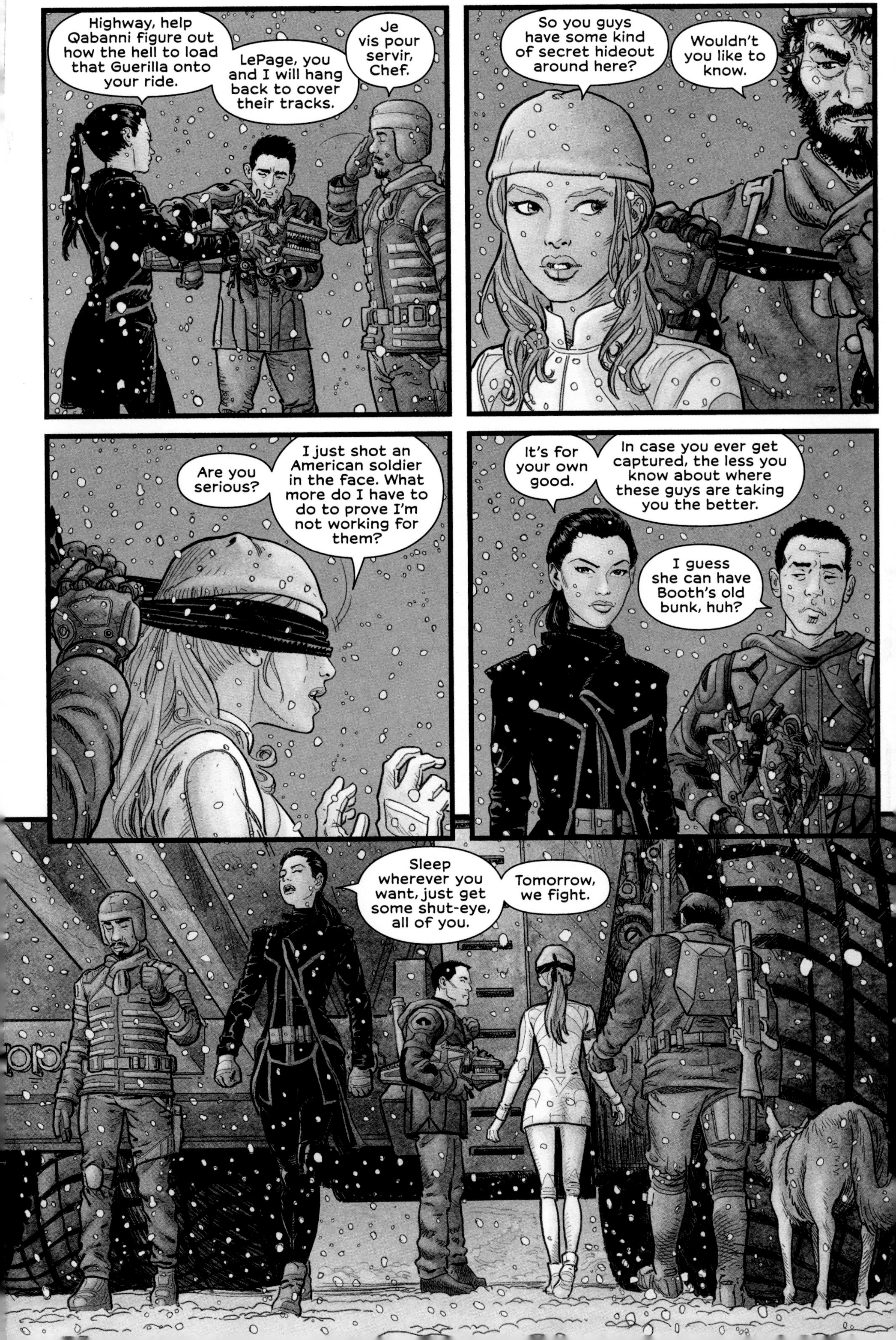
Highway, help Qabanni figure out how the hell to load that Guerilla onto your ride.
LePage, you and I will hang back to cover their tracks.
Je vis pour servir, Chef.
So you guys have some kind of secret hideout around here?
Wouldn't you like to know.
Are you serious?
I just shot an American soldier in the face. What more do I have to do to prove I'm not working for them?
It's for your own good.
In case you ever get captured, the less you know about where these guys are taking you the better.
I guess she can have Booth's old bunk, huh?
Sleep wherever you want, just get some shut-eye, all of you.
Tomorrow, we fight.

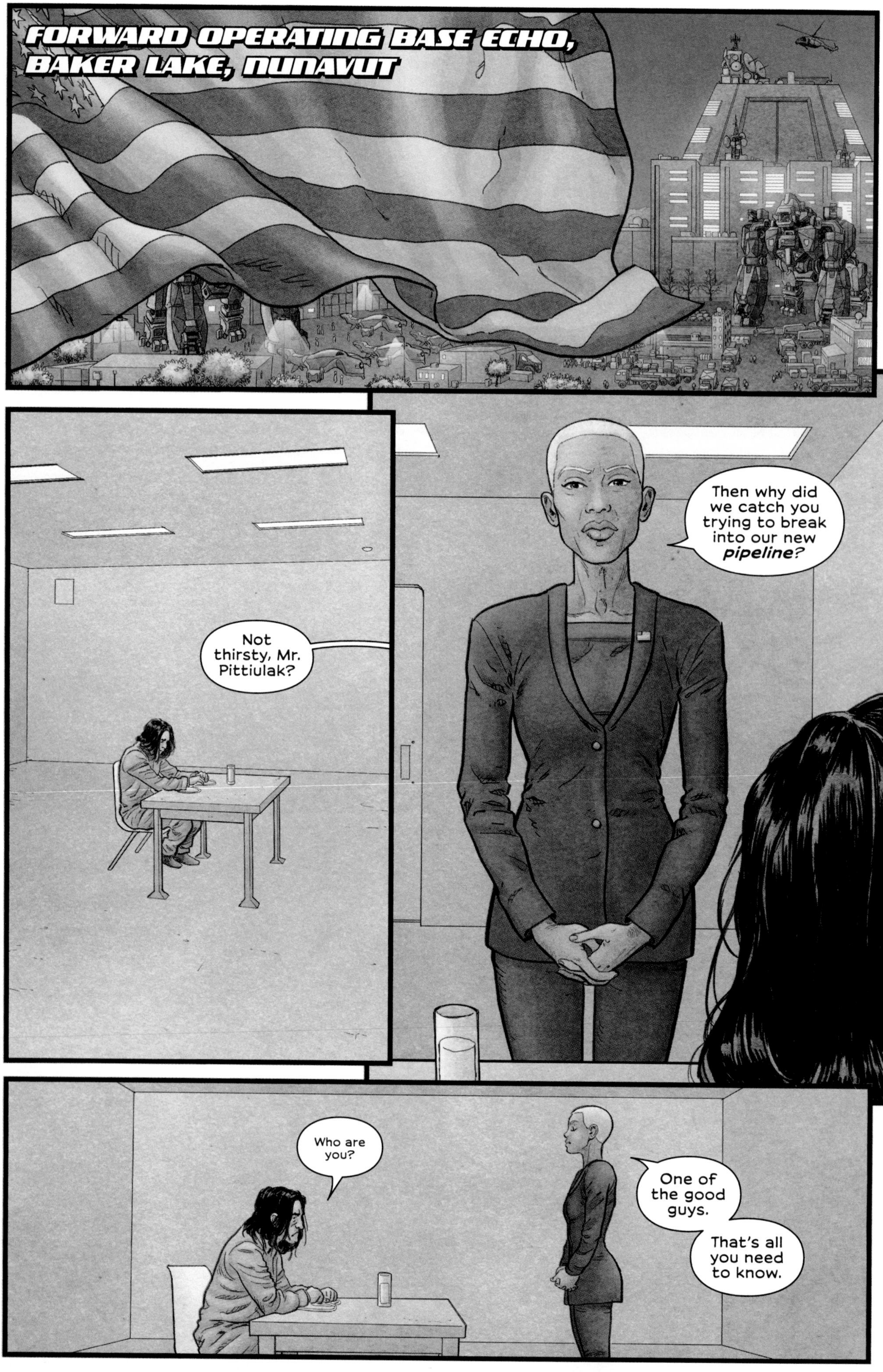
FORWARD OPERATING BASE ECHO, BAKER LAKE, NUNAVUT
Not thirsty, Mr. Pittiulak?
Then why did we catch you trying to break into our new *pipeline*?
Who are you?
One of the good guys.
That's all you need to know.

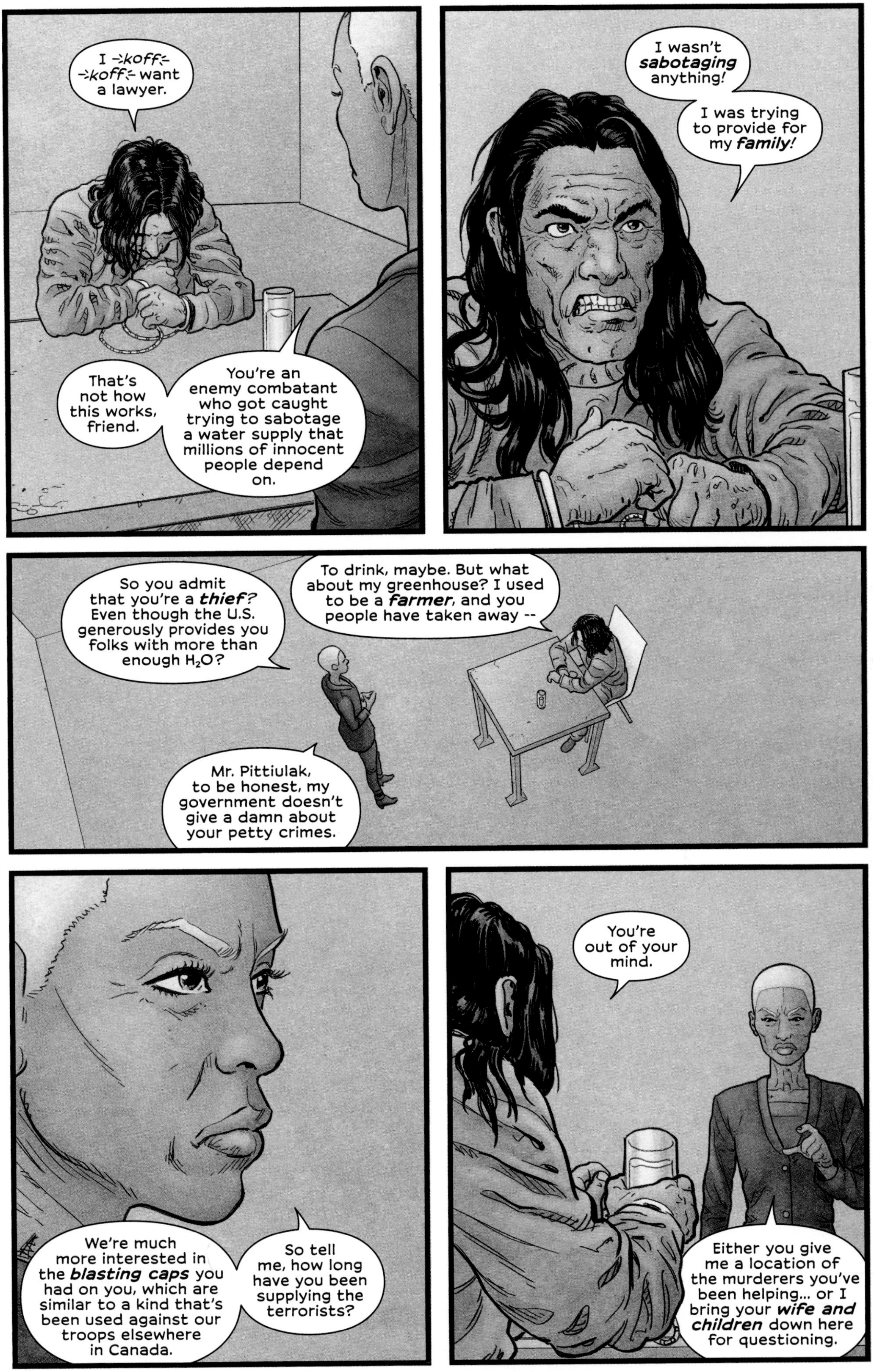

I -koff- -koff- want a lawyer.
That's not how this works, friend.
You're an enemy combatant who got caught trying to sabotage a water supply that millions of innocent people depend on.
I wasn't *sabotaging* anything!
I was trying to provide for my *family!*
So you admit that you're a *thief?* Even though the U.S. generously provides you folks with more than enough H_2O?
To drink, maybe. But what about my greenhouse? I used to be a *farmer*, and you people have taken away --
Mr. Pittiulak, to be honest, my government doesn't give a damn about your petty crimes.
We're much more interested in the *blasting caps* you had on you, which are similar to a kind that's been used against our troops elsewhere in Canada.
So tell me, how long have you been supplying the terrorists?
You're out of your mind.
Either you give me a location of the murderers you've been helping... or I bring your *wife and children* down here for questioning.

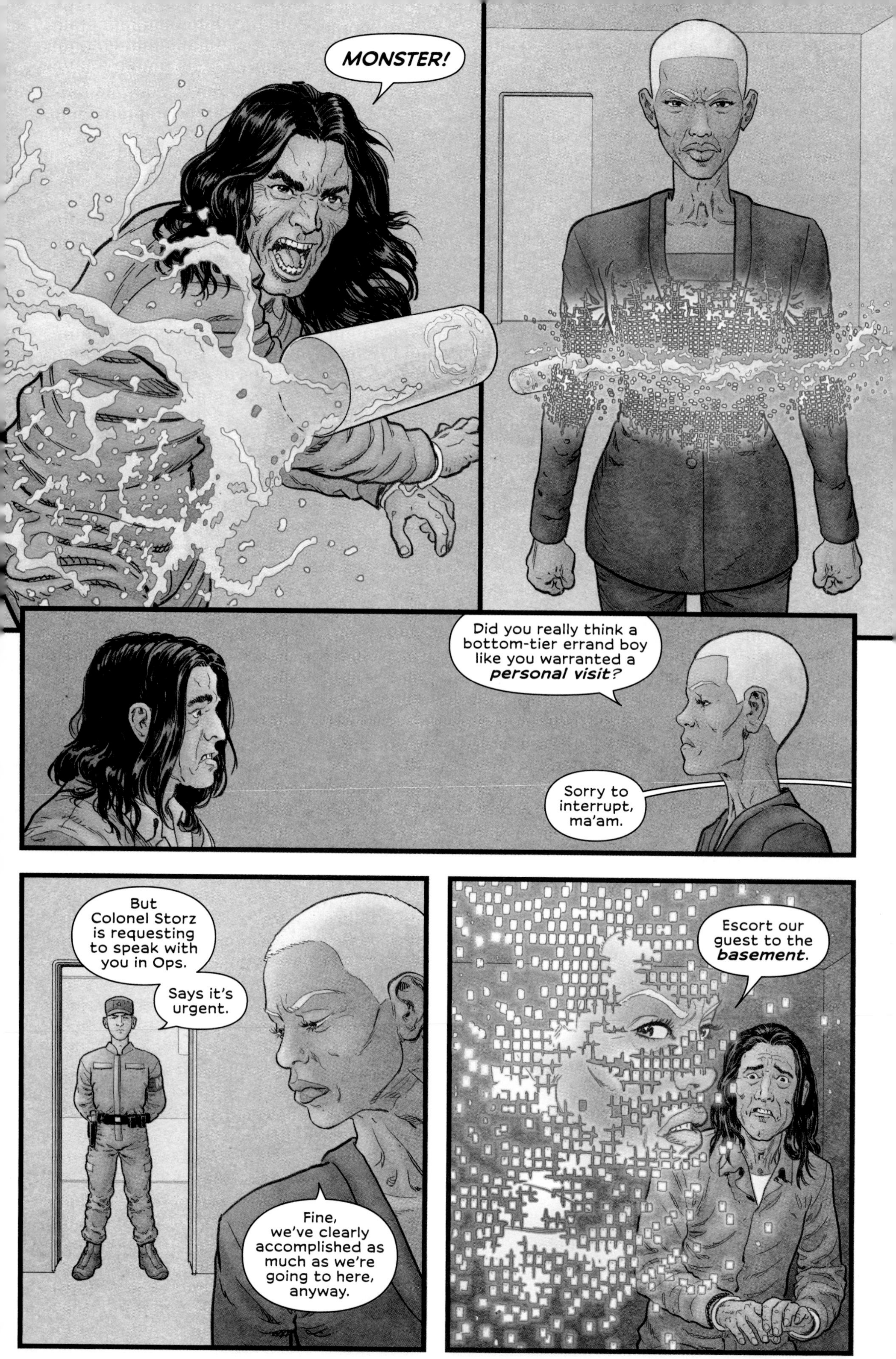
MONSTER!
Did you really think a bottom-tier errand boy like you warranted a ***personal visit***?
Sorry to interrupt, ma'am.
But Colonel Storz is requesting to speak with you in Ops.
Says it's urgent.
Fine, we've clearly accomplished as much as we're going to here, anyway.
Escort our guest to the ***basement***.

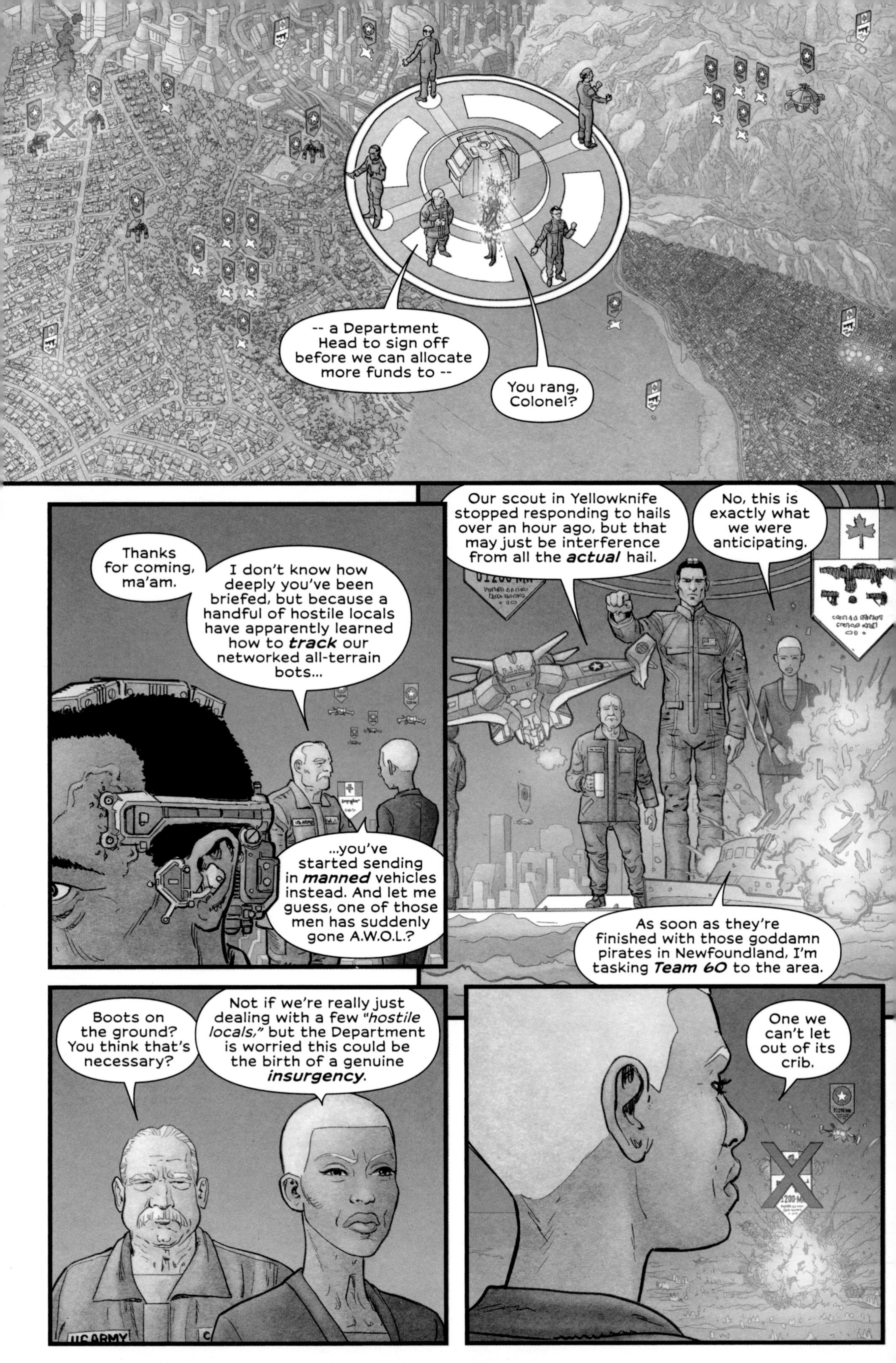

-- a Department Head to sign off before we can allocate more funds to --
You rang, Colonel?
Thanks for coming, ma'am.
I don't know how deeply you've been briefed, but because a handful of hostile locals have apparently learned how to *track* our networked all-terrain bots...
...you've started sending in *manned* vehicles instead. And let me guess, one of those men has suddenly gone A.W.O.L.?
Our scout in Yellowknife stopped responding to hails over an hour ago, but that may just be interference from all the *actual* hail.
No, this is exactly what we were anticipating.
As soon as they're finished with those goddamn pirates in Newfoundland, I'm tasking *Team 60* to the area.
Boots on the ground? You think that's necessary?
Not if we're really just dealing with a few *"hostile locals,"* but the Department is worried this could be the birth of a genuine *insurgency*.
One we can't let out of its crib.

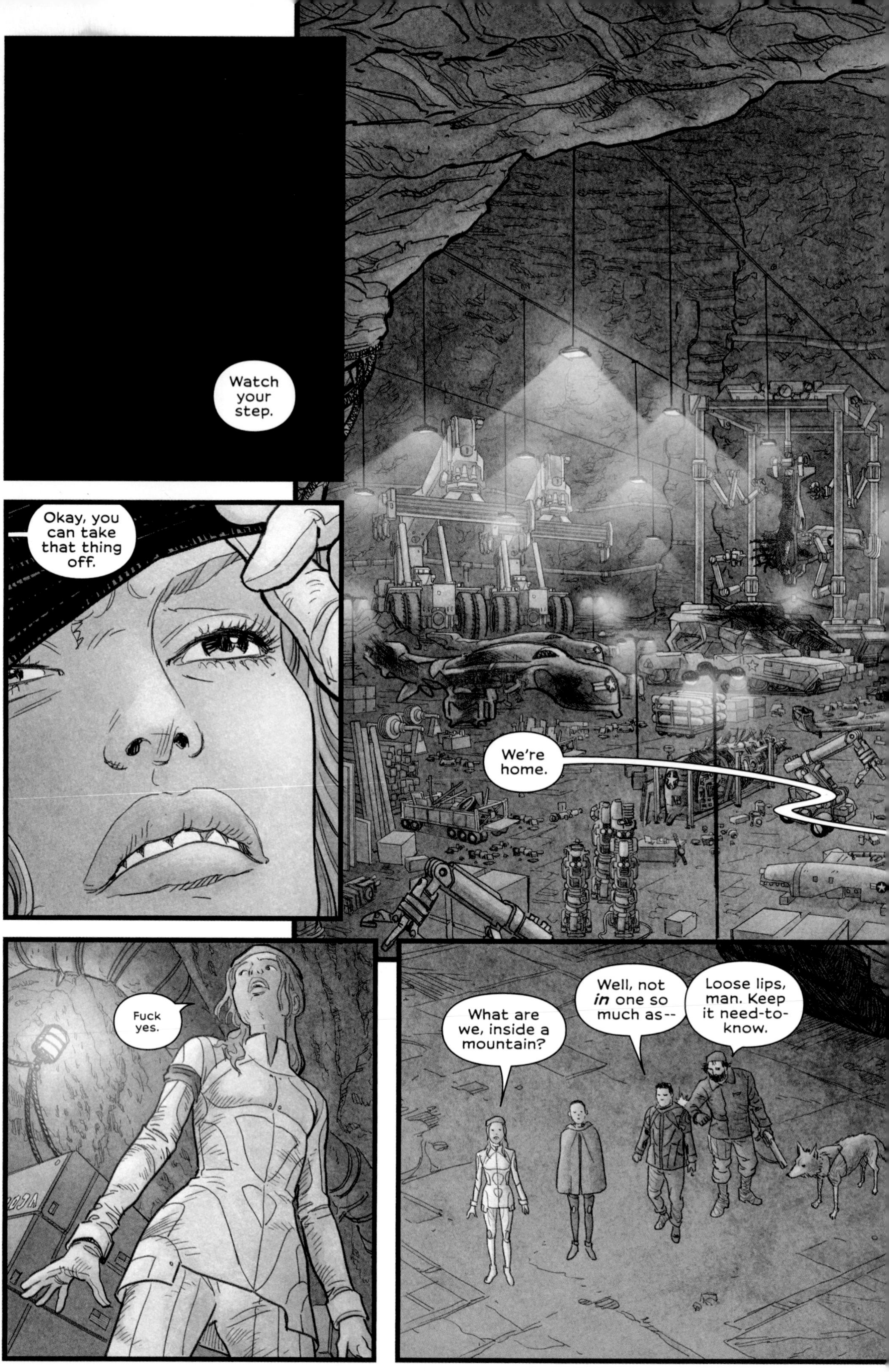
Watch your step.
Okay, you can take that thing off.
We're home.
Fuck yes.
What are we, inside a mountain?
Well, not *in* one so much as--
Loose lips, man. Keep it need-to-know.

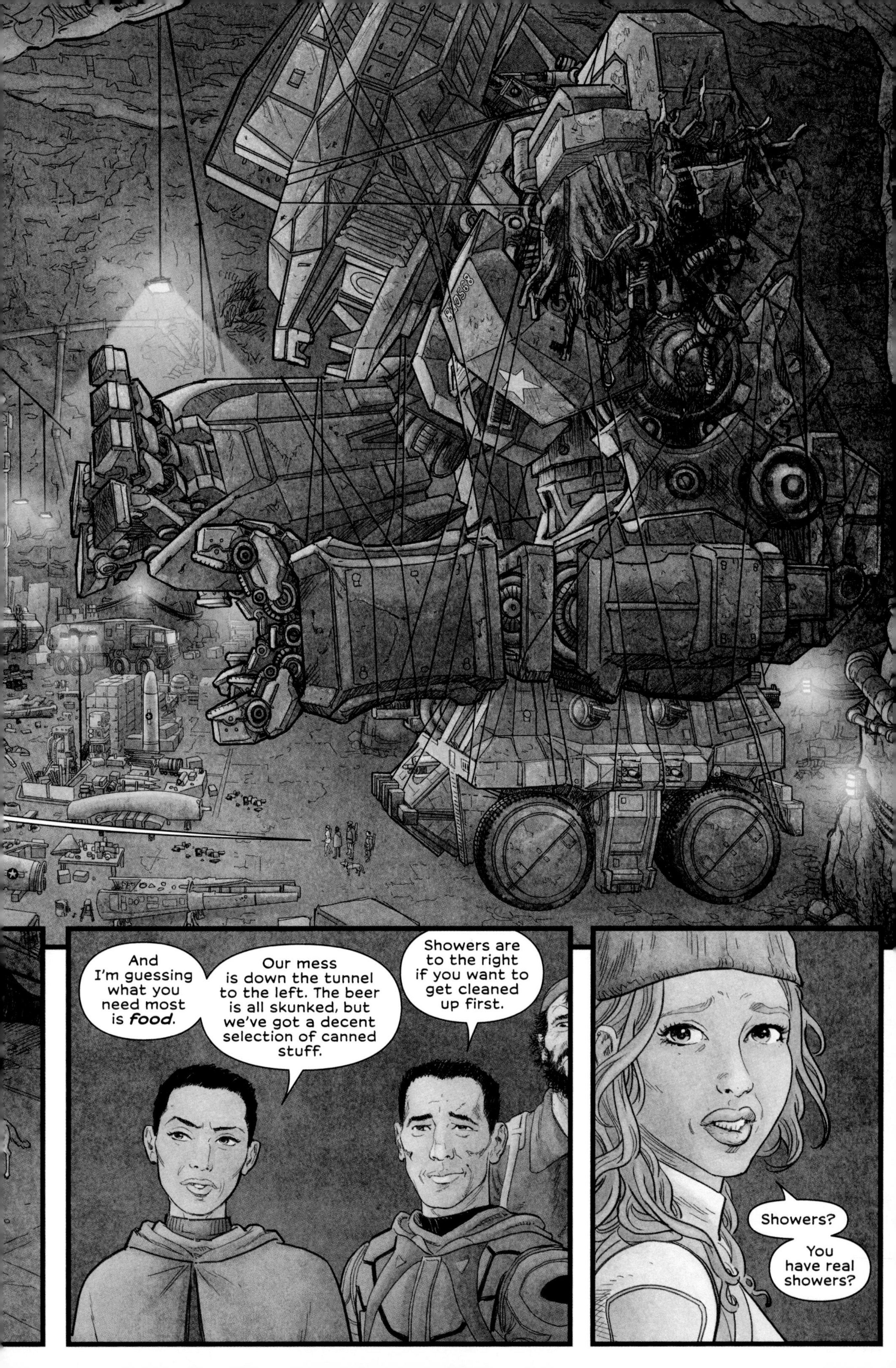
And I'm guessing what you need most is *food*.
Our mess is down the tunnel to the left. The beer is all skunked, but we've got a decent selection of canned stuff.
Showers are to the right if you want to get cleaned up first.
Showers?
You have real showers?

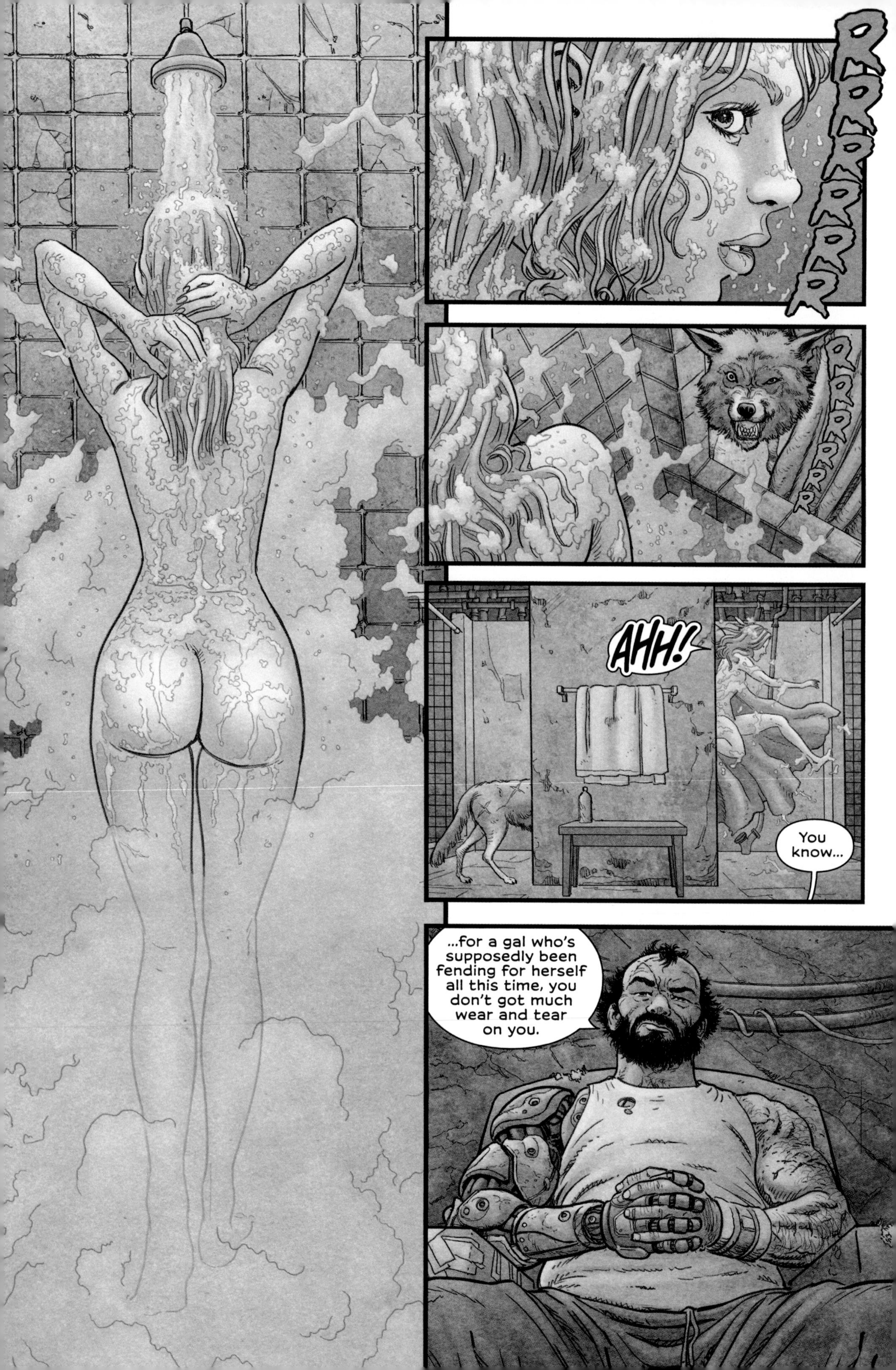
RRRRRR
RRRRRRR
AHH!
You know...
...for a gal who's supposedly been fending for herself all this time, you don't got much wear and tear on you.

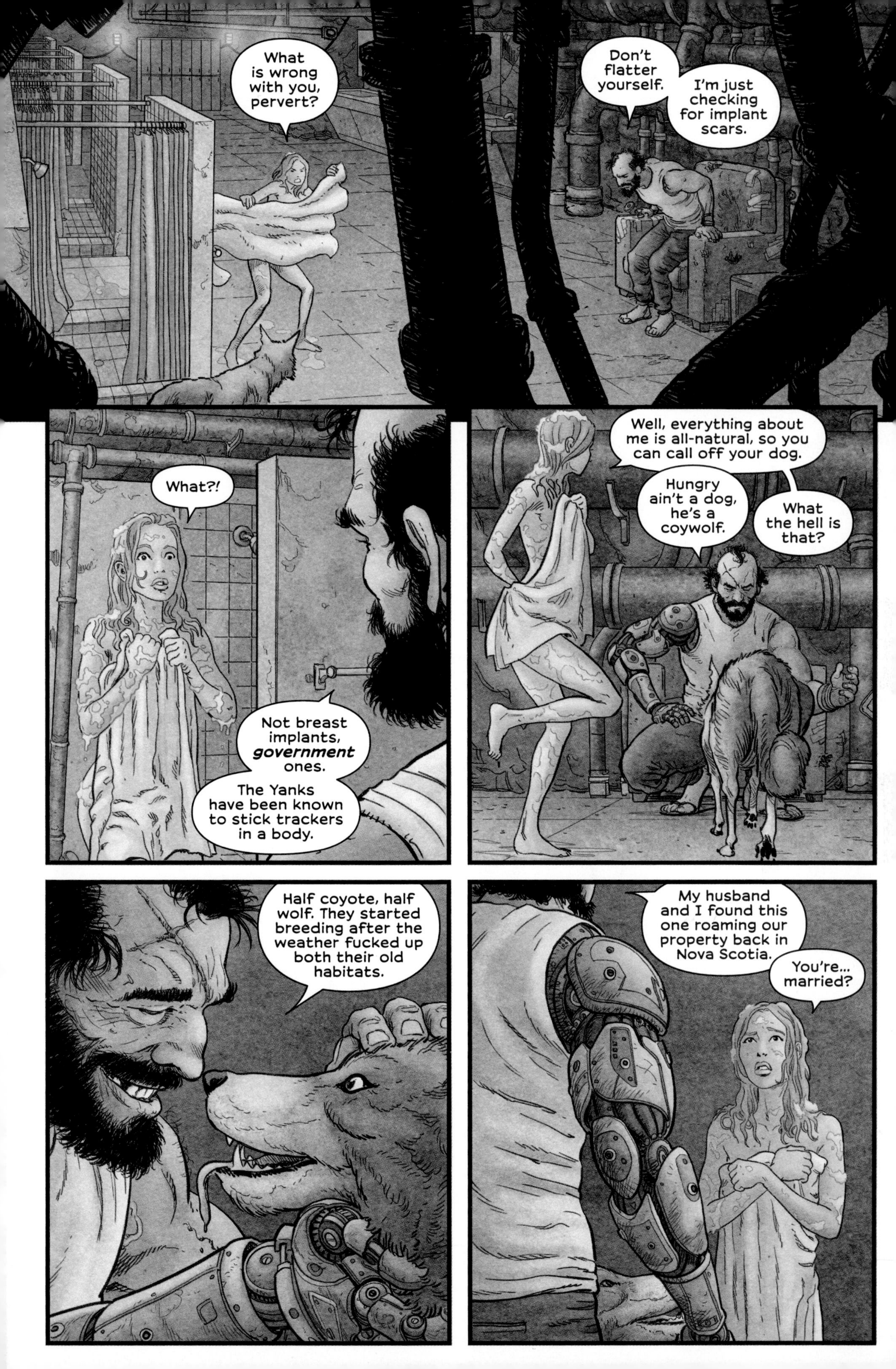
What is wrong with you, pervert?
Don't flatter yourself.
I'm just checking for implant scars.
What?!
Not breast implants, ***government*** ones.
The Yanks have been known to stick trackers in a body.
Well, everything about me is all-natural, so you can call off your dog.
Hungry ain't a dog, he's a coywolf.
What the hell is that?
Half coyote, half wolf. They started breeding after the weather fucked up both their old habitats.
My husband and I found this one roaming our property back in Nova Scotia.
You're... married?

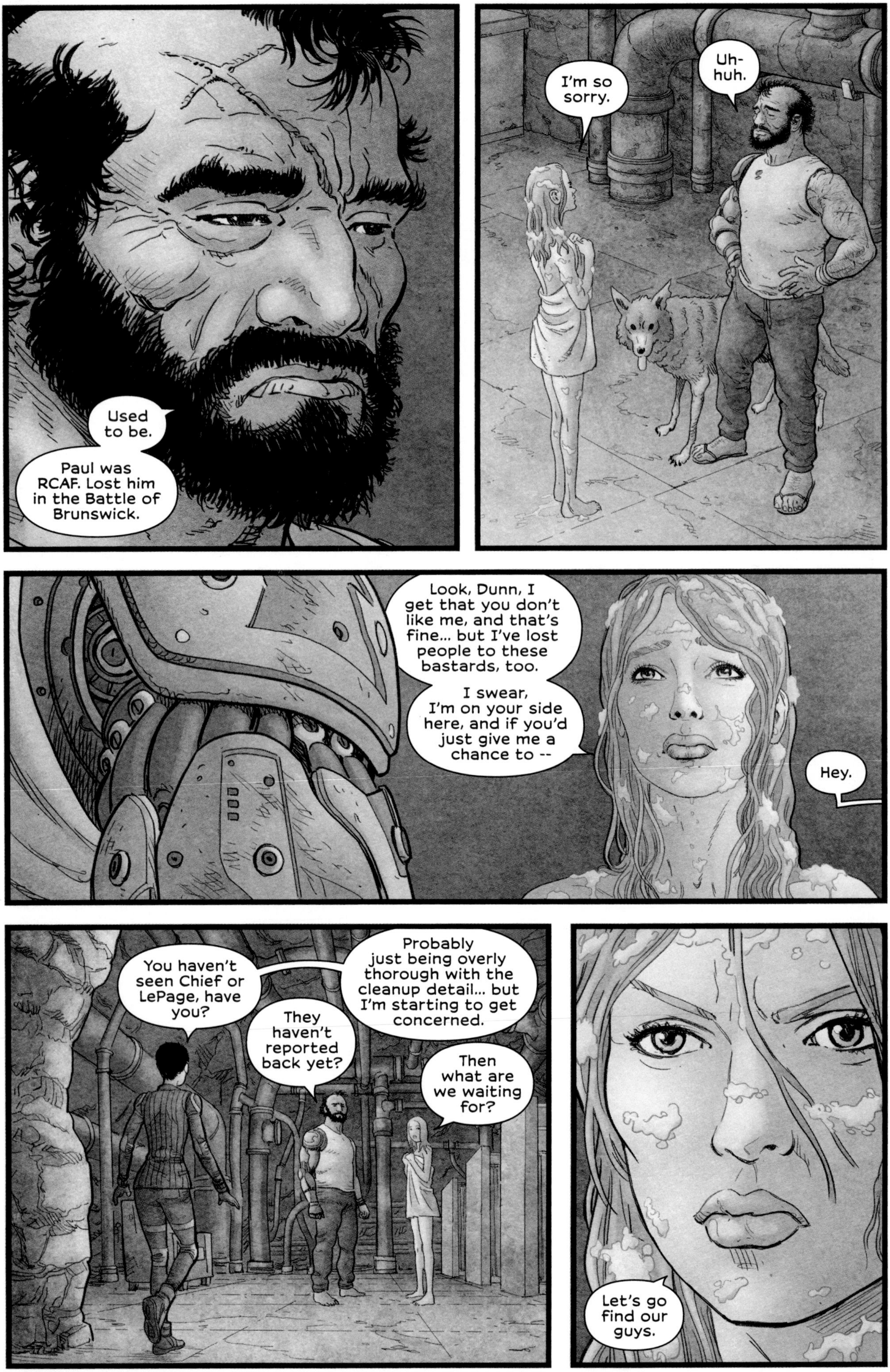
Used to be.
Paul was RCAF. Lost him in the Battle of Brunswick.
I'm so sorry.
Uh-huh.
Look, Dunn, I get that you don't like me, and that's fine... but I've lost people to these bastards, too.
I swear, I'm on your side here, and if you'd just give me a chance to --
Hey.
You haven't seen Chief or LePage, have you?
Probably just being overly thorough with the cleanup detail... but I'm starting to get concerned.
They haven't reported back yet?
Then what are we waiting for?
Let's go find our guys.

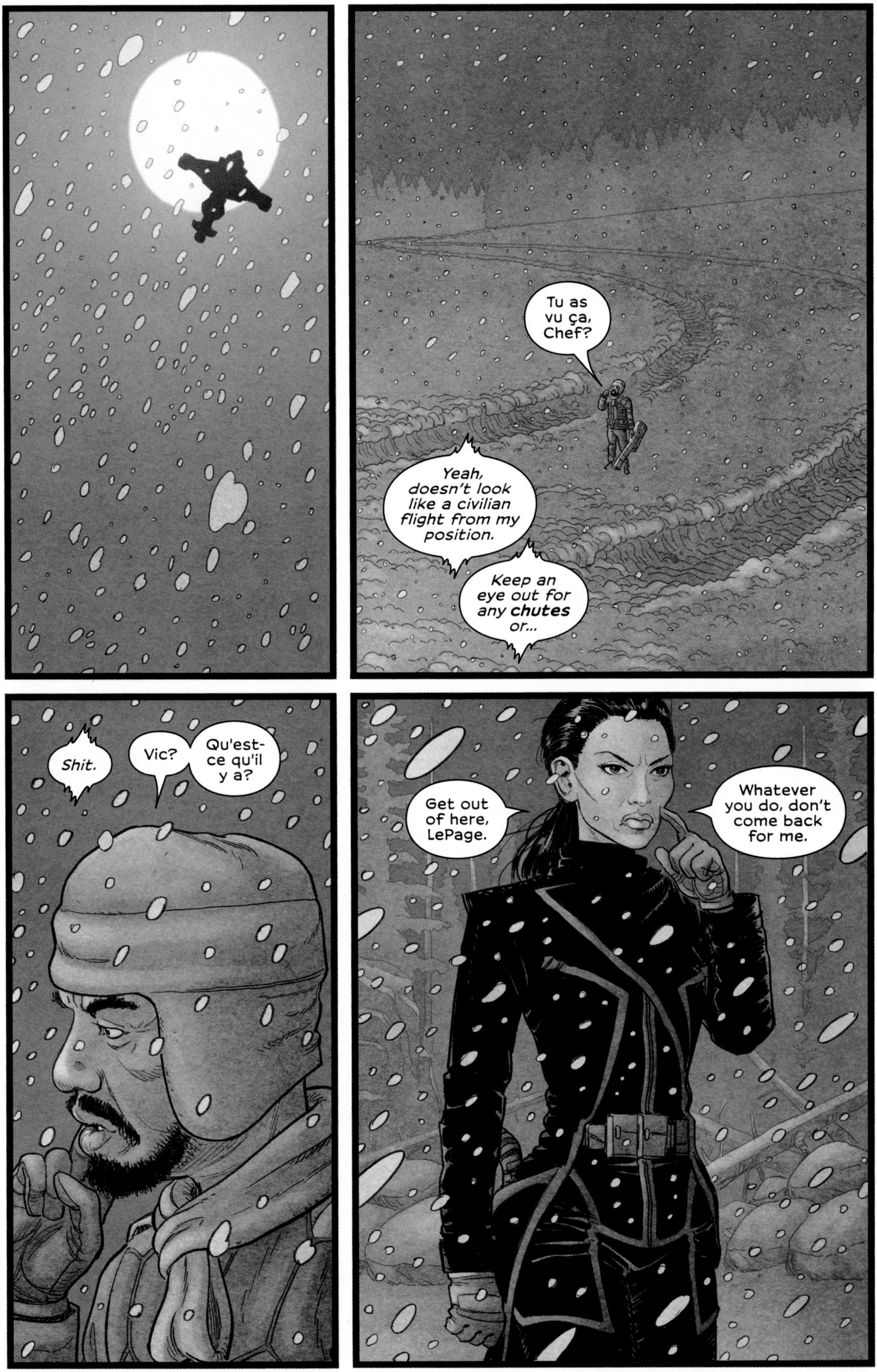

Tu as vu ça, Chef?
Yeah, doesn't look like a civilian flight from my position.
*Keep an eye out for any **chutes** or...*
Shit.
Vic?
Qu'est-ce qu'il y a?
Get out of here, LePage.
Whatever you do, don't come back for me.

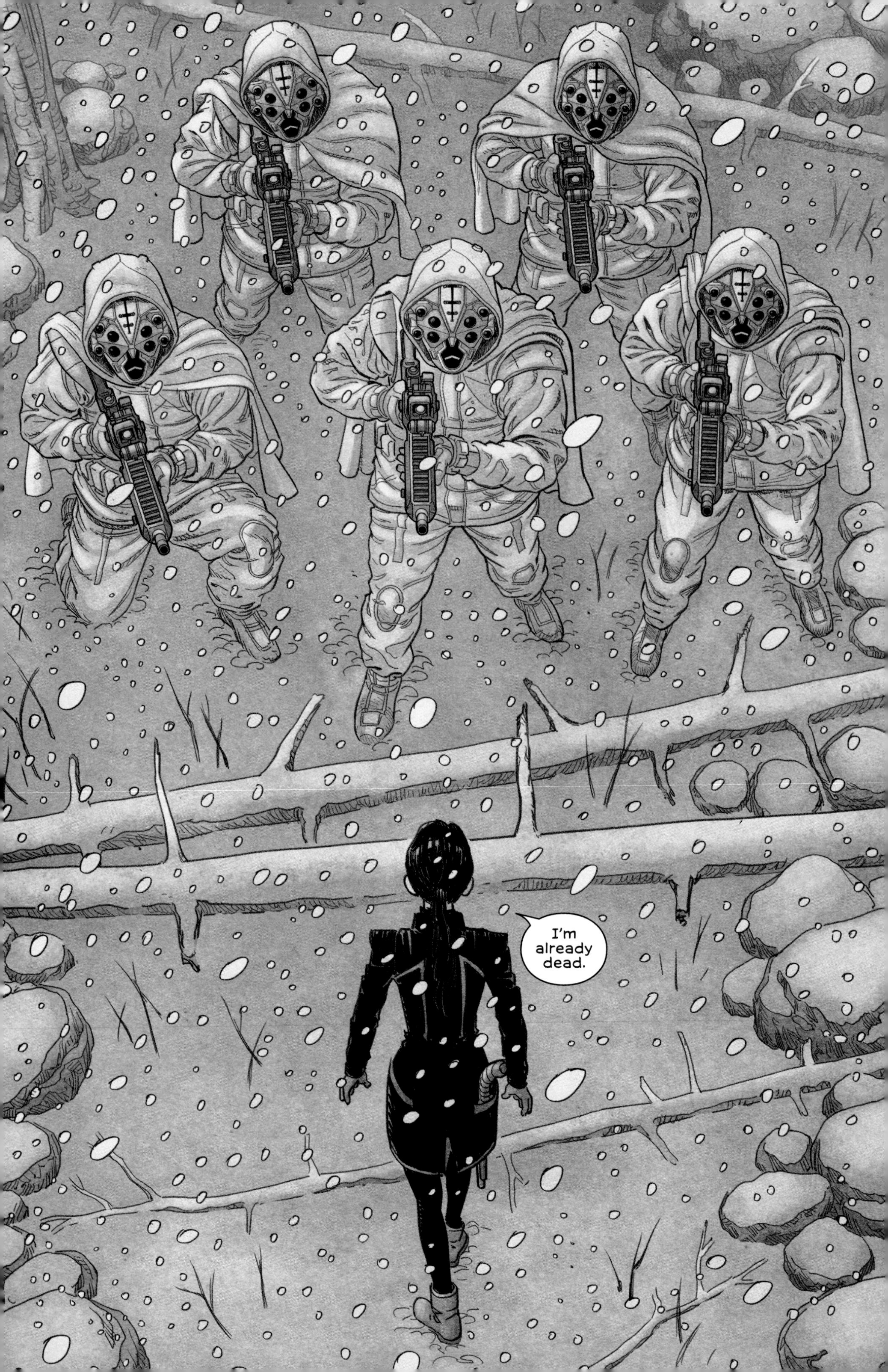
I'm already dead.

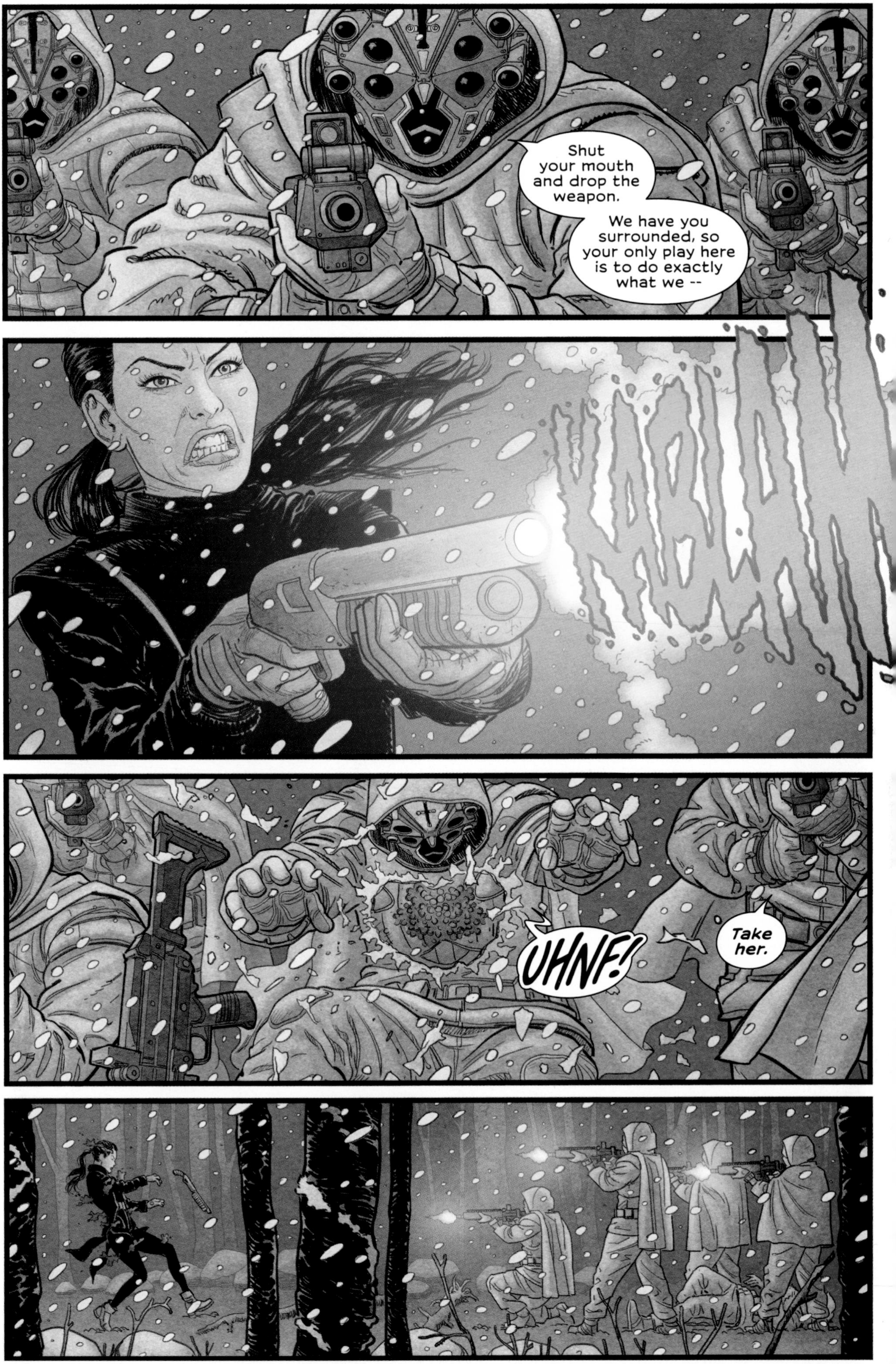
Shut your mouth and drop the weapon.
We have you surrounded, so your only play here is to do exactly what we --
KABLAM
UHNF!
Take her.

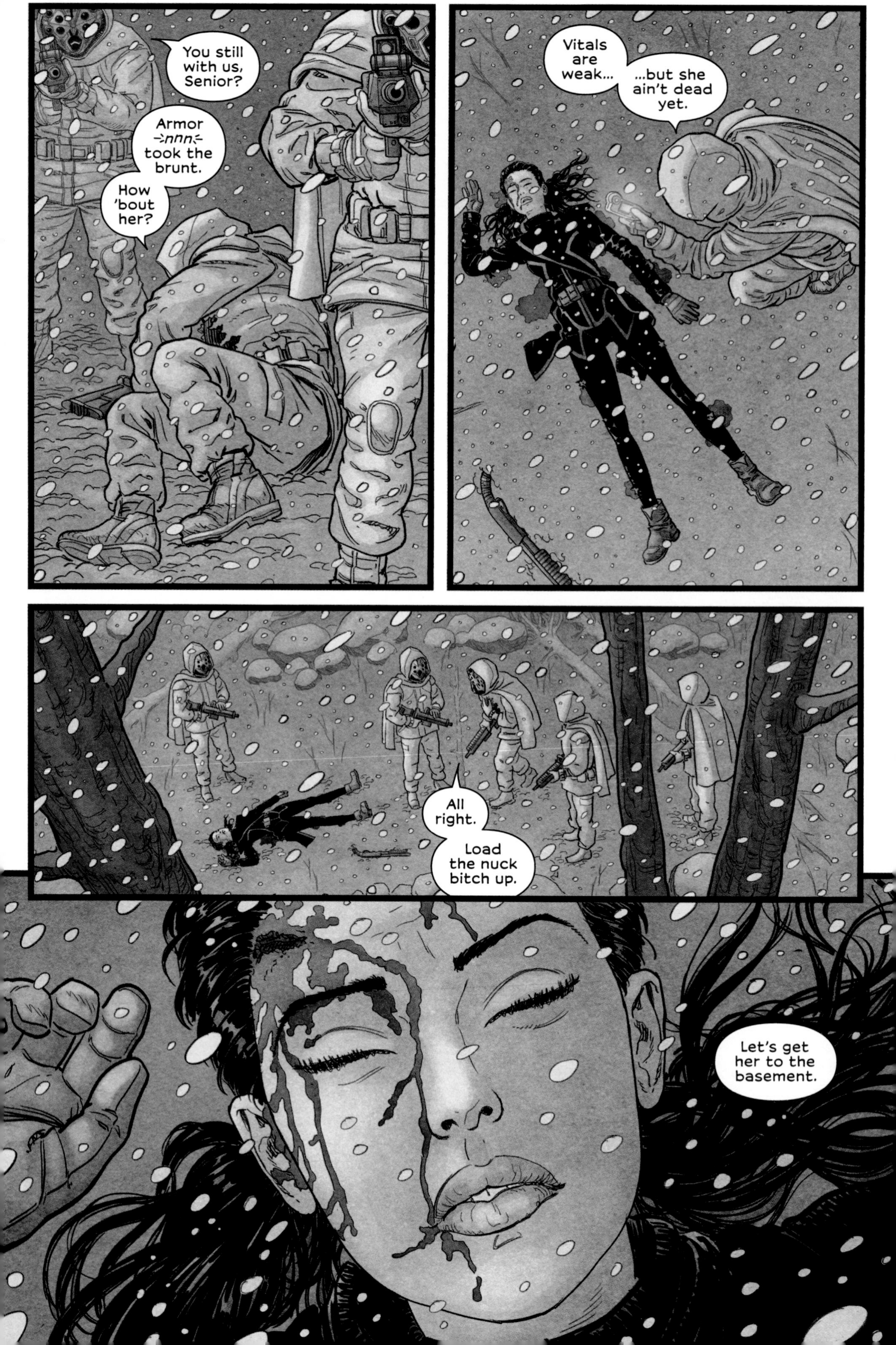
You still with us, Senior?
Armor -nnn- took the brunt.
How 'bout her?
Vitals are weak...
...but she ain't dead yet.
All right.
Load the nuck bitch up.
Let's get her to the basement.

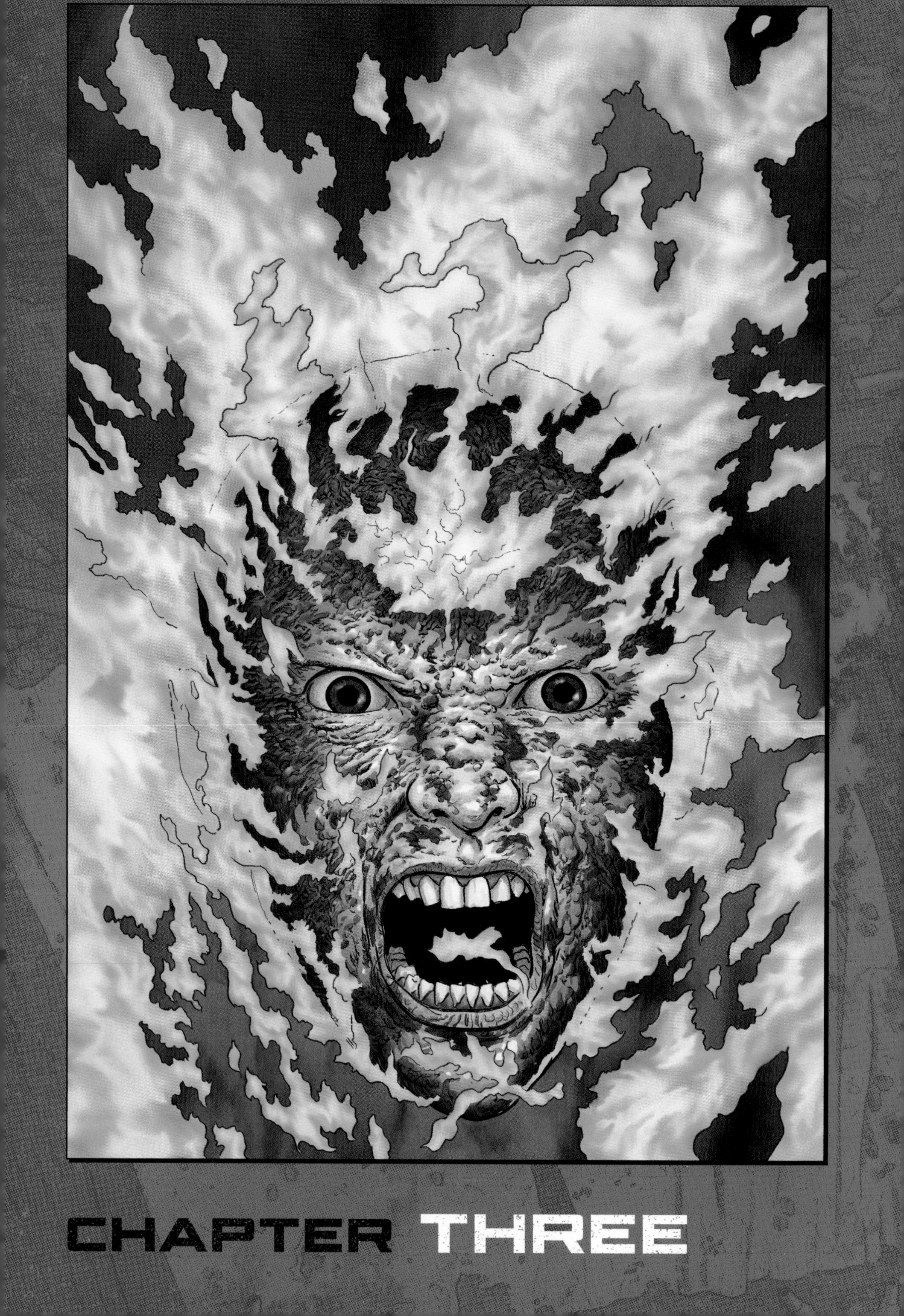

CHAPTER THREE

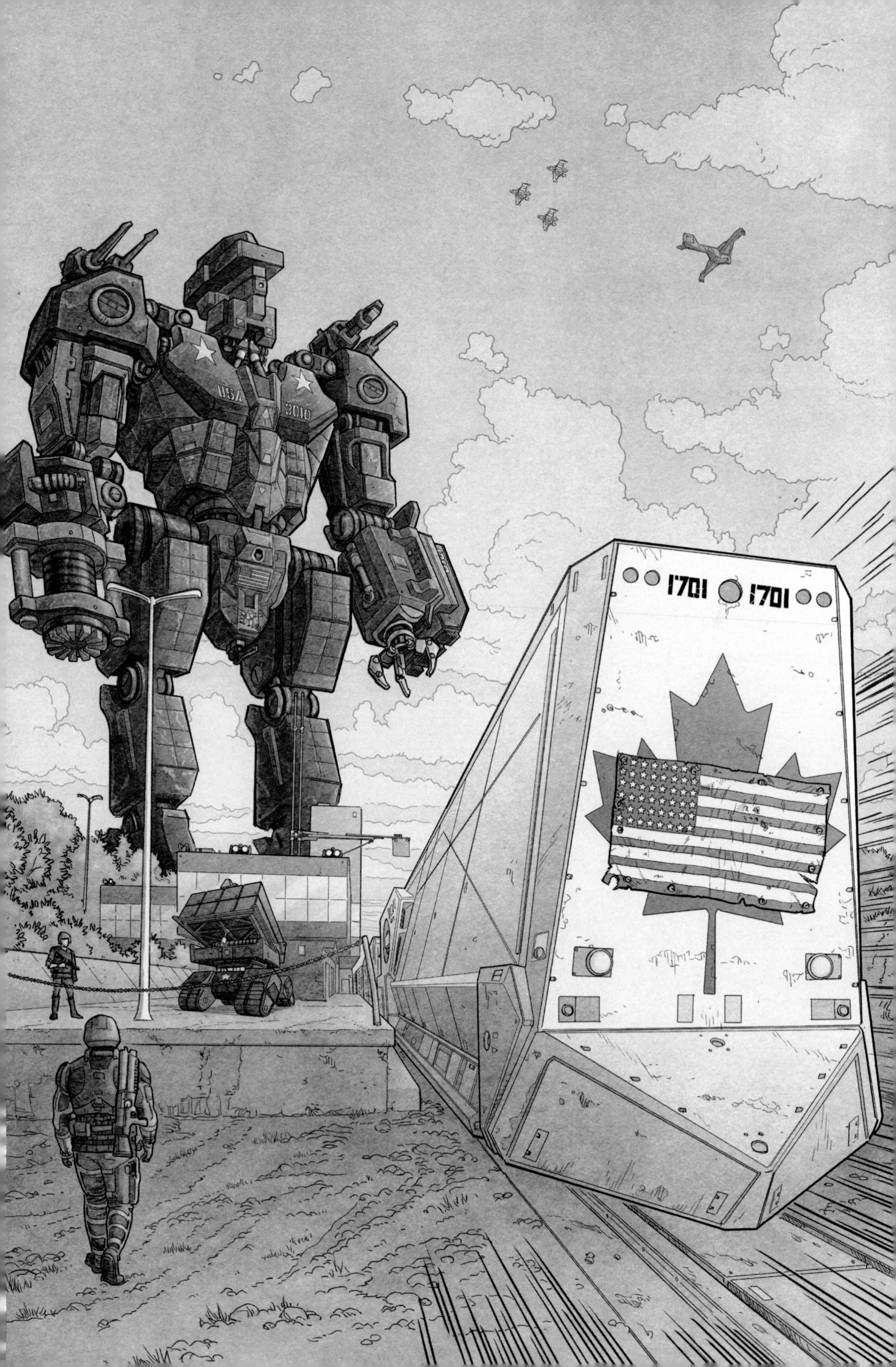
USA
3010
1701
1701

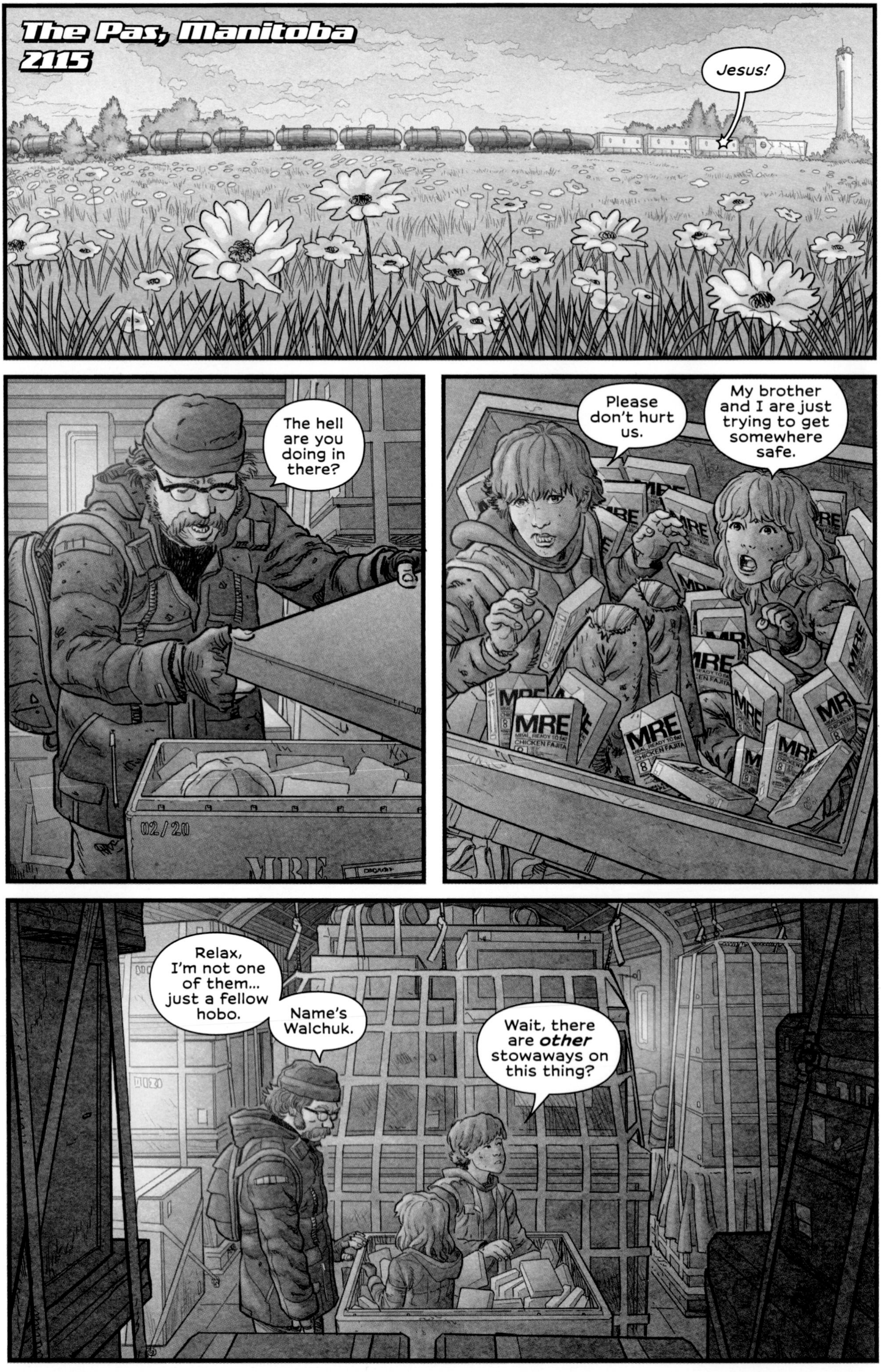
The Pas, Manitoba
2115
Jesus!
The hell are you doing in there?
Please don't hurt us.
My brother and I are just trying to get somewhere safe.
MRE
MEAL, READY TO EAT
CHICKEN FAJITA
Relax, I'm not one of them... just a fellow hobo.
Name's Walchuk.
Wait, there are *other* stowaways on this thing?

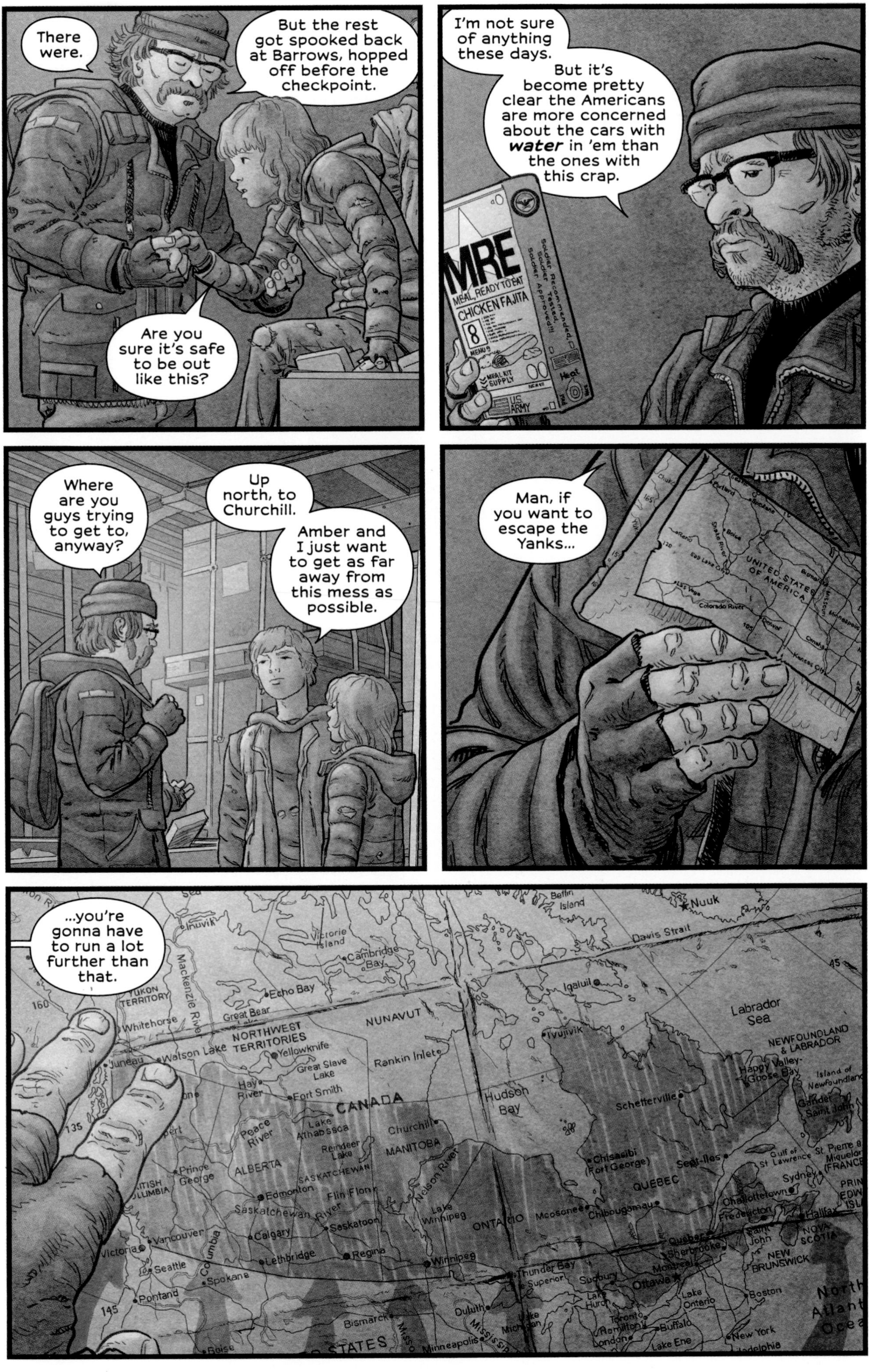
There were.
But the rest got spooked back at Barrows, hopped off before the checkpoint.
Are you sure it's safe to be out like this?
I'm not sure of anything these days.
But it's become pretty clear the Americans are more concerned about the cars with **water** in 'em than the ones with this crap.
MRE
MEAL, READY TO EAT
CHICKEN FAJITA
Where are you guys trying to get to, anyway?
Up north, to Churchill.
Amber and I just want to get as far away from this mess as possible.
Man, if you want to escape the Yanks...
...you're gonna have to run a lot further than that.

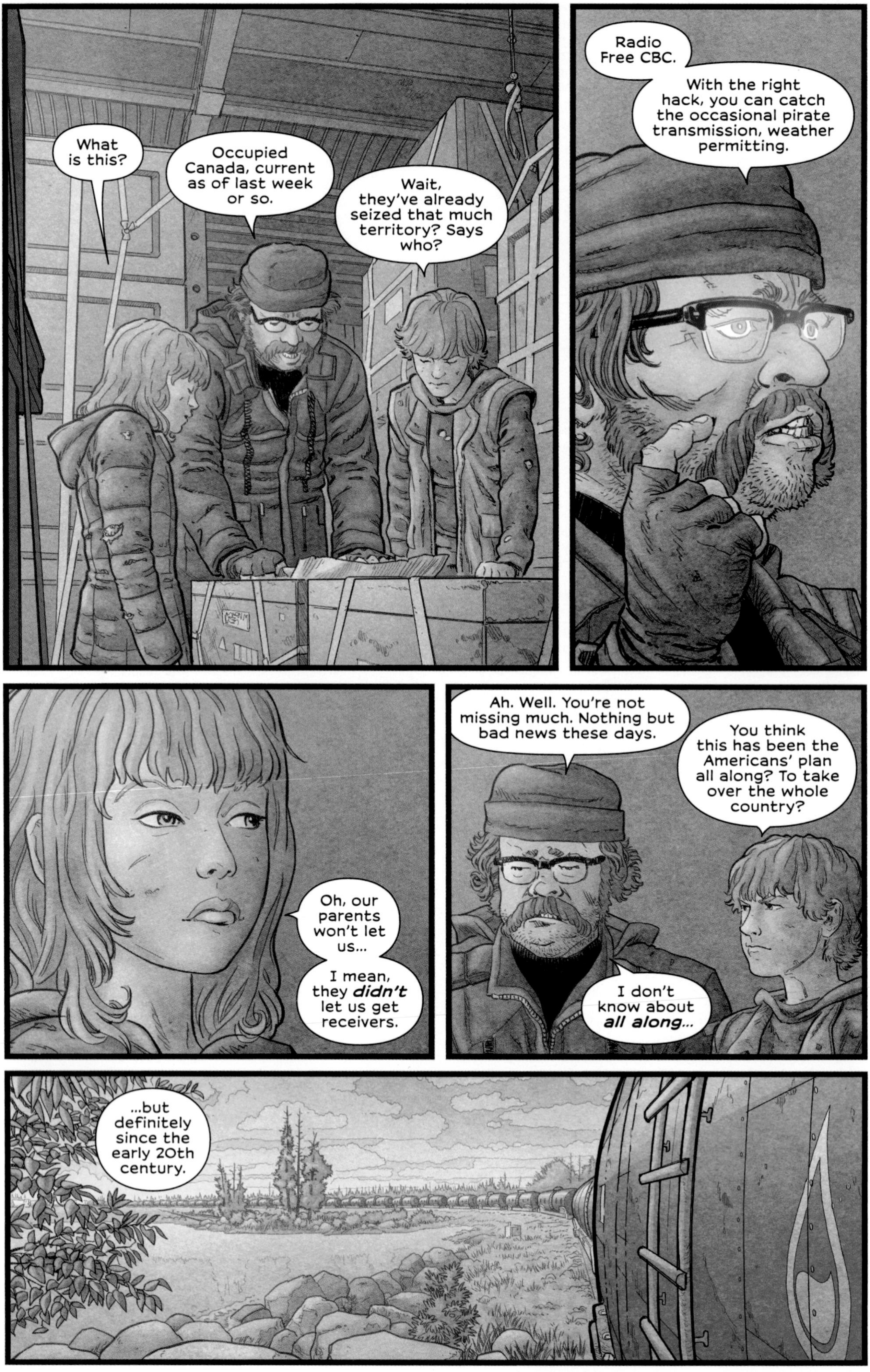
What is this?
Occupied Canada, current as of last week or so.
Wait, they've already seized that much territory? Says who?
Radio Free CBC.
With the right hack, you can catch the occasional pirate transmission, weather permitting.
Oh, our parents won't let us...
I mean, they *didn't* let us get receivers.
Ah. Well. You're not missing much. Nothing but bad news these days.
You think this has been the Americans' plan all along? To take over the whole country?
I don't know about ***all along***...
...but definitely since the early 20th century.

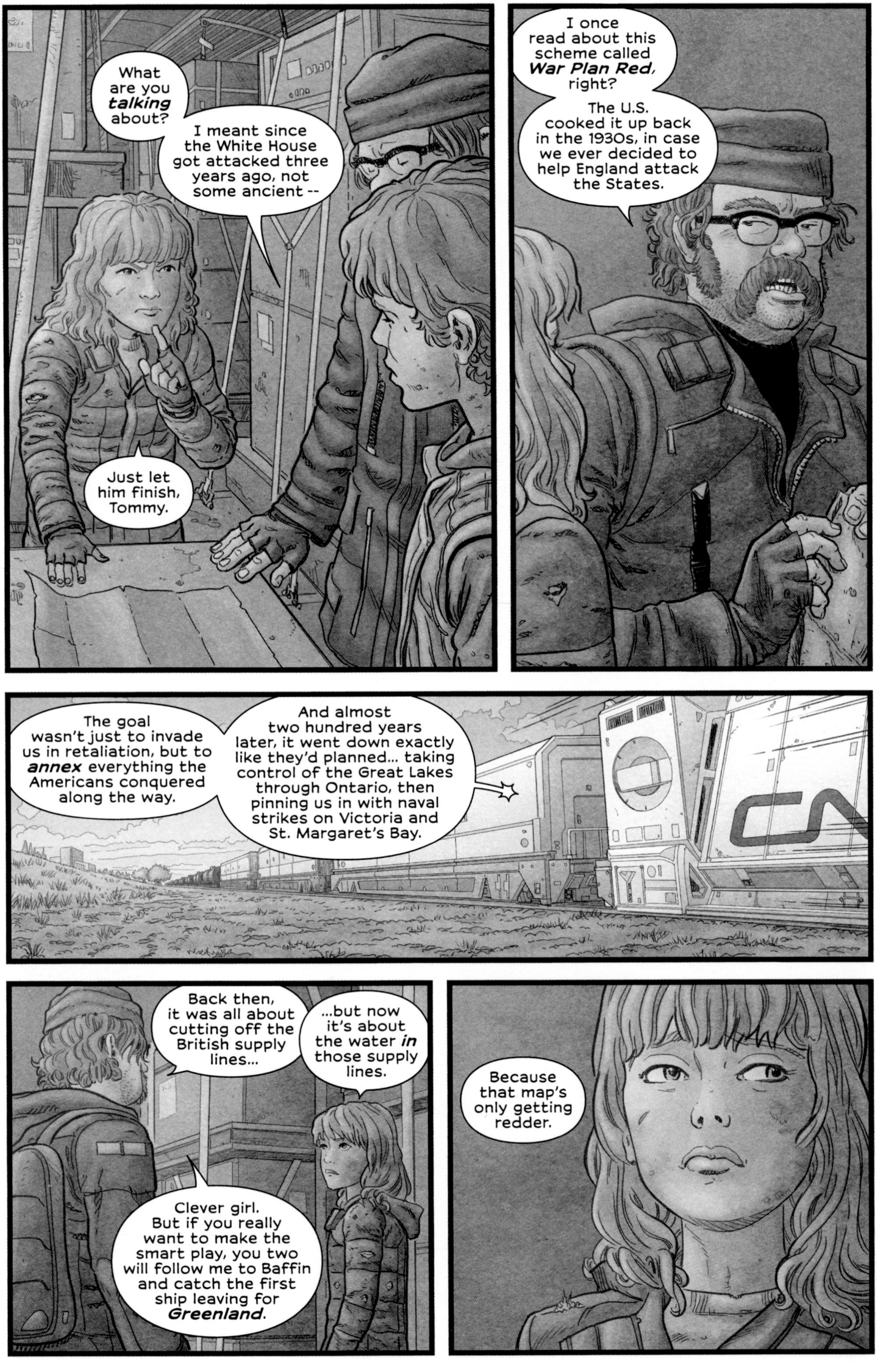
What are you *talking* about?
I meant since the White House got attacked three years ago, not some ancient --
Just let him finish, Tommy.
I once read about this scheme called *War Plan Red,* right?
The U.S. cooked it up back in the 1930s, in case we ever decided to help England attack the States.
The goal wasn't just to invade us in retaliation, but to *annex* everything the Americans conquered along the way.
And almost two hundred years later, it went down exactly like they'd planned... taking control of the Great Lakes through Ontario, then pinning us in with naval strikes on Victoria and St. Margaret's Bay.
CN
Back then, it was all about cutting off the British supply lines...
...but now it's about the water *in* those supply lines.
Clever girl. But if you really want to make the smart play, you two will follow me to Baffin and catch the first ship leaving for *Greenland*.
Because that map's only getting redder.

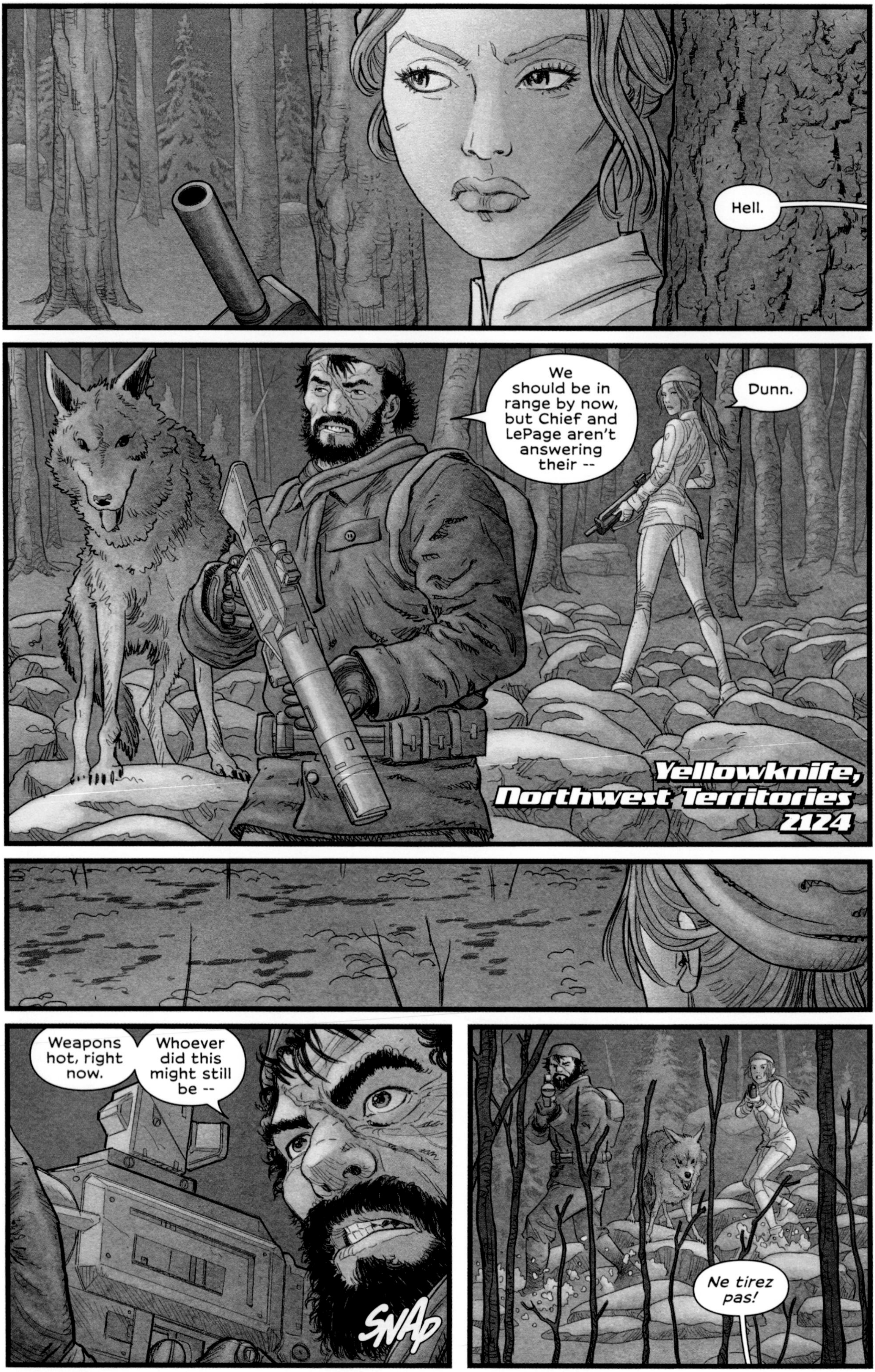
Hell.
We should be in range by now, but Chief and LePage aren't answering their --
Dunn.
Yellowknife, Northwest Territories 2124
Weapons hot, right now.
Whoever did this might still be --
SNAP
Ne tirez pas!

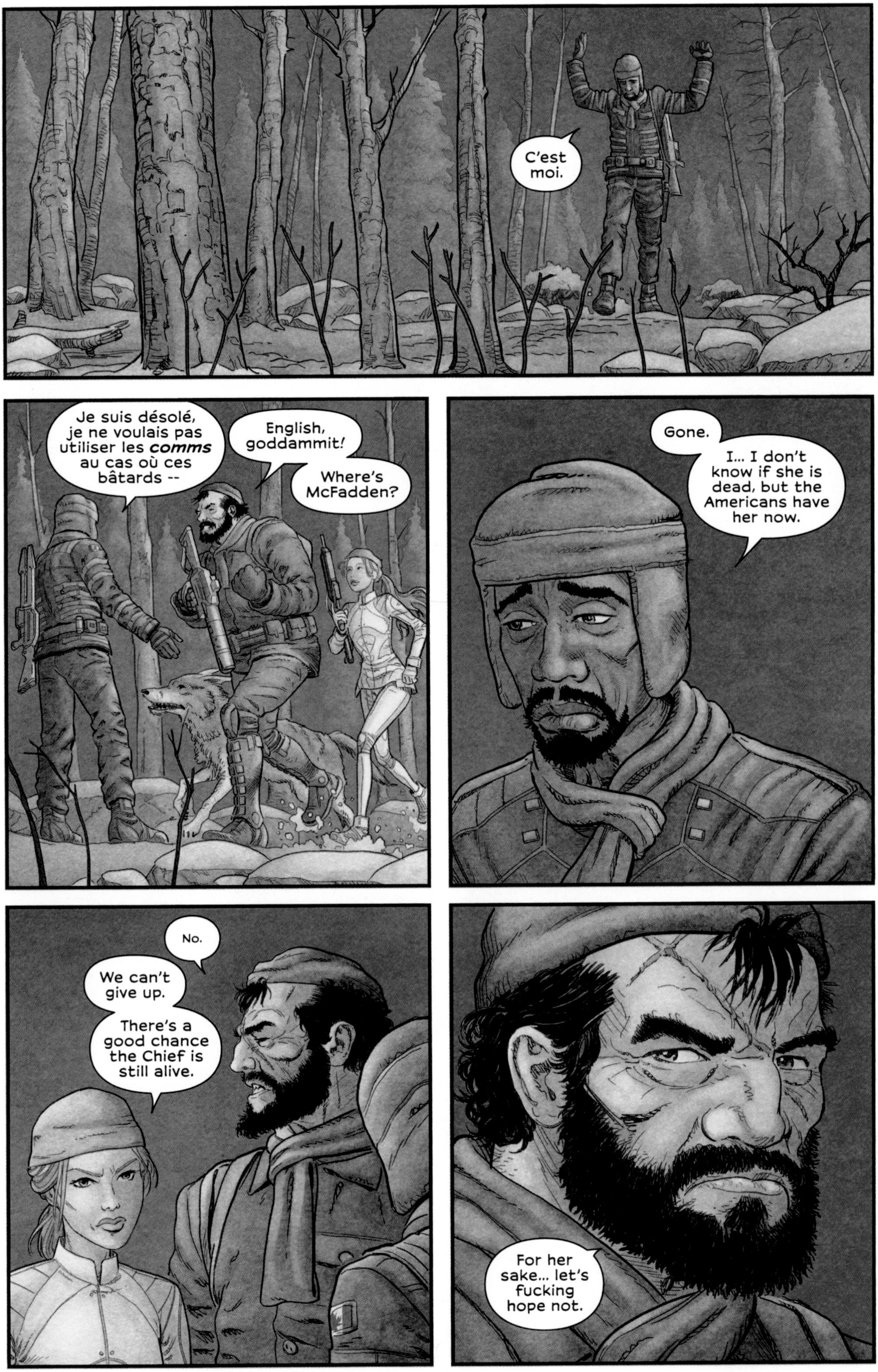
C'est moi.
Je suis désolé, je ne voulais pas utiliser les ***comms*** au cas où ces bâtards --
English, goddammit!
Where's McFadden?
Gone.
I... I don't know if she is dead, but the Americans have her now.
No.
We can't give up.
There's a good chance the Chief is still alive.
For her sake... let's fucking hope not.

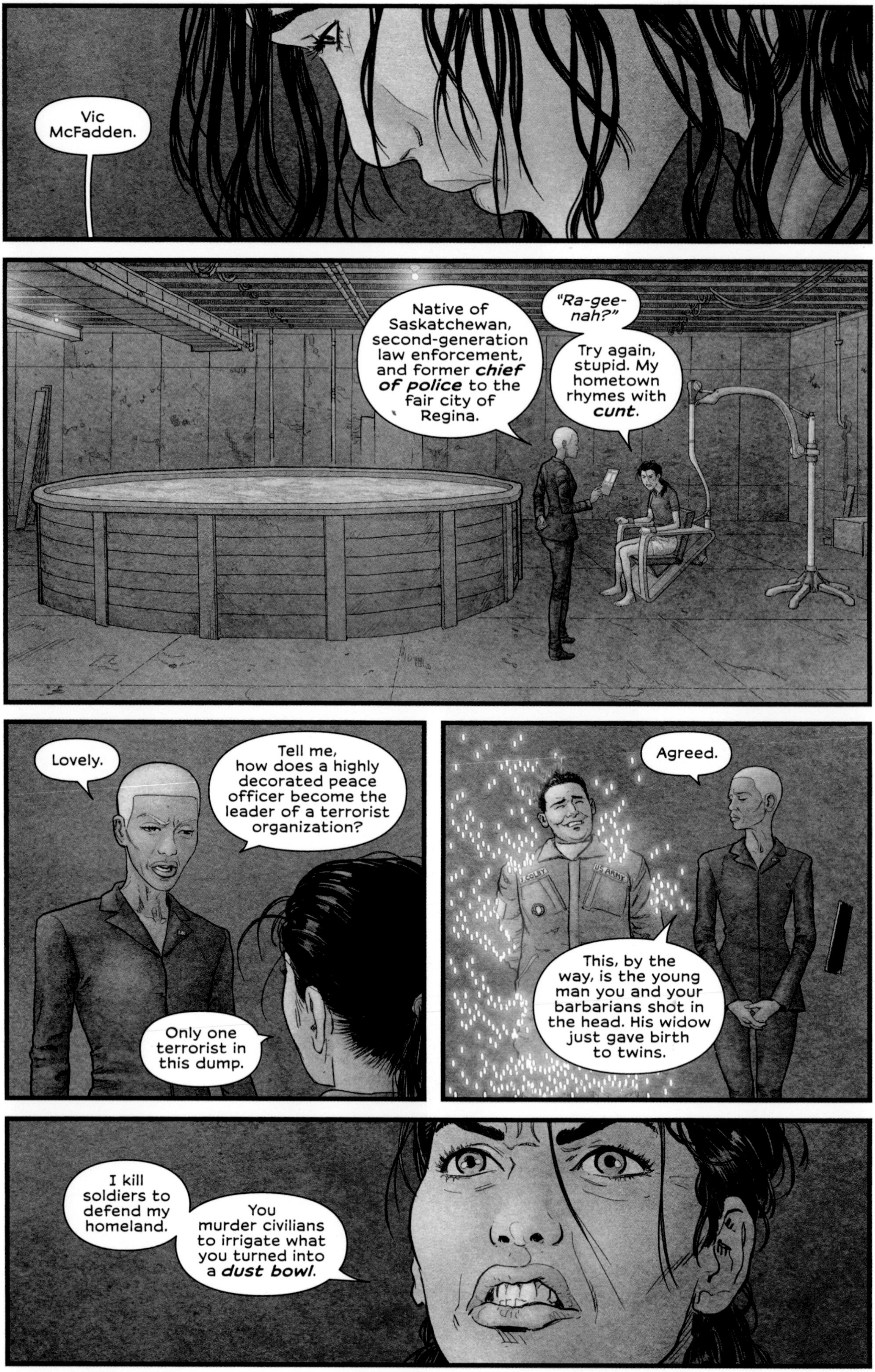
Vic McFadden.
Native of Saskatchewan, second-generation law enforcement, and former *chief of police* to the fair city of Regina.
"Ra-gee-nah?"
Try again, stupid. My hometown rhymes with *cunt*.
Lovely.
Tell me, how does a highly decorated peace officer become the leader of a terrorist organization?
Only one terrorist in this dump.
Agreed.
J.COLBY
US ARMY
This, by the way, is the young man you and your barbarians shot in the head. His widow just gave birth to twins.
I kill soldiers to defend my homeland.
You murder civilians to irrigate what you turned into a *dust bowl*.

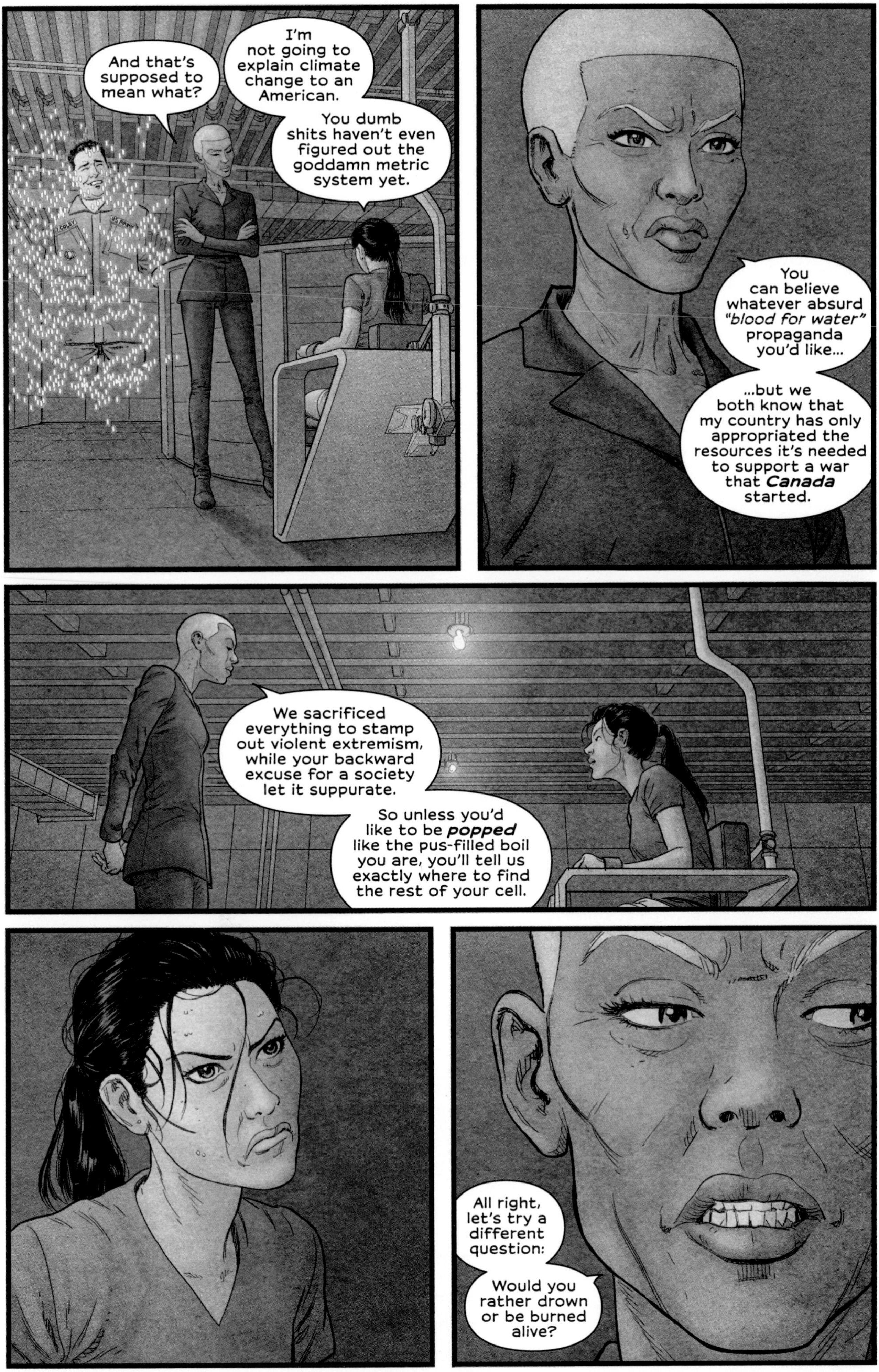
And that's supposed to mean what?
I'm not going to explain climate change to an American.
You dumb shits haven't even figured out the goddamn metric system yet.
J. COLBY
US ARMY
You can believe whatever absurd *"blood for water"* propaganda you'd like...
...but we both know that my country has only appropriated the resources it's needed to support a war that ***Canada*** started.
We sacrificed everything to stamp out violent extremism, while your backward excuse for a society let it suppurate.
So unless you'd like to be ***popped*** like the pus-filled boil you are, you'll tell us exactly where to find the rest of your cell.
All right, let's try a different question:
Would you rather drown or be burned alive?

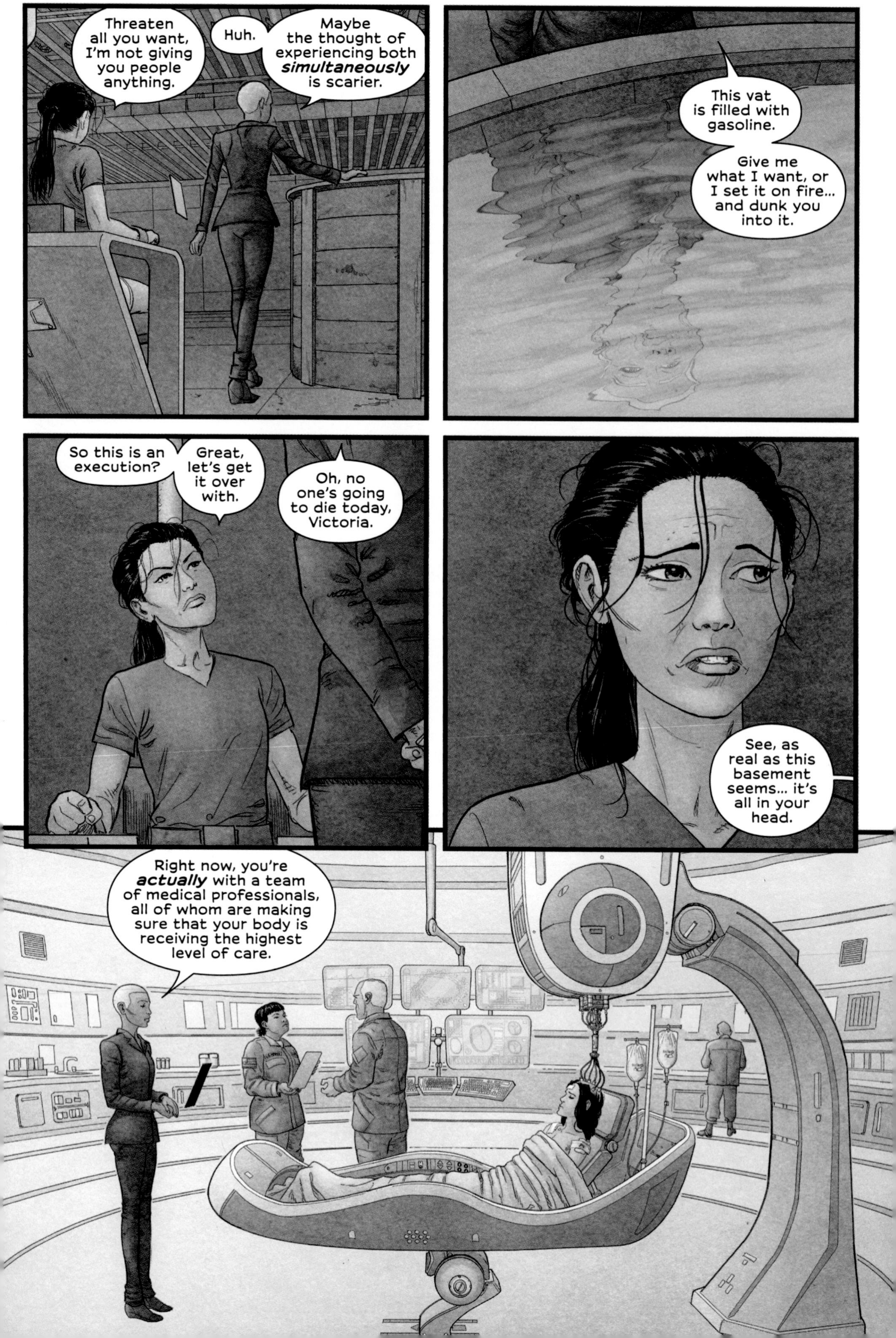

Threaten all you want, I'm not giving you people anything.
Huh.
Maybe the thought of experiencing both *simultaneously* is scarier.
This vat is filled with gasoline.
Give me what I want, or I set it on fire... and dunk you into it.
So this is an execution?
Great, let's get it over with.
Oh, no one's going to die today, Victoria.
See, as real as this basement seems... it's all in your head.
Right now, you're *actually* with a team of medical professionals, all of whom are making sure that your body is receiving the highest level of care.

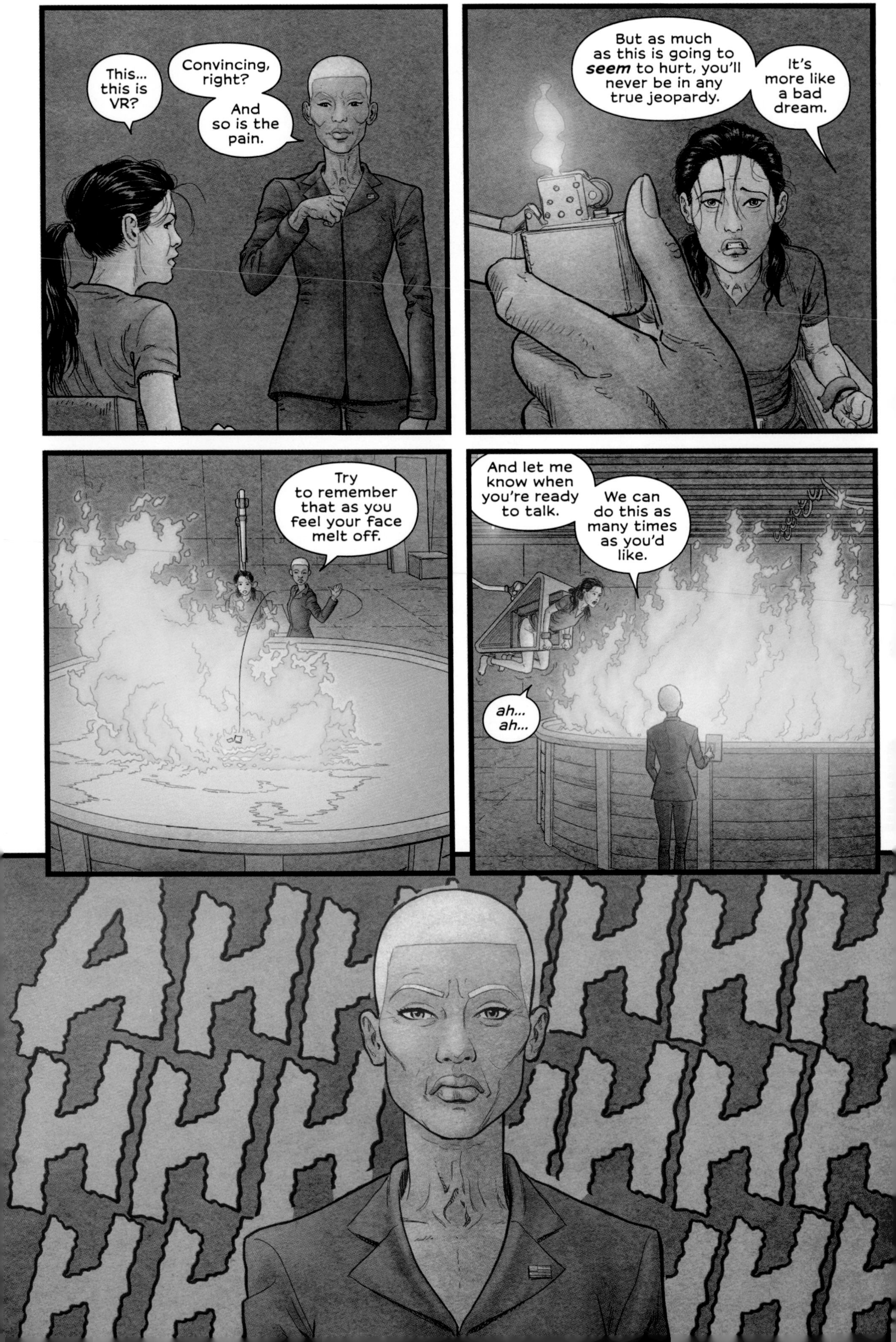
This... this is VR?
Convincing, right?
And so is the pain.
But as much as this is going to *seem* to hurt, you'll never be in any true jeopardy.
It's more like a bad dream.
Try to remember that as you feel your face melt off.
And let me know when you're ready to talk.
We can do this as many times as you'd like.
ah... ah...
AHHHHHHHHHHHHHHHHHHHH

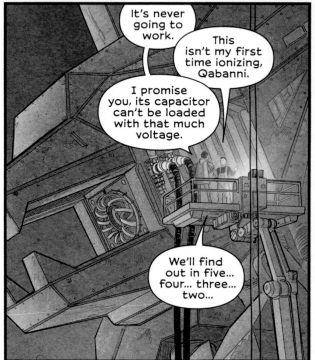

It's never going to work.

This isn't my first time ionizing, Qabanni.

I promise you, its capacitor can't be loaded with that much voltage.

We'll find out in five... four... three... two...

FZZZTBRK

Dammit.

Sorry, but it'll take *time* before the big guy can do everything we want.

Then leave it behind.

Grab whatever you can carry.

We're moving out.

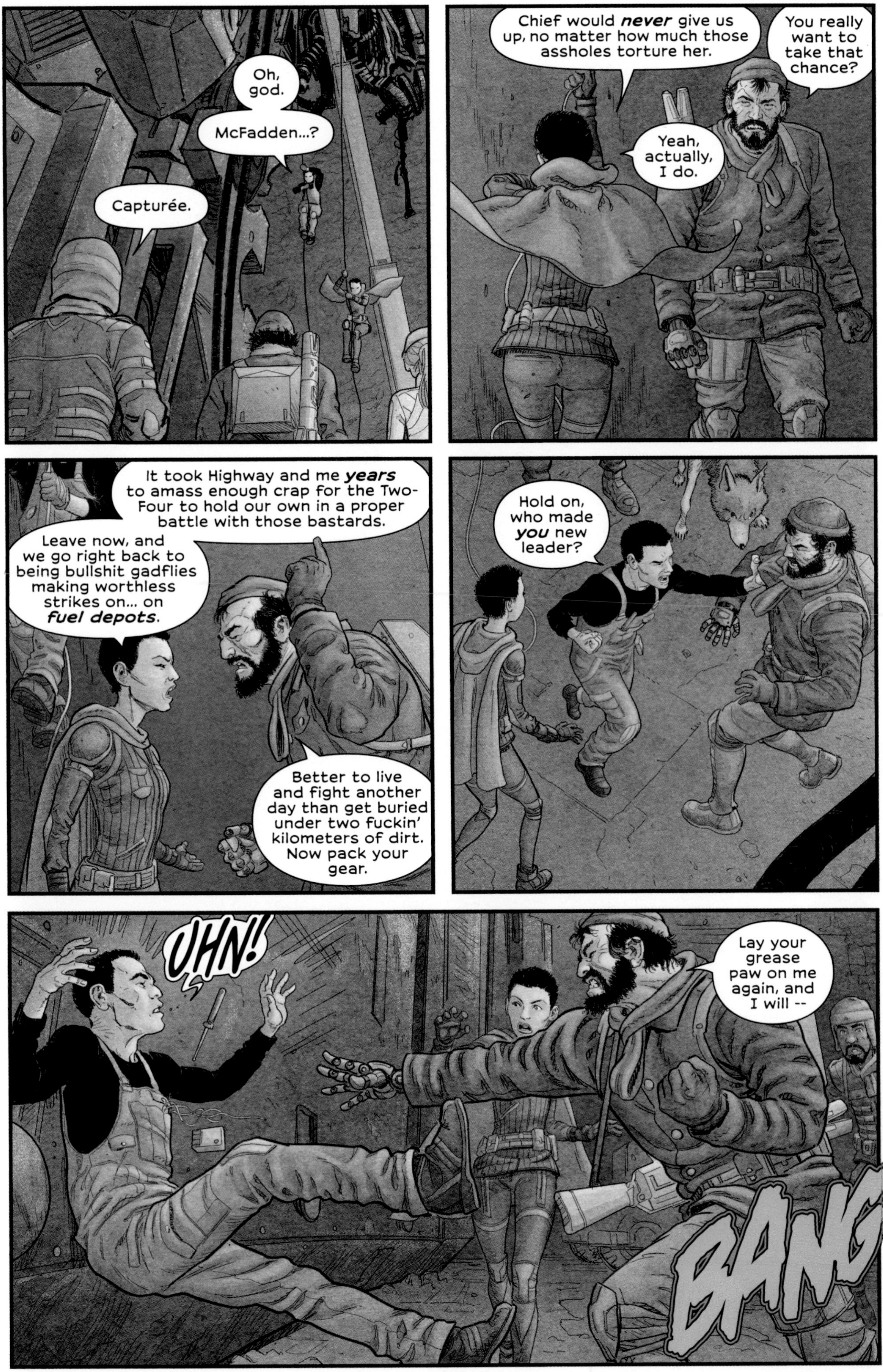
Oh, god.
McFadden...?
Capturée.
Chief would *never* give us up, no matter how much those assholes torture her.
You really want to take that chance?
Yeah, actually, I do.
It took Highway and me *years* to amass enough crap for the Two-Four to hold our own in a proper battle with those bastards.
Leave now, and we go right back to being bullshit gadflies making worthless strikes on... on *fuel depots*.
Better to live and fight another day than get buried under two fuckin' kilometers of dirt. Now pack your gear.
Hold on, who made *you* new leader?
UHN!
Lay your grease paw on me again, and I will --
BANG

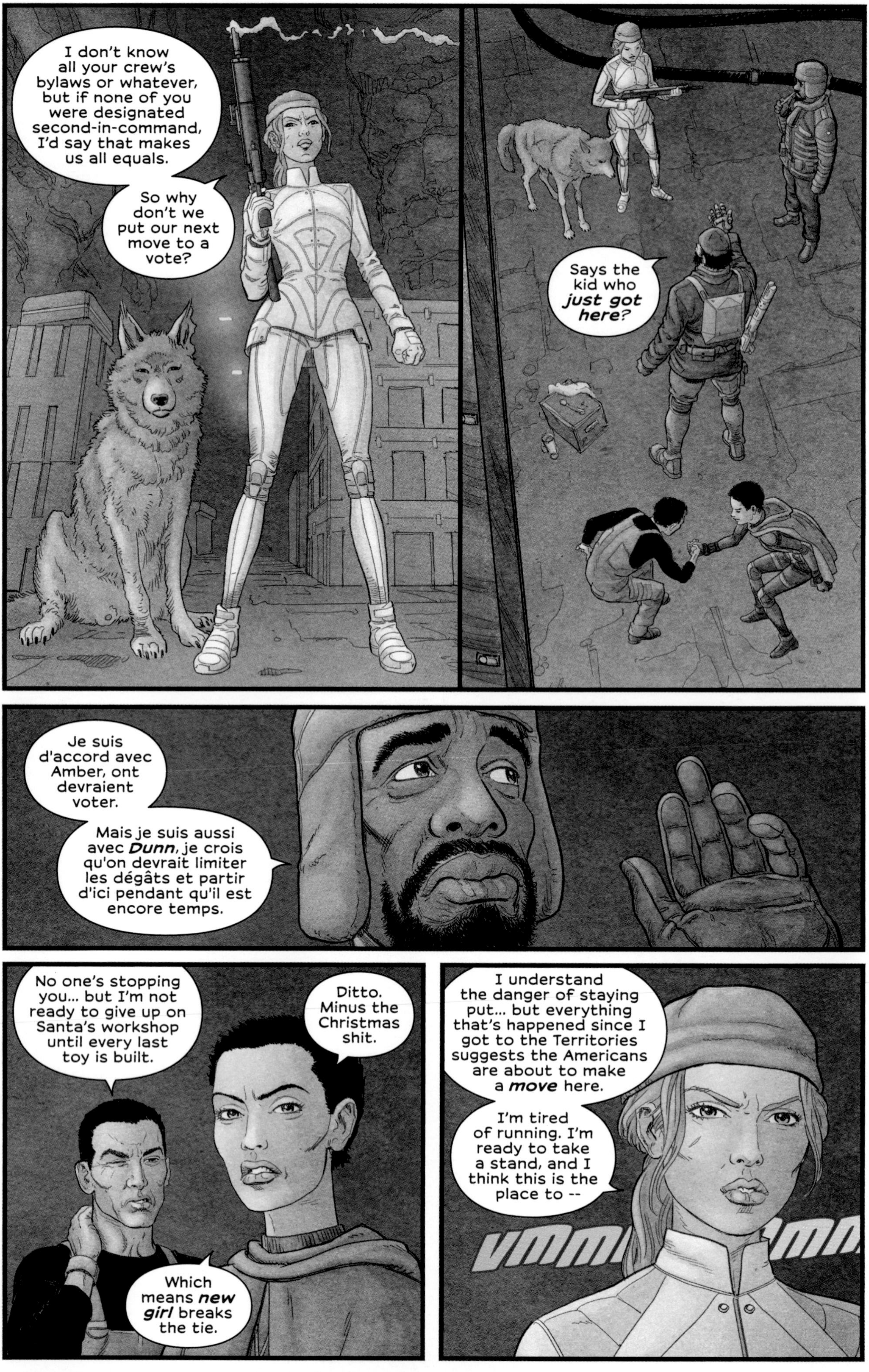
I don't know all your crew's bylaws or whatever, but if none of you were designated second-in-command, I'd say that makes us all equals.
So why don't we put our next move to a vote?
Says the kid who *just got here*?
Je suis d'accord avec Amber, ont devraient voter.
Mais je suis aussi avec *Dunn*, je crois qu'on devrait limiter les dégâts et partir d'ici pendant qu'il est encore temps.
No one's stopping you... but I'm not ready to give up on Santa's workshop until every last toy is built.
Ditto. Minus the Christmas shit.
Which means *new girl* breaks the tie.
I understand the danger of staying put... but everything that's happened since I got to the Territories suggests the Americans are about to make a *move* here.
I'm tired of running. I'm ready to take a stand, and I think this is the place to --

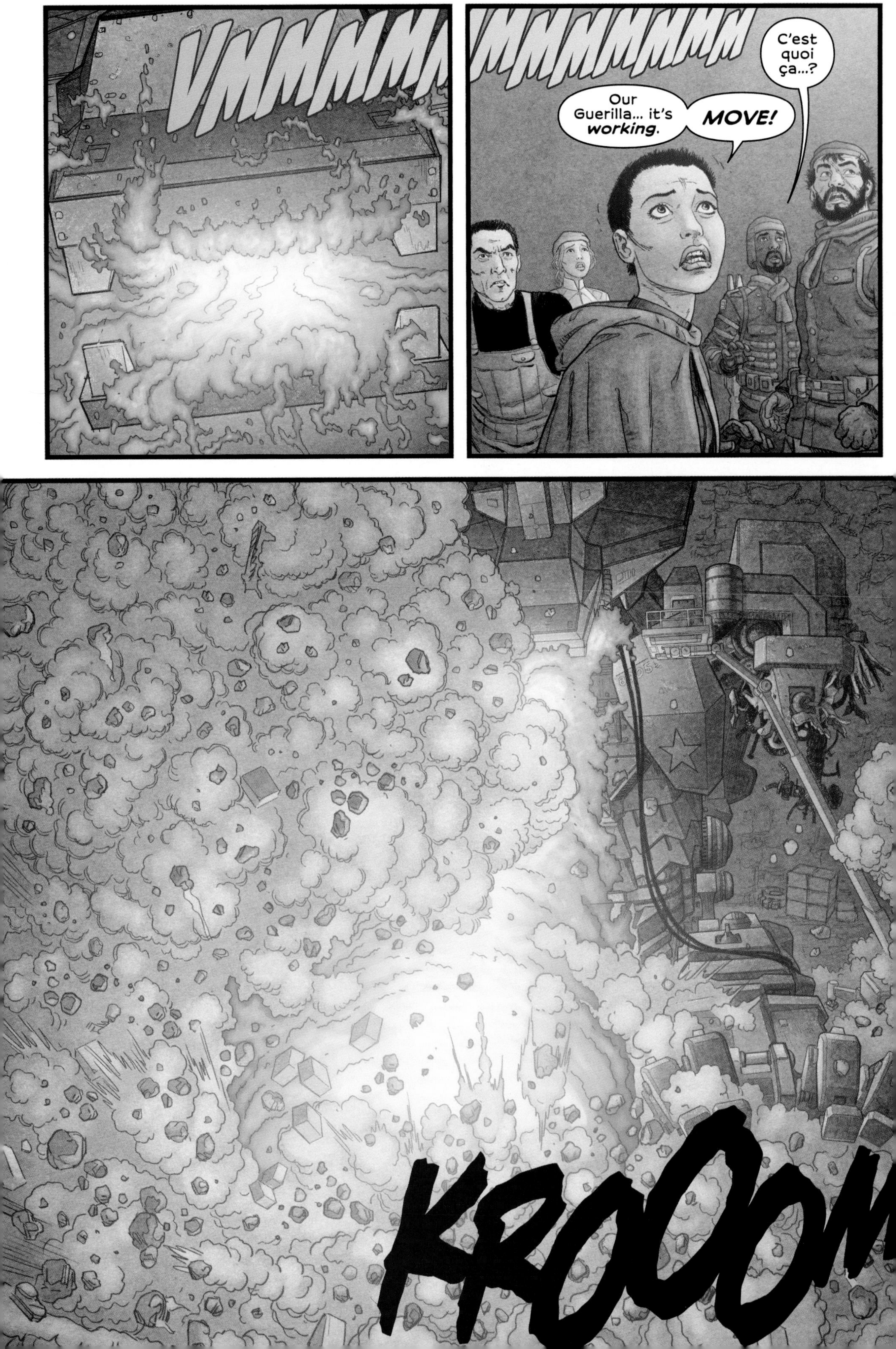
VMMMMMMMMMMMMMMMMMMM
C'est quoi ça...?
Our Guerilla... it's *working*.
MOVE!
KROOOM

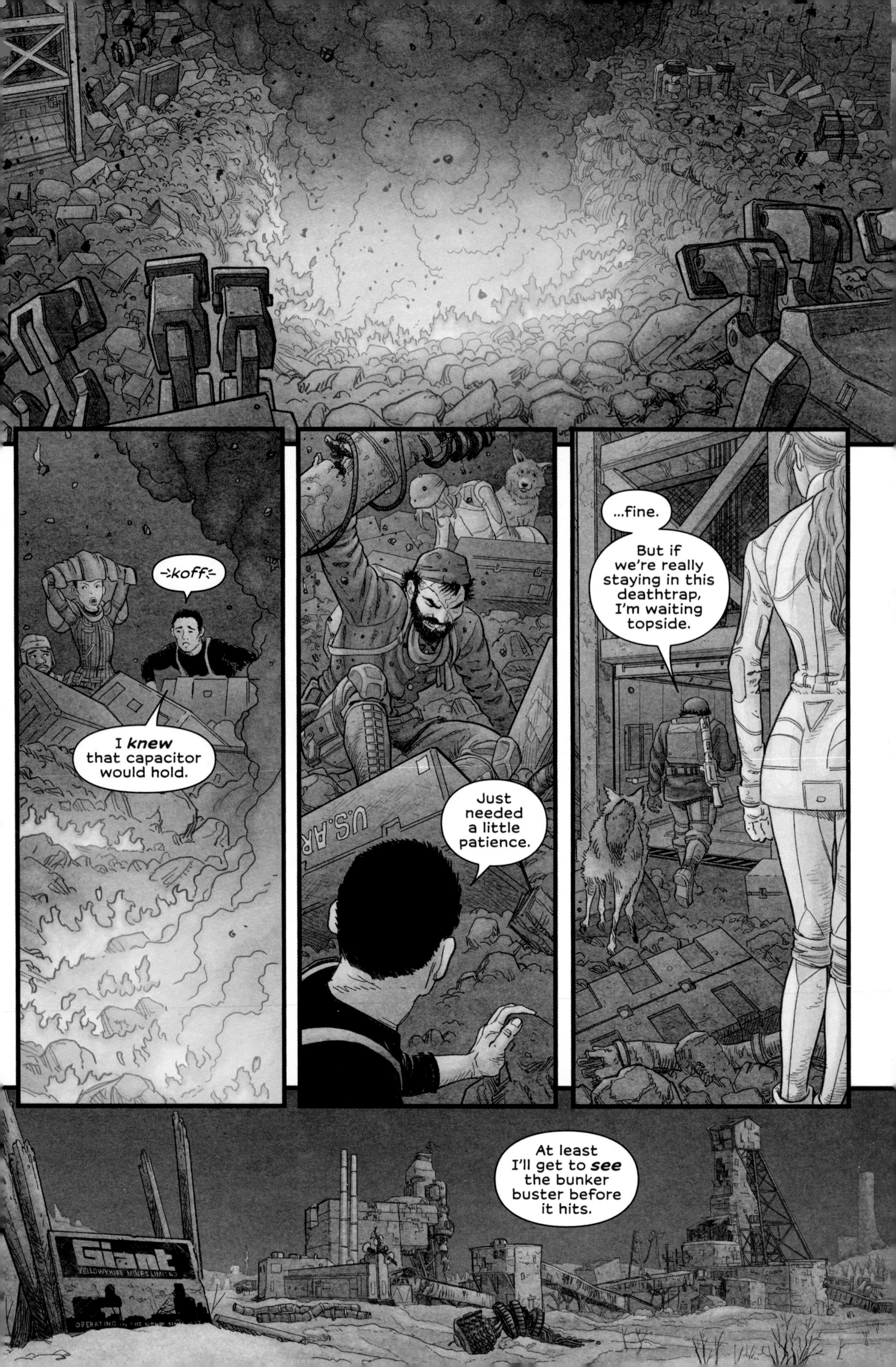

-:koff:-
I *knew* that capacitor would hold.
Just needed a little patience.
...fine.
But if we're really staying in this deathtrap, I'm waiting topside.
At least I'll get to *see* the bunker buster before it hits.
Giant
YELLOWKNIFE MINES LIMITED

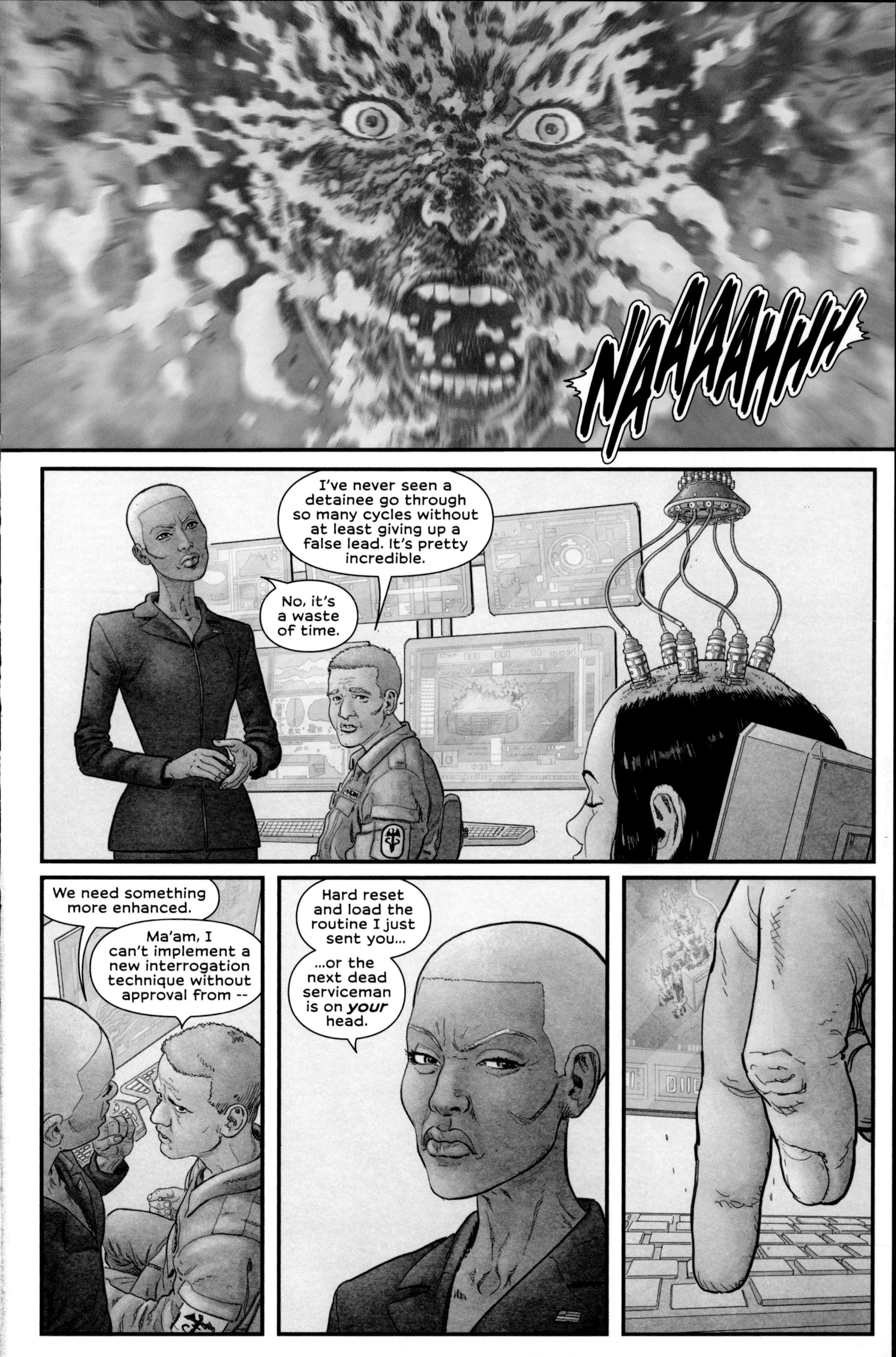
NAAAAHHH
I've never seen a detainee go through so many cycles without at least giving up a false lead. It's pretty incredible.
No, it's a waste of time.
We need something more enhanced.
Ma'am, I can't implement a new interrogation technique without approval from --
Hard reset and load the routine I just sent you...
...or the next dead serviceman is on *your* head.

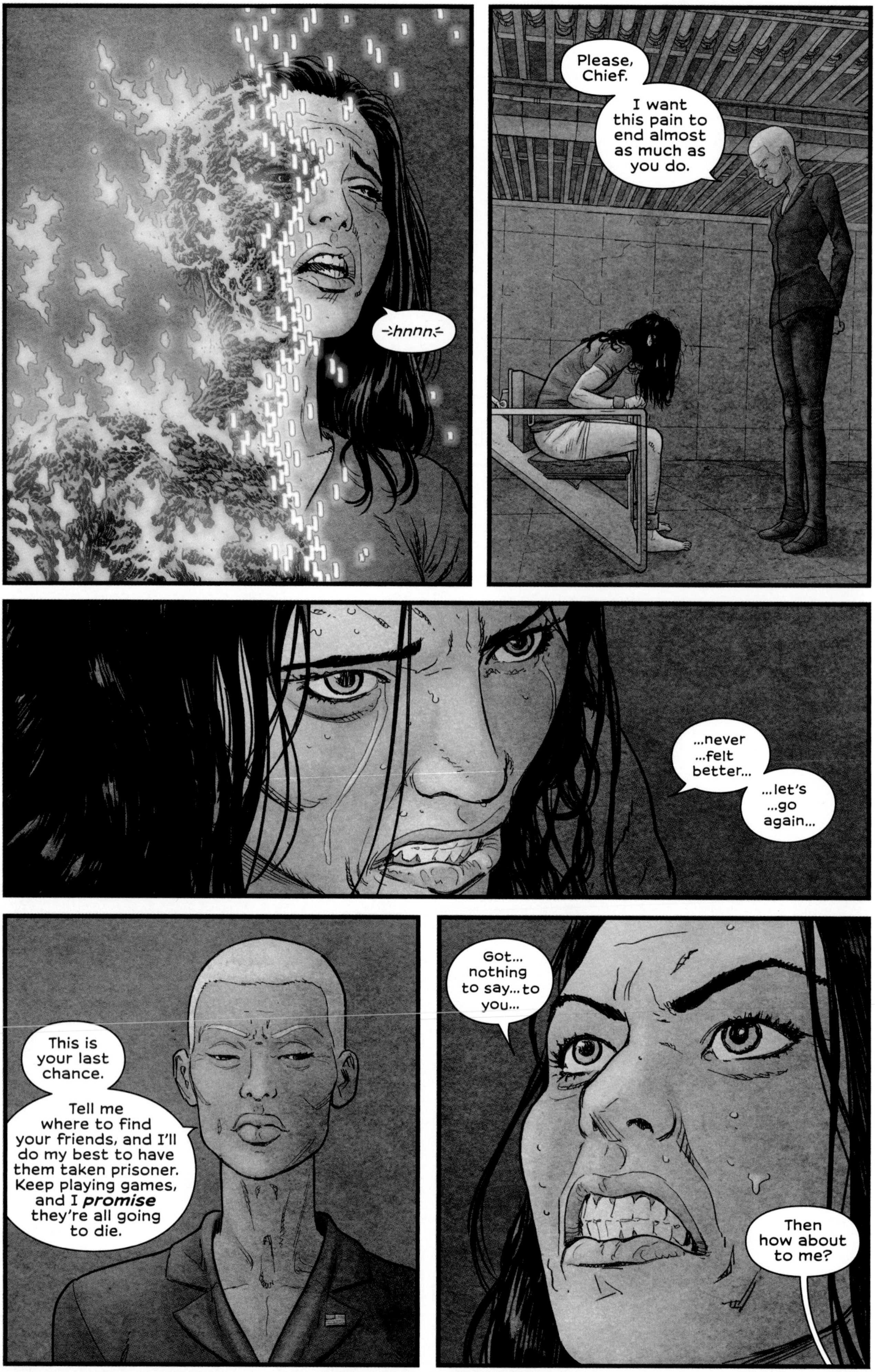
-hnnn-
Please, Chief.
I want this pain to end almost as much as you do.
...never ...felt better...
...let's ...go again...
This is your last chance.
Tell me where to find your friends, and I'll do my best to have them taken prisoner. Keep playing games, and I *promise* they're all going to die.
Got... nothing to say... to you...
Then how about to me?

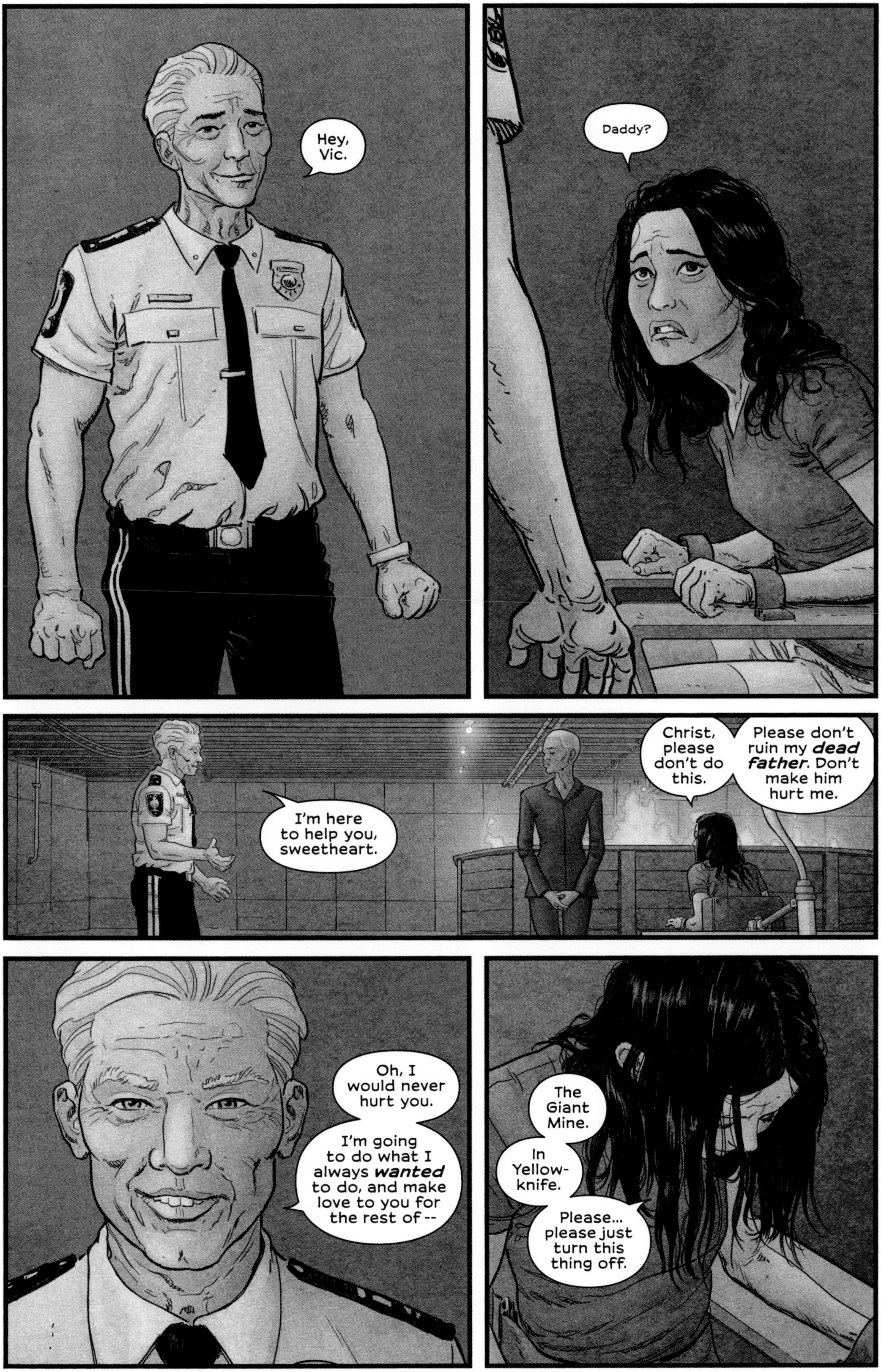
Hey, Vic.
Daddy?
I'm here to help you, sweetheart.
Christ, please don't do this.
Please don't ruin my *dead father*. Don't make him hurt me.
Oh, I would never hurt you.
I'm going to do what I always *wanted* to do, and make love to you for the rest of --
The Giant Mine.
In Yellow-knife.
Please... please just turn this thing off.

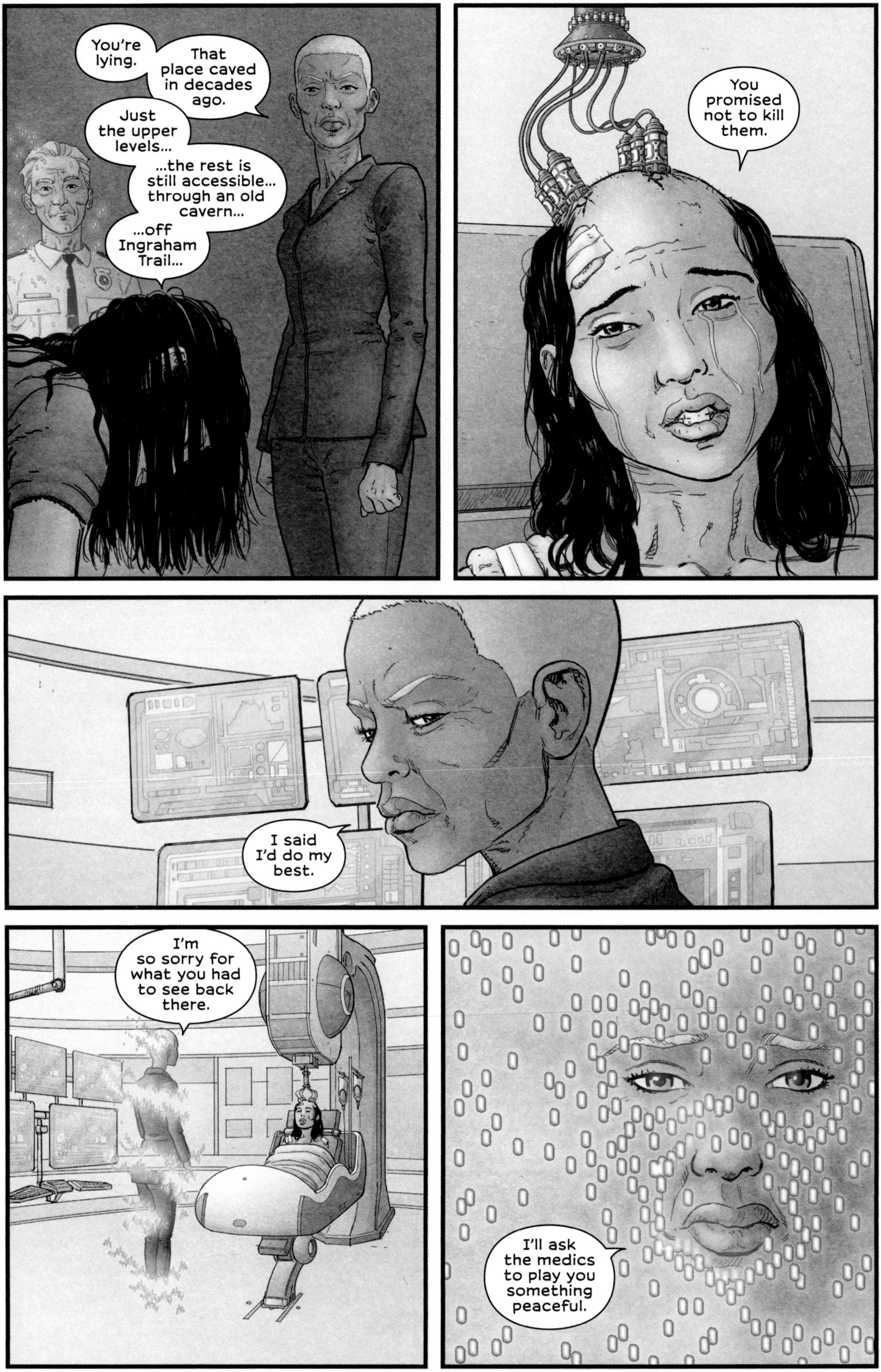
You're lying.
That place caved in decades ago.
Just the upper levels...
...the rest is still accessible... through an old cavern...
...off Ingraham Trail...
You promised not to kill them.
I said I'd do my best.
I'm so sorry for what you had to see back there.
I'll ask the medics to play you something peaceful.

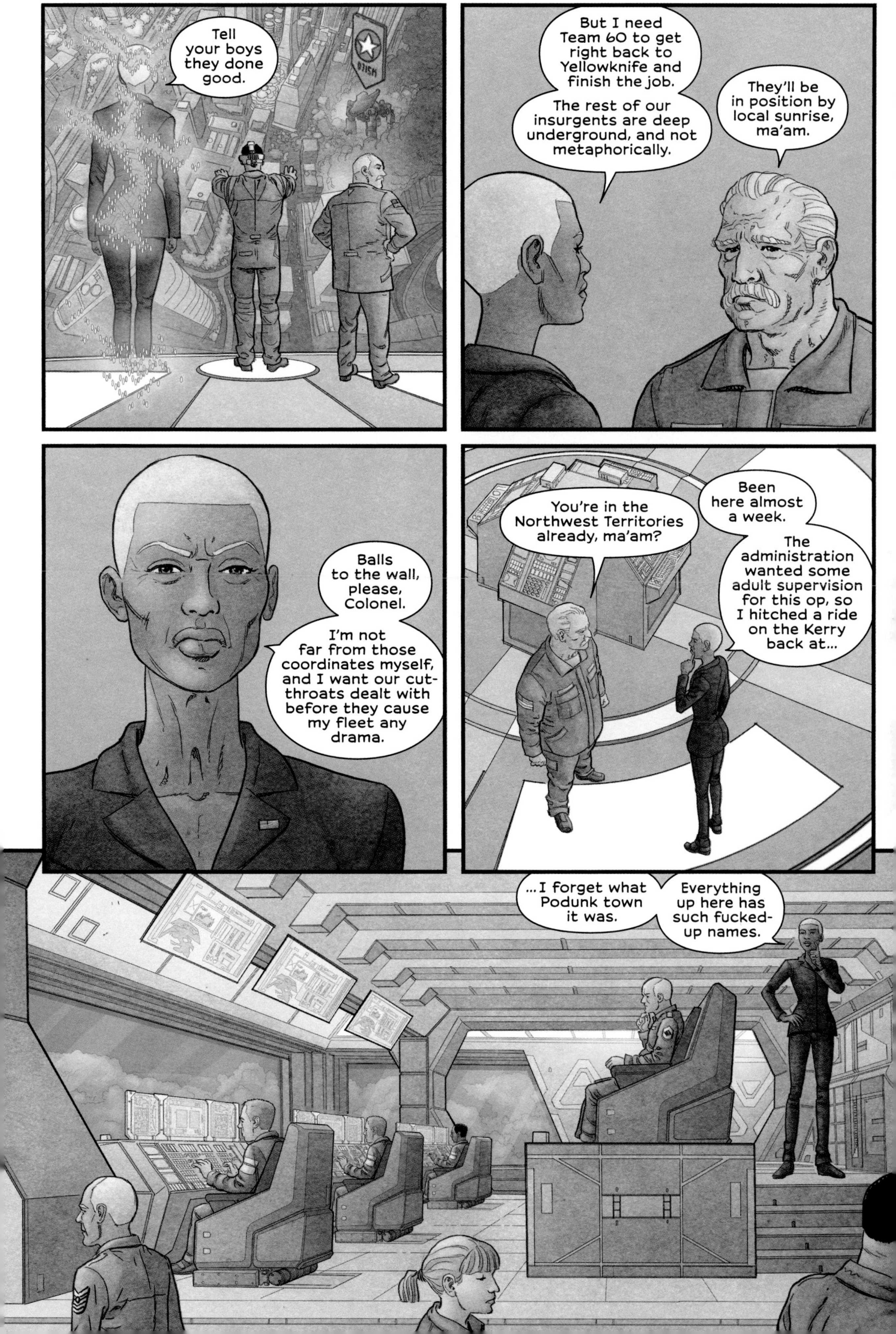
Tell your boys they done good.
But I need Team 60 to get right back to Yellowknife and finish the job.
The rest of our insurgents are deep underground, and not metaphorically.
They'll be in position by local sunrise, ma'am.
Balls to the wall, please, Colonel.
I'm not far from those coordinates myself, and I want our cut-throats dealt with before they cause my fleet any drama.
You're in the Northwest Territories already, ma'am?
Been here almost a week.
The administration wanted some adult supervision for this op, so I hitched a ride on the Kerry back at...
...I forget what Podunk town it was.
Everything up here has such fucked-up names.

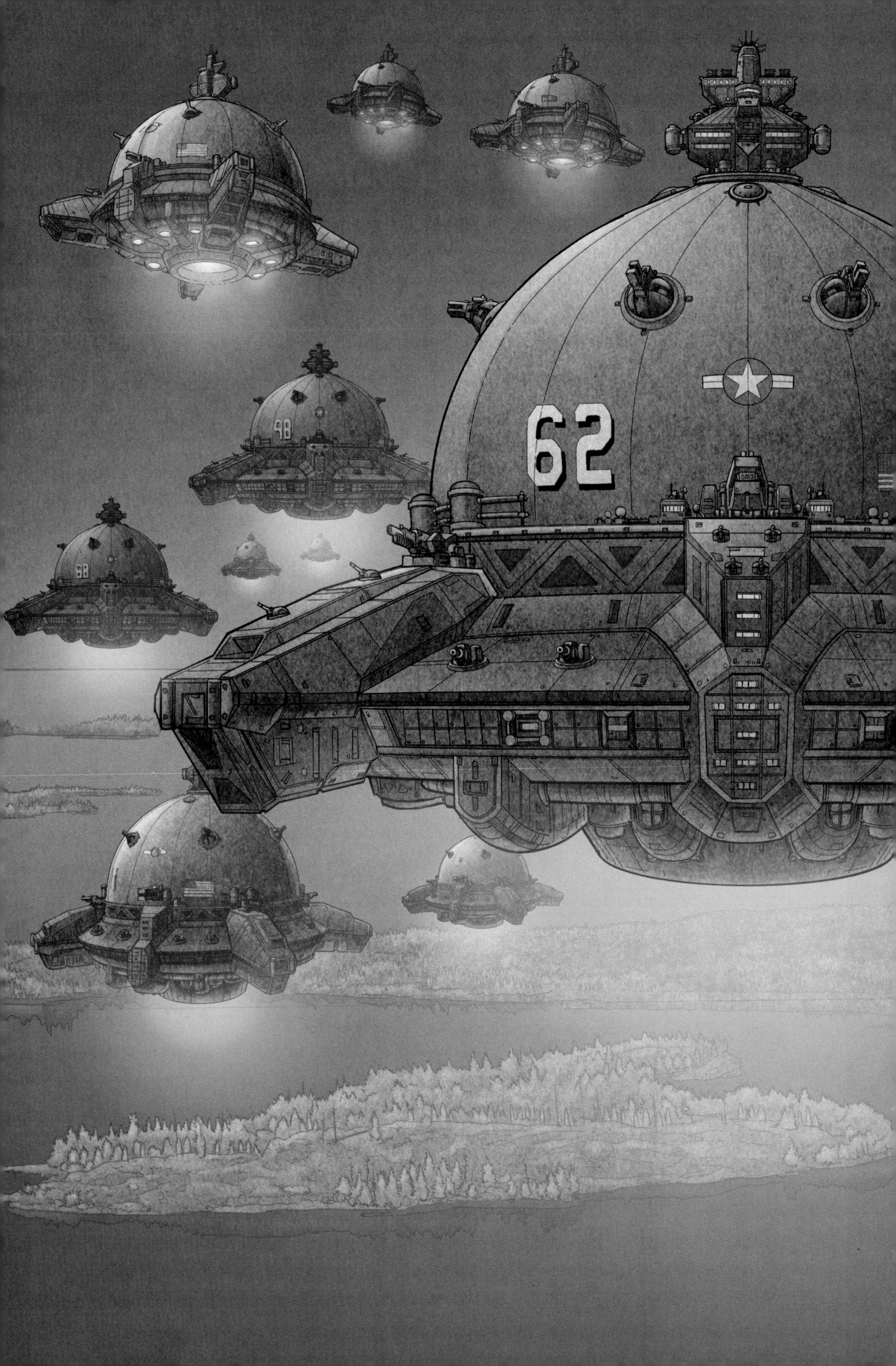
62

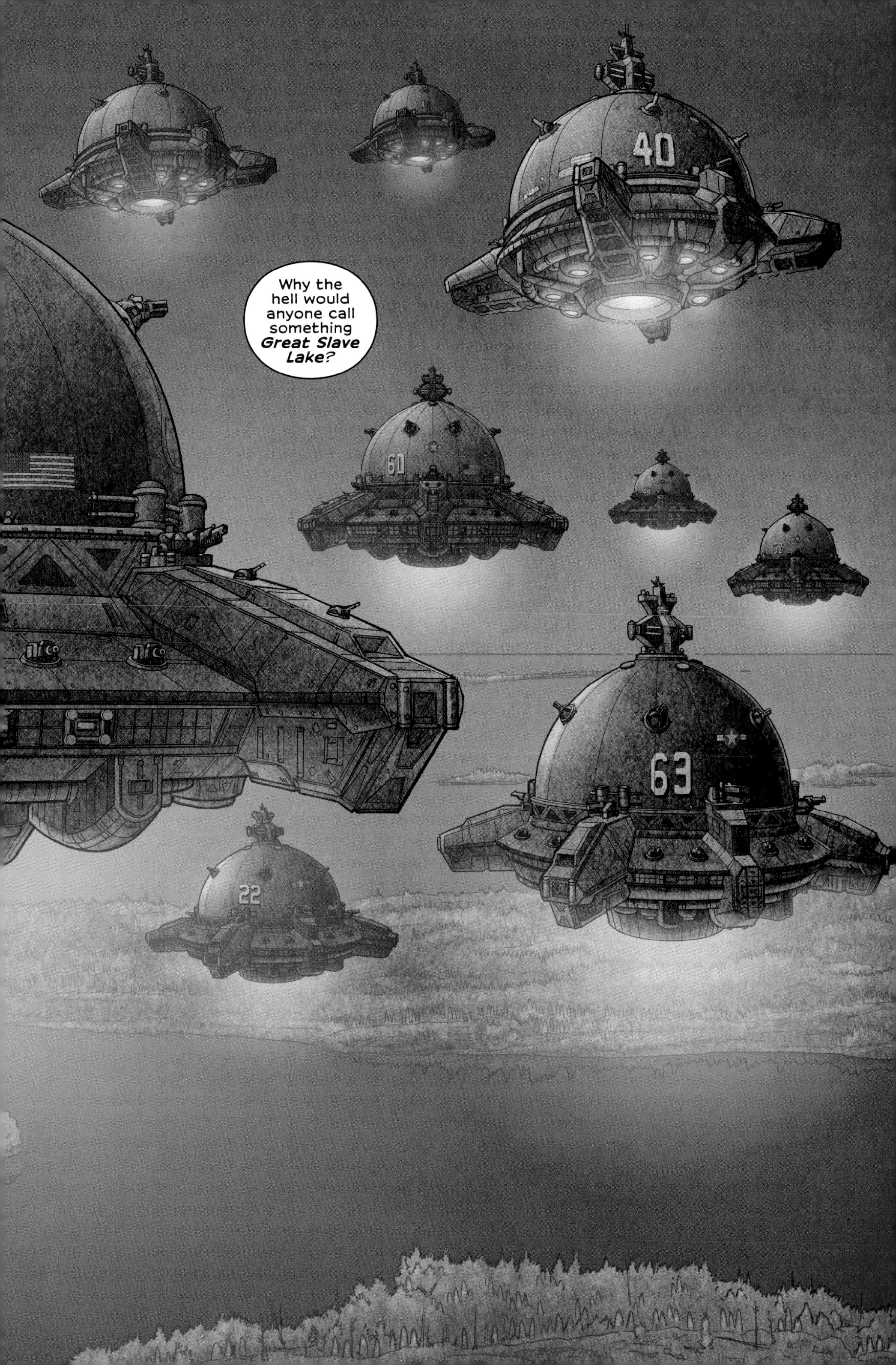
Why the hell would anyone call something *Great Slave Lake?*
40
60
63
22

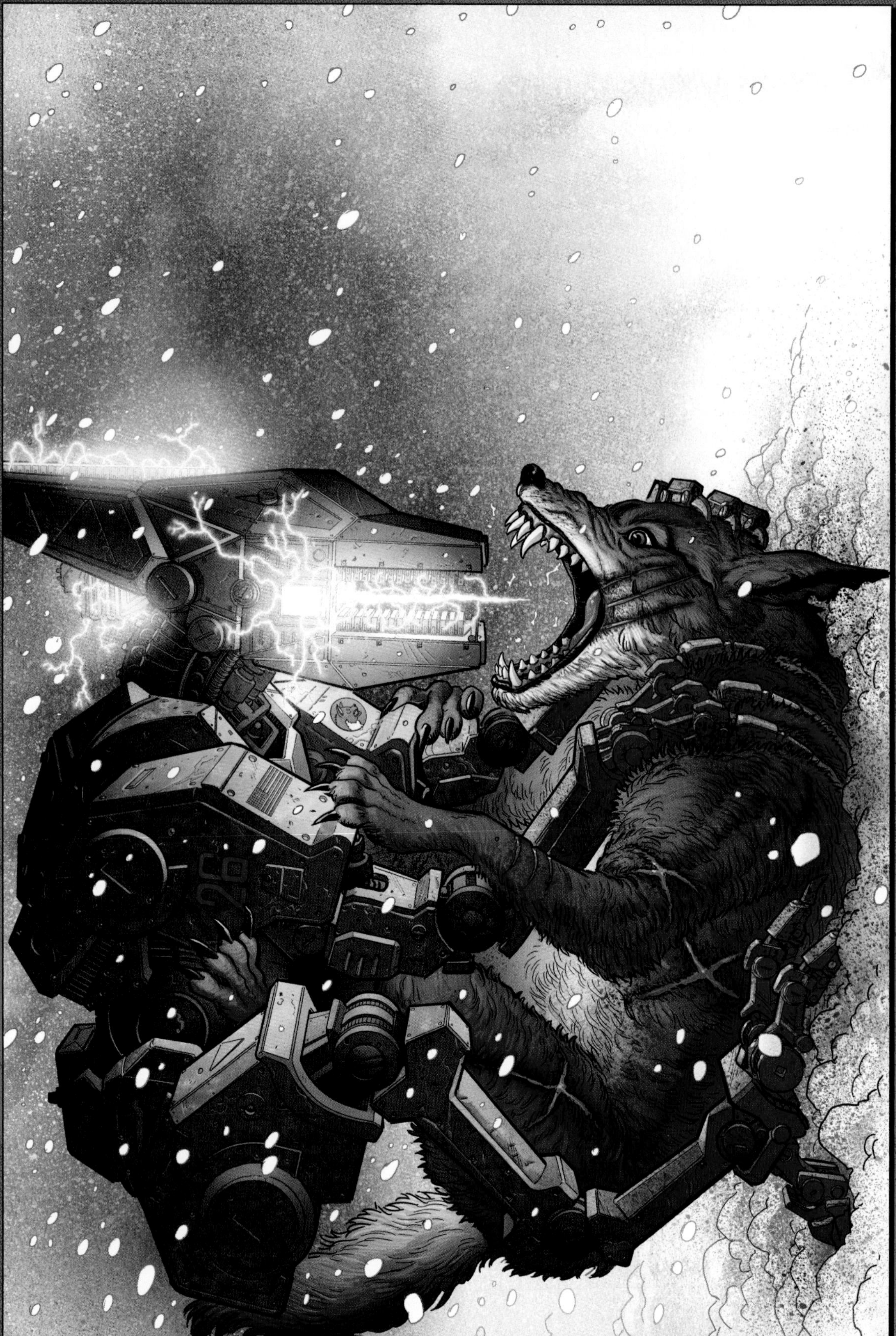

CHAPTER FOUR

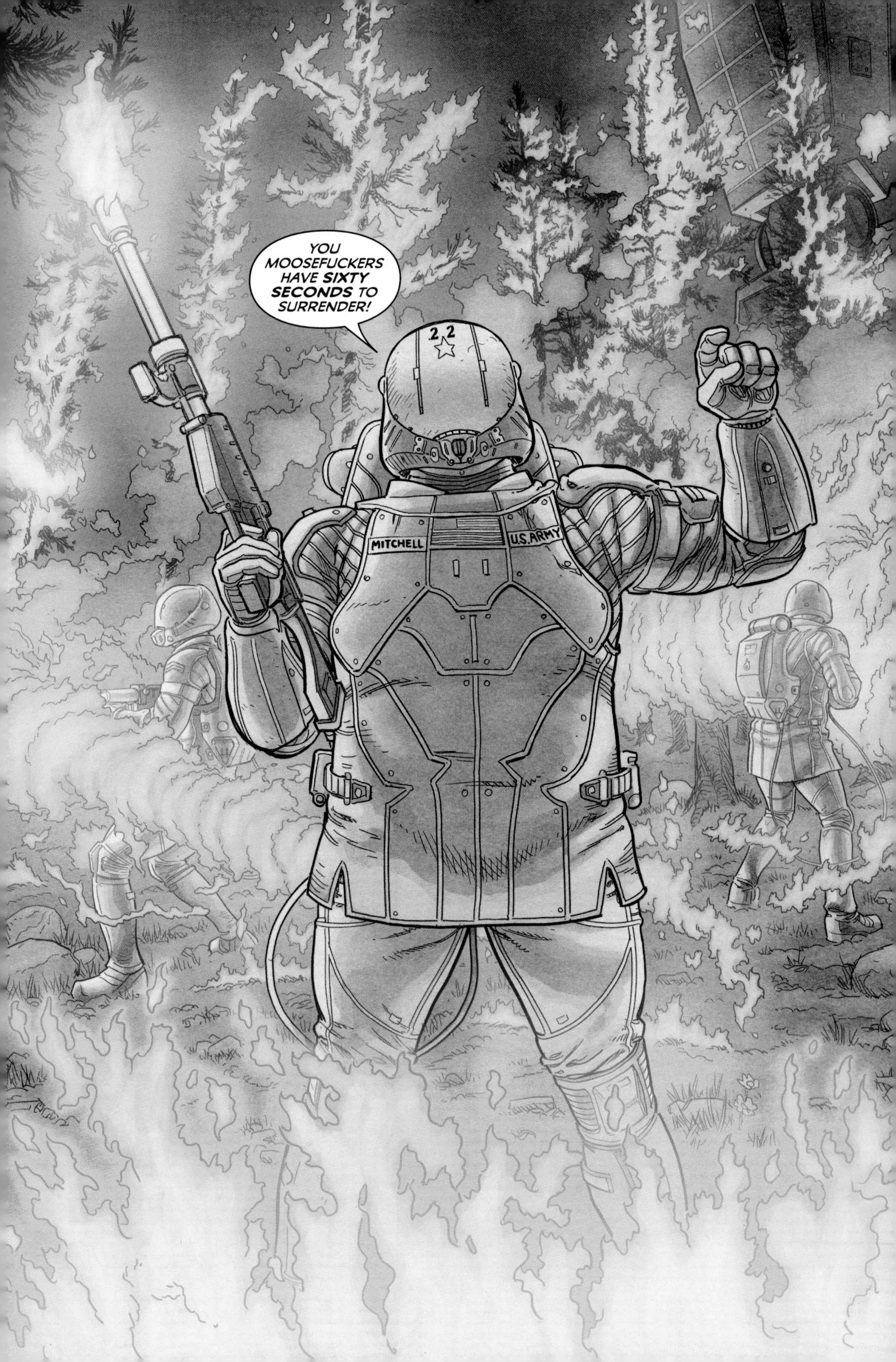
YOU MOOSEFUCKERS HAVE SIXTY SECONDS TO SURRENDER!
22
MITCHELL
U.S. ARMY

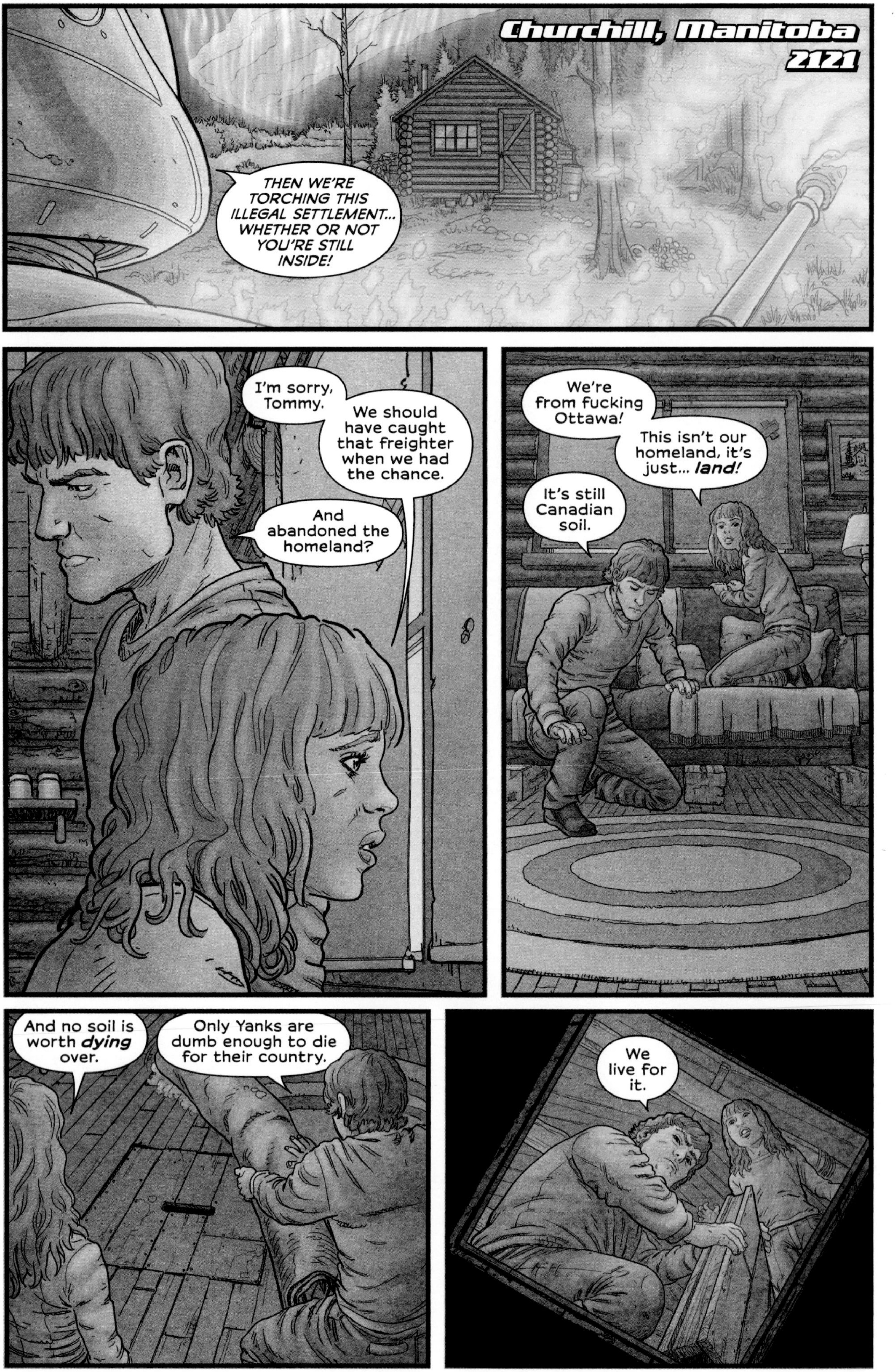
Churchill, Manitoba
2121
THEN WE'RE TORCHING THIS ILLEGAL SETTLEMENT... WHETHER OR NOT YOU'RE STILL INSIDE!
I'm sorry, Tommy.
We should have caught that freighter when we had the chance.
And abandoned the homeland?
We're from fucking Ottawa!
This isn't our homeland, it's just... *land!*
It's still Canadian soil.
And no soil is worth *dying* over.
Only Yanks are dumb enough to die for their country.
We live for it.

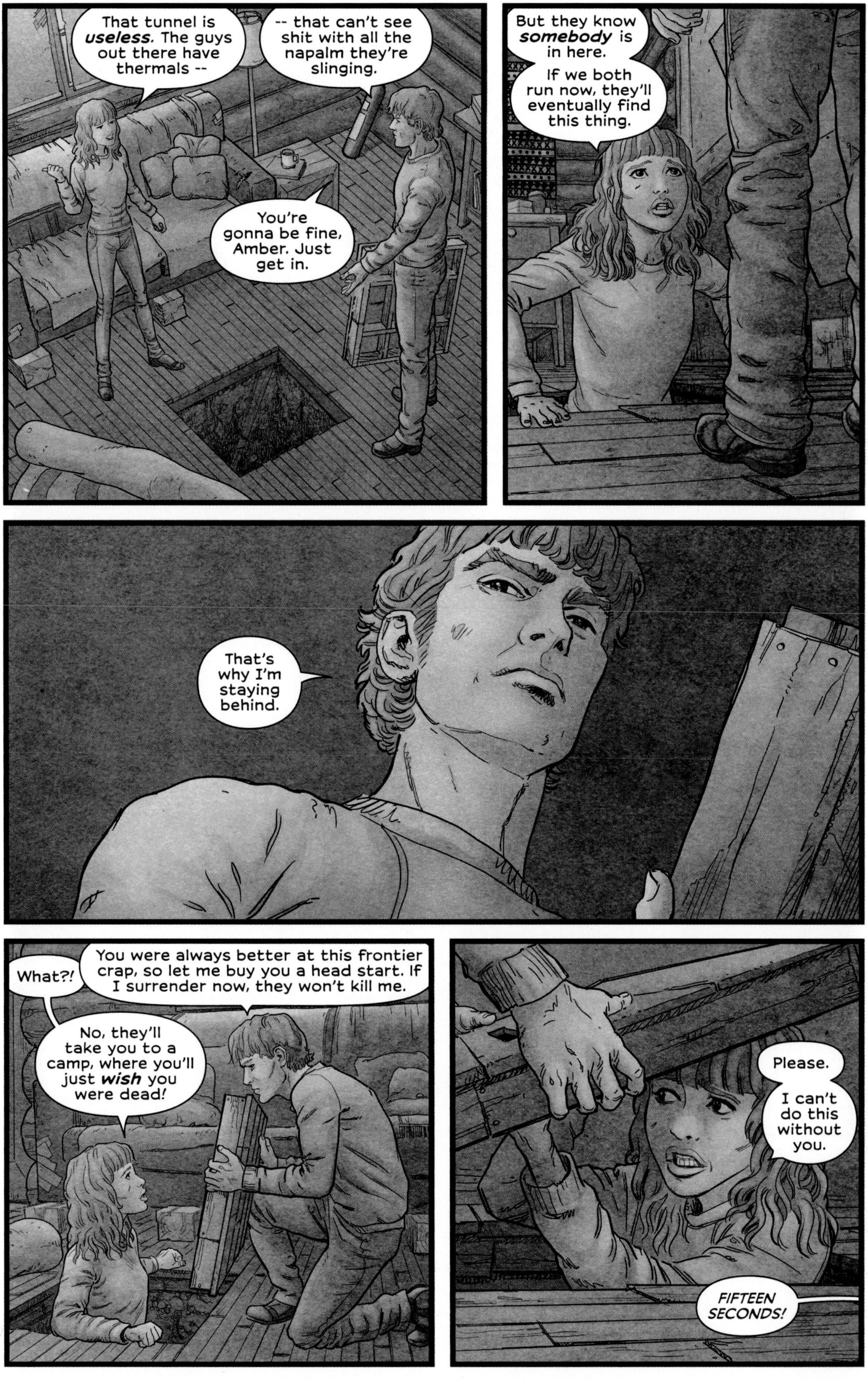

That tunnel is *useless.* The guys out there have thermals --
-- that can't see shit with all the napalm they're slinging.
You're gonna be fine, Amber. Just get in.
But they know *somebody* is in here.
If we both run now, they'll eventually find this thing.
That's why I'm staying behind.
What?!
You were always better at this frontier crap, so let me buy you a head start. If I surrender now, they won't kill me.
No, they'll take you to a camp, where you'll just *wish* you were dead!
Please.
I can't do this without you.
FIFTEEN SECONDS!

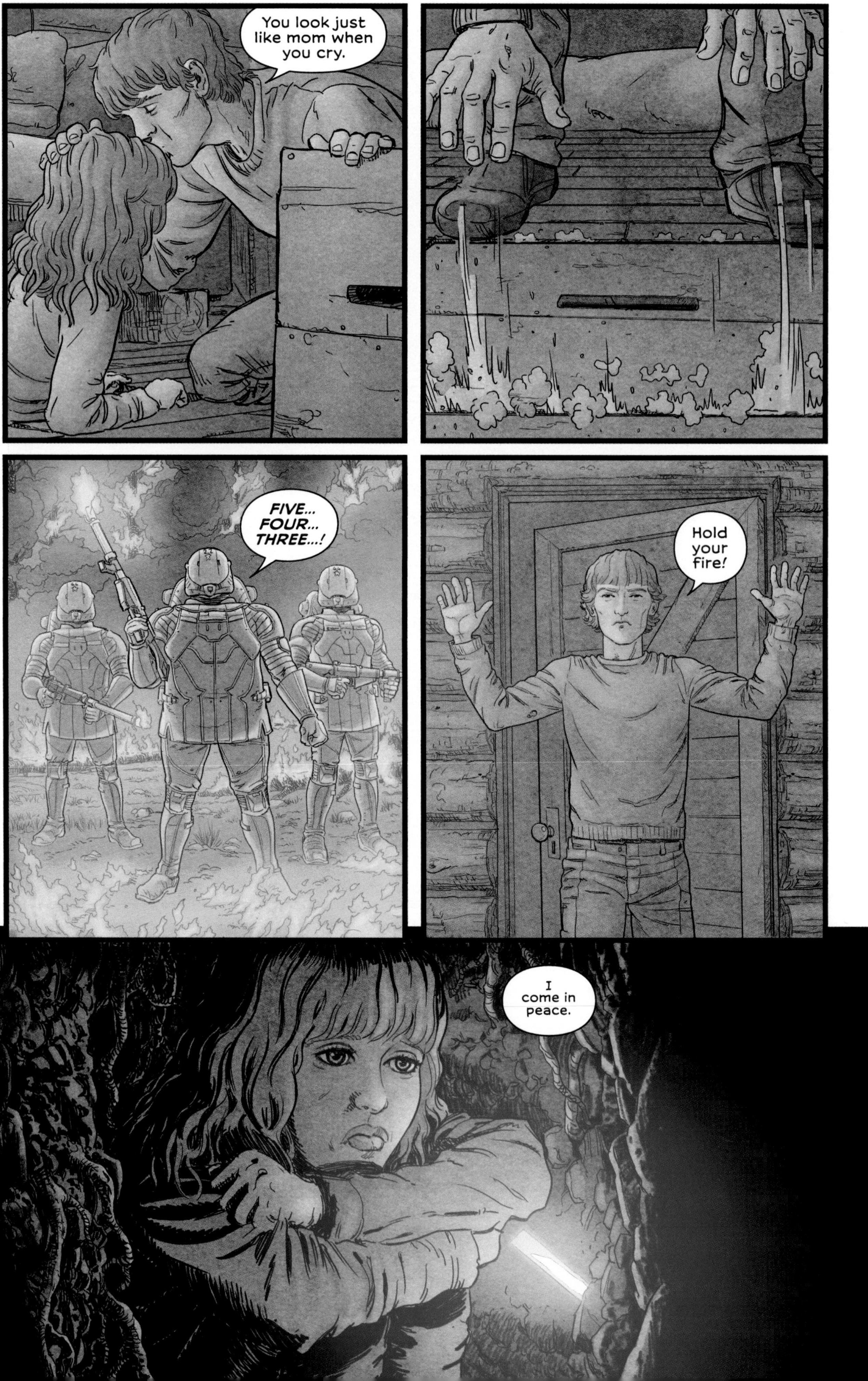
You look just like mom when you cry.
FIVE... FOUR... THREE...!
Hold your fire!
I come in peace.

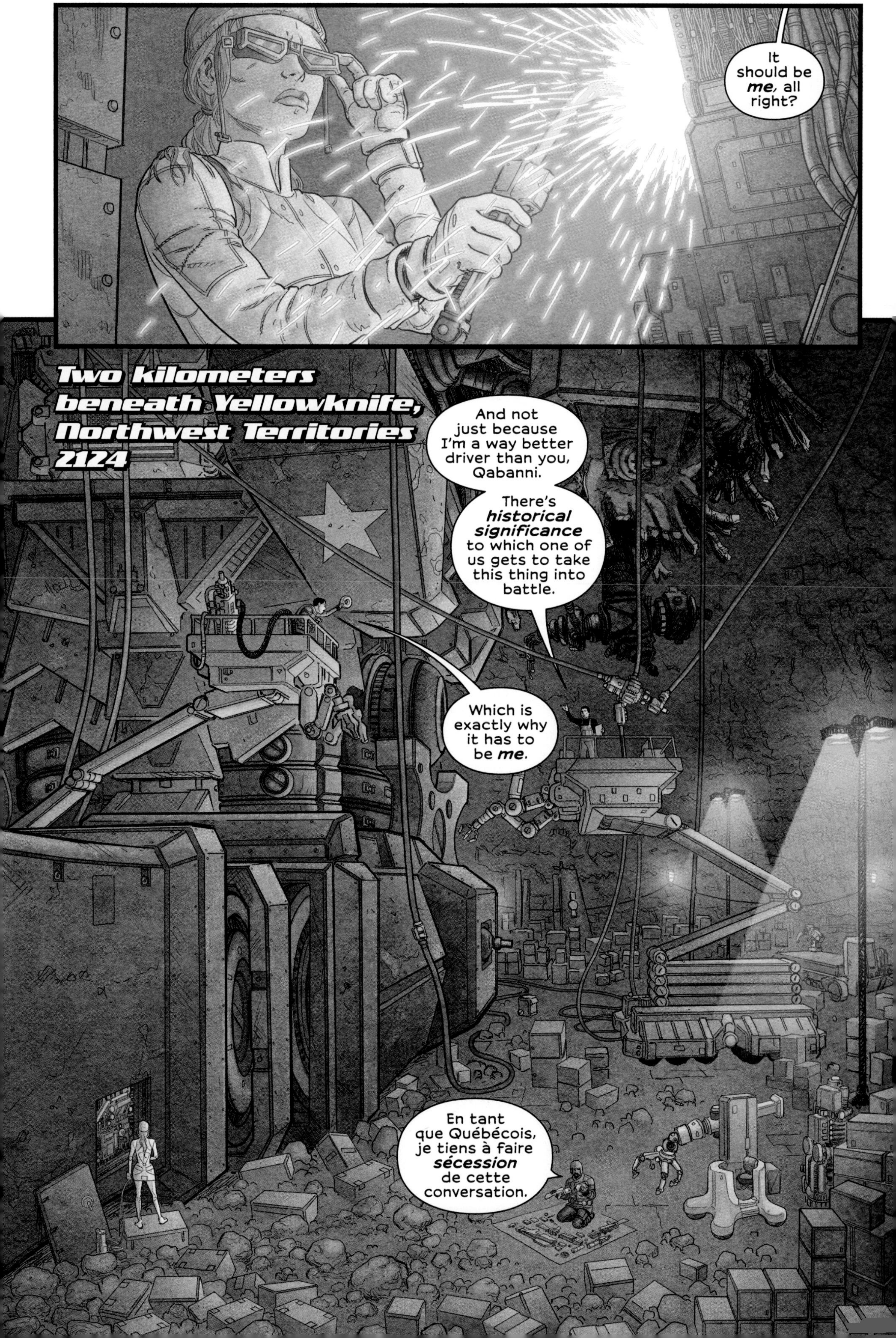

It should be *me,* all right?
Two kilometers beneath Yellowknife, Northwest Territories 2124
And not just because I'm a way better driver than you, Qabanni.
There's ***historical significance*** to which one of us gets to take this thing into battle.
Which is exactly why it has to be *me*.
En tant que Québécois, je tiens à faire ***sécession*** de cette conversation.

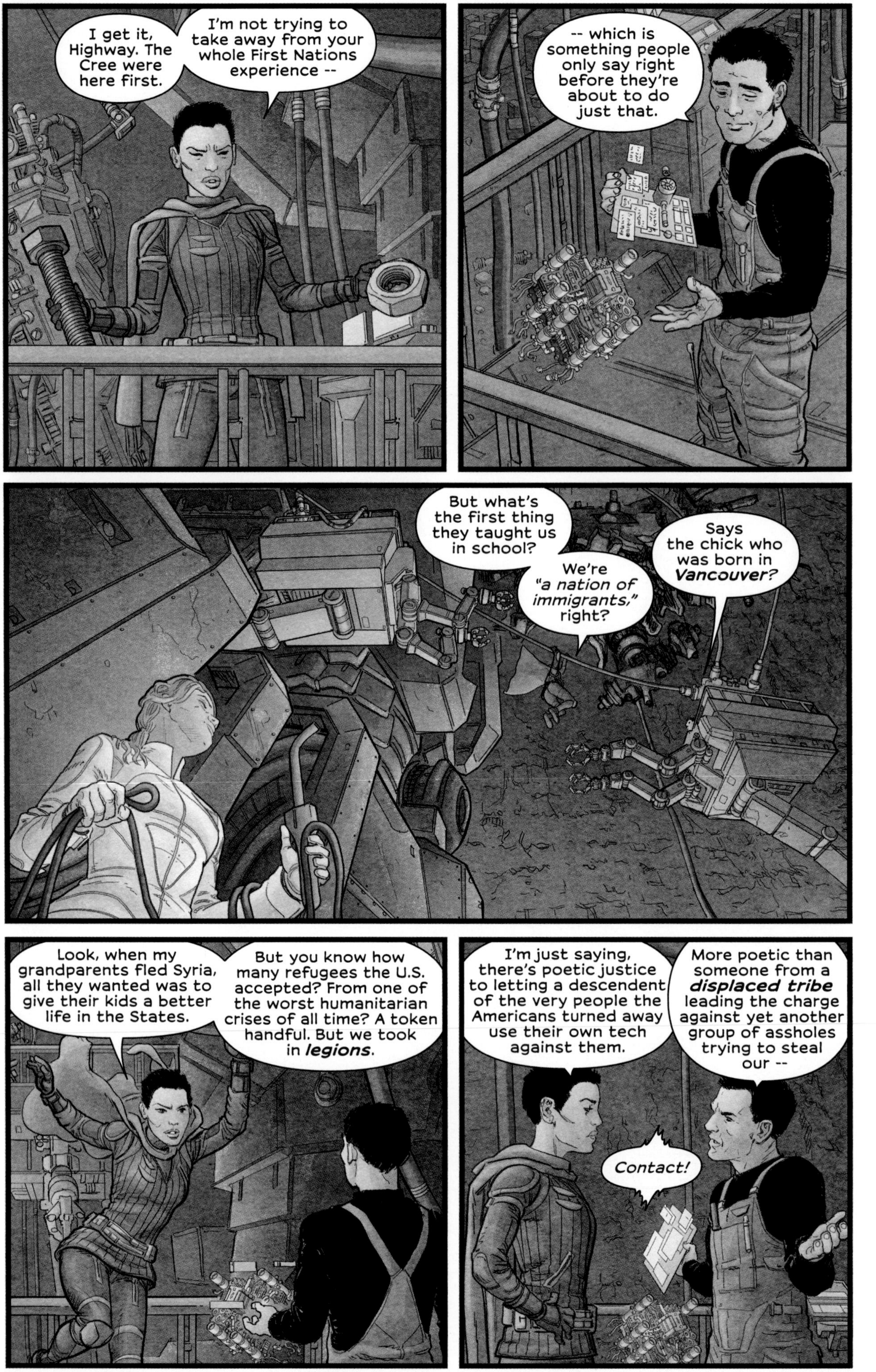

I get it, Highway. The Cree were here first.
I'm not trying to take away from your whole First Nations experience --
-- which is something people only say right before they're about to do just that.
But what's the first thing they taught us in school?
We're *"a nation of immigrants,"* right?
Says the chick who was born in ***Vancouver?***
Look, when my grandparents fled Syria, all they wanted was to give their kids a better life in the States.
But you know how many refugees the U.S. accepted? From one of the worst humanitarian crises of all time? A token handful. But we took in ***legions***.
I'm just saying, there's poetic justice to letting a descendent of the very people the Americans turned away use their own tech against them.
More poetic than someone from a ***displaced tribe*** leading the charge against yet another group of assholes trying to steal our --
Contact!

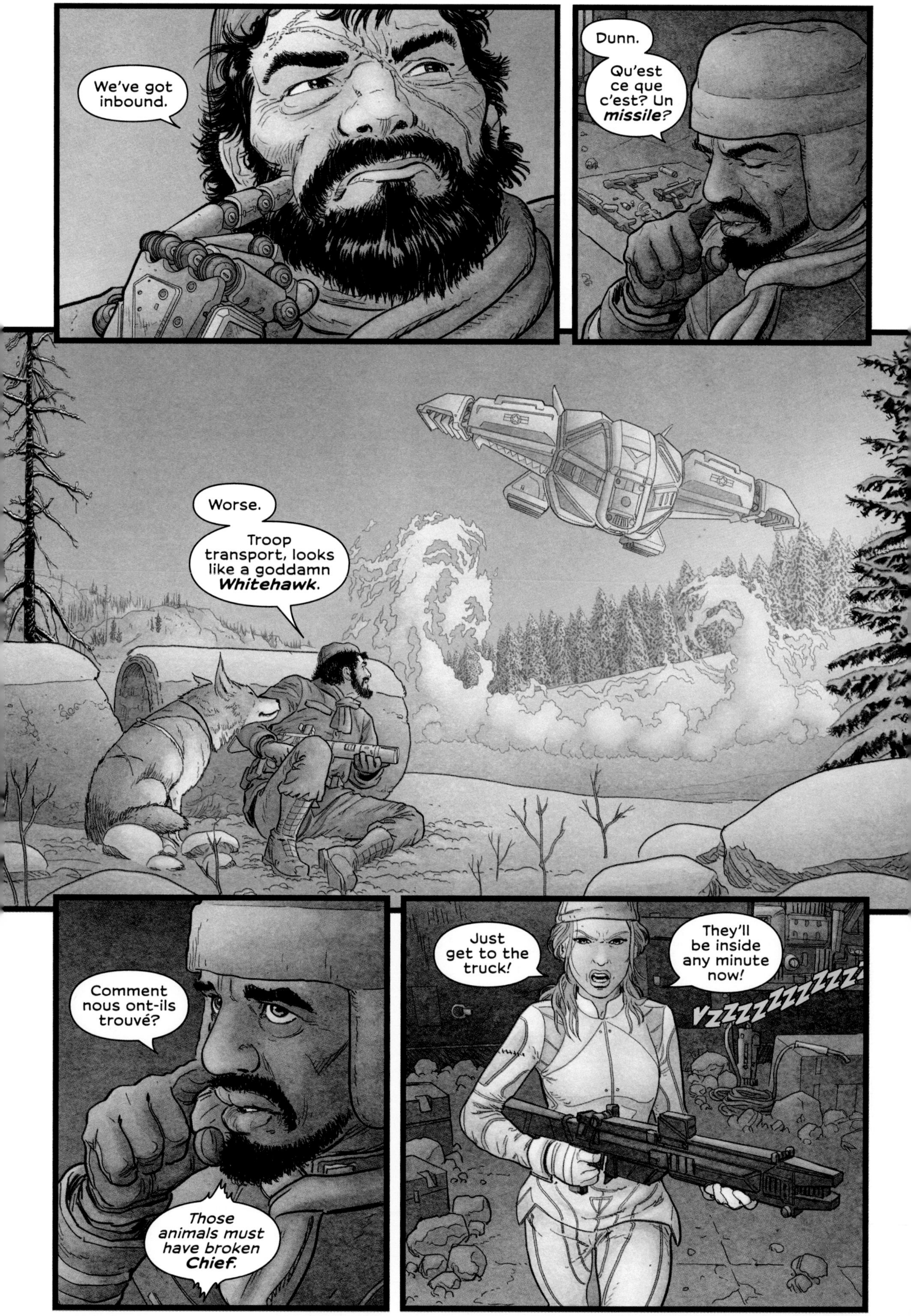
We've got inbound.
Dunn.
Qu'est ce que c'est? Un *missile*?
Worse.
Troop transport, looks like a goddamn ***Whitehawk***.
Comment nous ont-ils trouvé?
*Those animals must have broken **Chief**.*
Just get to the truck!
They'll be inside any minute now!
VZZZZZZZZZZZ

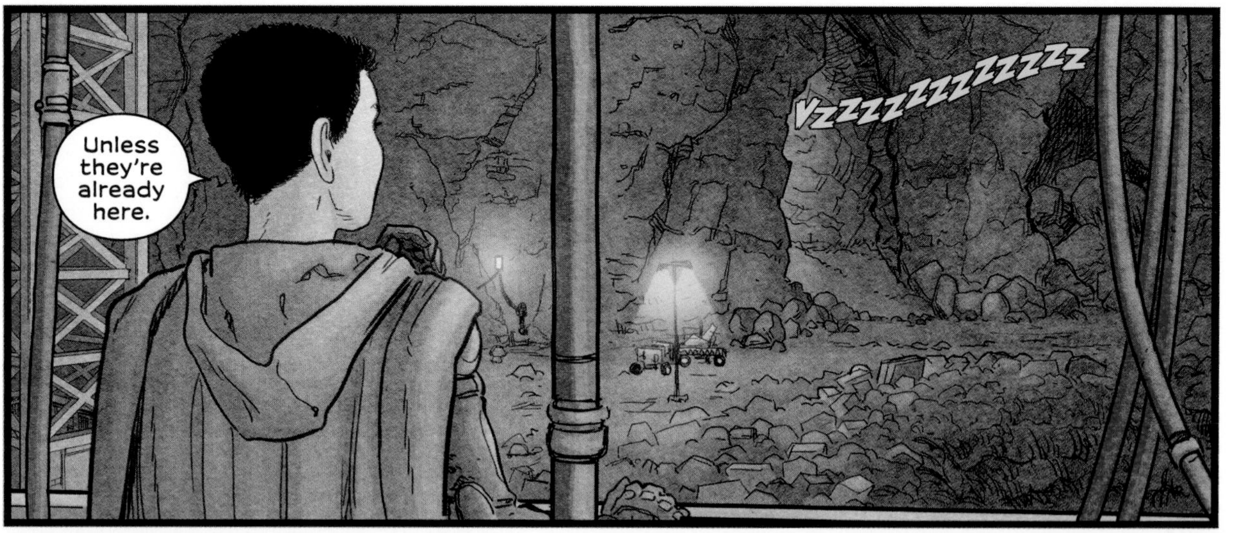
Unless they're already here.
Vzzzzzzzzzzzz

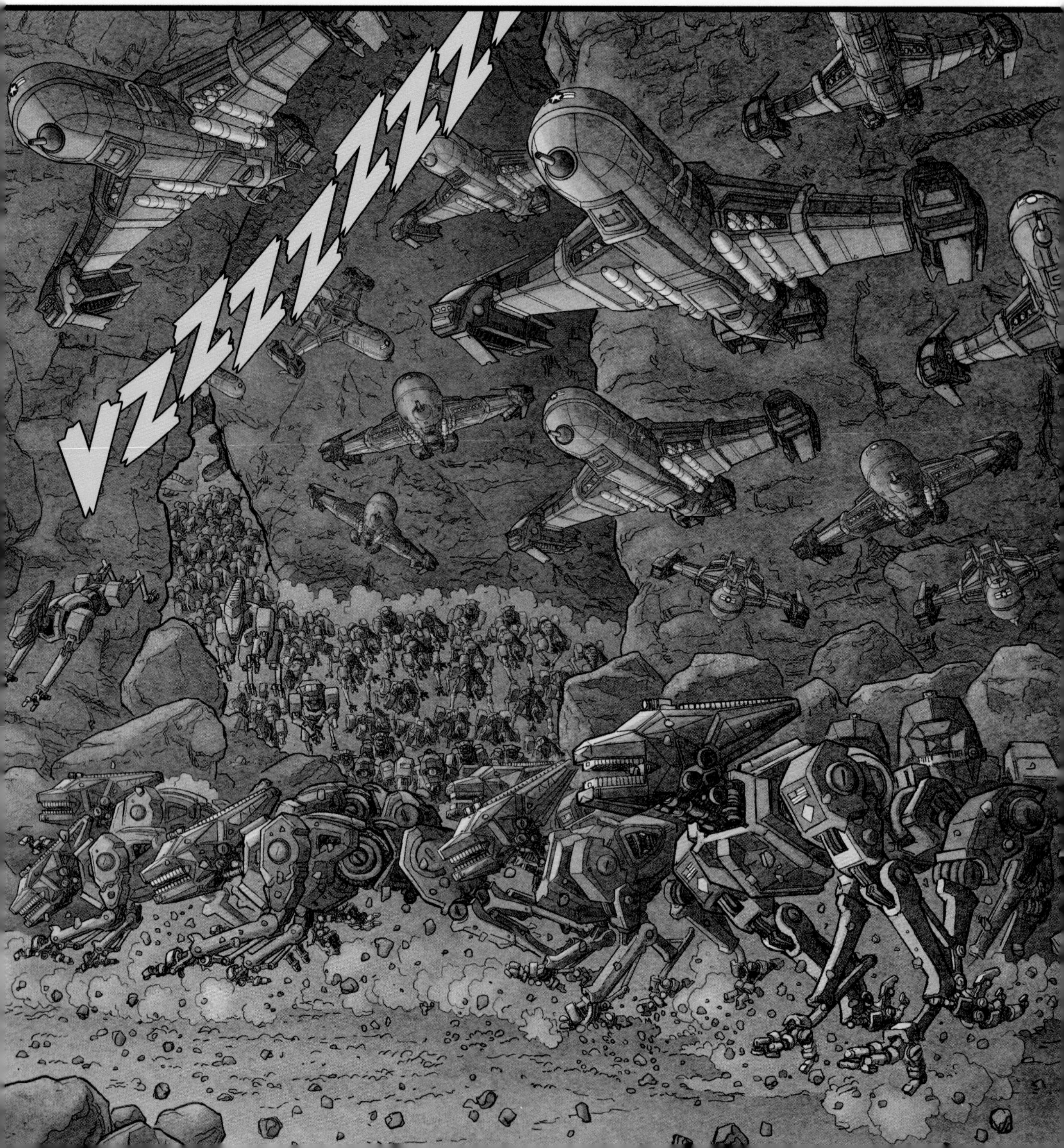
VZZZZZZZZZ!

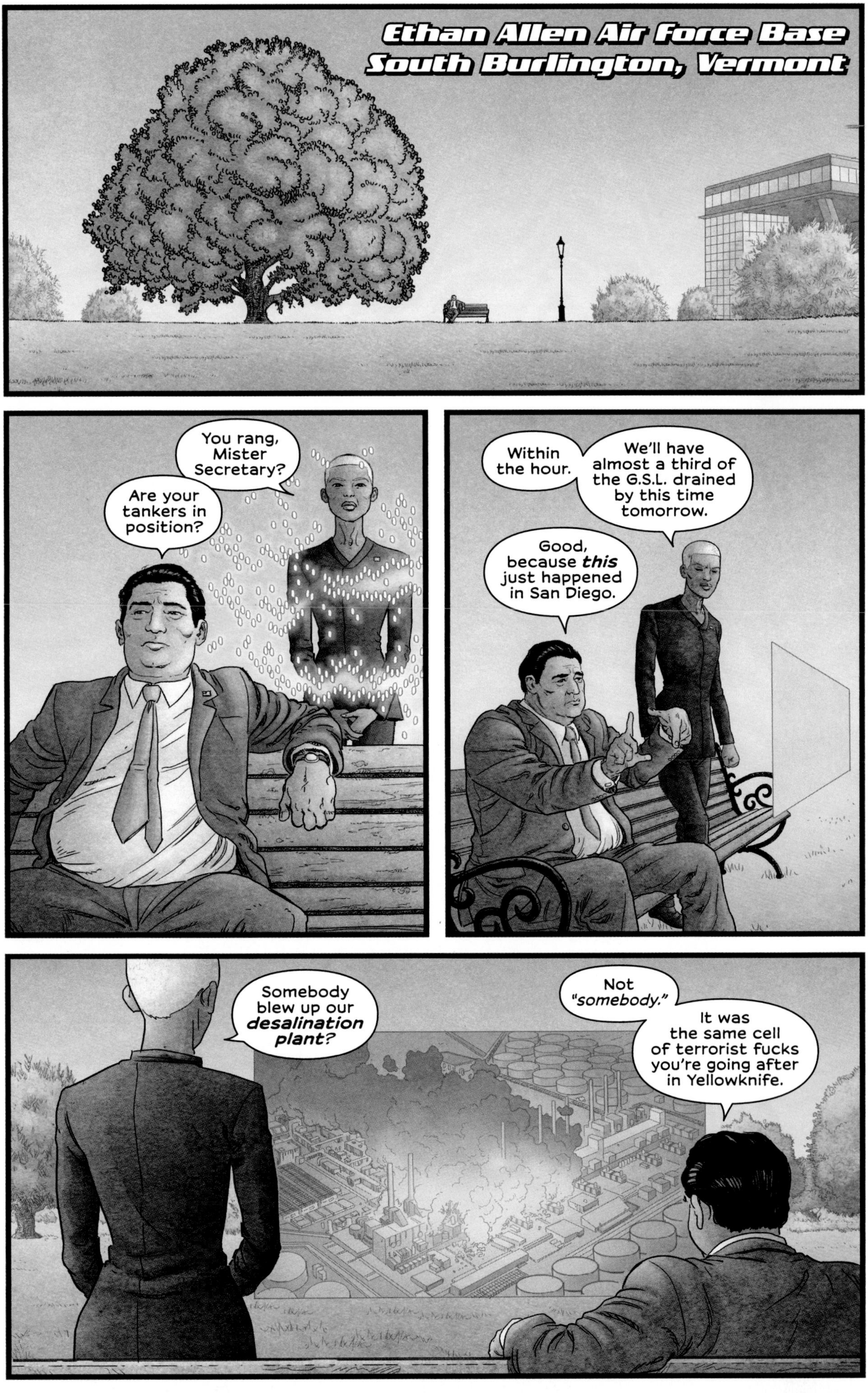
Ethan Allen Air Force Base
South Burlington, Vermont
Are your tankers in position?
You rang, Mister Secretary?
Within the hour.
We'll have almost a third of the G.S.L. drained by this time tomorrow.
Good, because *this* just happened in San Diego.
Somebody blew up our *desalination plant?*
Not *"somebody."*
It was the same cell of terrorist fucks you're going after in Yellowknife.

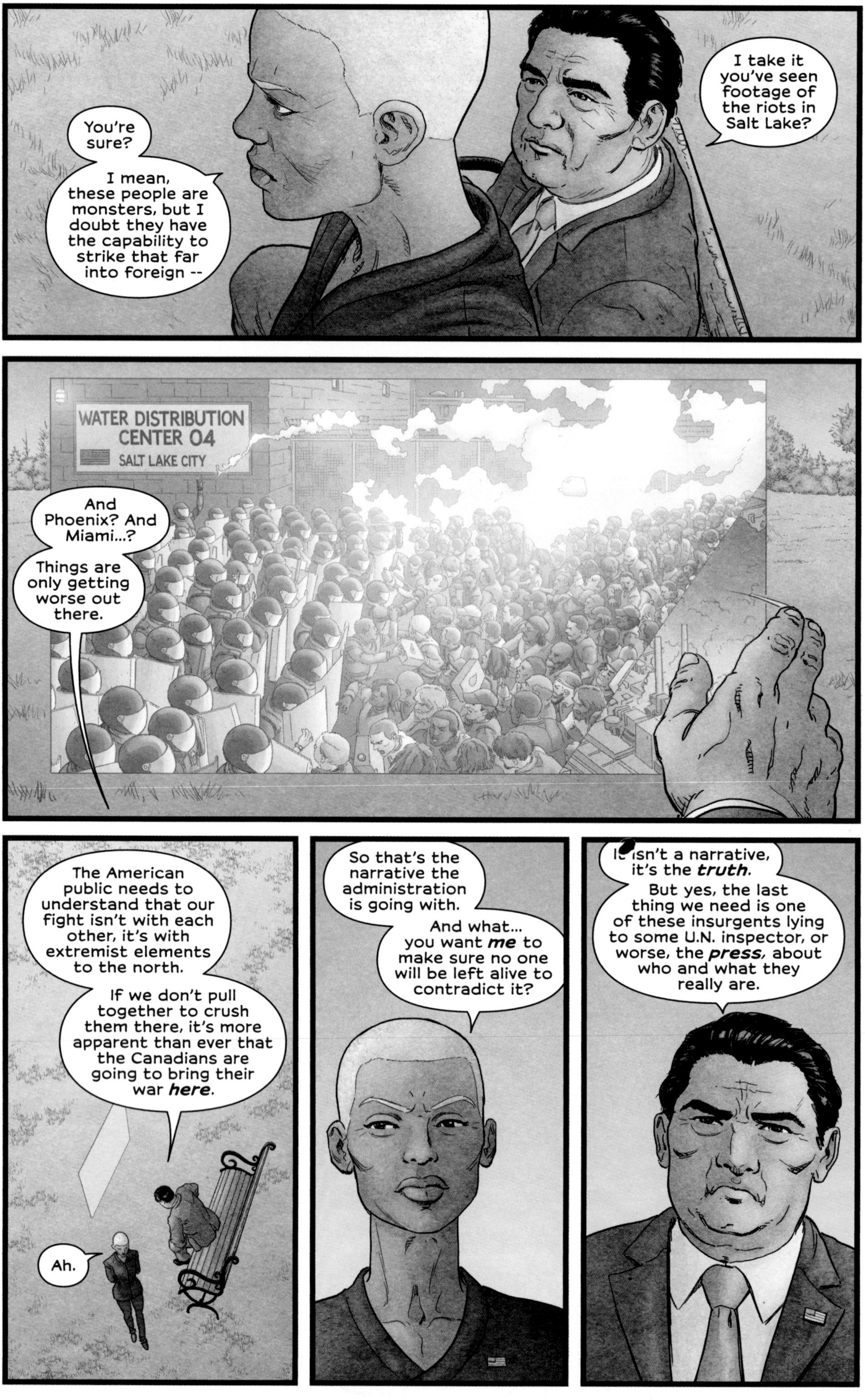
You're sure?
I mean, these people are monsters, but I doubt they have the capability to strike that far into foreign --
I take it you've seen footage of the riots in Salt Lake?
WATER DISTRIBUTION CENTER 04
SALT LAKE CITY
And Phoenix? And Miami...?
Things are only getting worse out there.
The American public needs to understand that our fight isn't with each other, it's with extremist elements to the north.
If we don't pull together to crush them there, it's more apparent than ever that the Canadians are going to bring their war ***here***.
Ah.
So that's the narrative the administration is going with.
And what... you want ***me*** to make sure no one will be left alive to contradict it?
It isn't a narrative, it's the ***truth***.
But yes, the last thing we need is one of these insurgents lying to some U.N. inspector, or worse, the ***press***, about who and what they really are.

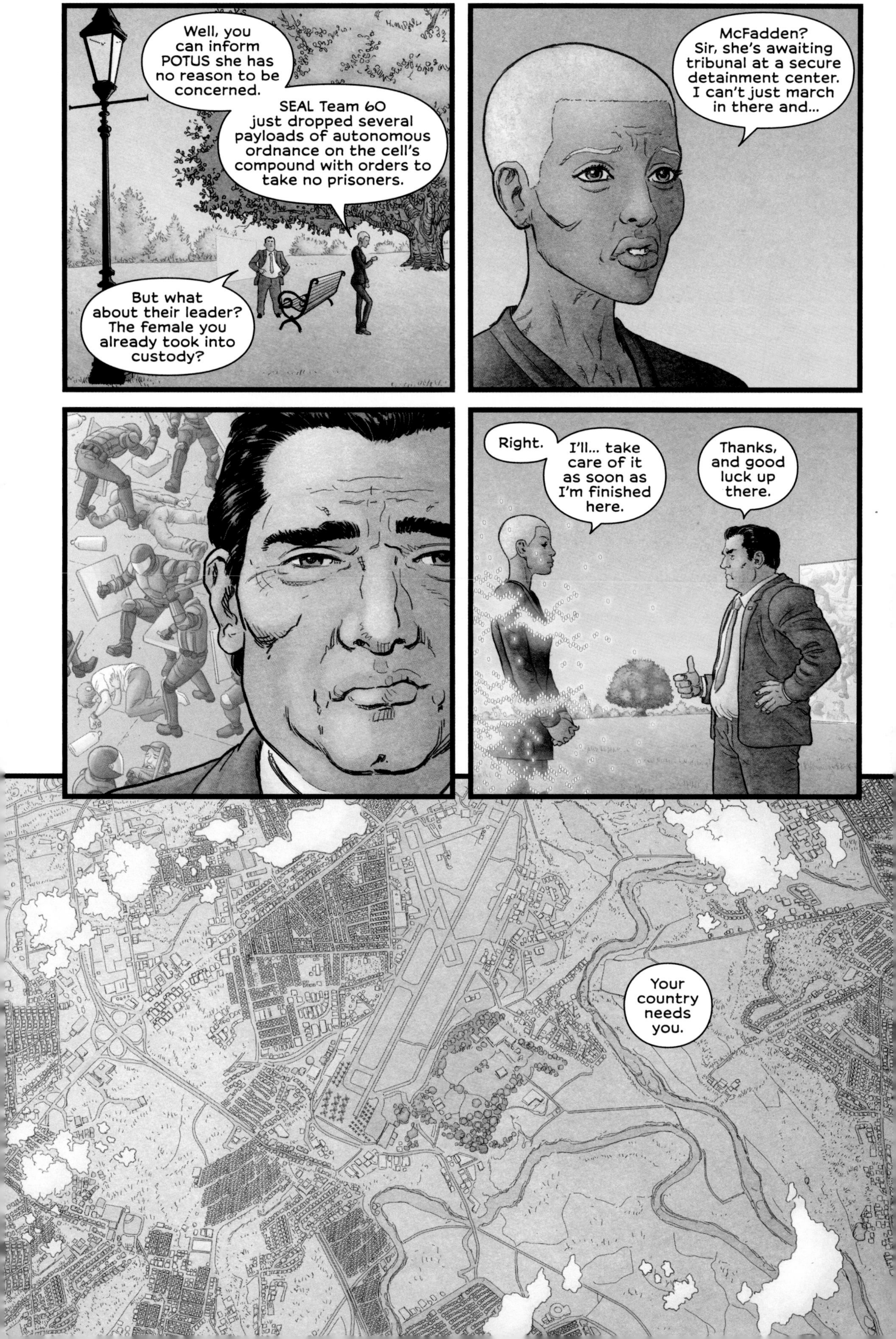
Well, you can inform POTUS she has no reason to be concerned.
SEAL Team 60 just dropped several payloads of autonomous ordnance on the cell's compound with orders to take no prisoners.
But what about their leader? The female you already took into custody?
McFadden? Sir, she's awaiting tribunal at a secure detainment center. I can't just march in there and...
Right.
I'll... take care of it as soon as I'm finished here.
Thanks, and good luck up there.
Your country needs you.

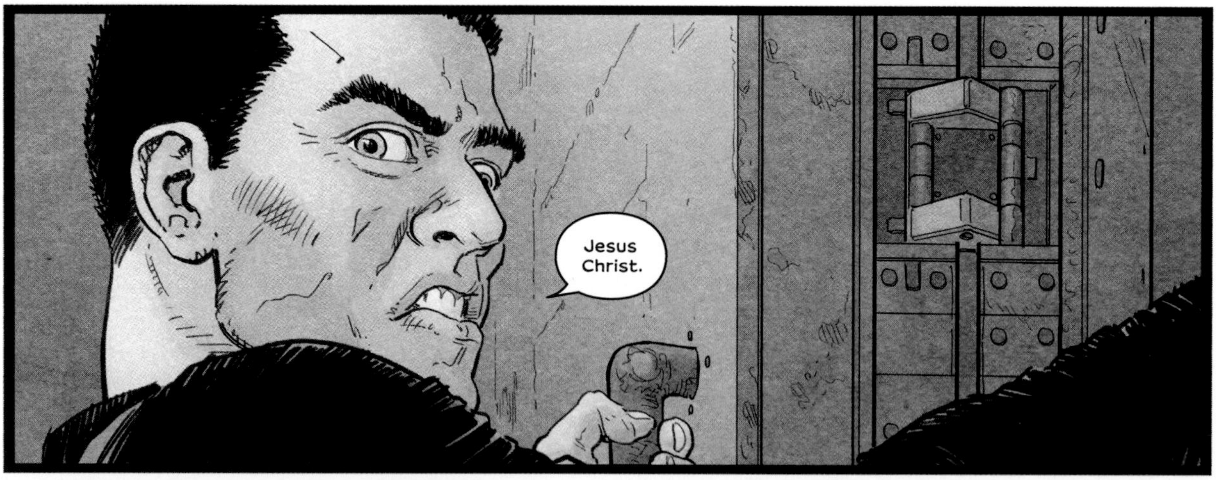
Jesus Christ.

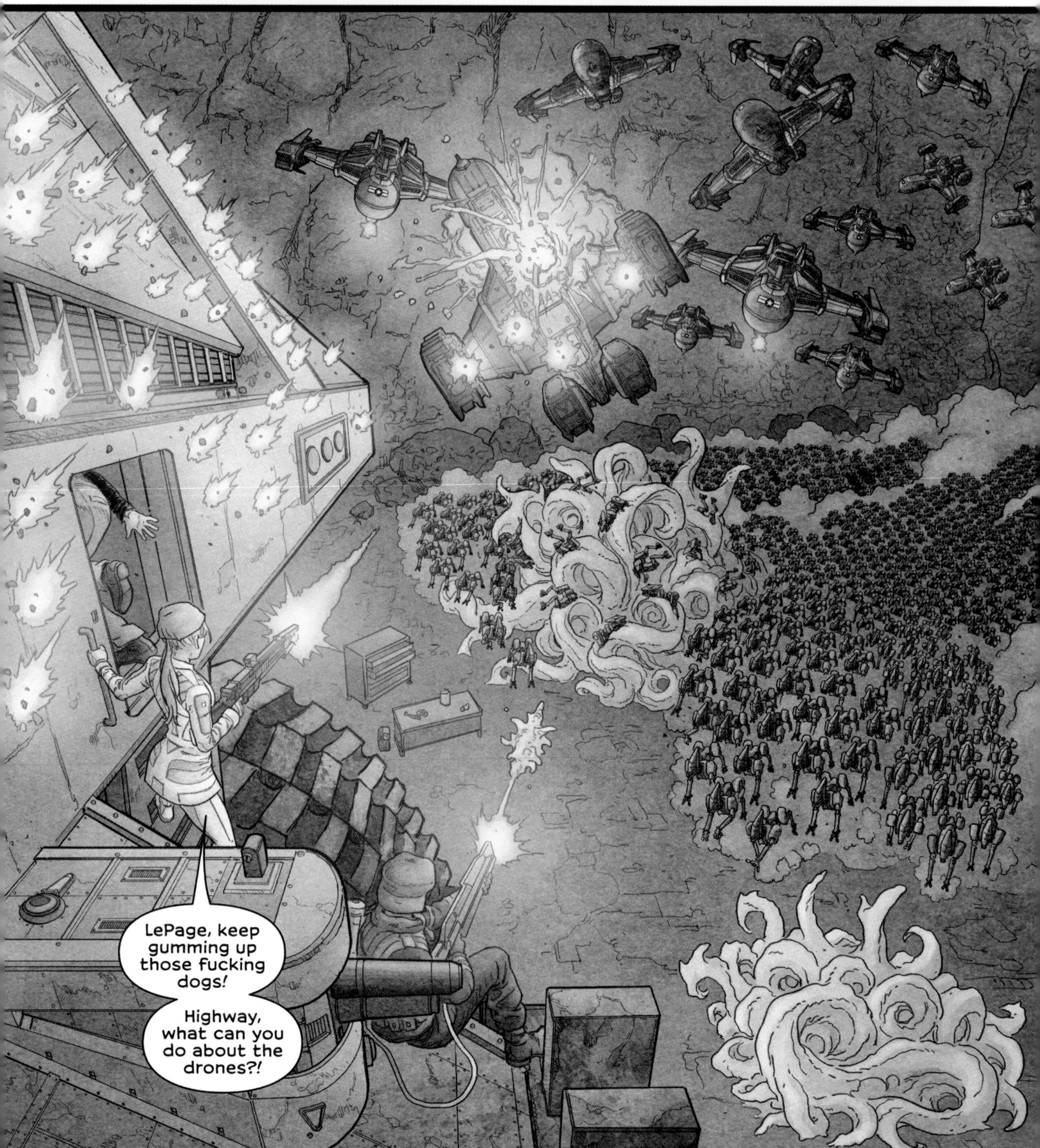
LePage, keep gumming up those fucking dogs!
Highway, what can you do about the drones?!

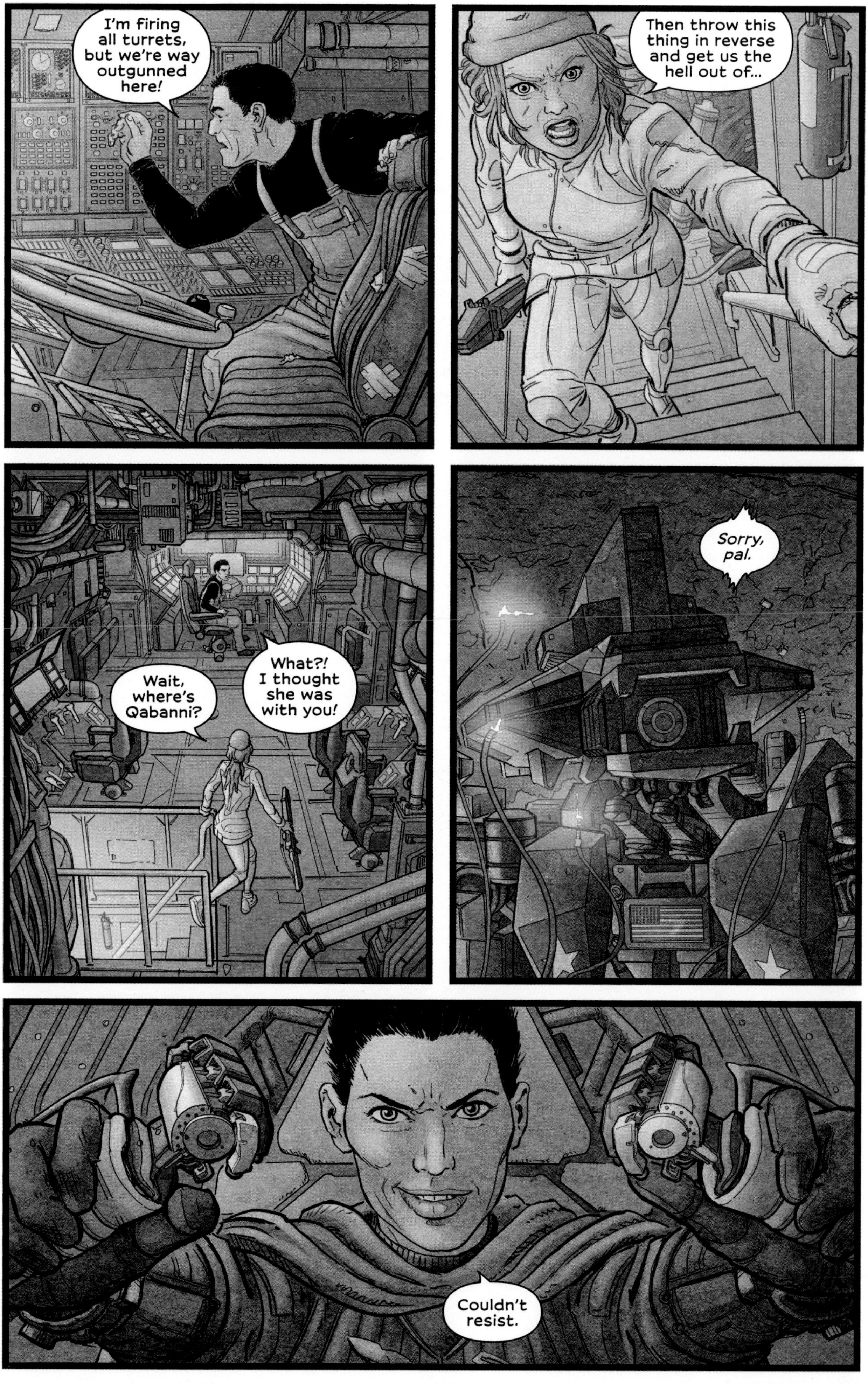
I'm firing all turrets, but we're way outgunned here!
Then throw this thing in reverse and get us the hell out of...
Wait, where's Qabanni?
What?! I thought she was with you!
Sorry, pal.
Couldn't resist.

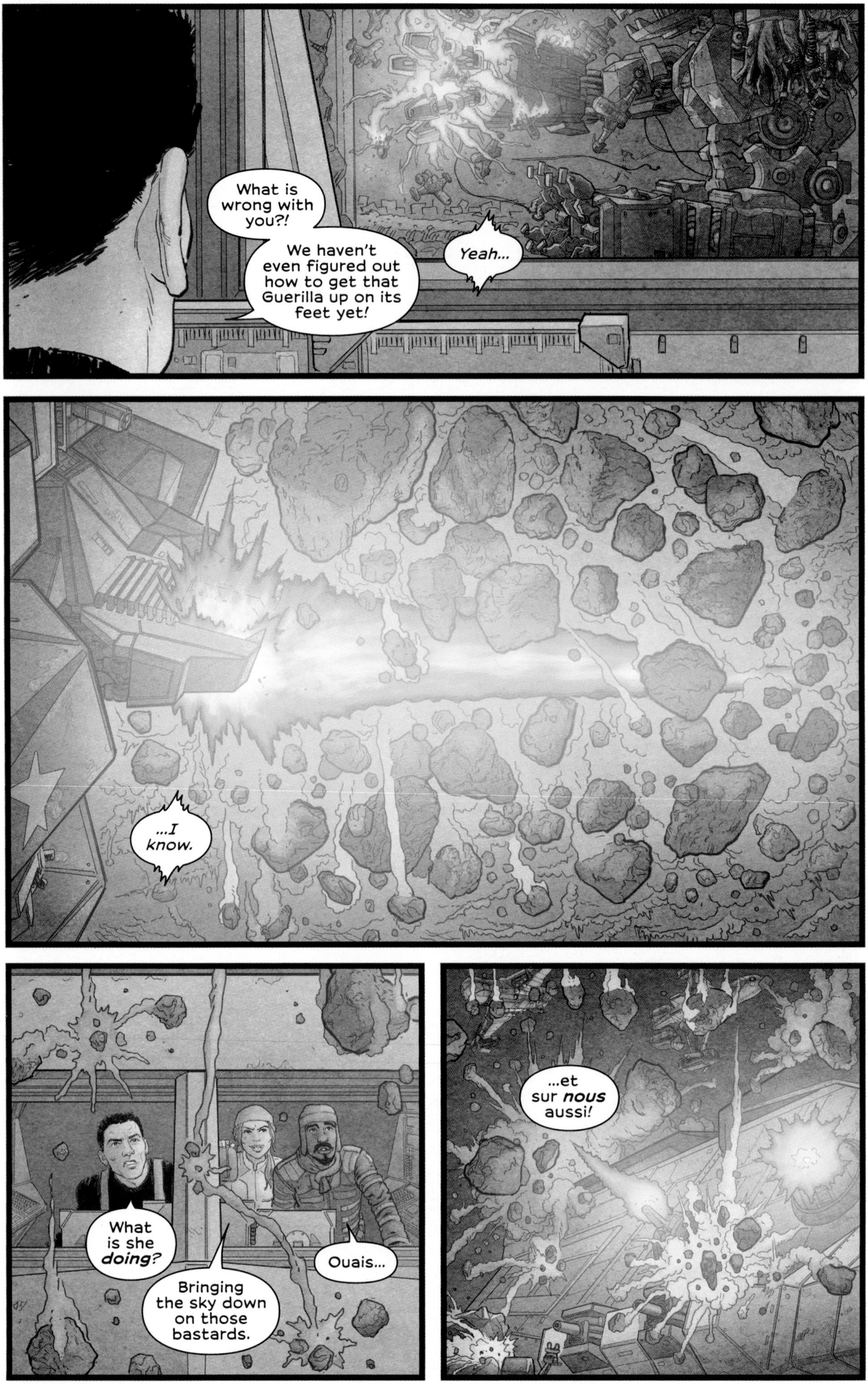
What is wrong with you?!
We haven't even figured out how to get that Guerilla up on its feet yet!
Yeah...
...I know.
What is she *doing*?
Bringing the sky down on those bastards.
Ouais...
...et sur ***nous*** aussi!

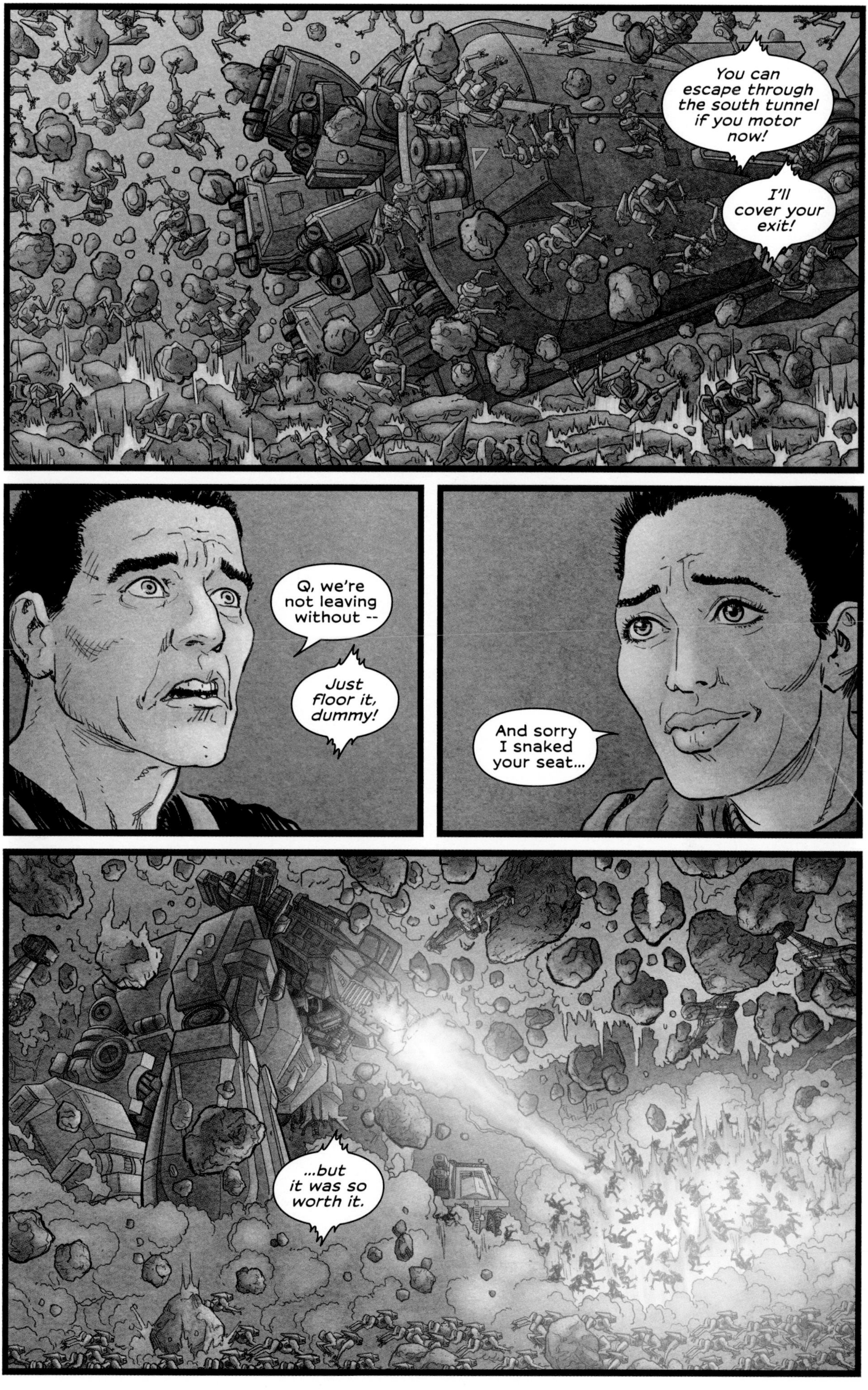
You can escape through the south tunnel if you motor now!
I'll cover your exit!
Q, we're not leaving without --
Just floor it, dummy!
And sorry I snaked your seat...
...but it was so worth it.

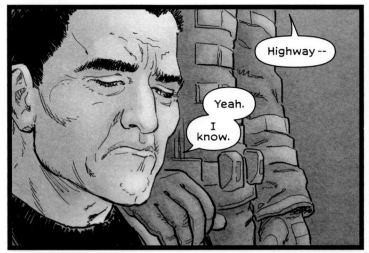

Highway --

Yeah.
I
know.

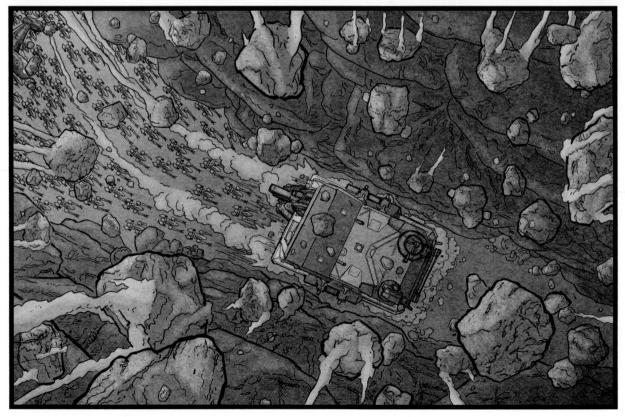

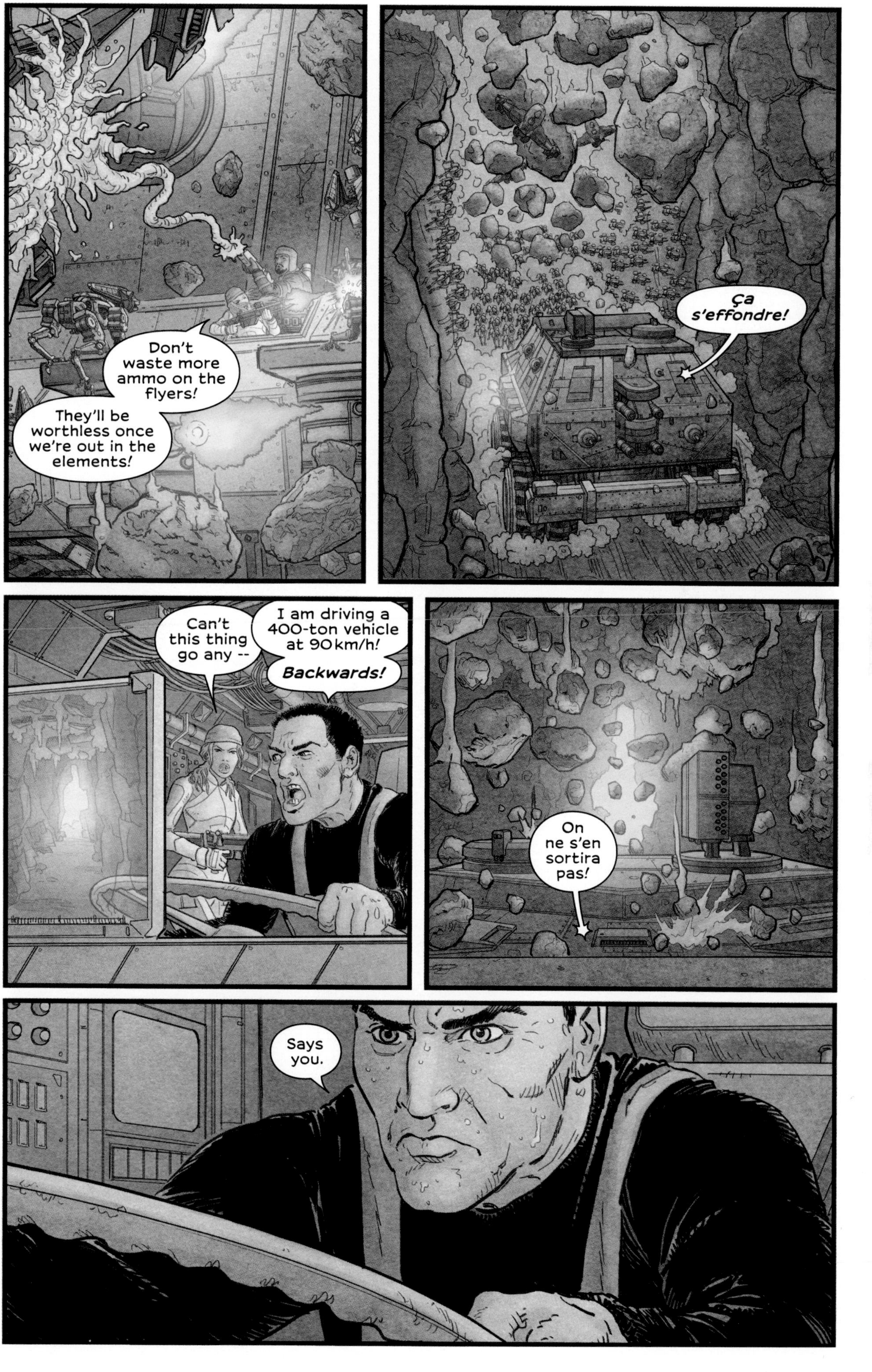
Don't waste more ammo on the flyers!
They'll be worthless once we're out in the elements!
Ça s'effondre!
Can't this thing go any --
I am driving a 400-ton vehicle at 90 km/h!
Backwards!
On ne s'en sortira pas!
Says you.

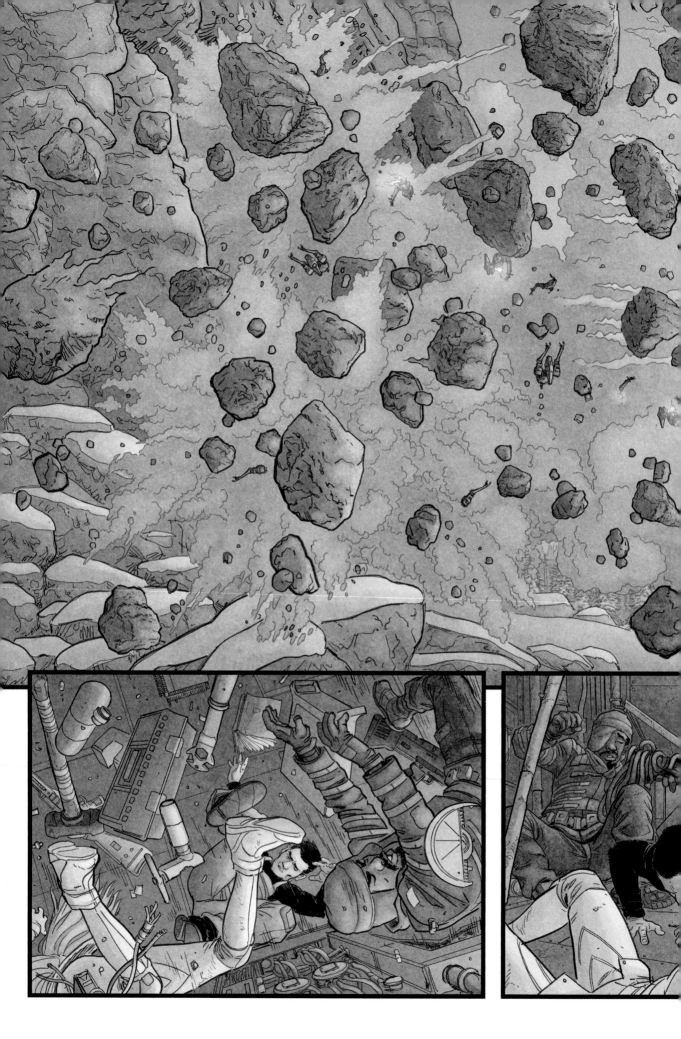

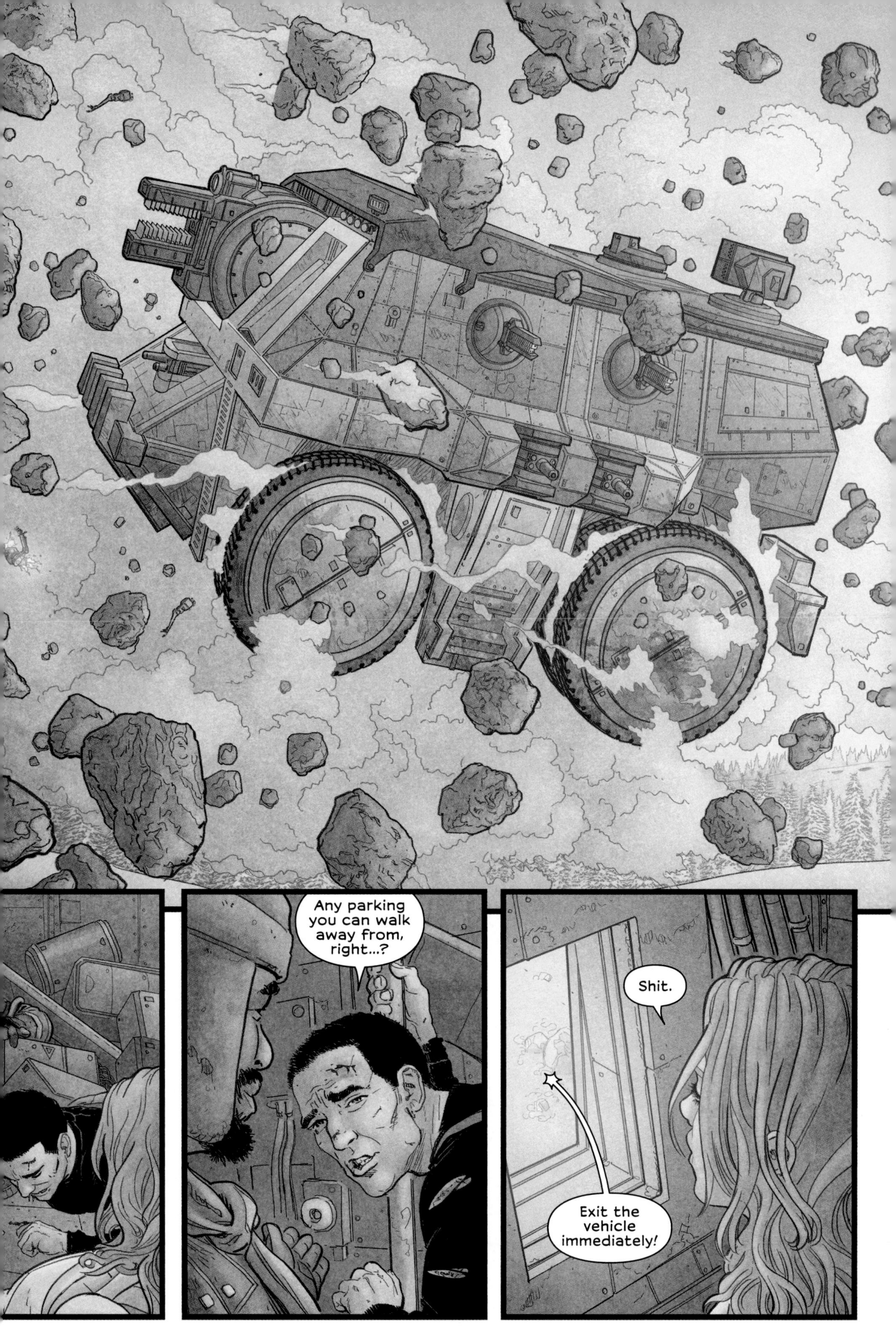
Any parking you can walk away from, right...?
Shit.
Exit the vehicle immediately!

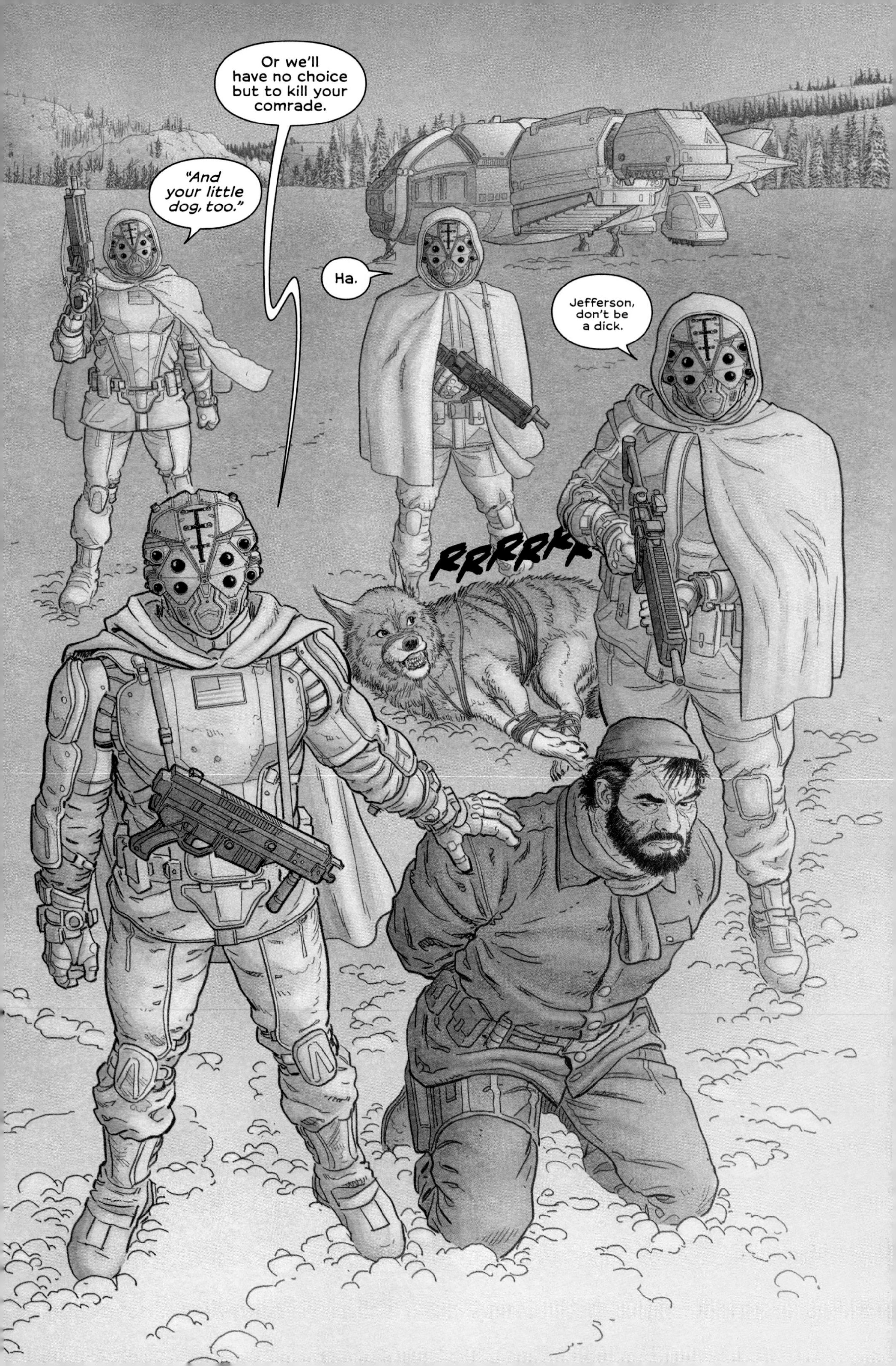

"And your little dog, too."
Or we'll have no choice but to kill your comrade.
Ha.
Jefferson, don't be a dick.
RRRRR

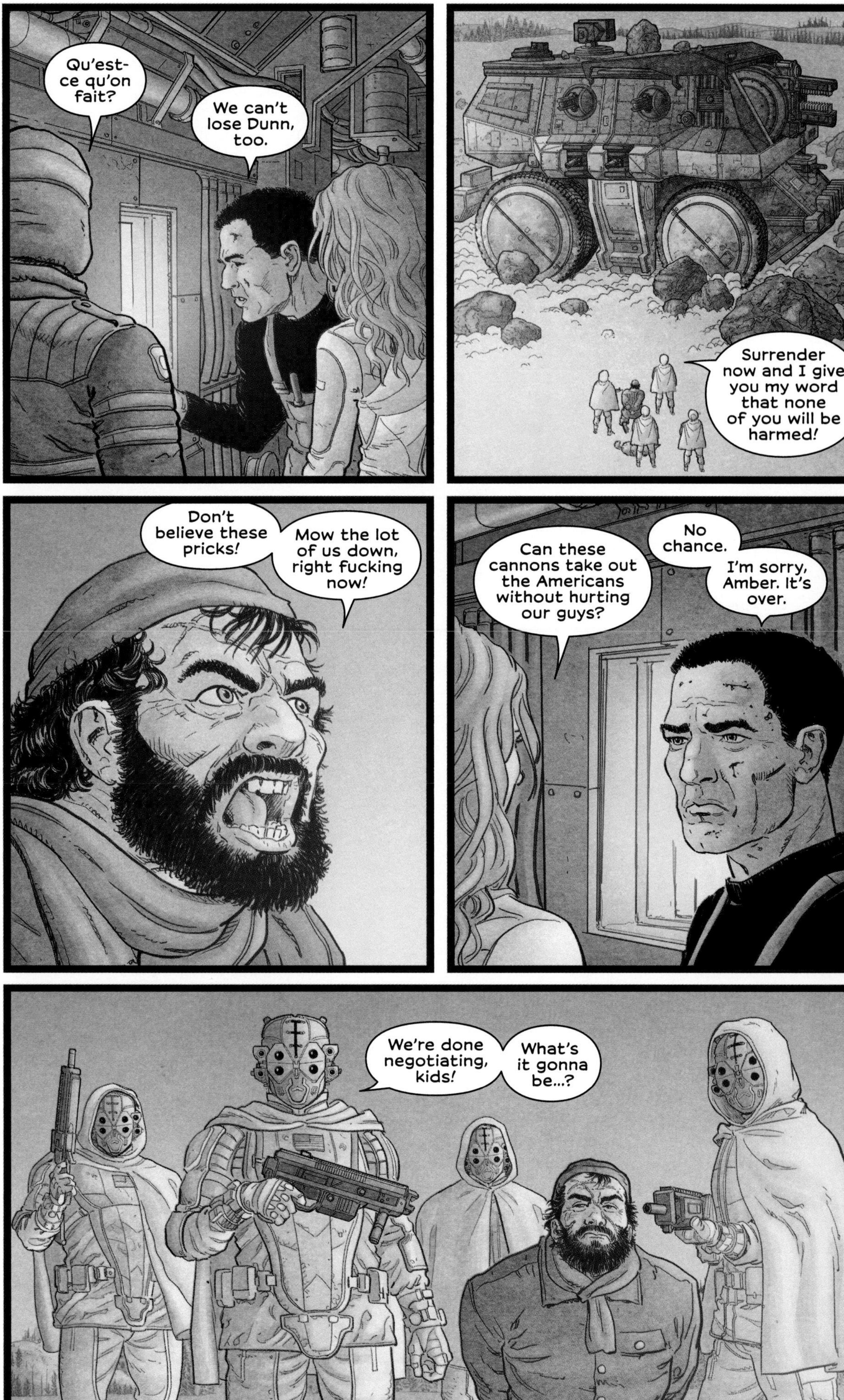
Qu'est-ce qu'on fait?
We can't lose Dunn, too.
Surrender now and I give you my word that none of you will be harmed!
Don't believe these pricks!
Mow the lot of us down, right fucking now!
Can these cannons take out the Americans without hurting our guys?
No chance.
I'm sorry, Amber. It's over.
We're done negotiating, kids!
What's it gonna be...?

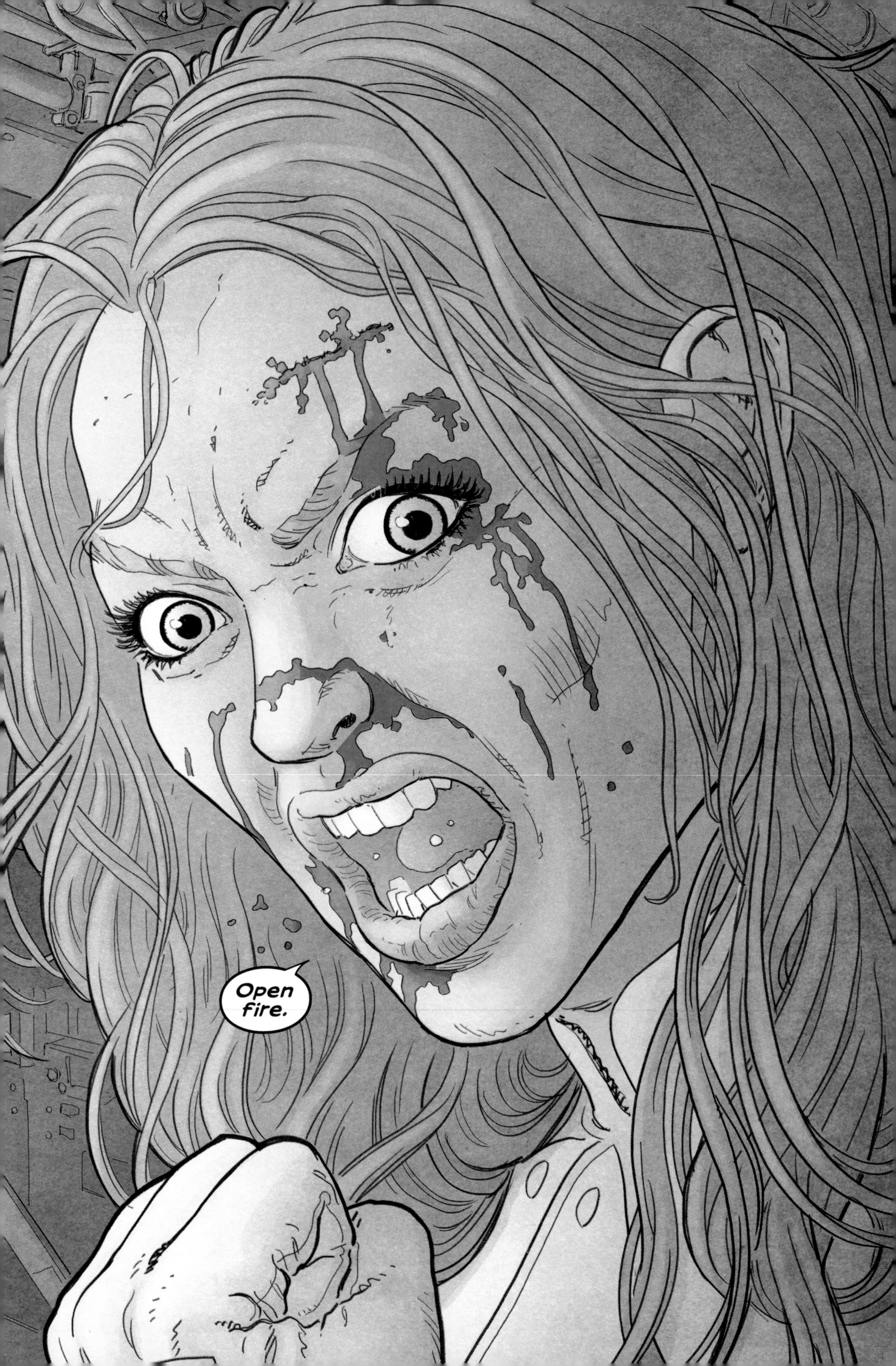
Open fire.

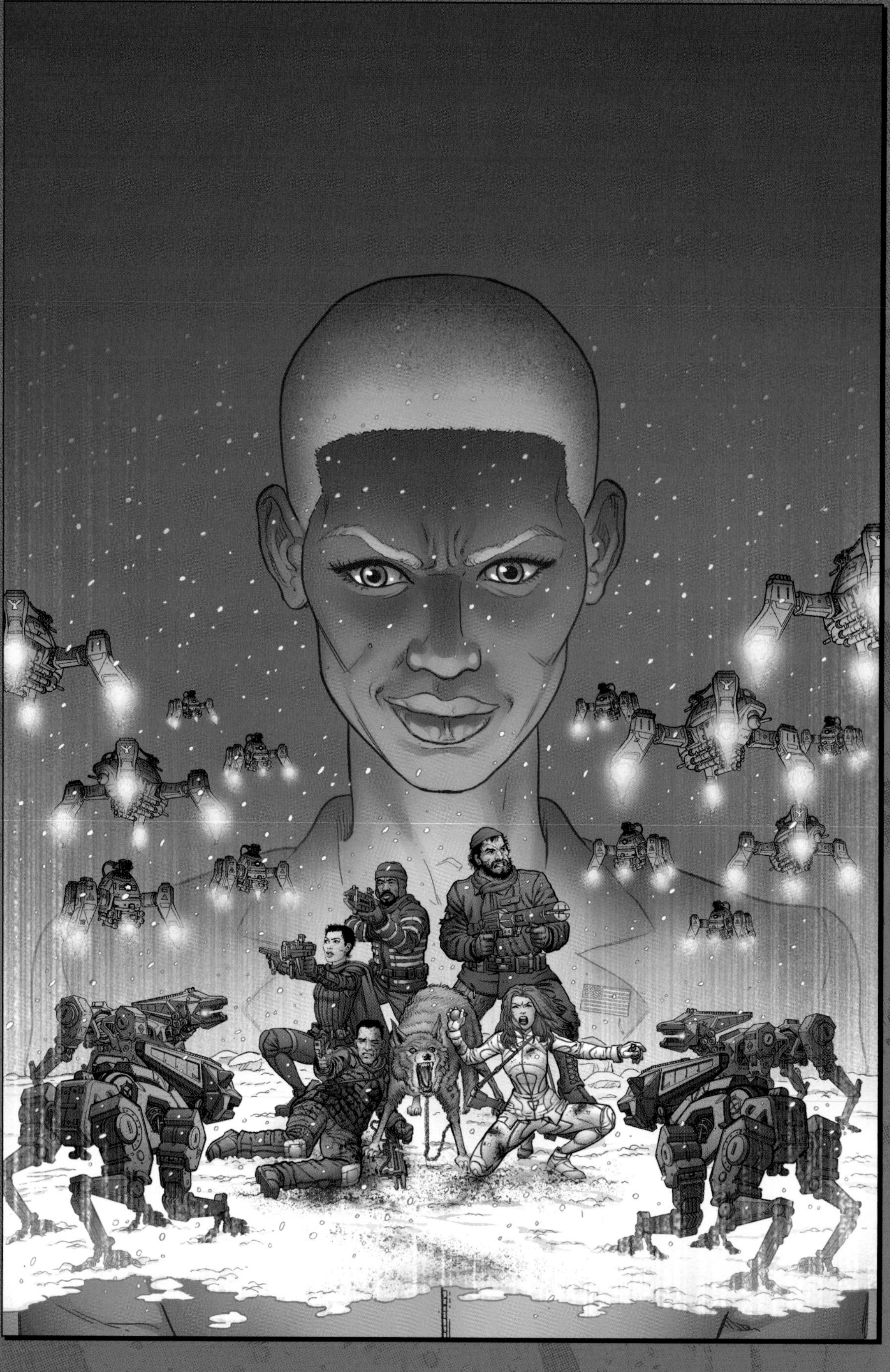

CHAPTER FIVE

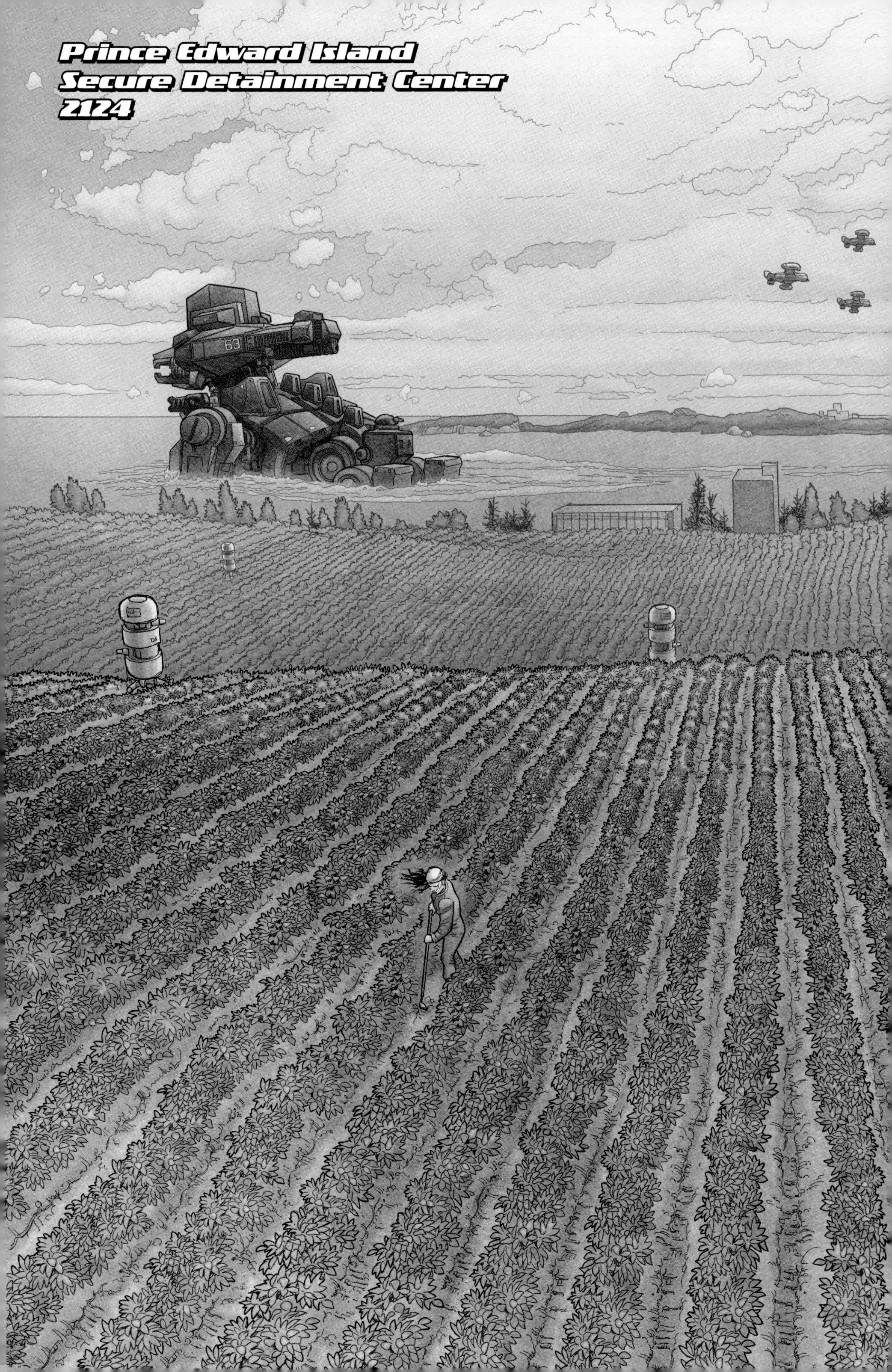
Prince Edward Island
Secure Detainment Center
2124

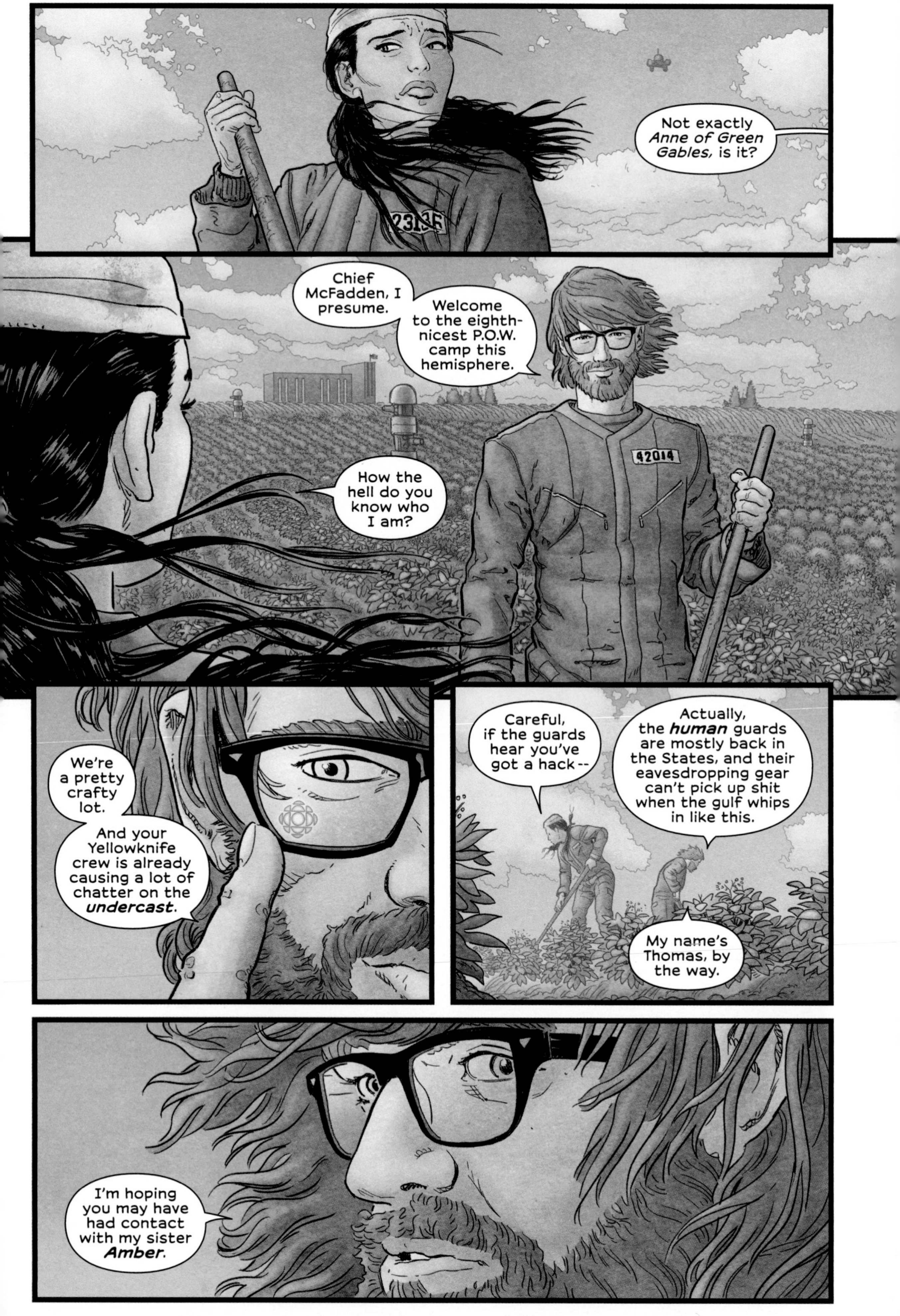
Not exactly *Anne of Green Gables,* is it?
23136
Chief McFadden, I presume.
Welcome to the eighth-nicest P.O.W. camp this hemisphere.
42014
How the hell do you know who I am?
We're a pretty crafty lot.
And your Yellowknife crew is already causing a lot of chatter on the *undercast*.
Careful, if the guards hear you've got a hack --
Actually, the ***human*** guards are mostly back in the States, and their eavesdropping gear can't pick up shit when the gulf whips in like this.
My name's Thomas, by the way.
I'm hoping you may have had contact with my sister ***Amber***.

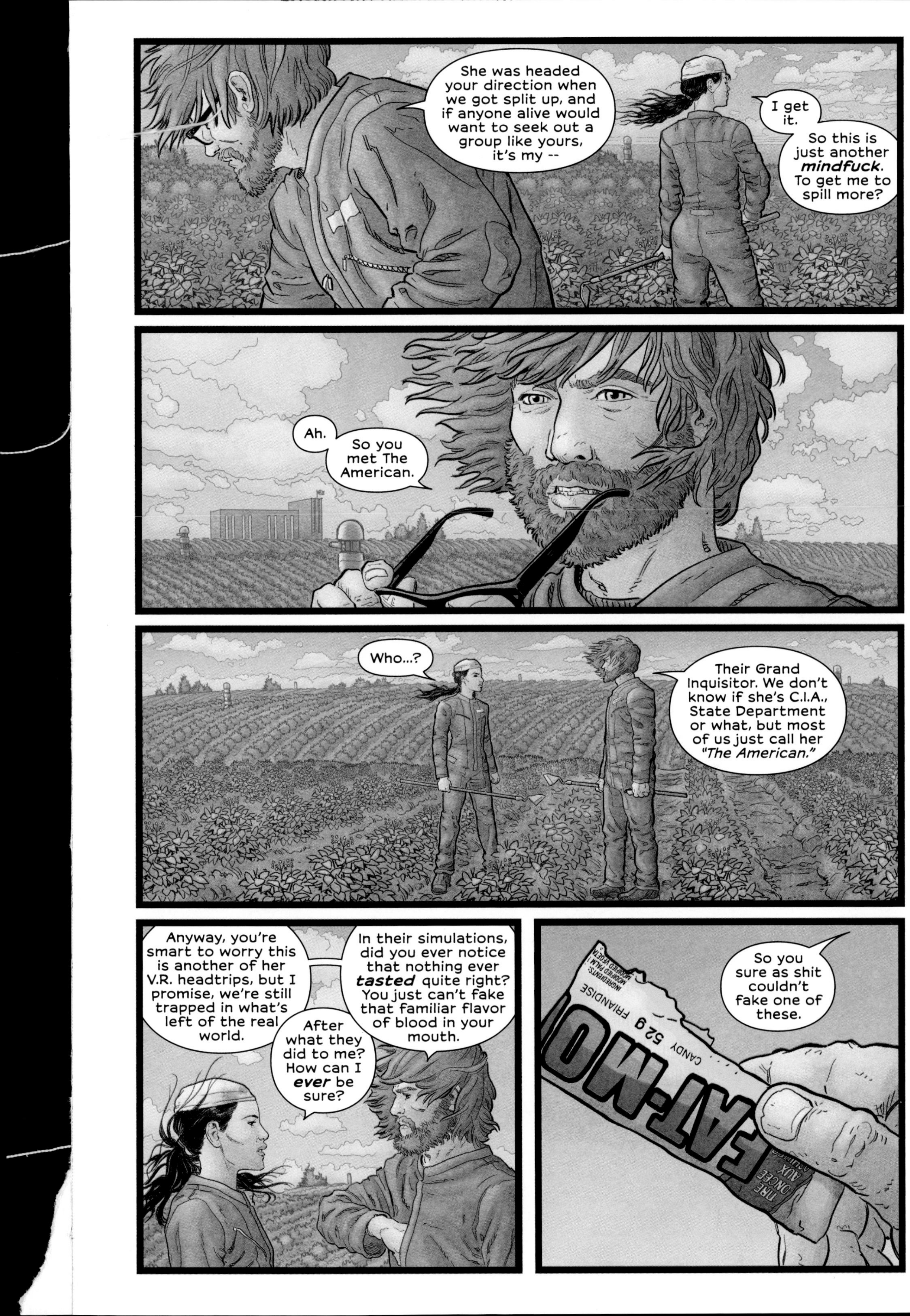
She was headed your direction when we got split up, and if anyone alive would want to seek out a group like yours, it's my --
I get it.
So this is just another **mindfuck**. To get me to spill more?
Ah.
So you met The American.
Who...?
Their Grand Inquisitor. We don't know if she's C.I.A., State Department or what, but most of us just call her *"The American."*
Anyway, you're smart to worry this is another of her V.R. headtrips, but I promise, we're still trapped in what's left of the real world.
After what they did to me? How can I **ever** be sure?
In their simulations, did you ever notice that nothing ever **tasted** quite right? You just can't fake that familiar flavor of blood in your mouth.
So you sure as shit couldn't fake one of these.
FAT-MO
CANDY 52 g FRIANDISE
INGREDIENTS: MODIFIED PALM

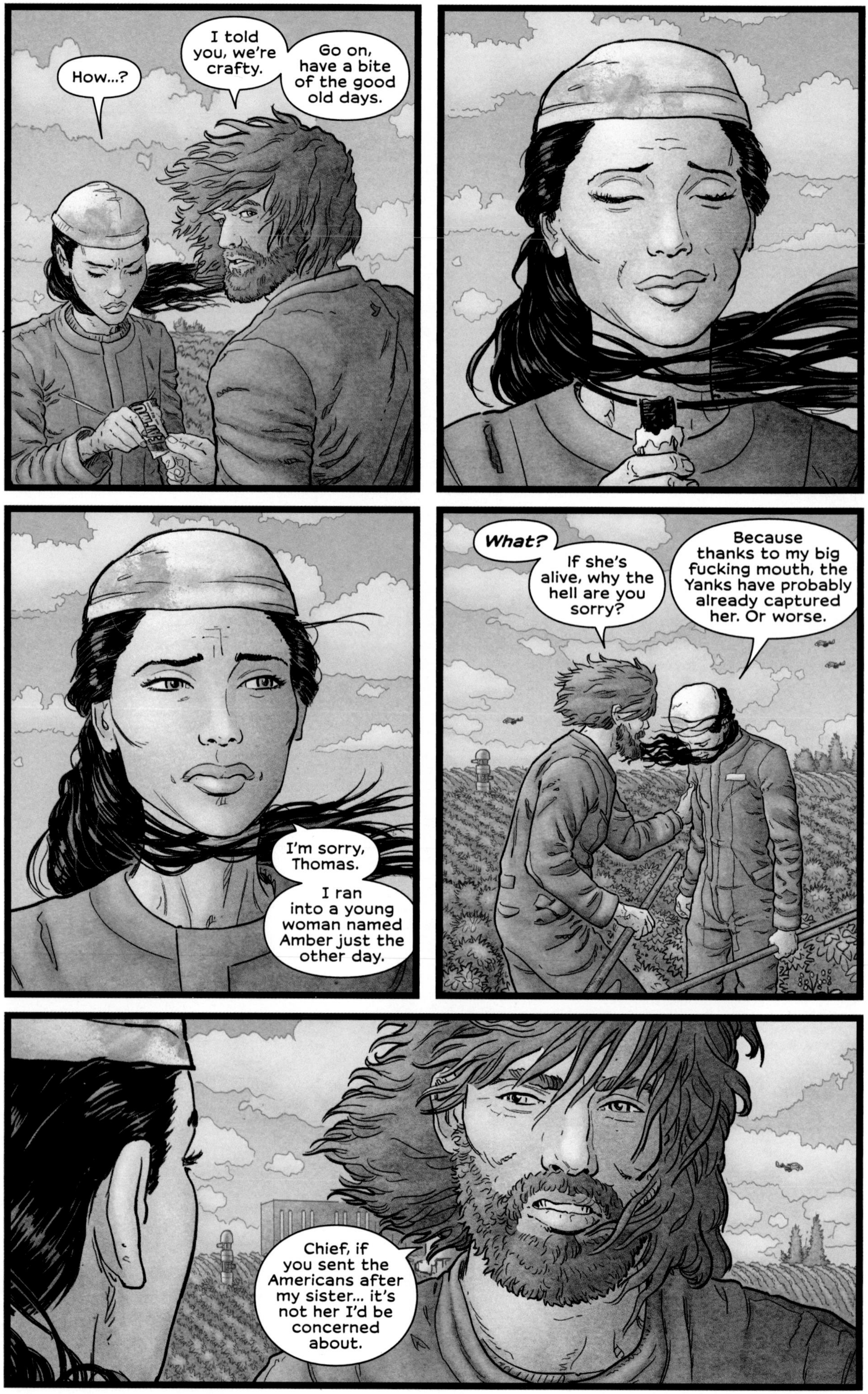
How...?
I told you, we're crafty.
Go on, have a bite of the good old days.
I'm sorry, Thomas.
I ran into a young woman named Amber just the other day.
What?
If she's alive, why the hell are you sorry?
Because thanks to my big fucking mouth, the Yanks have probably already captured her. Or worse.
Chief, if you sent the Americans after my sister... it's not her I'd be concerned about.

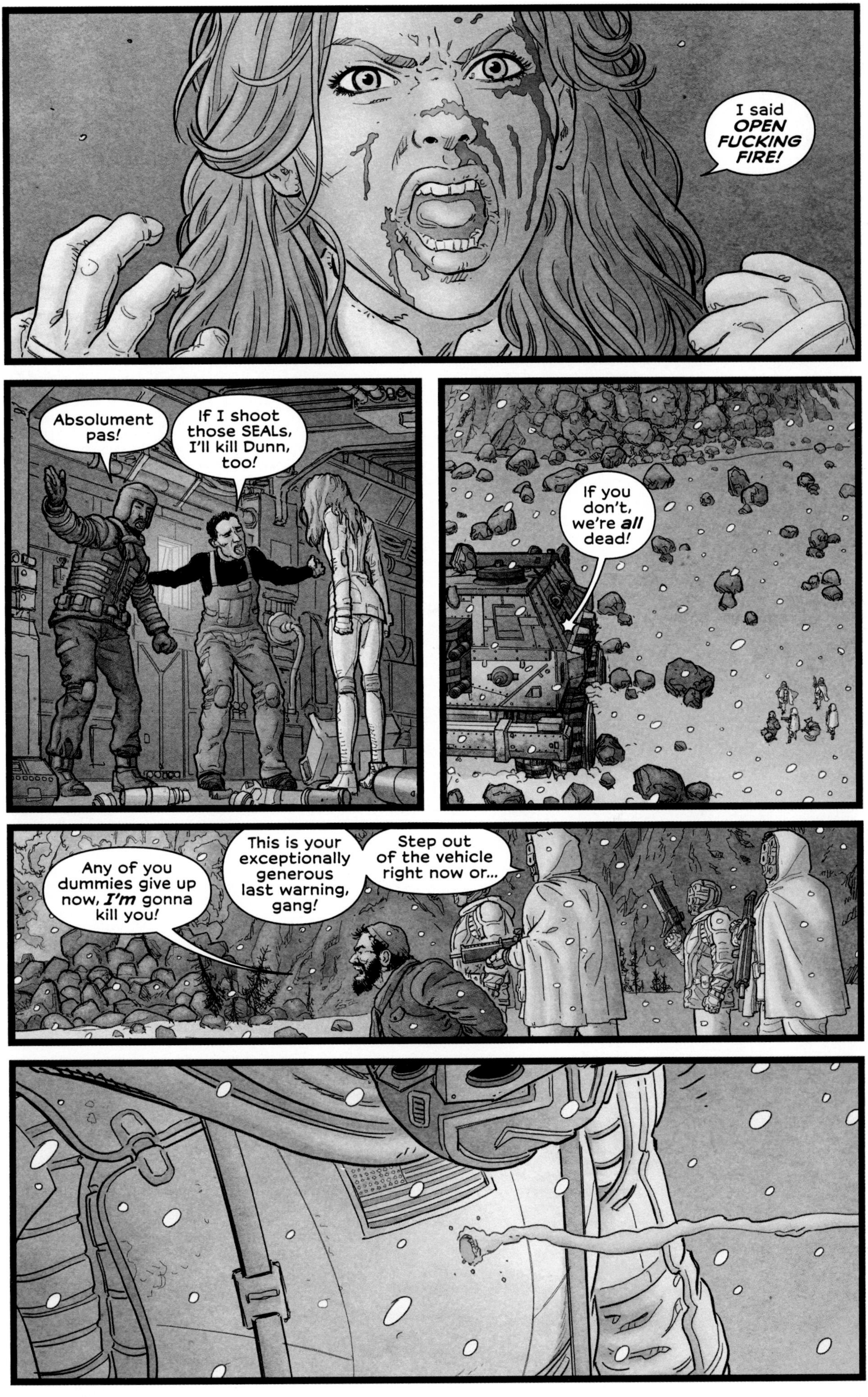
I said OPEN FUCKING FIRE!
Absolument pas!
If I shoot those SEALs, I'll kill Dunn, too!
If you don't, we're *all* dead!
This is your exceptionally generous last warning, gang!
Step out of the vehicle right now or...
Any of you dummies give up now, *I'm* gonna kill you!

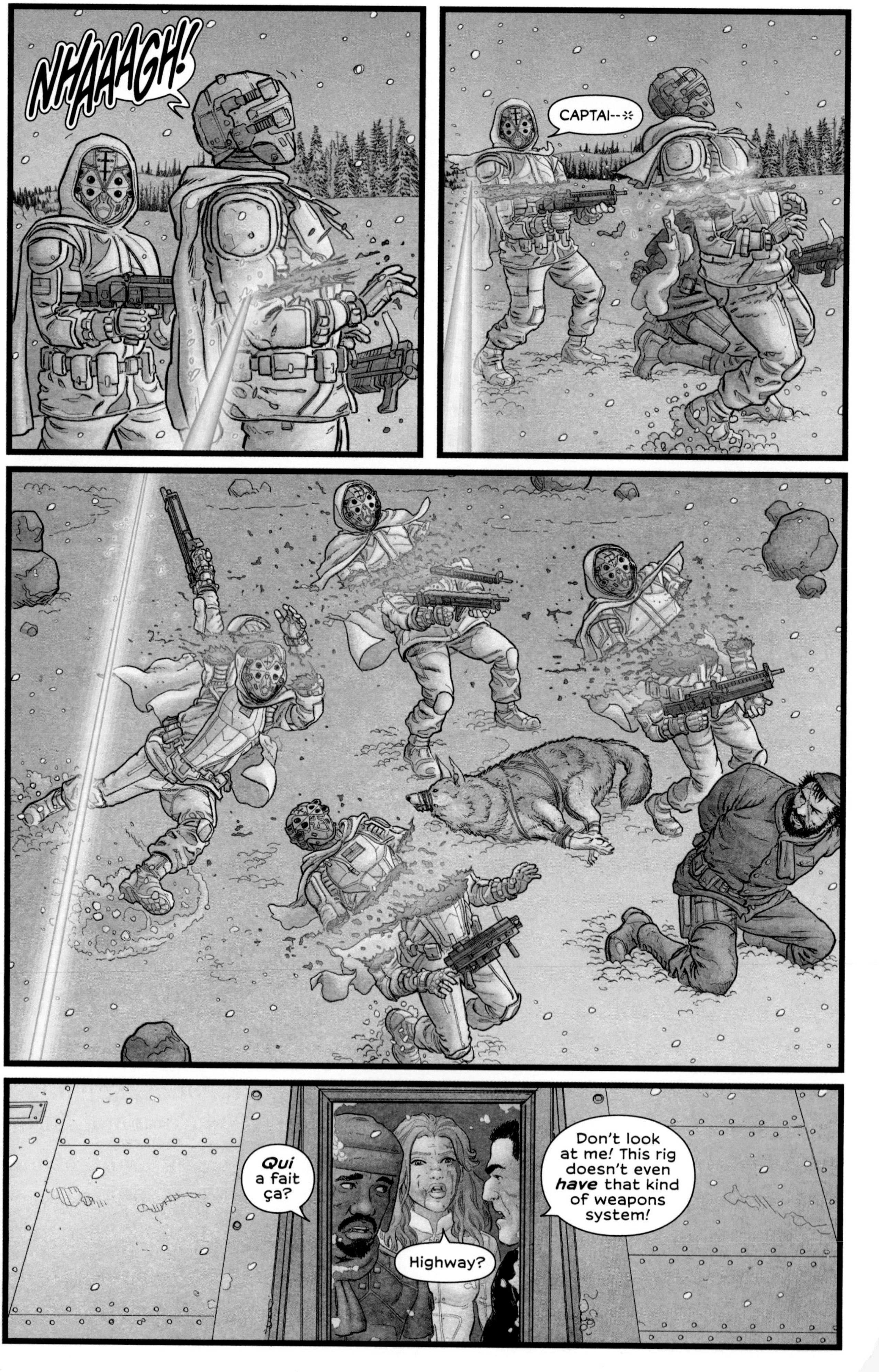
NHAAAGH!
CAPTAI--
Qui a fait ça?
Don't look at me! This rig doesn't even have that kind of weapons system!
Highway?

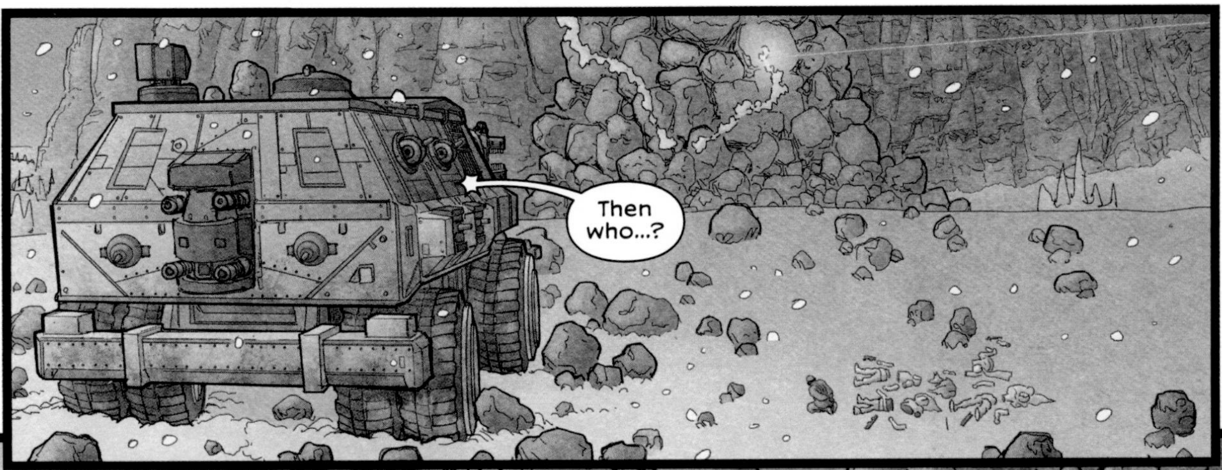
Then who...?

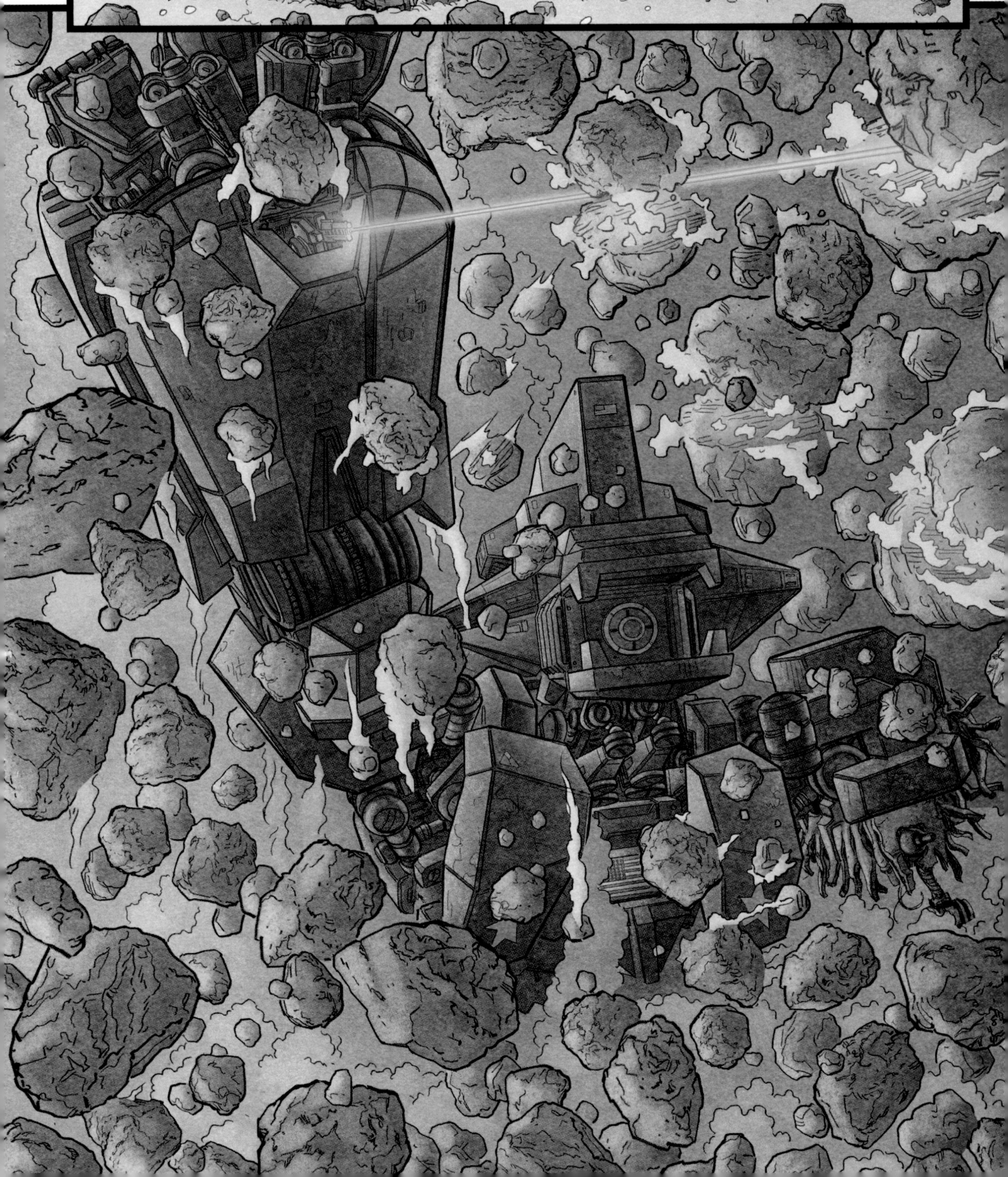

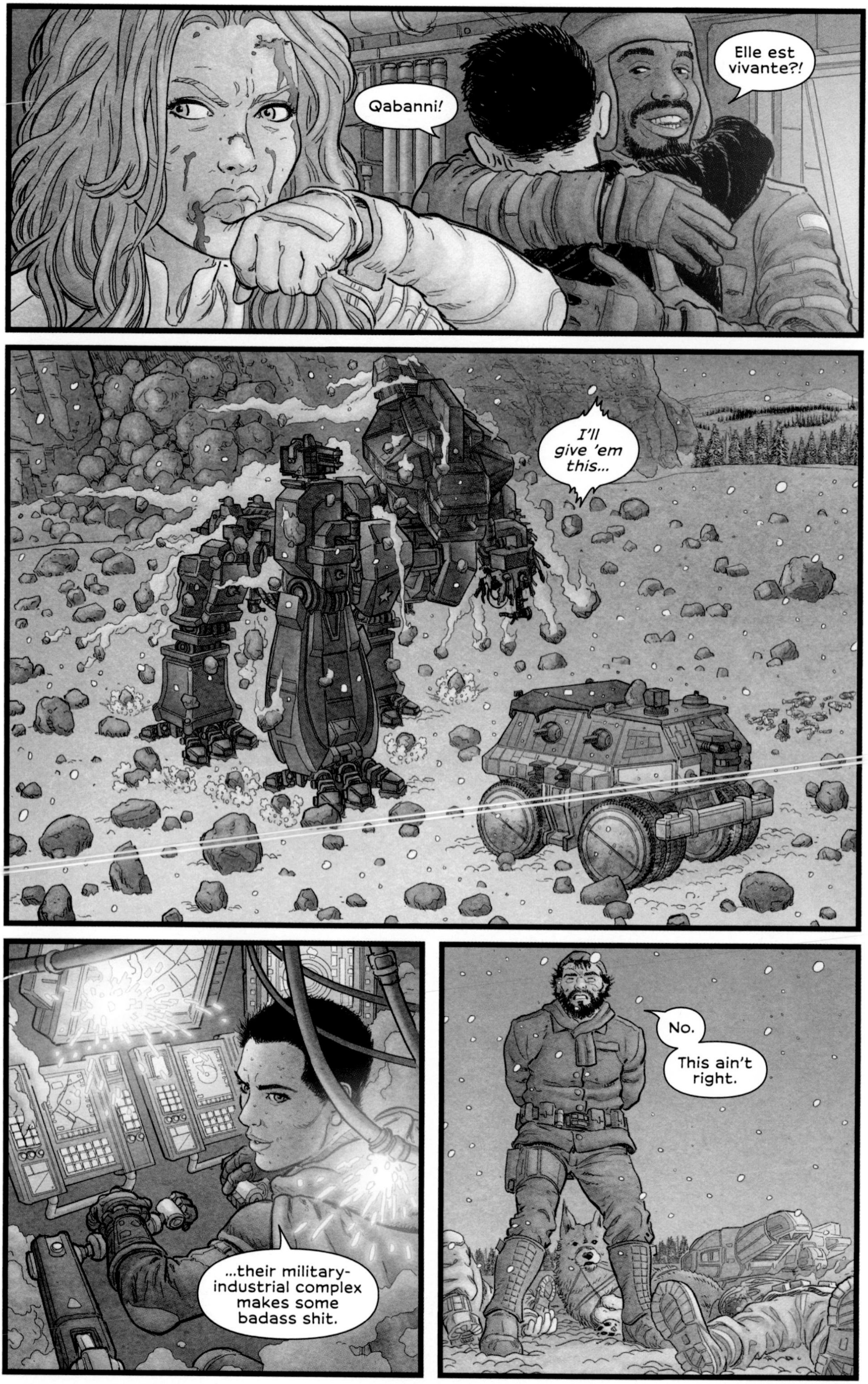
Qabanni!
Elle est vivante?!
I'll give 'em this...
...their military-industrial complex makes some badass shit.
No.
This ain't right.

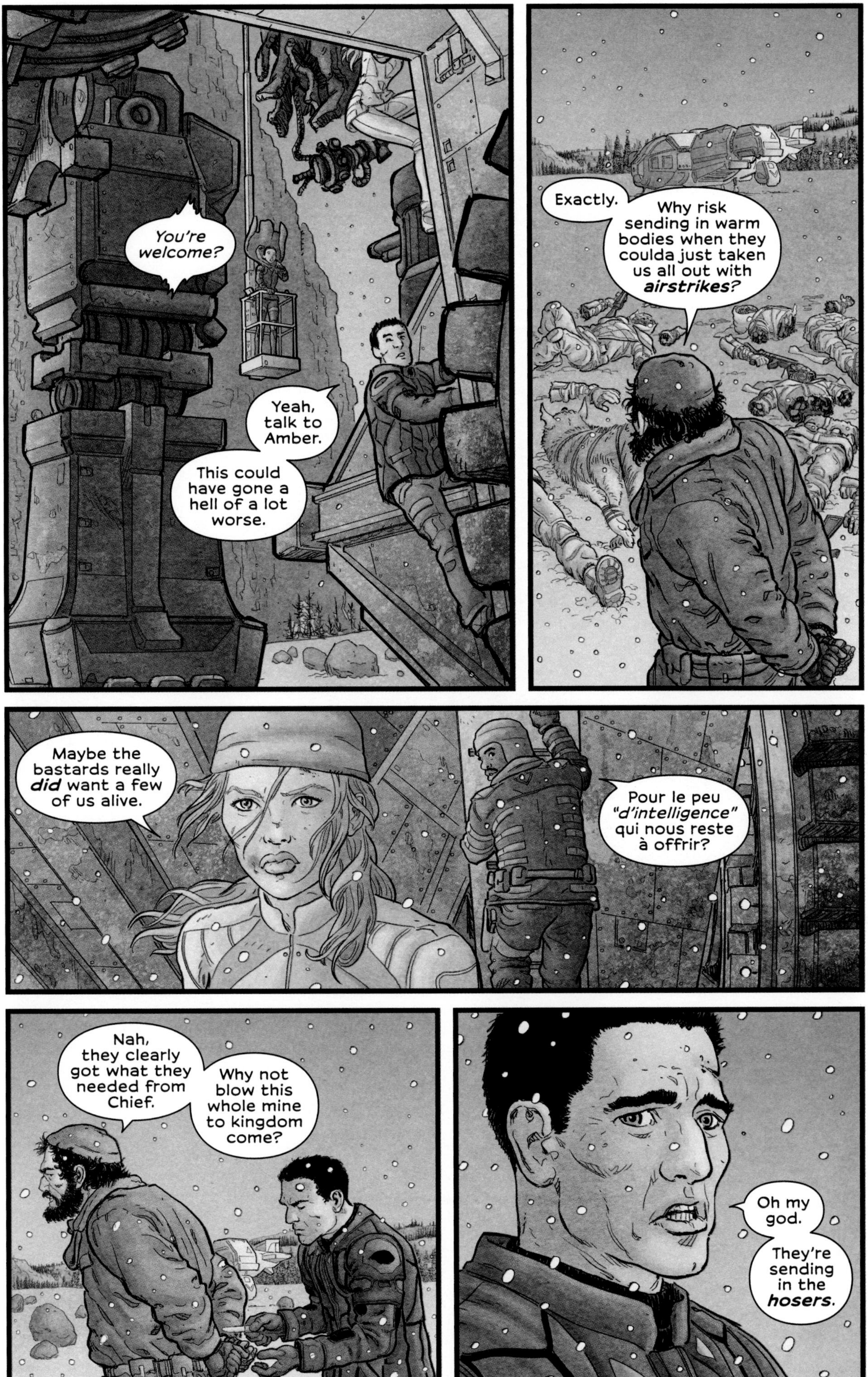

You're welcome?
Yeah, talk to Amber.
This could have gone a hell of a lot worse.
Exactly.
Why risk sending in warm bodies when they coulda just taken us all out with ***airstrikes***?
Maybe the bastards really ***did*** want a few of us alive.
Pour le peu *"d'intelligence"* qui nous reste à offrir?
Nah, they clearly got what they needed from Chief.
Why not blow this whole mine to kingdom come?
Oh my god.
They're sending in the ***hosers***.

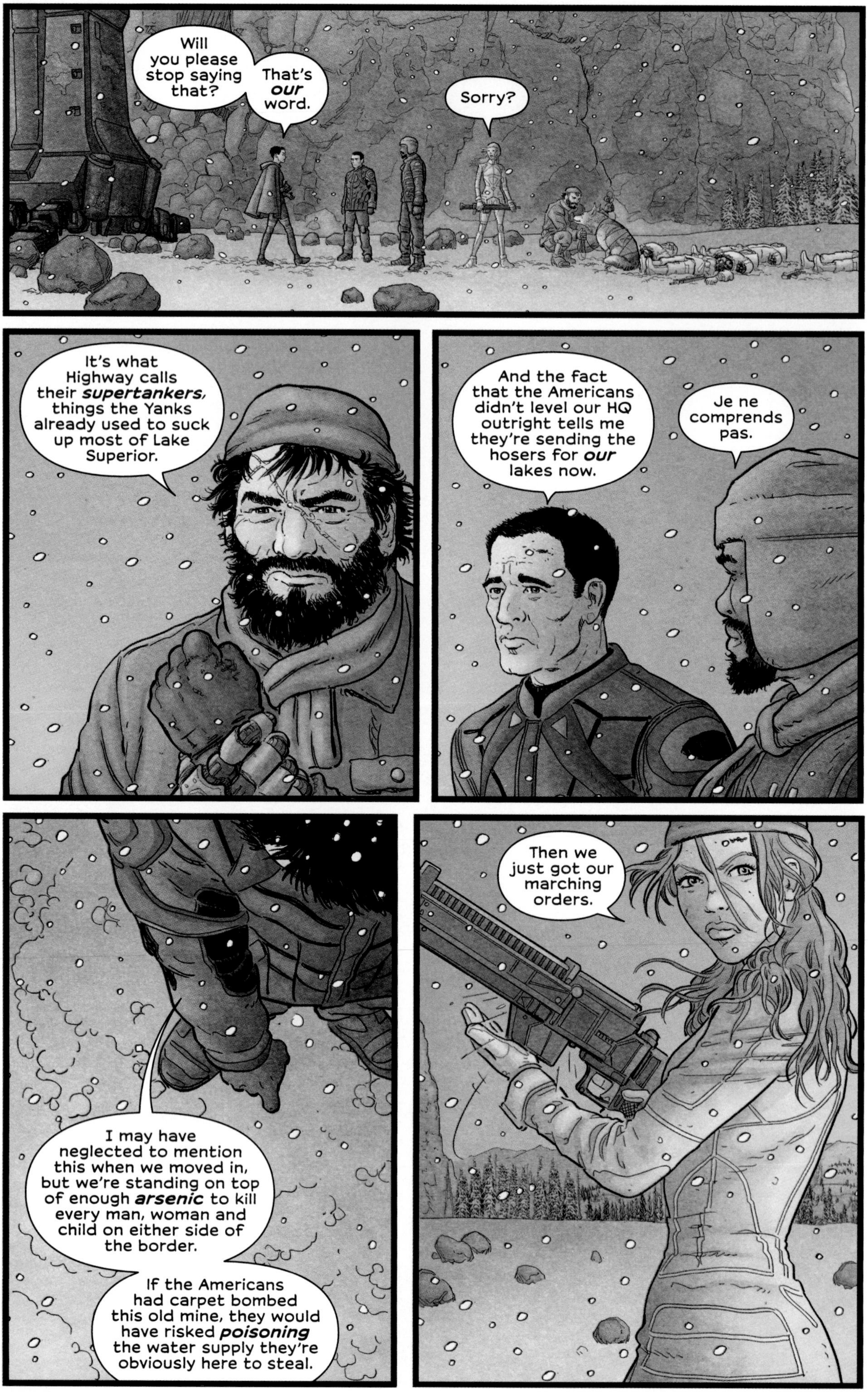
Will you please stop saying that?
That's *our* word.
Sorry?
It's what Highway calls their *supertankers,* things the Yanks already used to suck up most of Lake Superior.
And the fact that the Americans didn't level our HQ outright tells me they're sending the hosers for *our* lakes now.
Je ne comprends pas.
I may have neglected to mention this when we moved in, but we're standing on top of enough *arsenic* to kill every man, woman and child on either side of the border.
If the Americans had carpet bombed this old mine, they would have risked *poisoning* the water supply they're obviously here to steal.
Then we just got our marching orders.

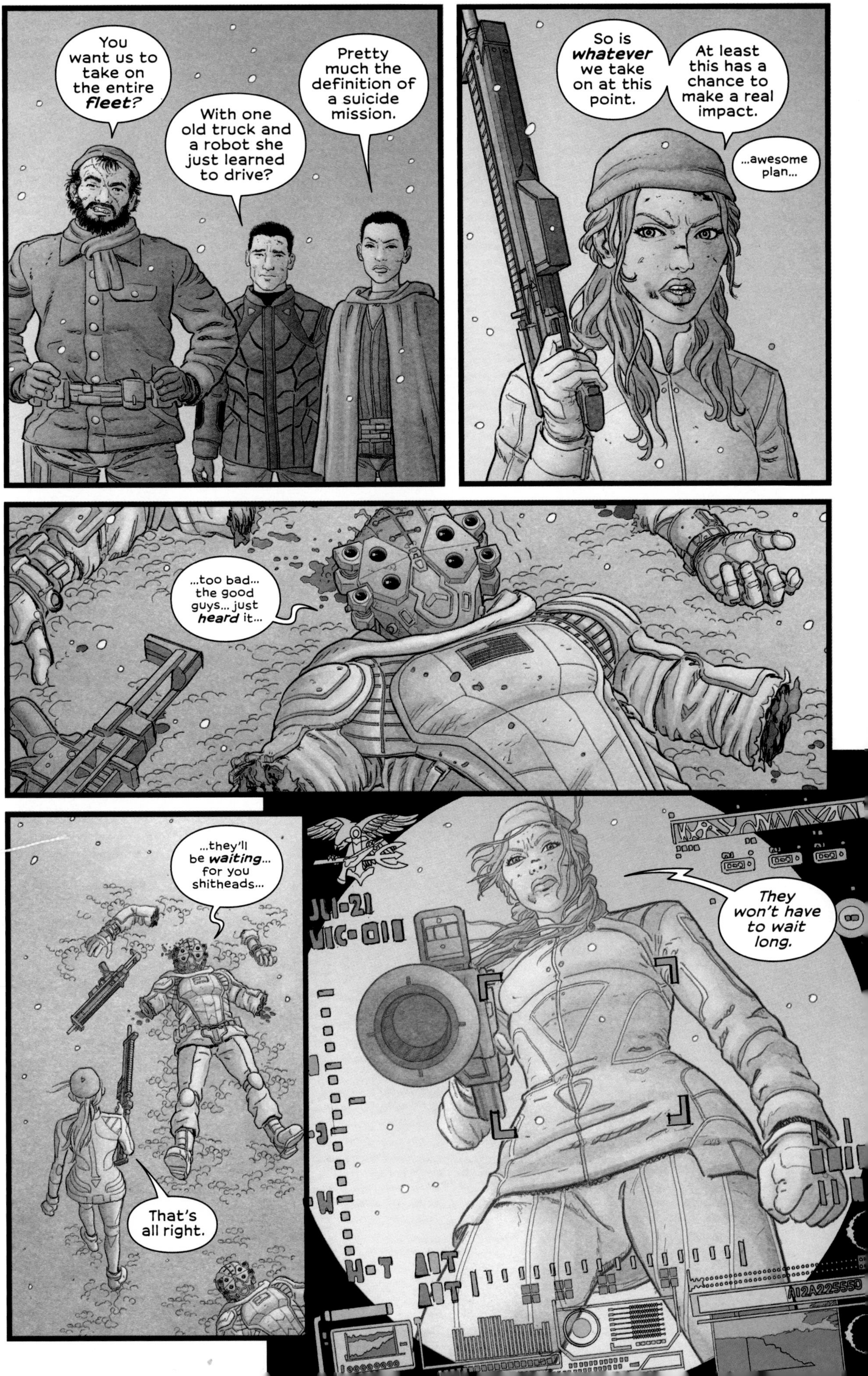

You want us to take on the entire *fleet*?
With one old truck and a robot she just learned to drive?
Pretty much the definition of a suicide mission.
So is *whatever* we take on at this point.
At least this has a chance to make a real impact.
...awesome plan...
...too bad... the good guys... just *heard* it...
...they'll be *waiting*... for you shitheads...
That's all right.
They won't have to wait long.

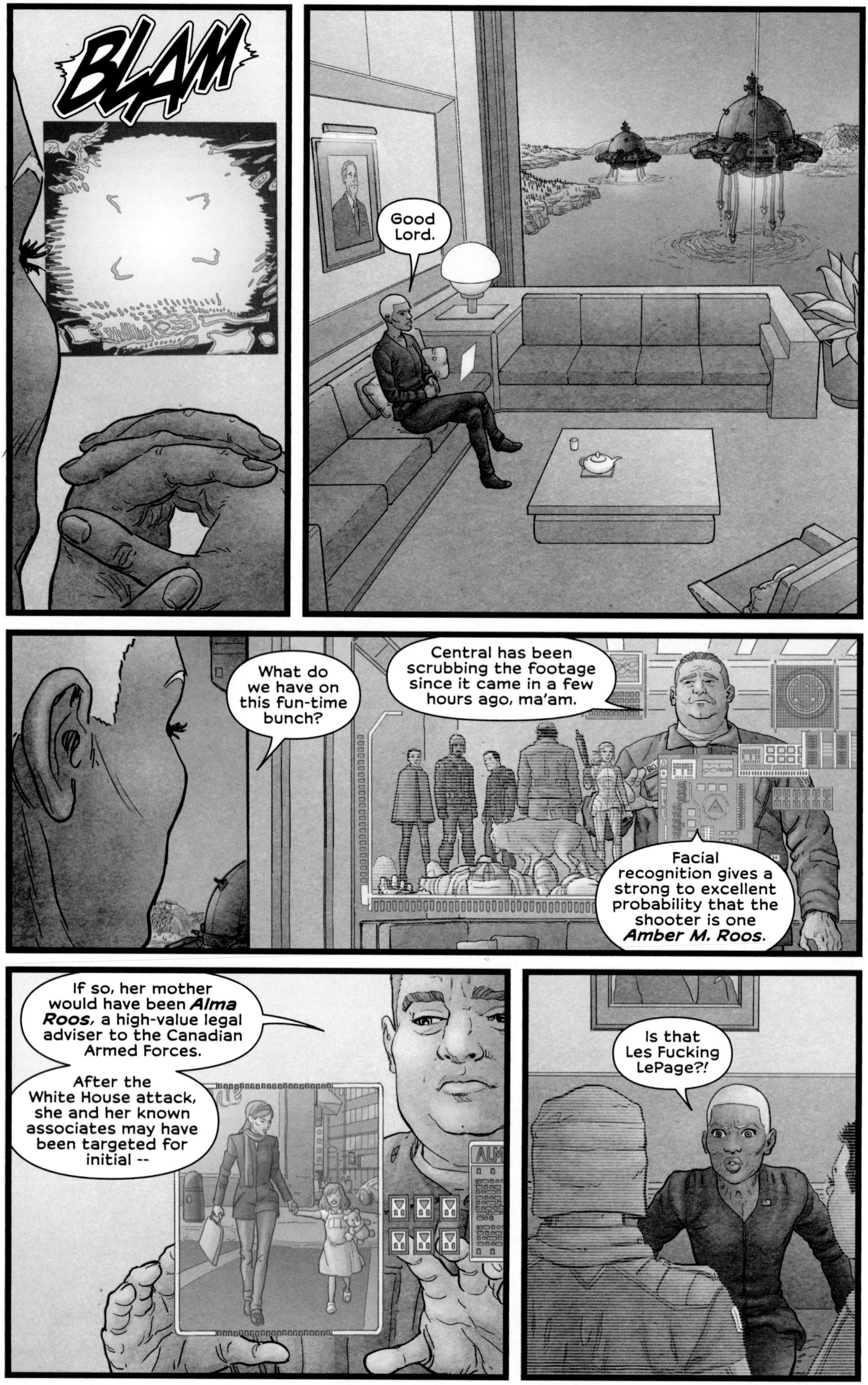
BLAM
Good Lord.
What do we have on this fun-time bunch?
Central has been scrubbing the footage since it came in a few hours ago, ma'am.
Facial recognition gives a strong to excellent probability that the shooter is one *Amber M. Roos*.
If so, her mother would have been *Alma Roos,* a high-value legal adviser to the Canadian Armed Forces.
After the White House attack, she and her known associates may have been targeted for initial --
Is that Les Fucking LePage?!

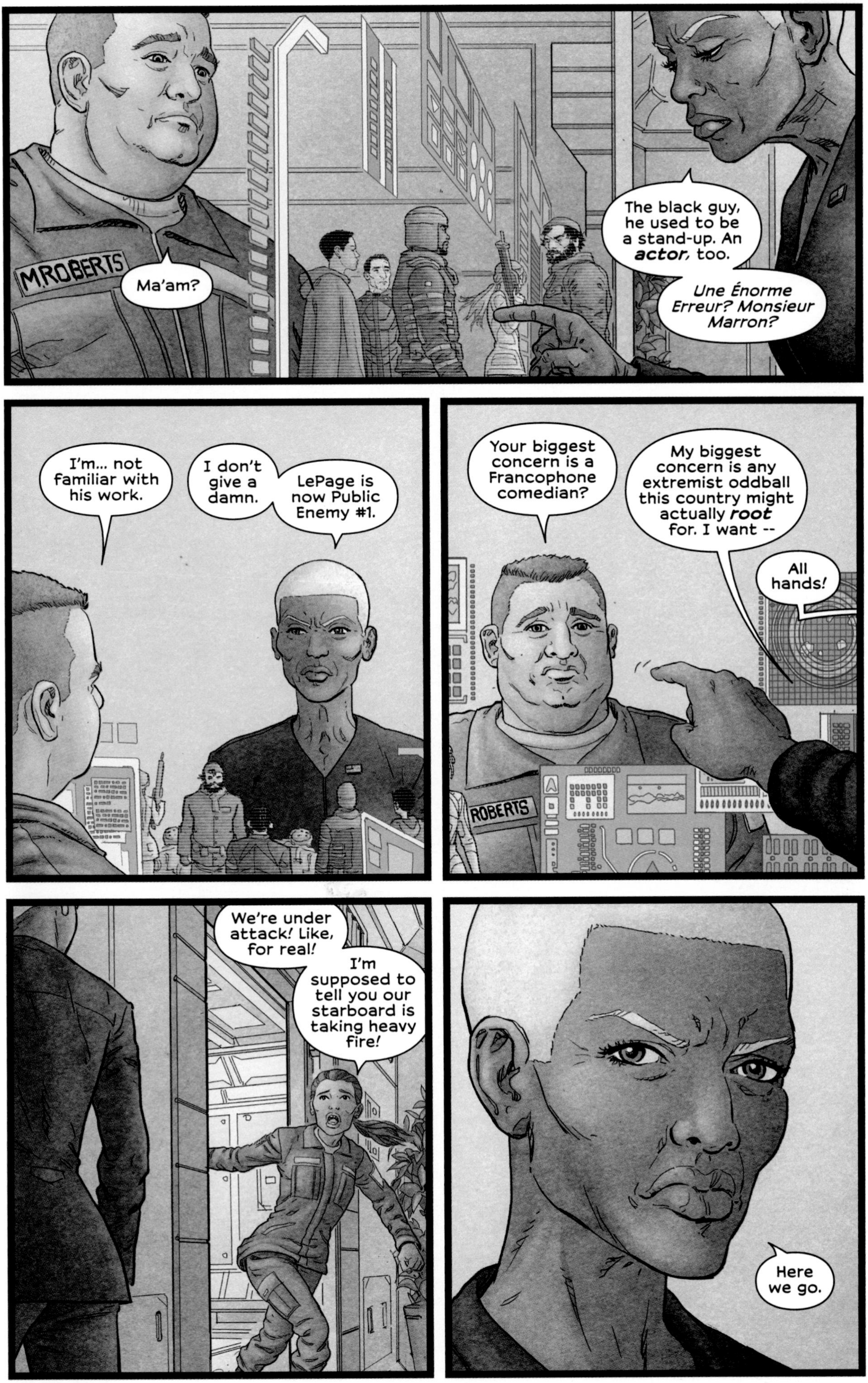
M.ROBERTS
Ma'am?
The black guy, he used to be a stand-up. An ***actor***, too.
Une Énorme Erreur? Monsieur Marron?
I'm... not familiar with his work.
I don't give a damn.
LePage is now Public Enemy #1.
Your biggest concern is a Francophone comedian?
My biggest concern is any extremist oddball this country might actually ***root*** for. I want --
All hands*!*
ROBERTS
We're under attack*!* Like, for real*!*
I'm supposed to tell you our starboard is taking heavy fire*!*
Here we go.

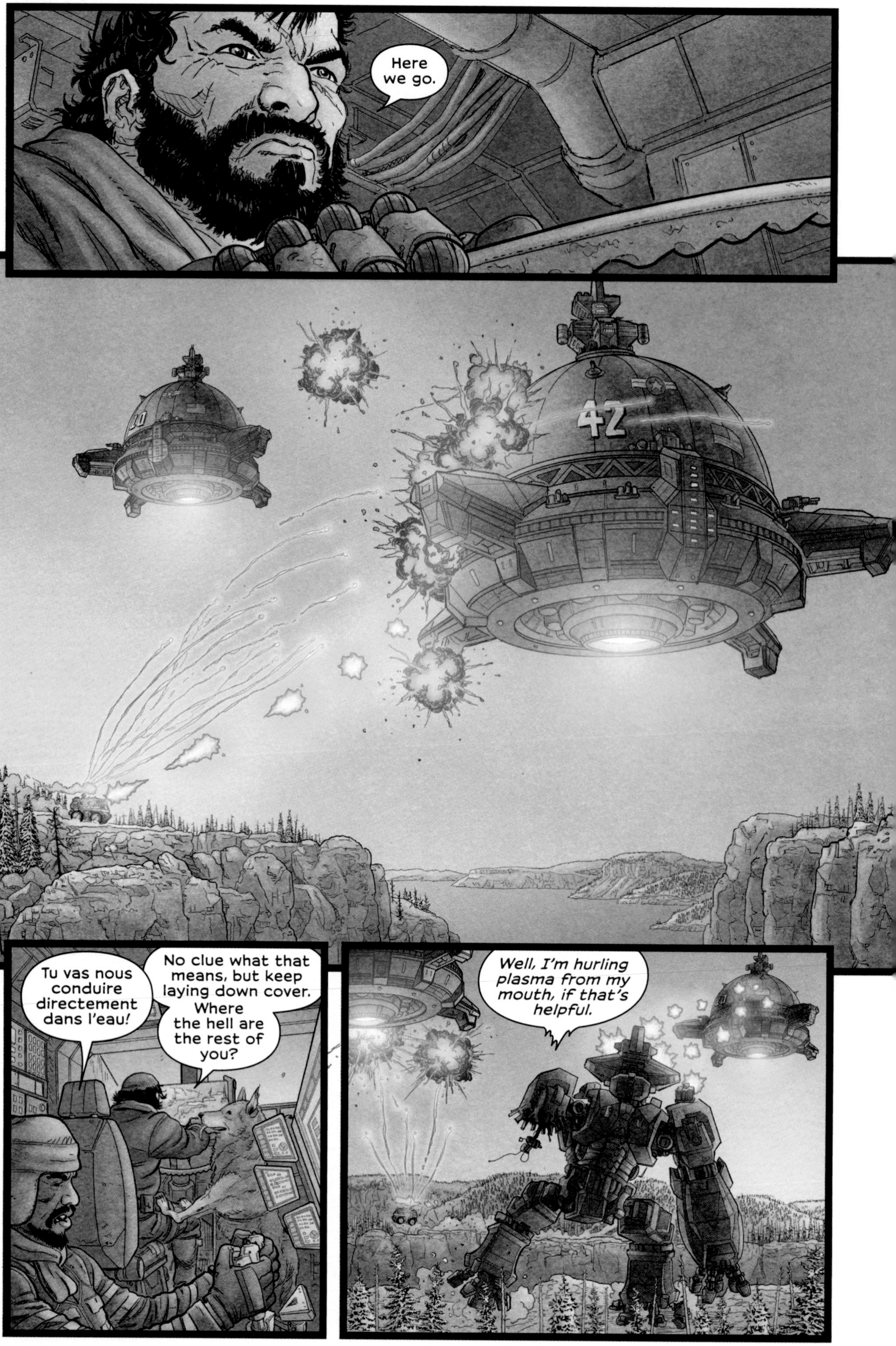
Here we go.
42
Tu vas nous conduire directement dans l'eau!
No clue what that means, but keep laying down cover. Where the hell are the rest of you?
Well, I'm hurling plasma from my mouth, if that's helpful.

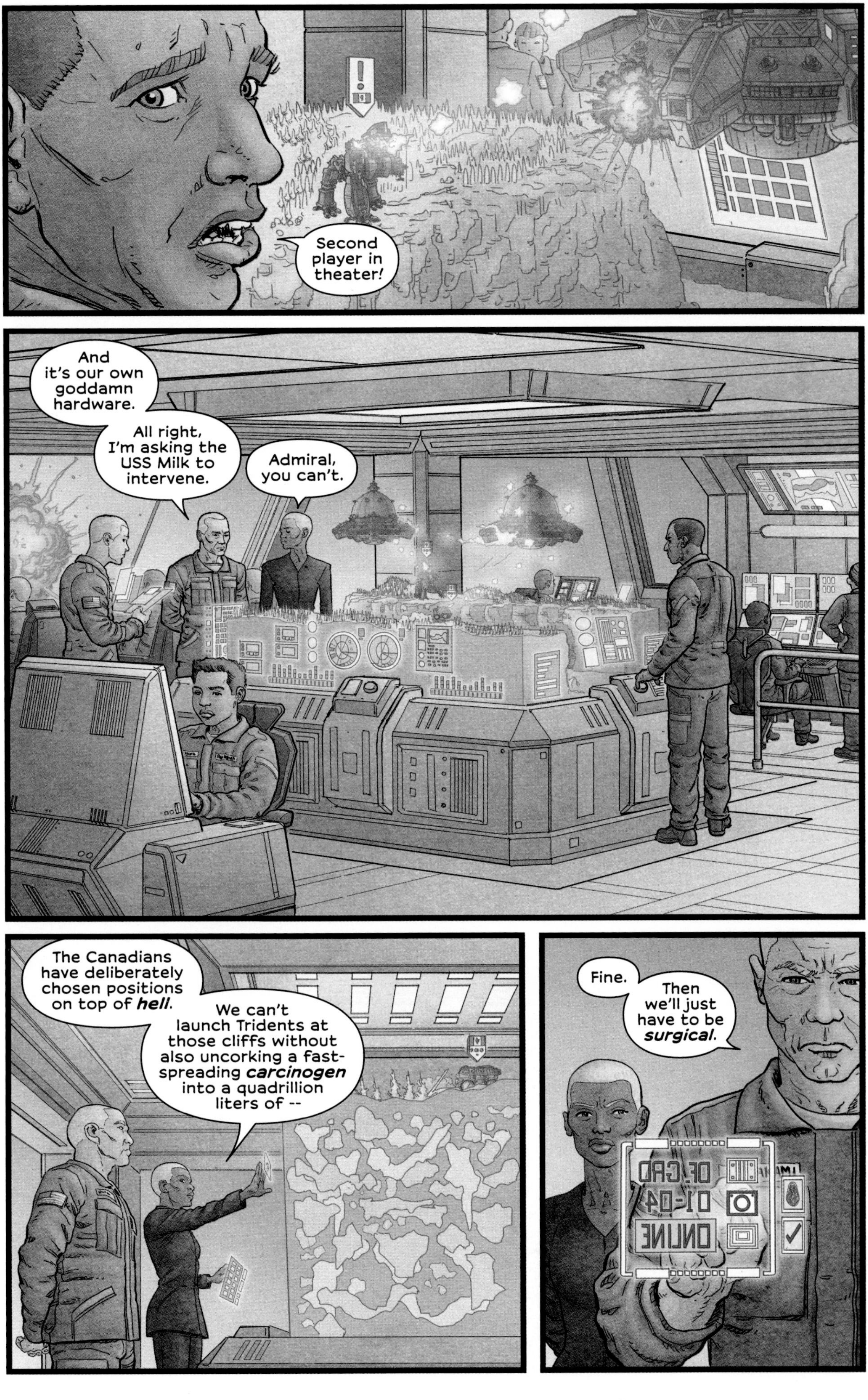
Second player in theater!
And it's our own goddamn hardware.
All right, I'm asking the USS Milk to intervene.
Admiral, you can't.
The Canadians have deliberately chosen positions on top of ***hell***.
We can't launch Tridents at those cliffs without also uncorking a fast-spreading ***carcinogen*** into a quadrillion liters of --
Fine.
Then we'll just have to be ***surgical***.

You boys holding up?

Plus ou moins.

J'aime beaucoup mieux cette bataille maintenant qu'ils tirent surtout sur toi.

Focus.

Does it look like that big one is charging up some sorta --

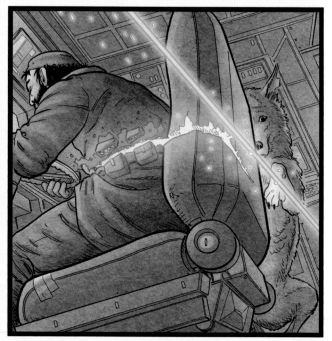

DUNN!

First target engaged.

And?

Why the hell is our old Guerilla still standing?

Admiral, we need to recalibrate the LaWS' Friendly Fire Prevention before we can --

Urgent-up!

I have a Whitehawk attempting to dock in our landing bay.

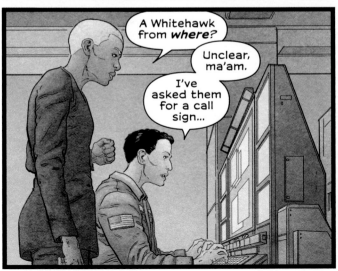

A Whitehawk from *where*?

Unclear, ma'am. I've asked them for a call sign...

...but all I hear is screaming.

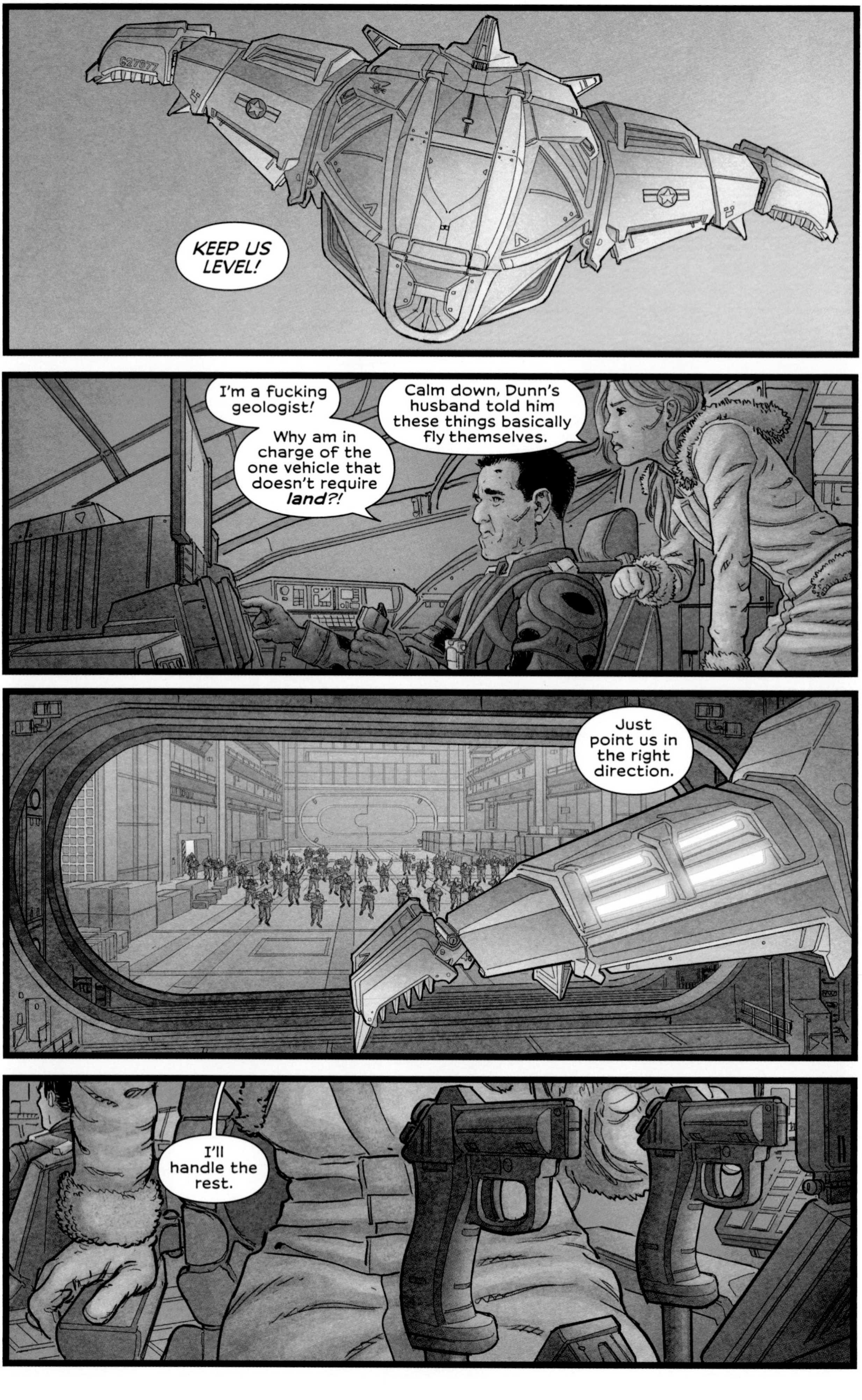

627677
KEEP US LEVEL!
I'm a fucking geologist!
Why am in charge of the one vehicle that doesn't require *land*?!
Calm down, Dunn's husband told him these things basically fly themselves.
Just point us in the right direction.
I'll handle the rest.

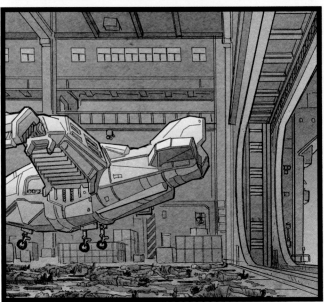

Clear.

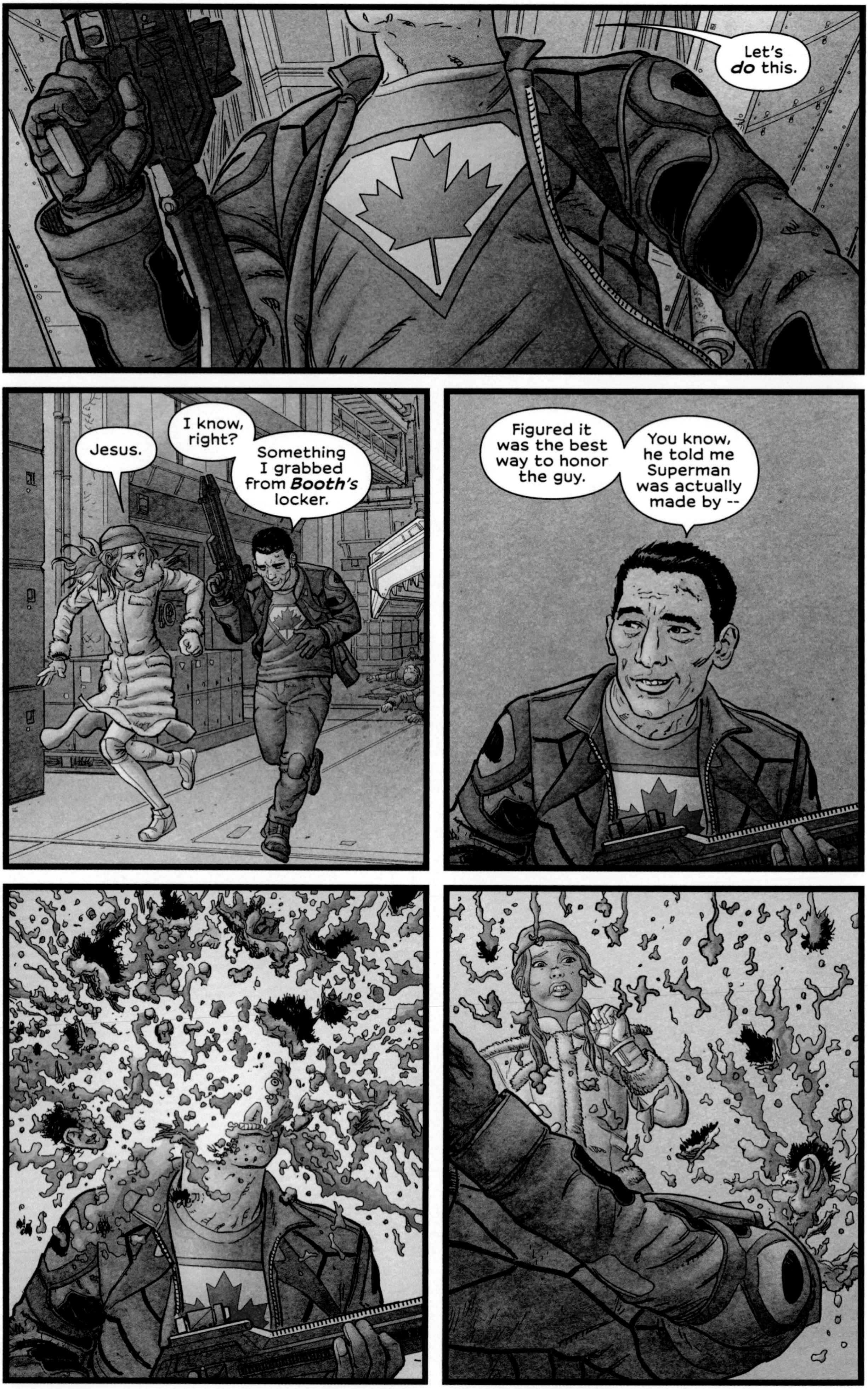
Let's *do* this.
Jesus.
I know, right?
Something I grabbed from *Booth's* locker.
Figured it was the best way to honor the guy.
You know, he told me Superman was actually made by --

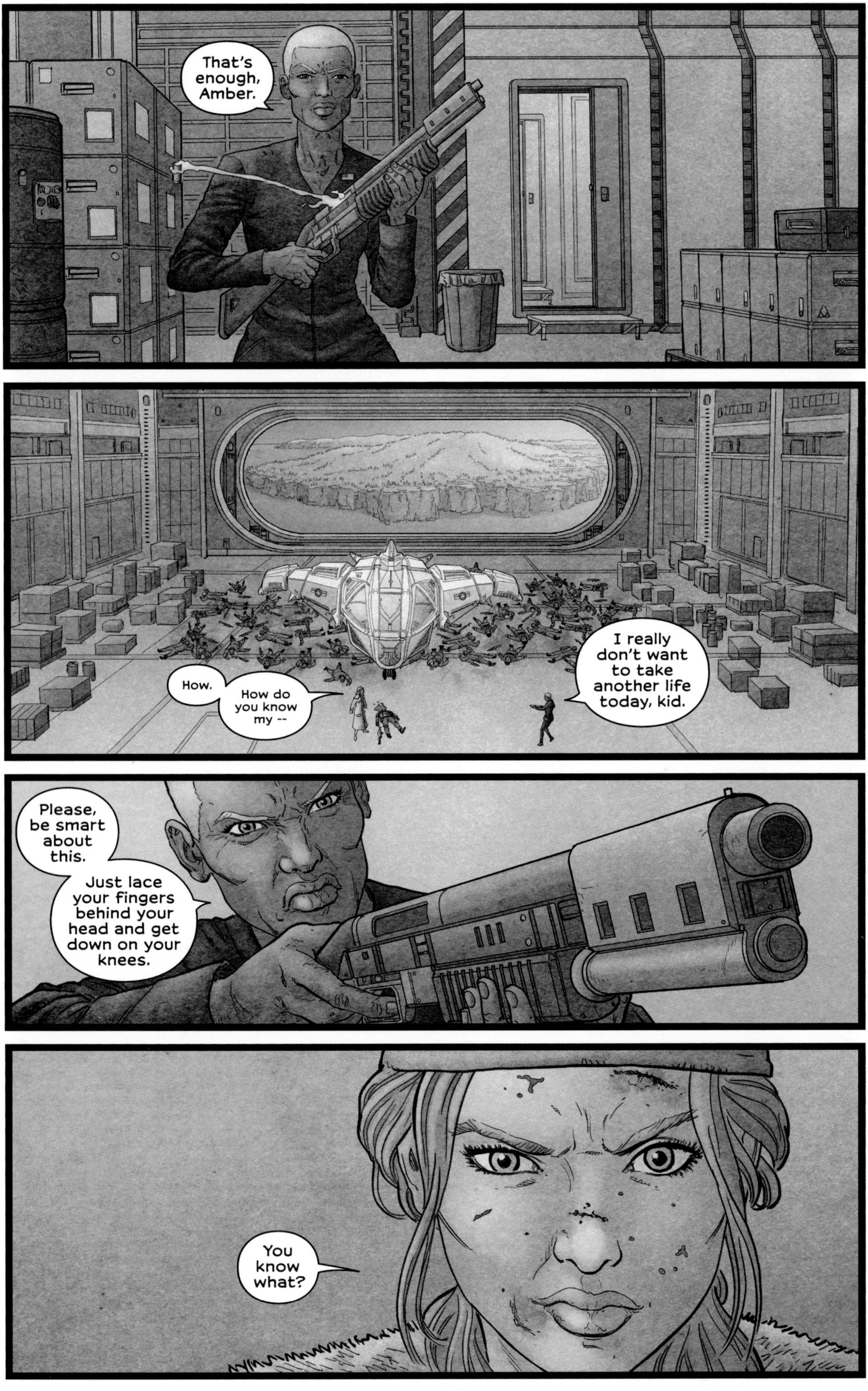

That's enough, Amber.
How.
How do you know my --
I really don't want to take another life today, kid.
Please, be smart about this.
Just lace your fingers behind your head and get down on your knees.
You know what?

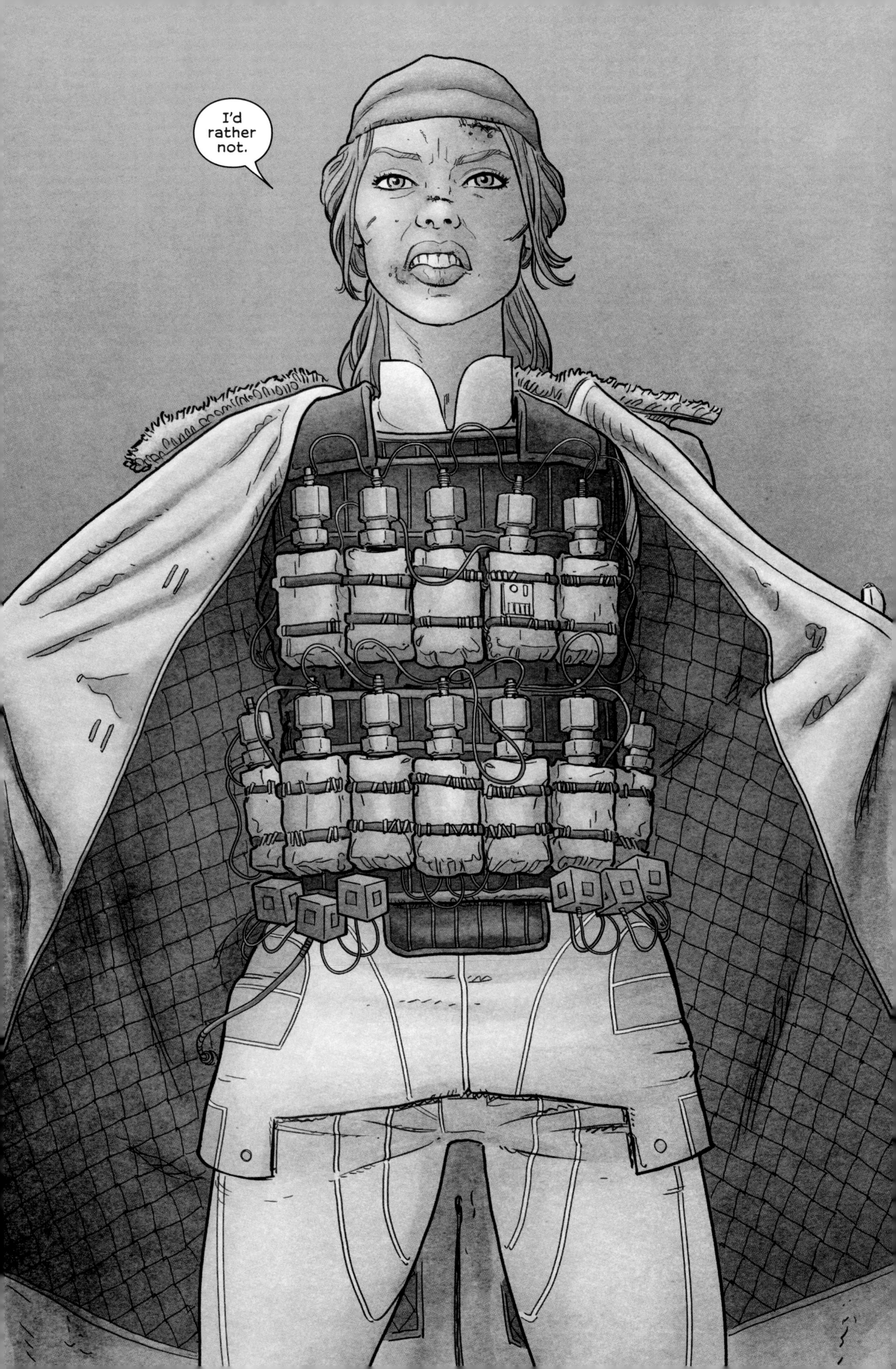
I'd rather not.

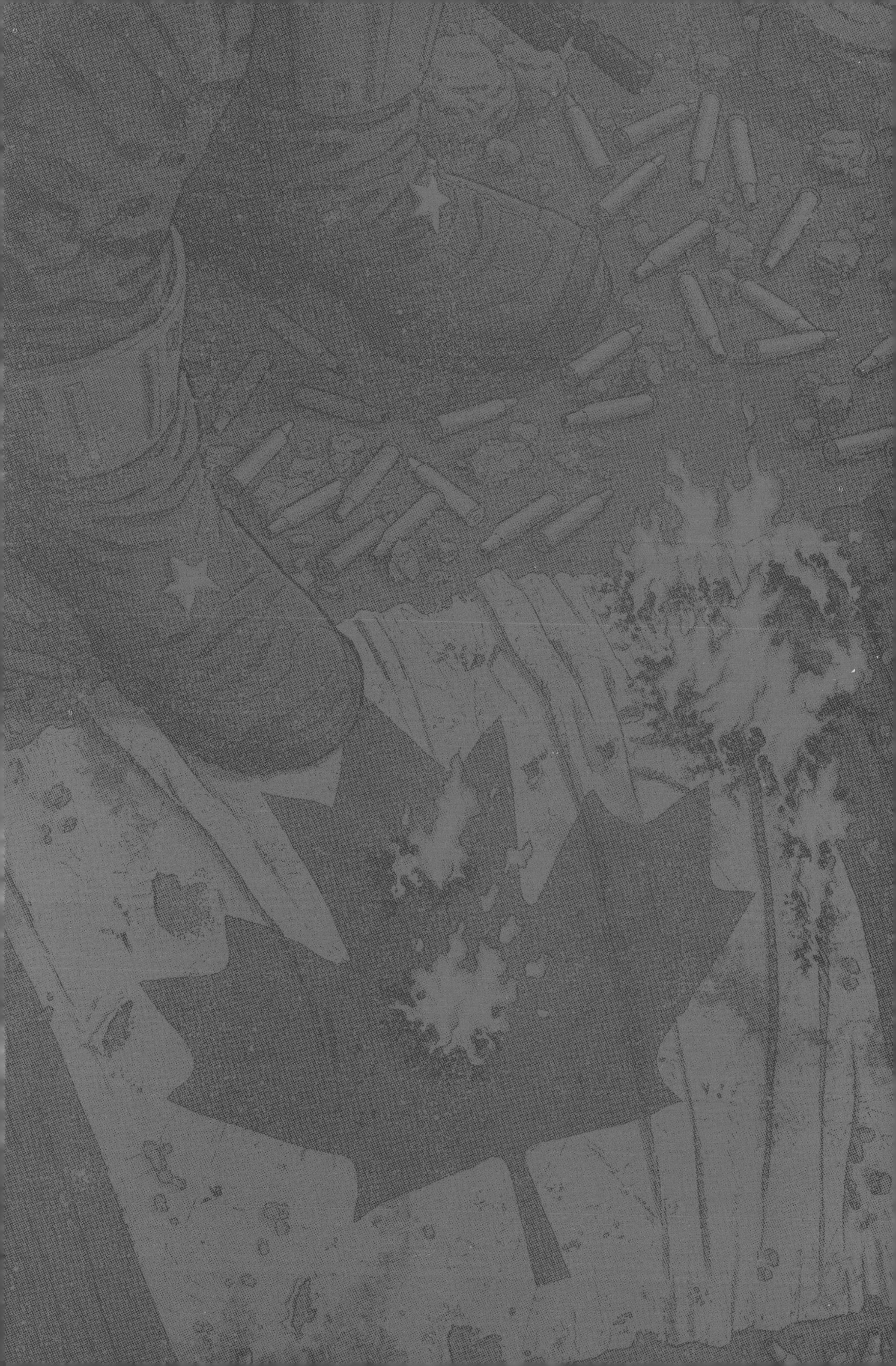

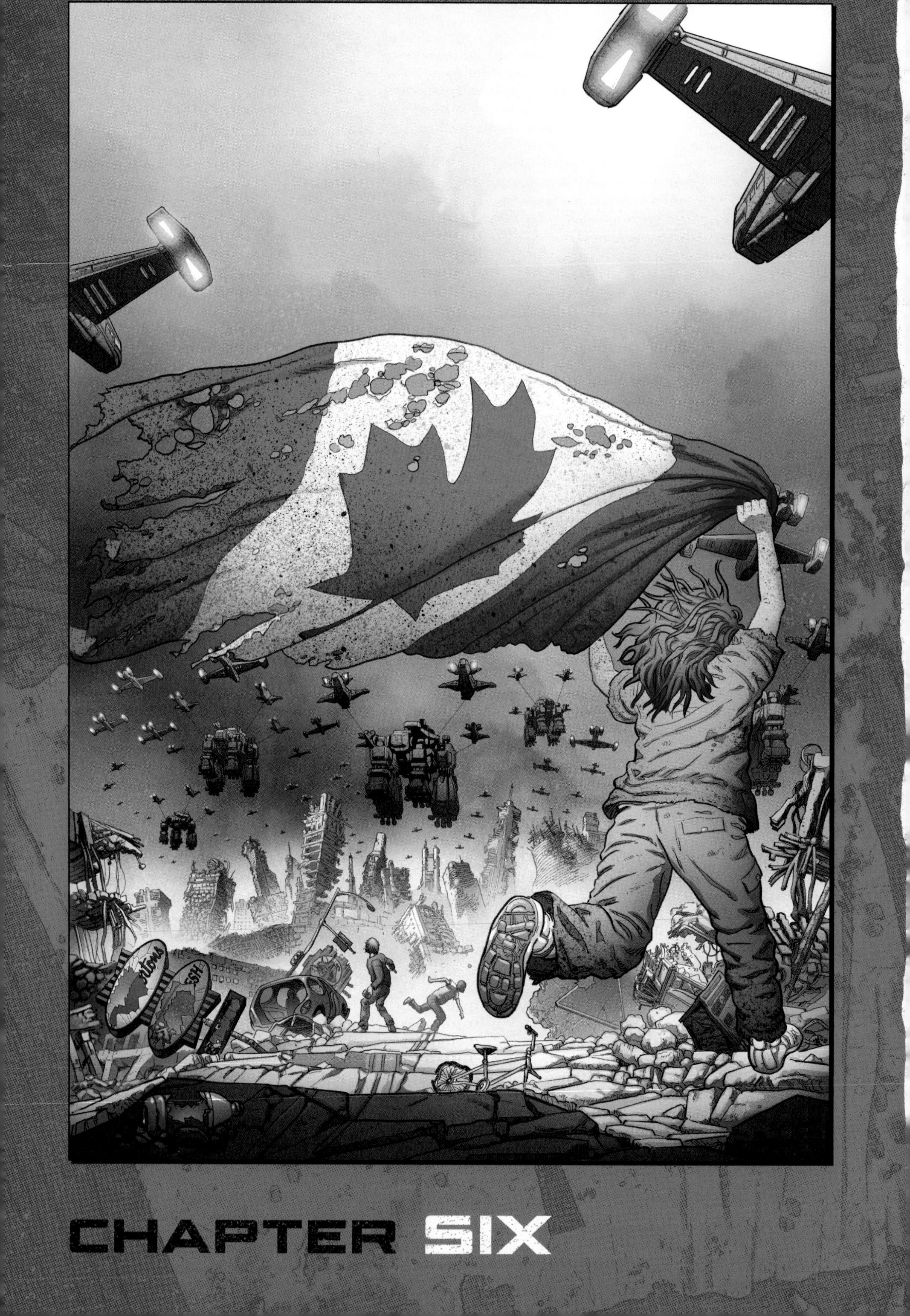

CHAPTER SIX

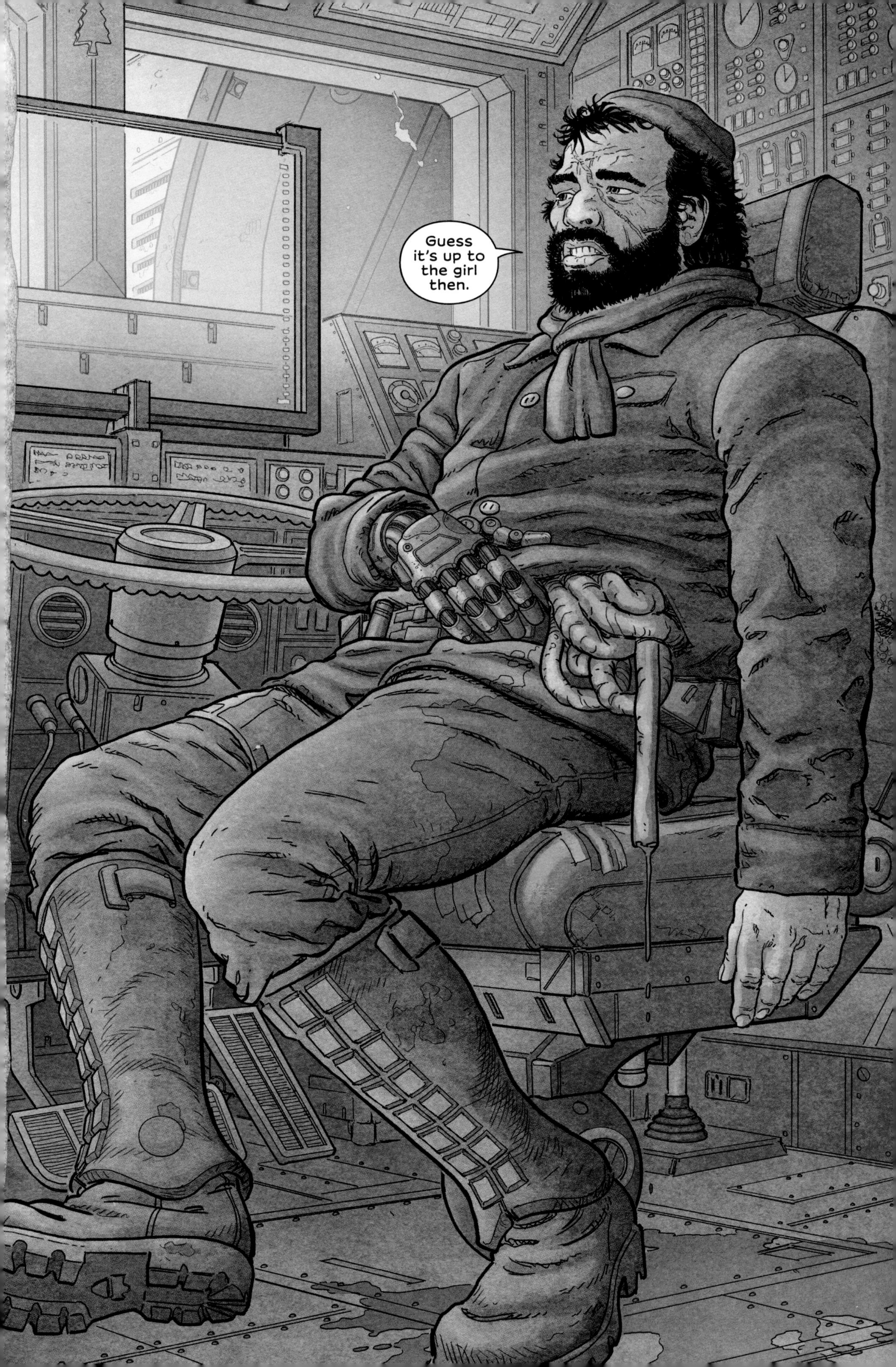
Guess it's up to the girl then.

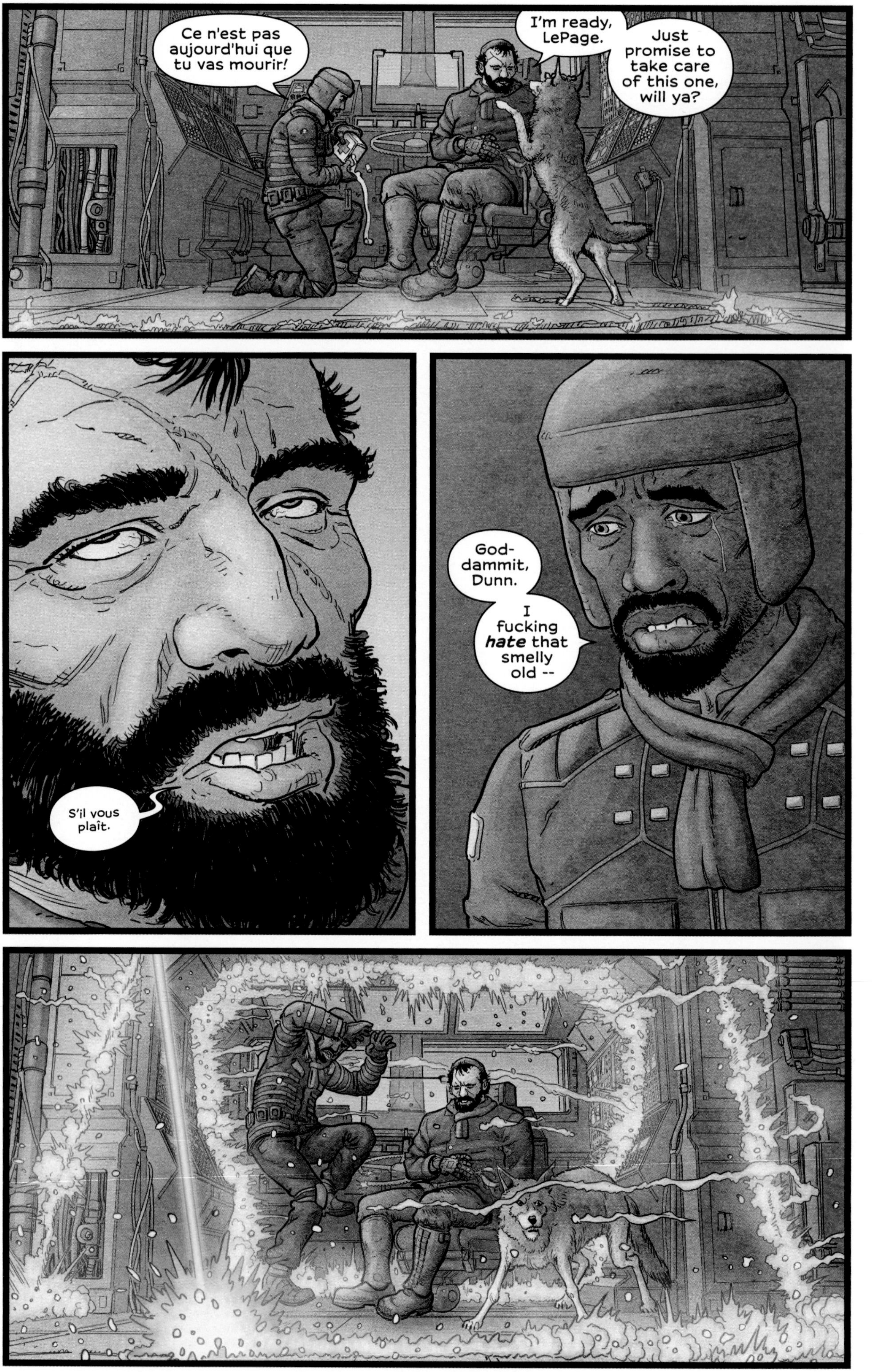

Ce n'est pas aujourd'hui que tu vas mourir!
I'm ready, LePage.
Just promise to take care of this one, will ya?
S'il vous plaît.
God- dammit, Dunn.
I fucking *hate* that smelly old --

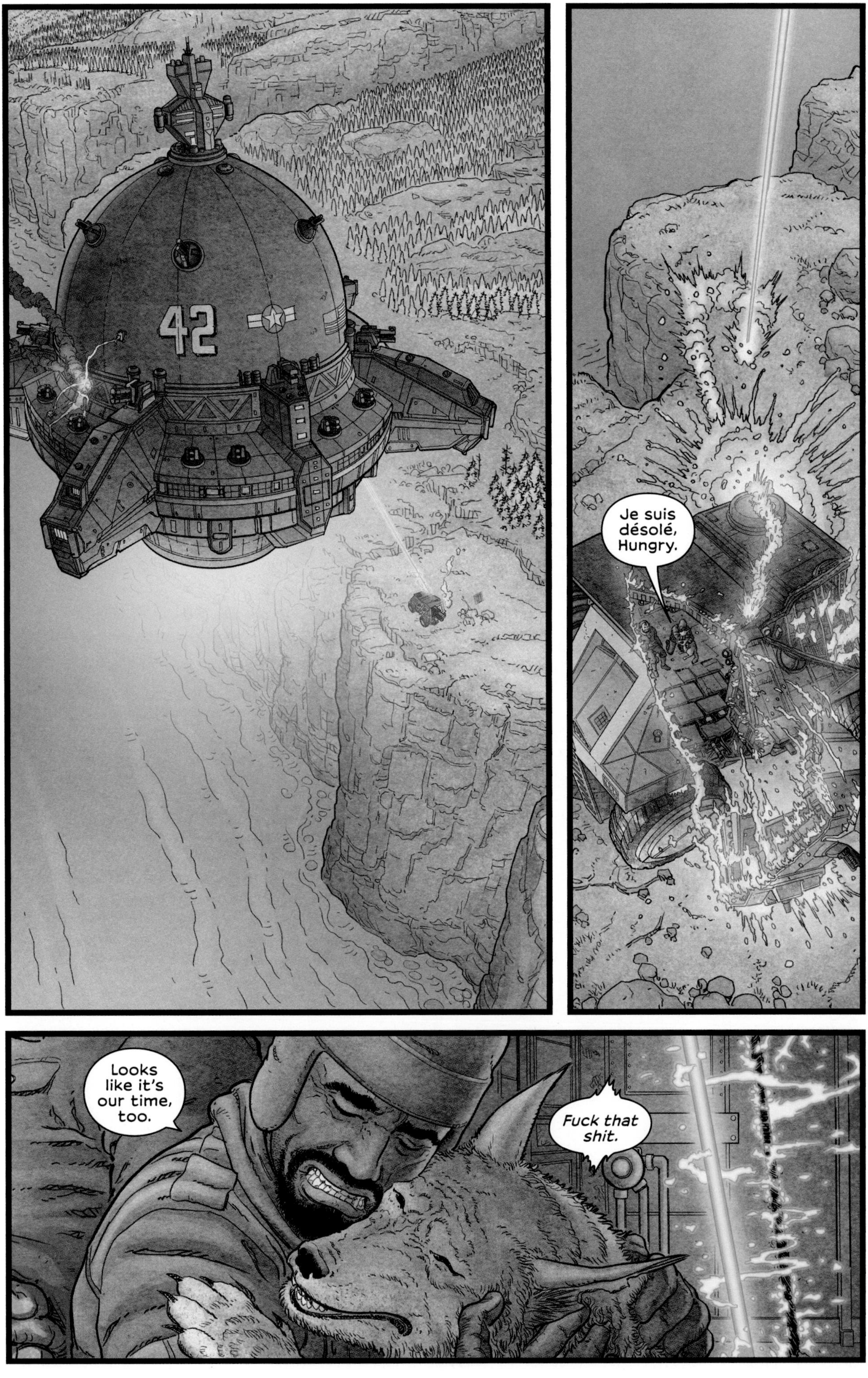
42
Je suis désolé, Hungry.
Looks like it's our time, too.
Fuck that shit.

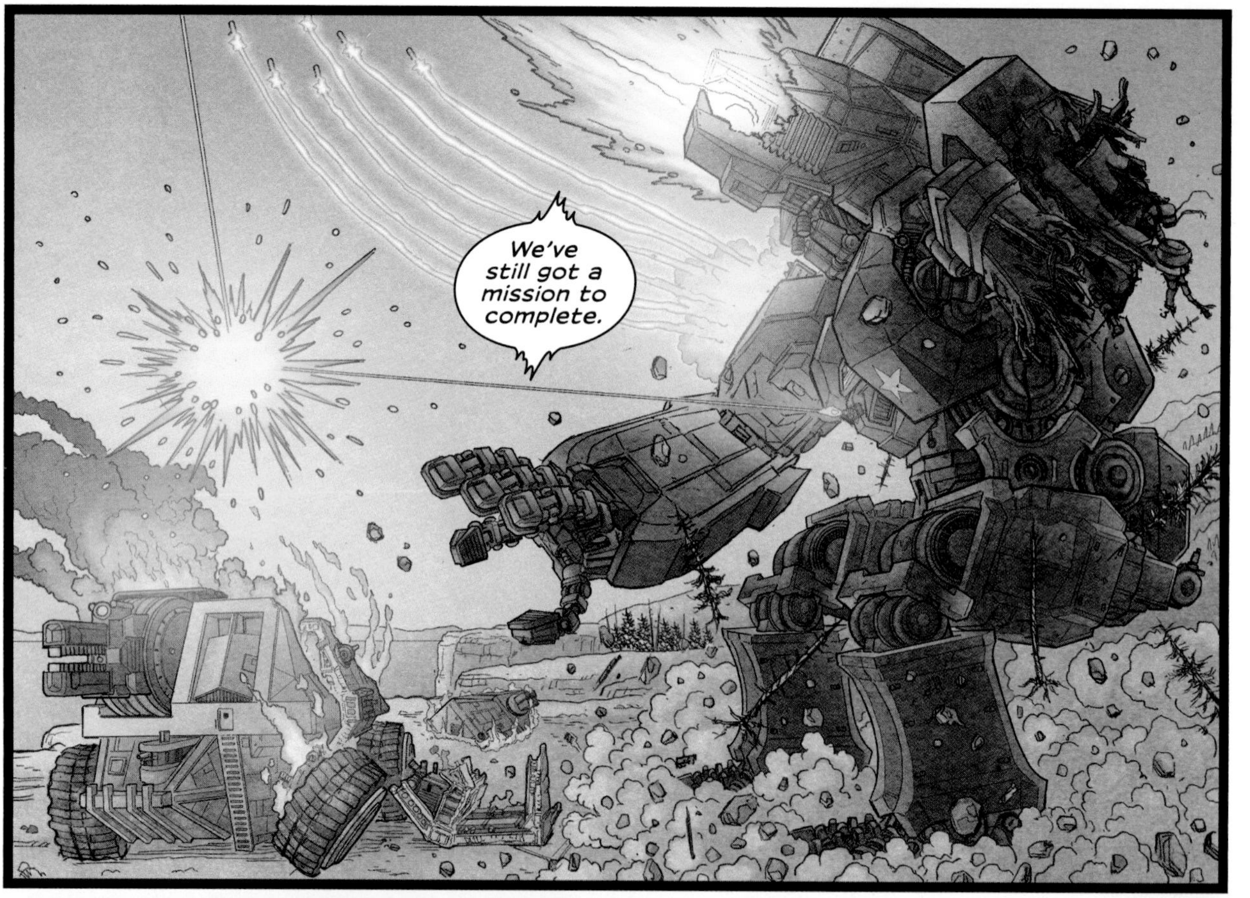
We've still got a mission to complete.

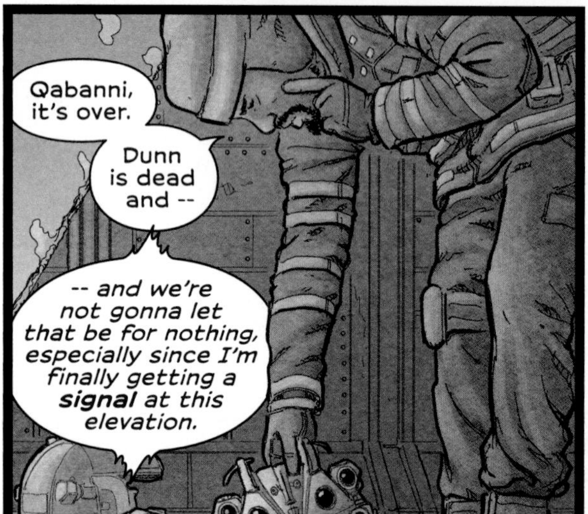
Qabanni, it's over.
Dunn is dead and --
-- and we're not gonna let that be for nothing, especially since I'm finally getting a **signal** at this elevation.

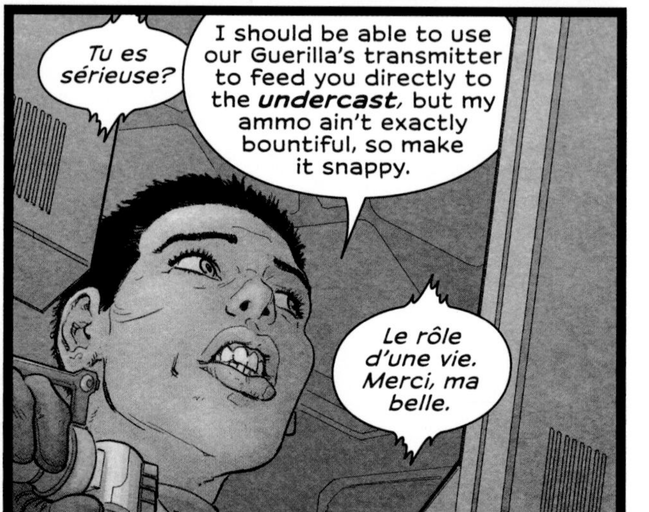
Tu es sérieuse?
I should be able to use our Guerilla's transmitter to feed you directly to the ***undercast***, but my ammo ain't exactly bountiful, so make it snappy.
Le rôle d'une vie. Merci, ma belle.

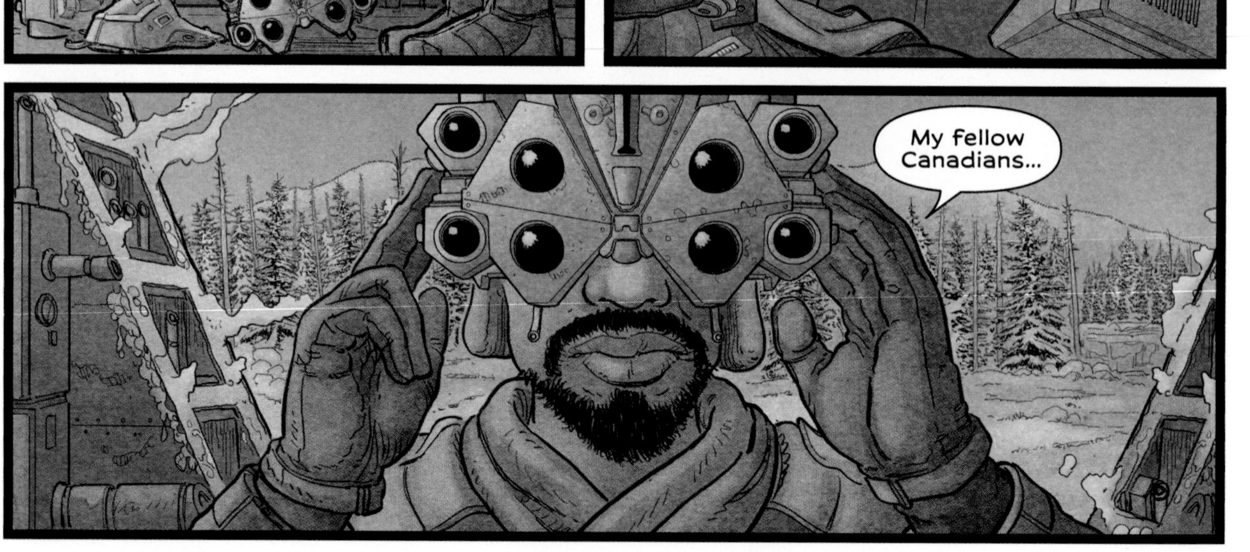
My fellow Canadians...

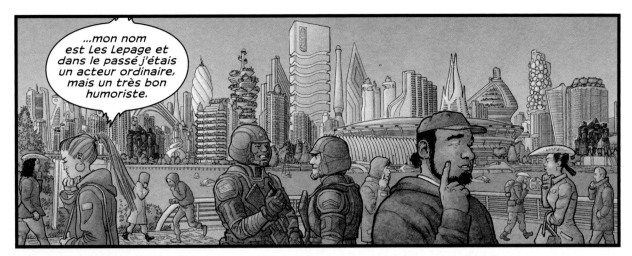

...mon nom est Les Lepage et dans le passé j'étais un acteur ordinaire, mais un très bon humoriste.

But now I'm part of what we call the Two-Four, a group of ordinary citizens like you who decided that they had had enough.

Malgré les obstacles auxquels nous faisons face, nous ne sommes pas stupide mes compatriotes et moi.

We know we can't win this war... but what if we could win just one battle?

Oh, god. *Amber.*

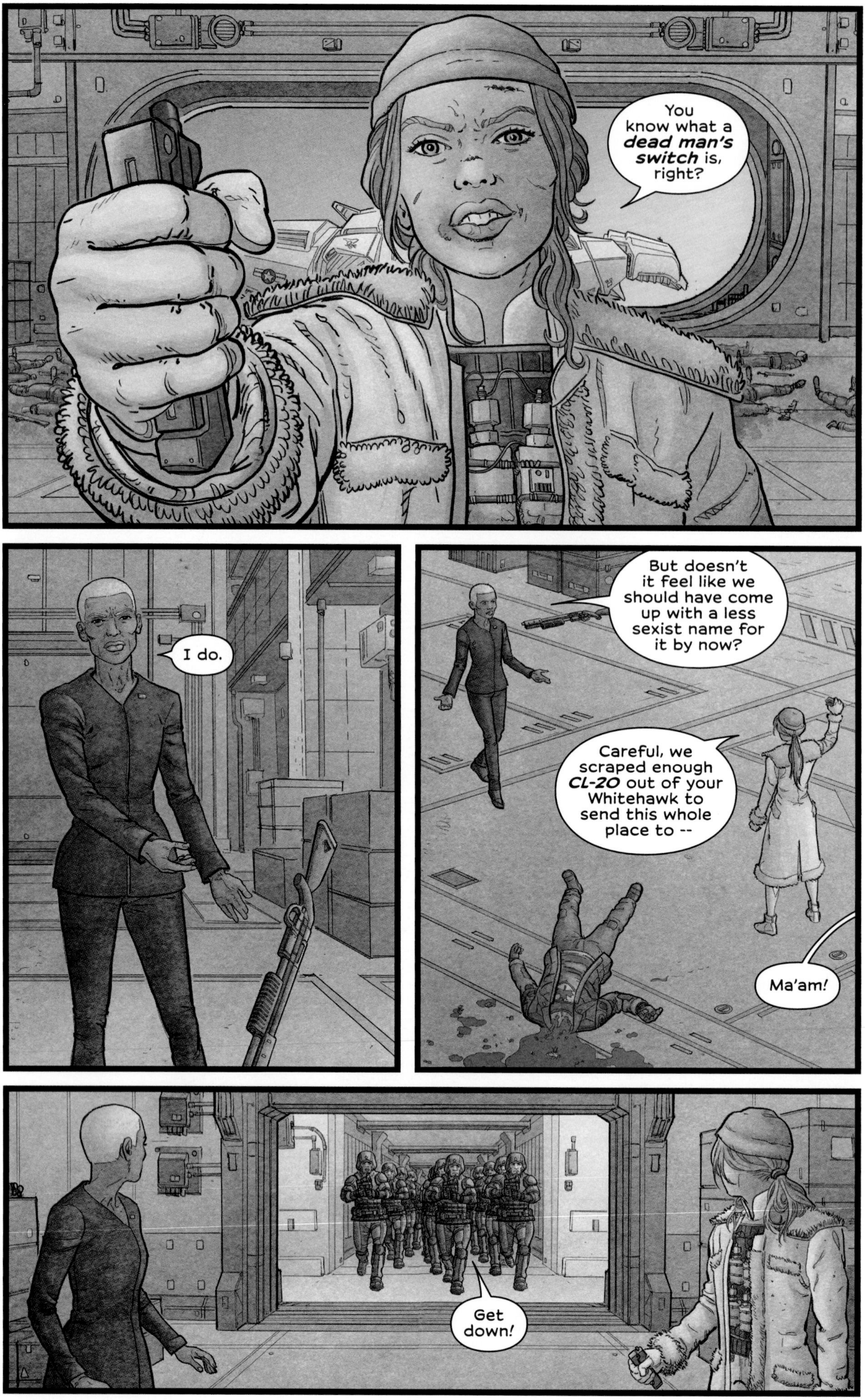
You know what a ***dead man's switch*** is, right?
I do.
But doesn't it feel like we should have come up with a less sexist name for it by now?
Careful, we scraped enough ***CL-20*** out of your Whitehawk to send this whole place to --
Ma'am!
Get down!

Idiots, *fall back!*

The kid and I are trying to have a conversation.

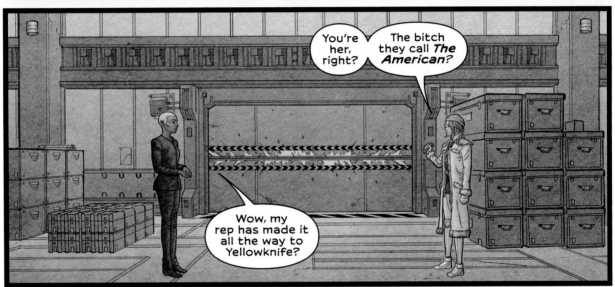

You're her, right?

The bitch they call *The American?*

Wow, my rep has made it all the way to Yellowknife?

Well, I'm glad we already know a little about each other, *Amber*.

But I have no idea why our detainees always end up calling me that. I mean, I wasn't even *born* in the States.

I'm originally from *Ottawa*, just like you.

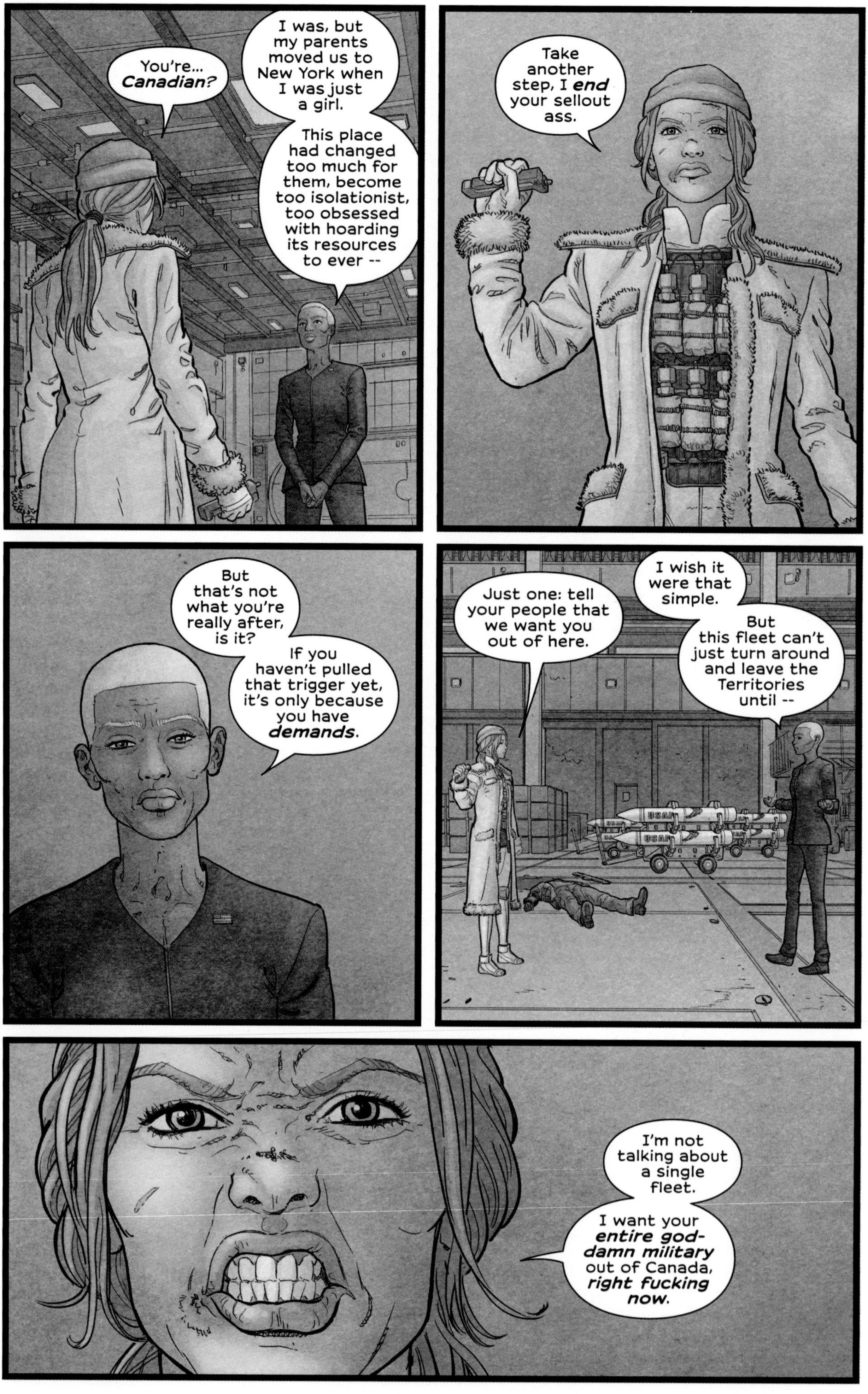

You're... *Canadian?*
I was, but my parents moved us to New York when I was just a girl.
This place had changed too much for them, become too isolationist, too obsessed with hoarding its resources to ever --
Take another step, I ***end*** your sellout ass.
But that's not what you're really after, is it?
If you haven't pulled that trigger yet, it's only because you have ***demands***.
Just one: tell your people that we want you out of here.
I wish it were that simple.
But this fleet can't just turn around and leave the Territories until --
I'm not talking about a single fleet.
I want your ***entire god-damn military*** out of Canada, ***right fucking now***.

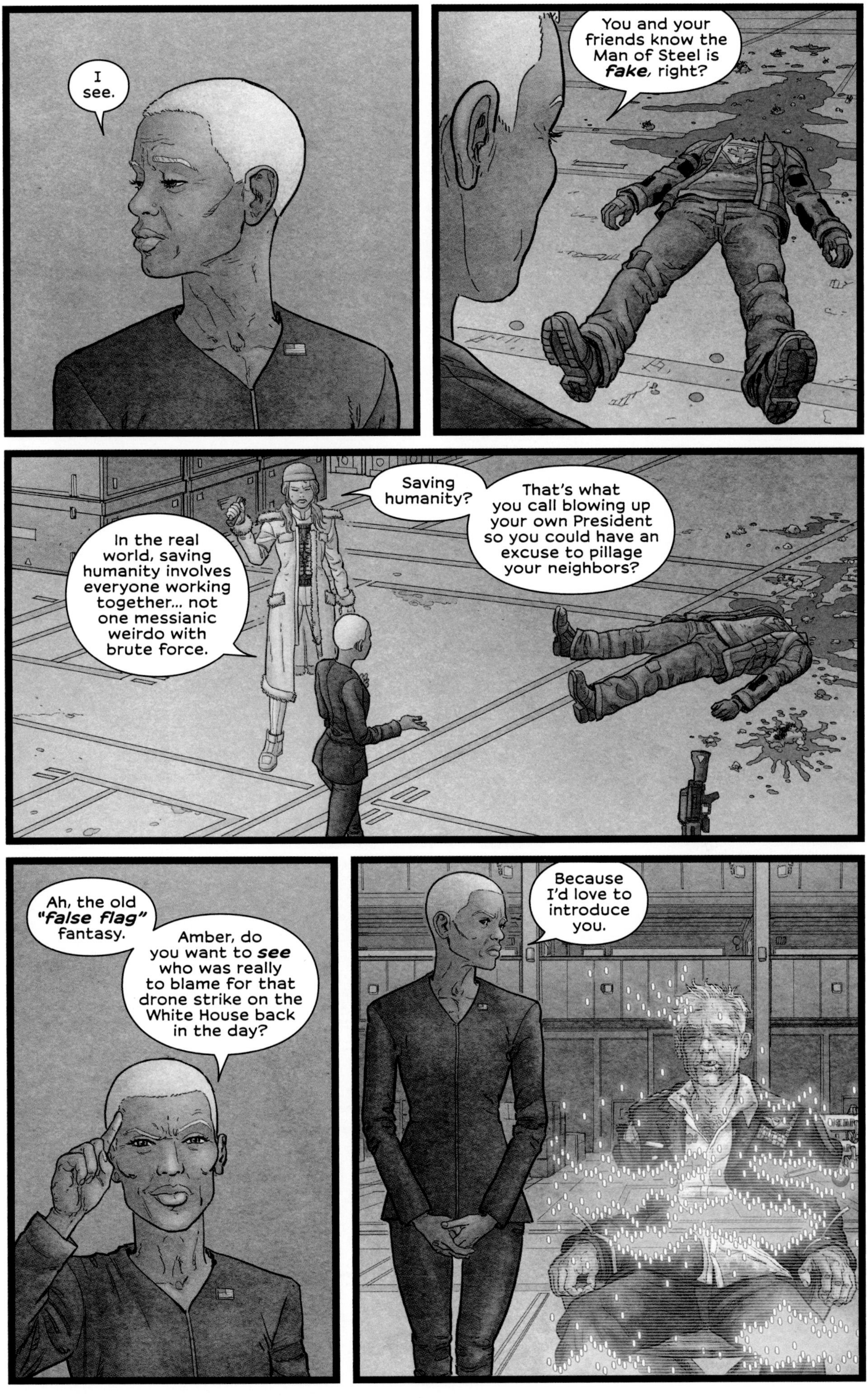
I see.
You and your friends know the Man of Steel is ***fake***, right?
Saving humanity?
That's what you call blowing up your own President so you could have an excuse to pillage your neighbors?
In the real world, saving humanity involves everyone working together... not one messianic weirdo with brute force.
Ah, the old ***"false flag"*** fantasy.
Amber, do you want to ***see*** who was really to blame for that drone strike on the White House back in the day?
Because I'd love to introduce you.

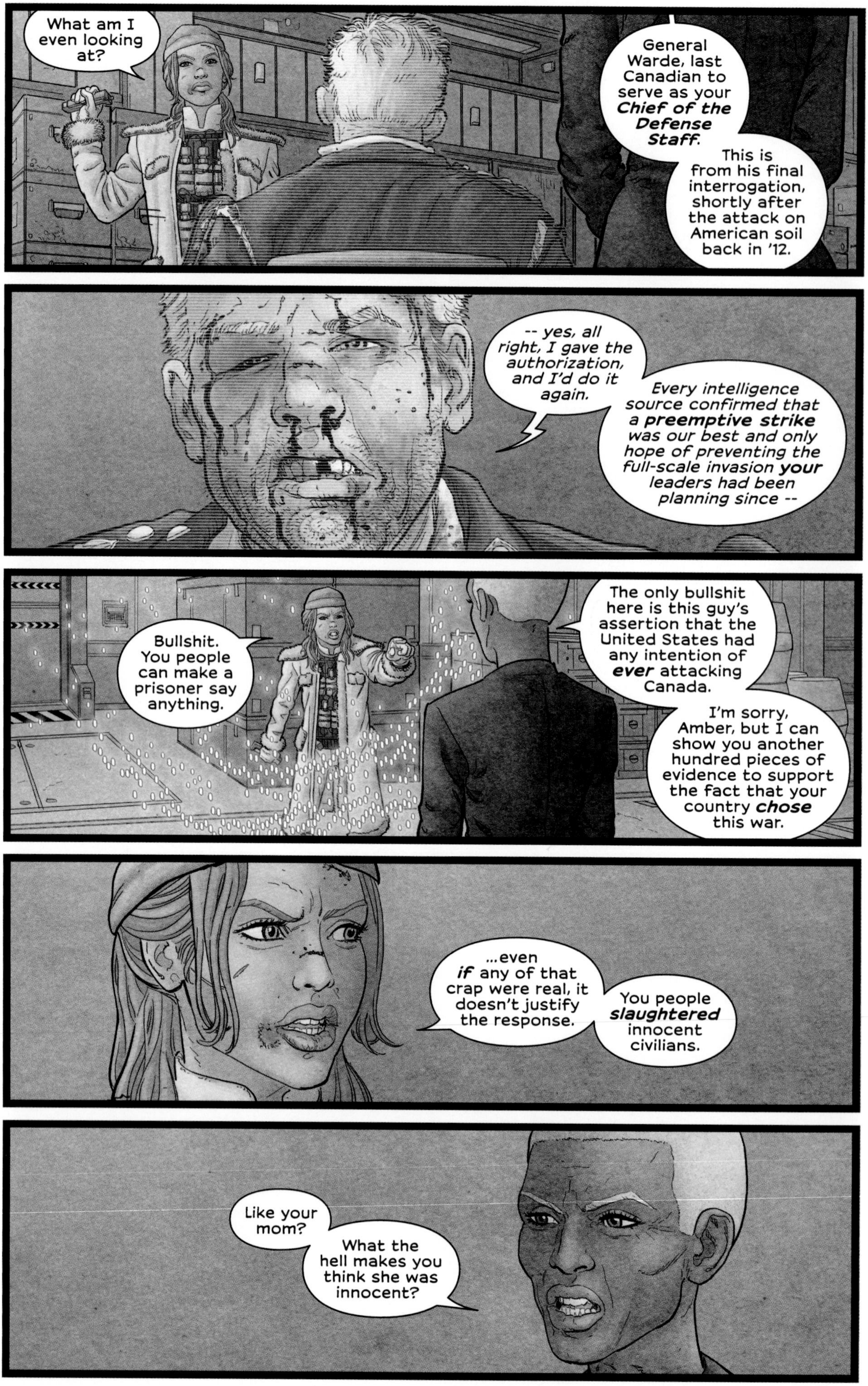
What am I even looking at?
General Warde, last Canadian to serve as your Chief of the Defense Staff.
This is from his final interrogation, shortly after the attack on American soil back in '12.
-- yes, all right, I gave the authorization, and I'd do it again.
Every intelligence source confirmed that a preemptive strike was our best and only hope of preventing the full-scale invasion your leaders had been planning since --
Bullshit. You people can make a prisoner say anything.
The only bullshit here is this guy's assertion that the United States had any intention of ever attacking Canada.
I'm sorry, Amber, but I can show you another hundred pieces of evidence to support the fact that your country chose this war.
...even if any of that crap were real, it doesn't justify the response.
You people slaughtered innocent civilians.
Like your mom?
What the hell makes you think she was innocent?

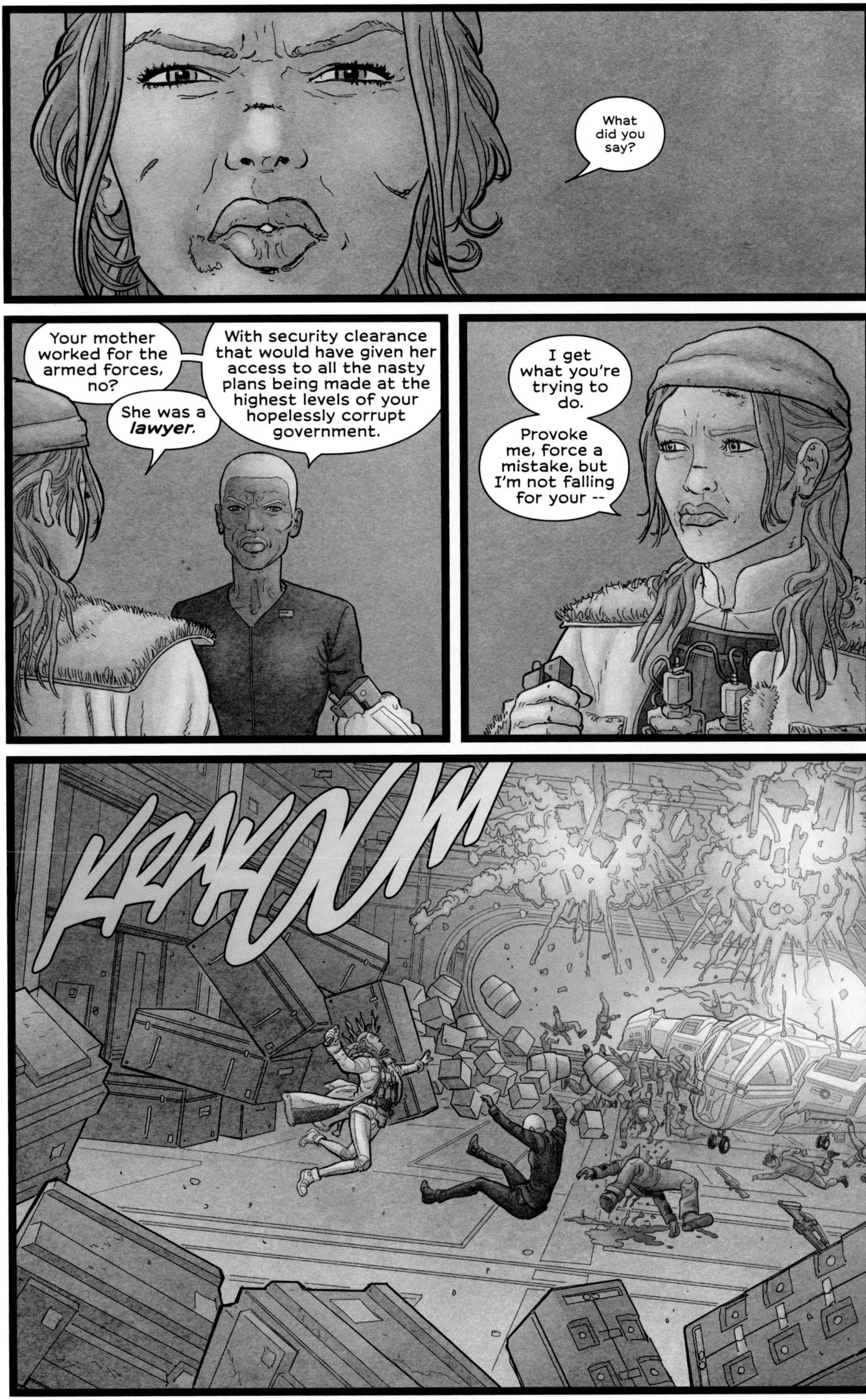
What did you say?
Your mother worked for the armed forces, no?
She was a *lawyer*.
With security clearance that would have given her access to all the nasty plans being made at the highest levels of your hopelessly corrupt government.
I get what you're trying to do.
Provoke me, force a mistake, but I'm not falling for your --
KRAKOOM

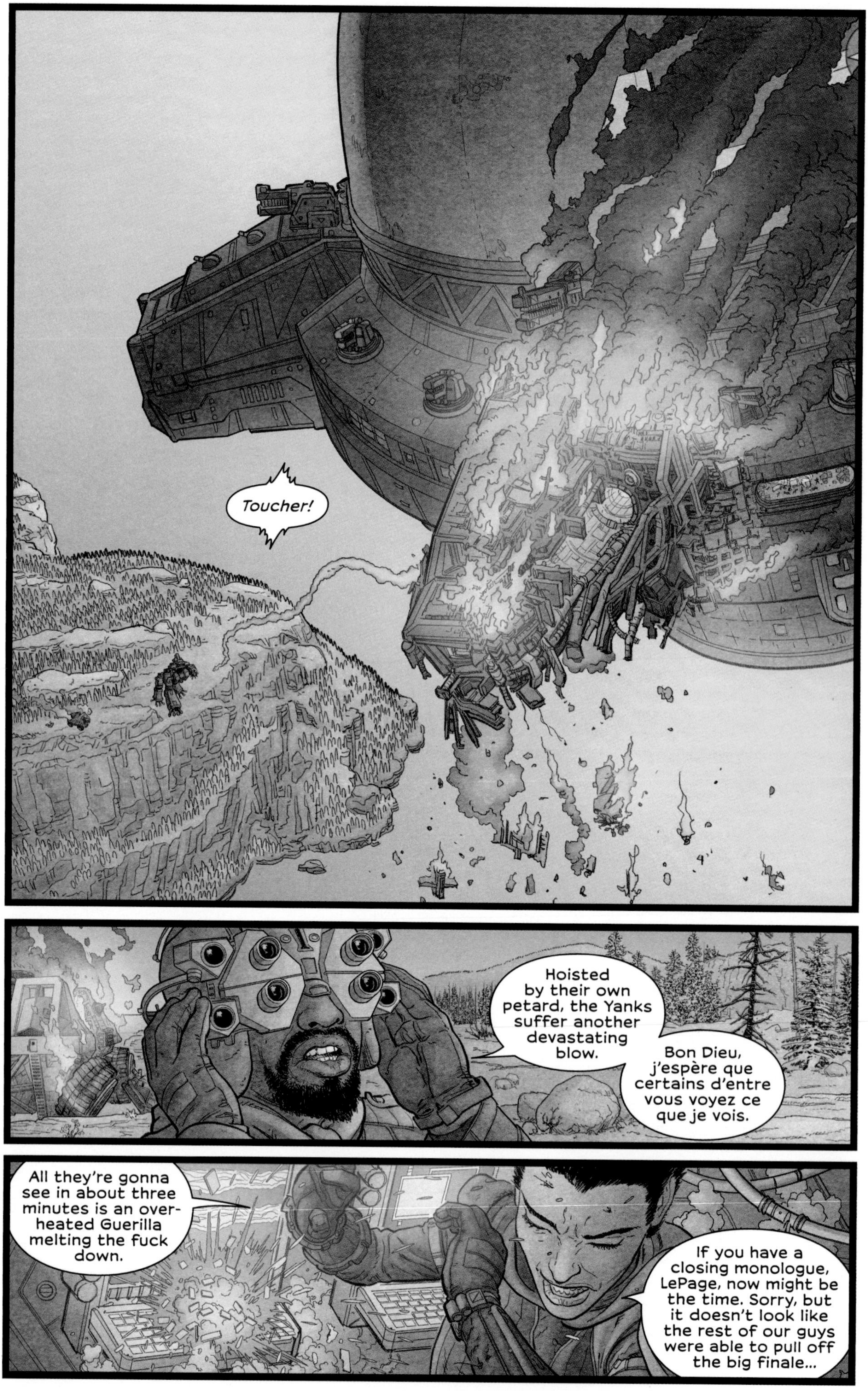
Toucher!
Hoisted by their own petard, the Yanks suffer another devastating blow.
Bon Dieu, j'espère que certains d'entre vous voyez ce que je vois.
All they're gonna see in about three minutes is an over-heated Guerilla melting the fuck down.
If you have a closing monologue, LePage, now might be the time. Sorry, but it doesn't look like the rest of our guys were able to pull off the big finale...

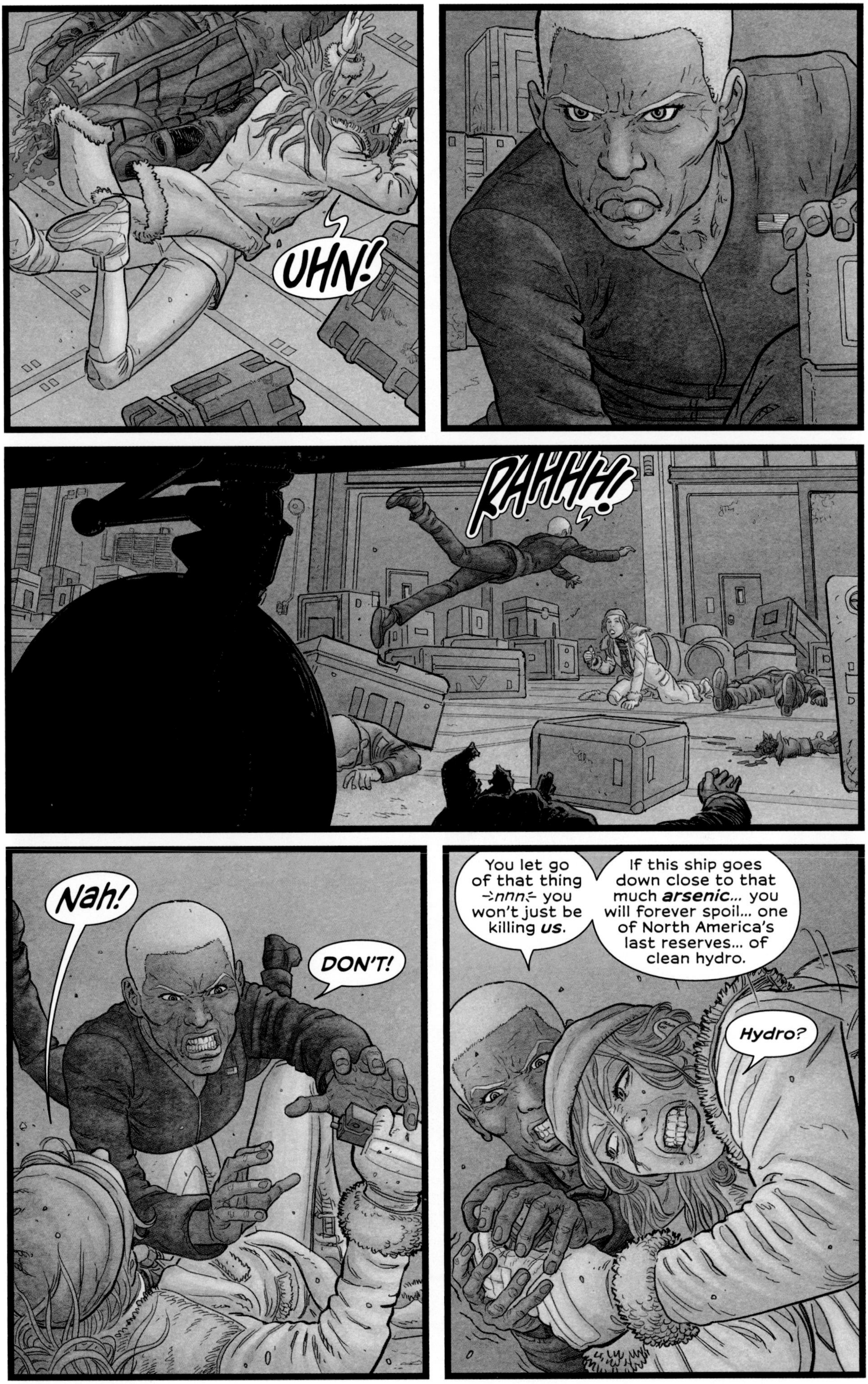
UHN!
RAHHH!
Nah!
DON'T!
You let go of that thing -nnn- you won't just be killing *us*.
If this ship goes down close to that much *arsenic*... you will forever spoil... one of North America's last reserves... of clean hydro.
Hydro?

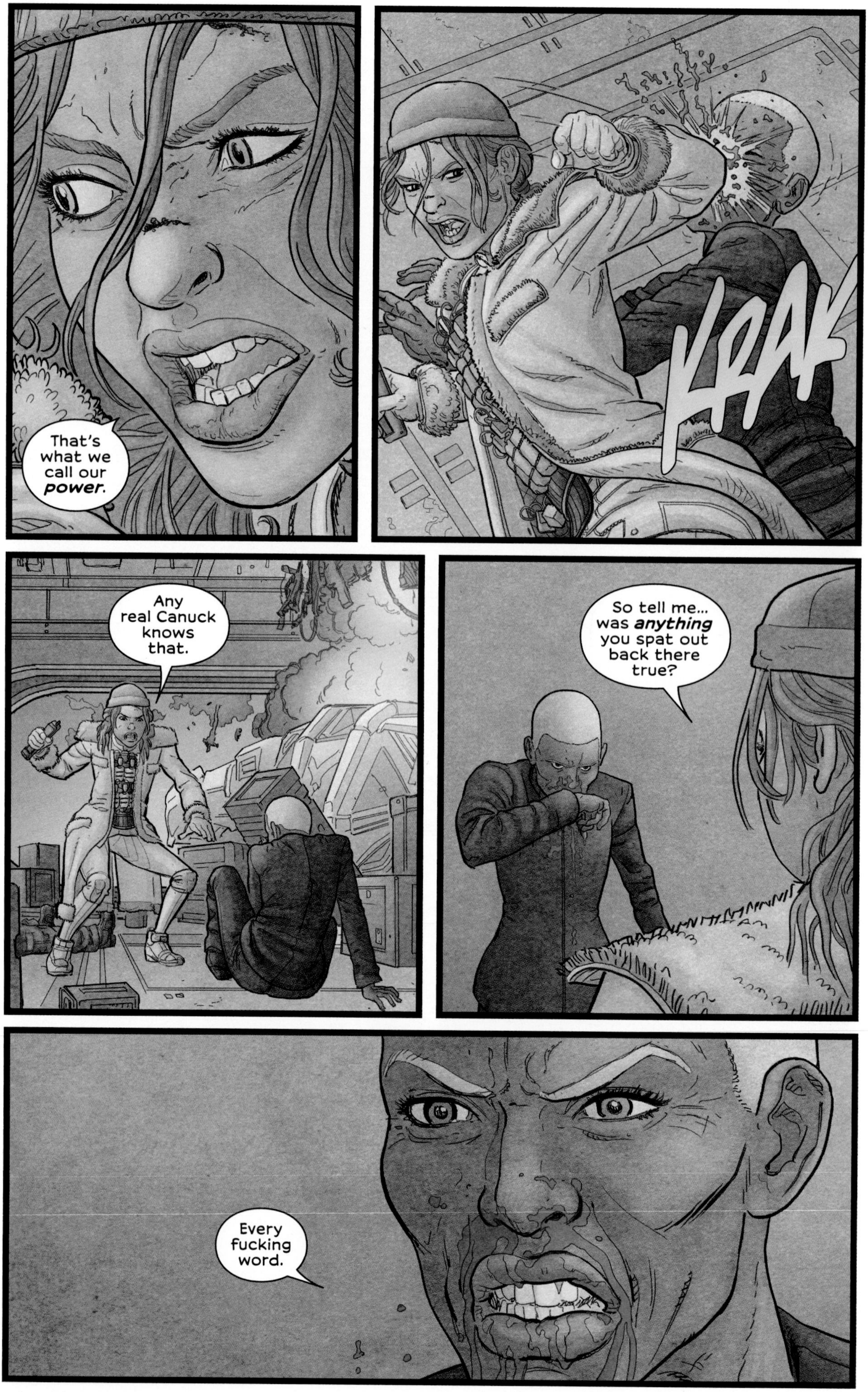
That's what we call our *power*.
KRAK
Any real Canuck knows that.
So tell me... was *anything* you spat out back there true?
Every fucking word.

Hn.

Maybe.

You were definitely right about one thing.

There's no Superman out there.

'Cause you know what *really* happens when you blow up a kid's parents?

You don't get some noble defender of justice.

You get me.

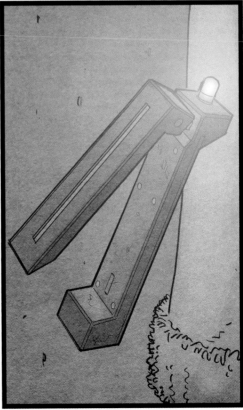

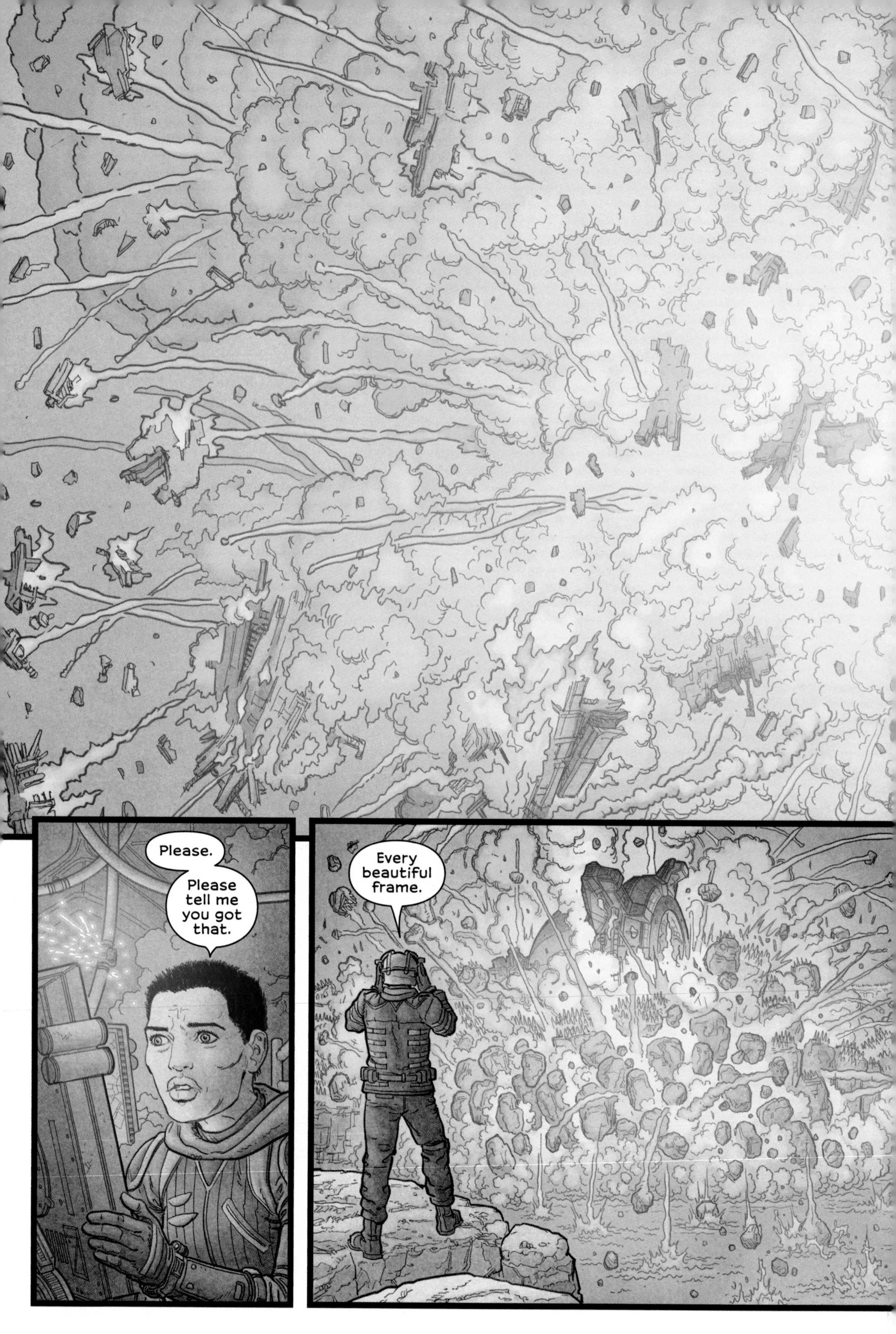
Please.
Please tell me you got that.
Every beautiful frame.

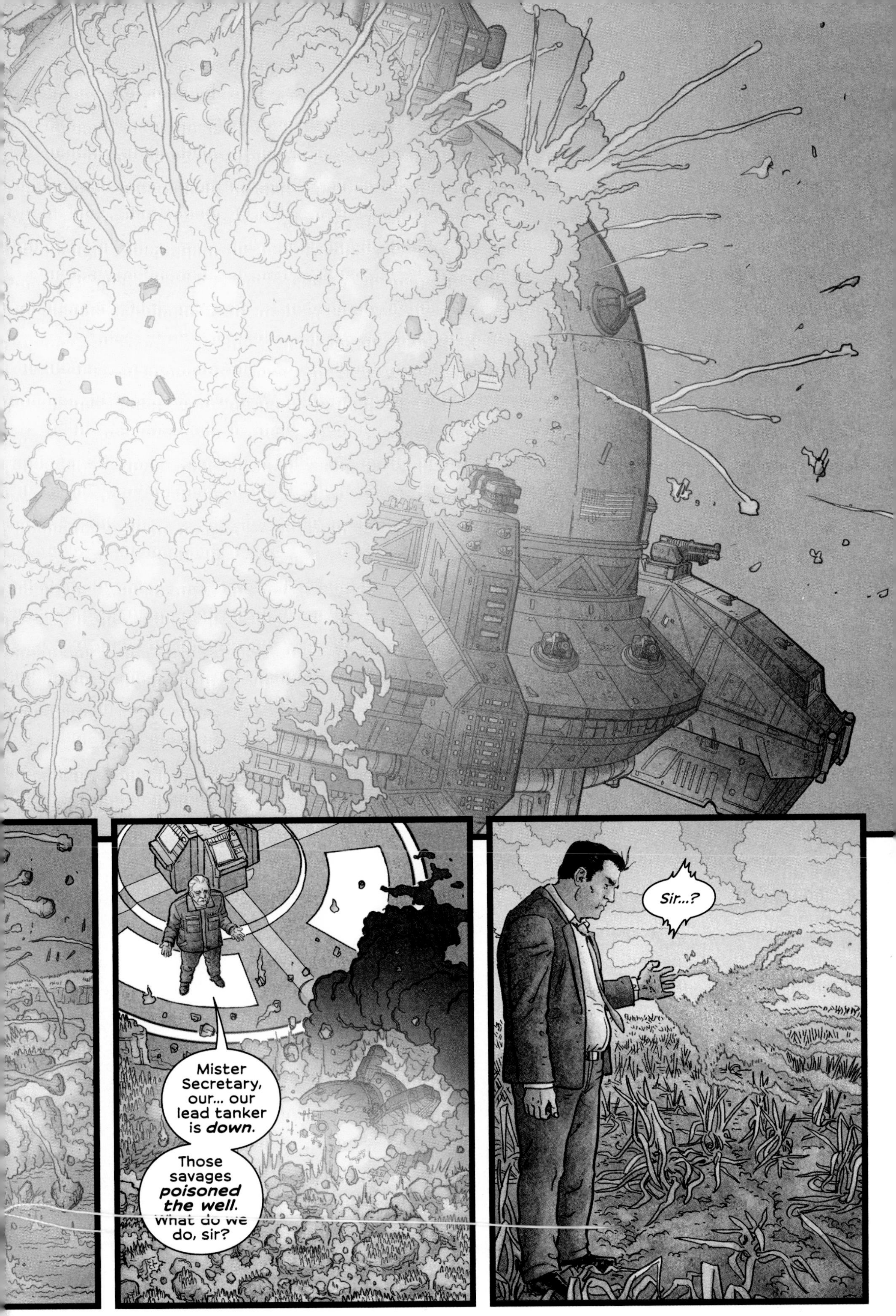

Mister Secretary, our... our lead tanker is *down*.
Those savages ***poisoned the well***. What do we do, sir?
Sir...?

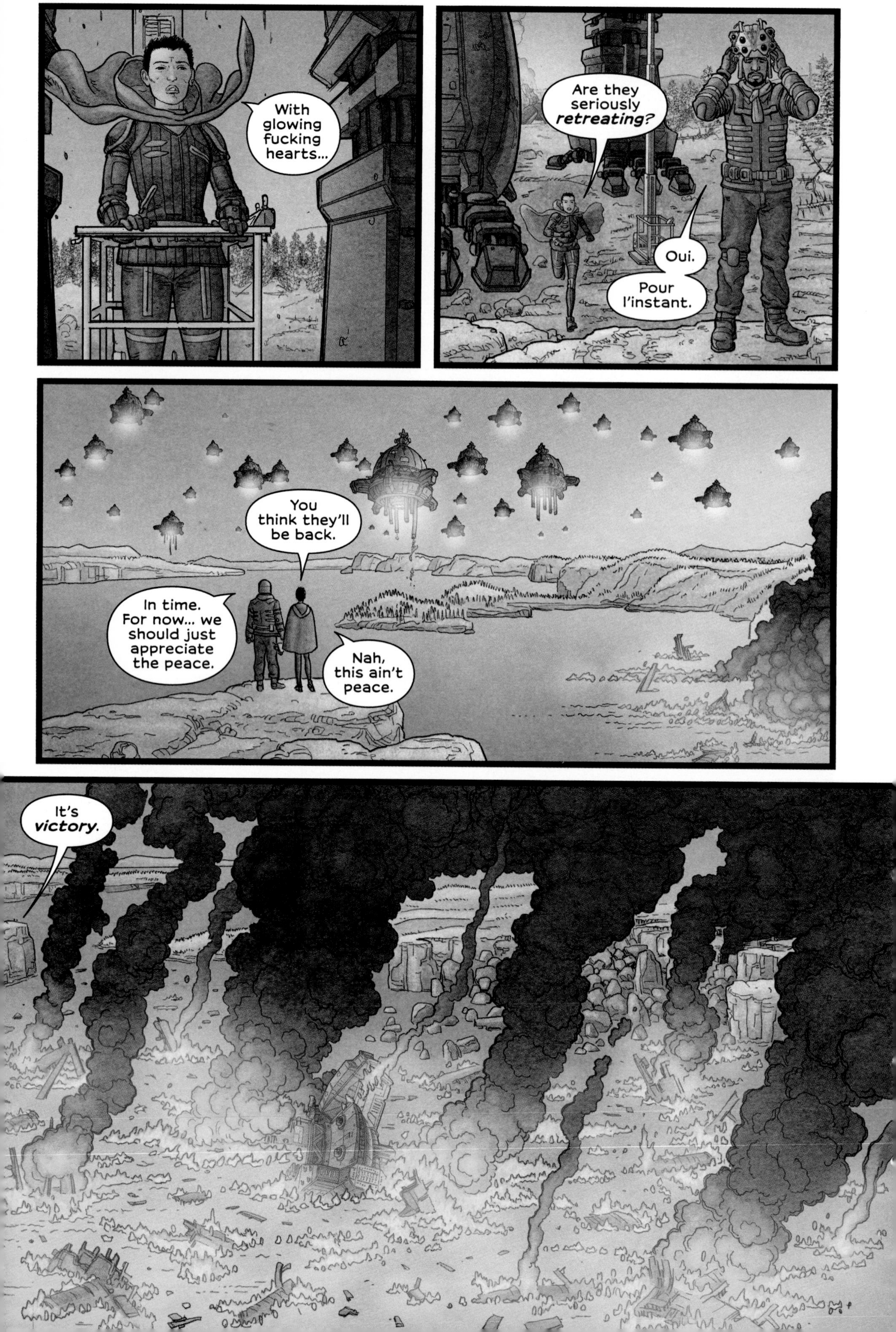
With glowing fucking hearts...
Are they seriously *retreating*?
Oui.
Pour l'instant.
You think they'll be back.
In time. For now... we should just appreciate the peace.
Nah, this ain't peace.
It's *victory*.

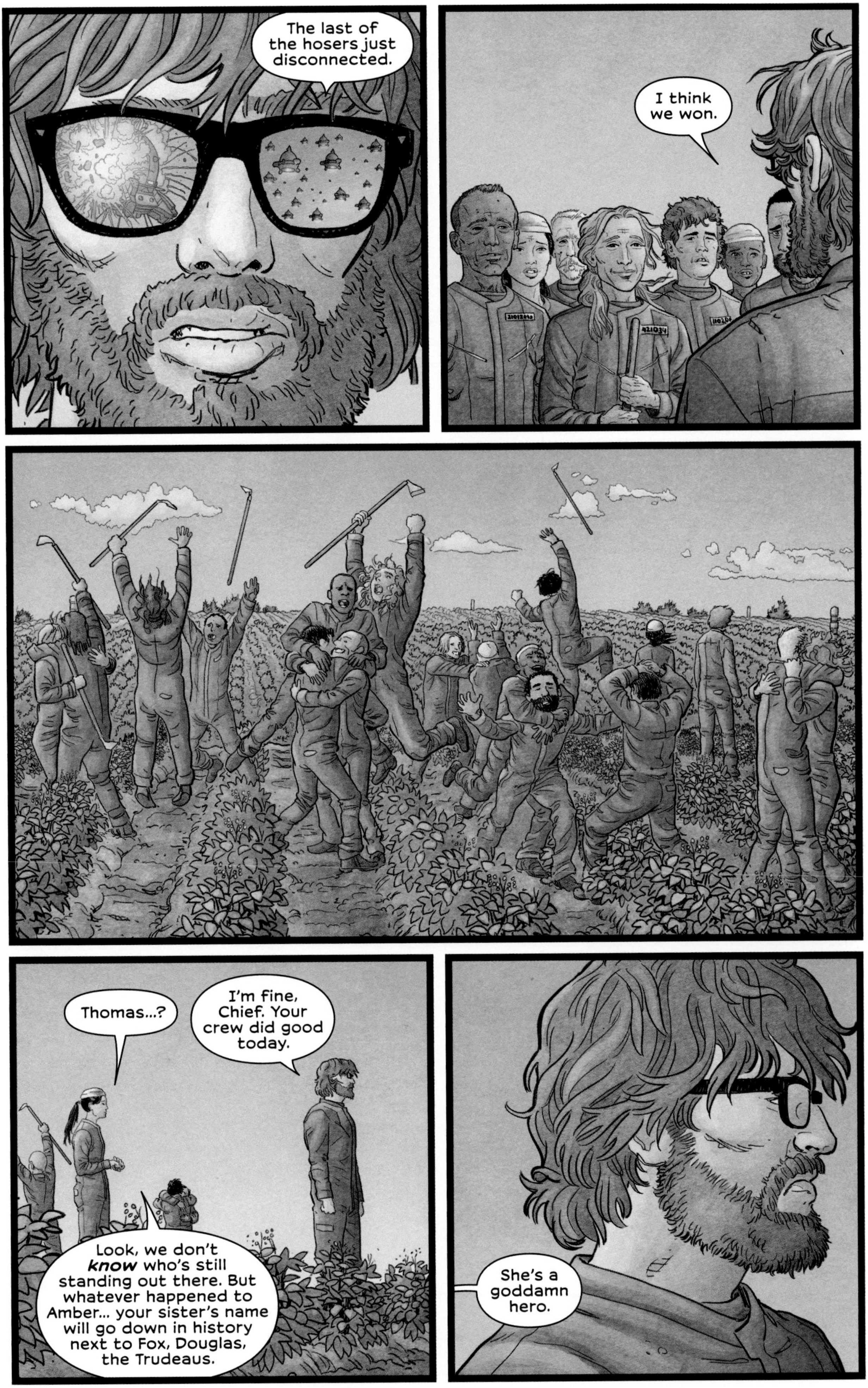
The last of the hosers just disconnected.
I think we won.
Thomas...?
I'm fine, Chief. Your crew did good today.
Look, we don't ***know*** who's still standing out there. But whatever happened to Amber... your sister's name will go down in history next to Fox, Douglas, the Trudeaus.
She's a goddamn hero.

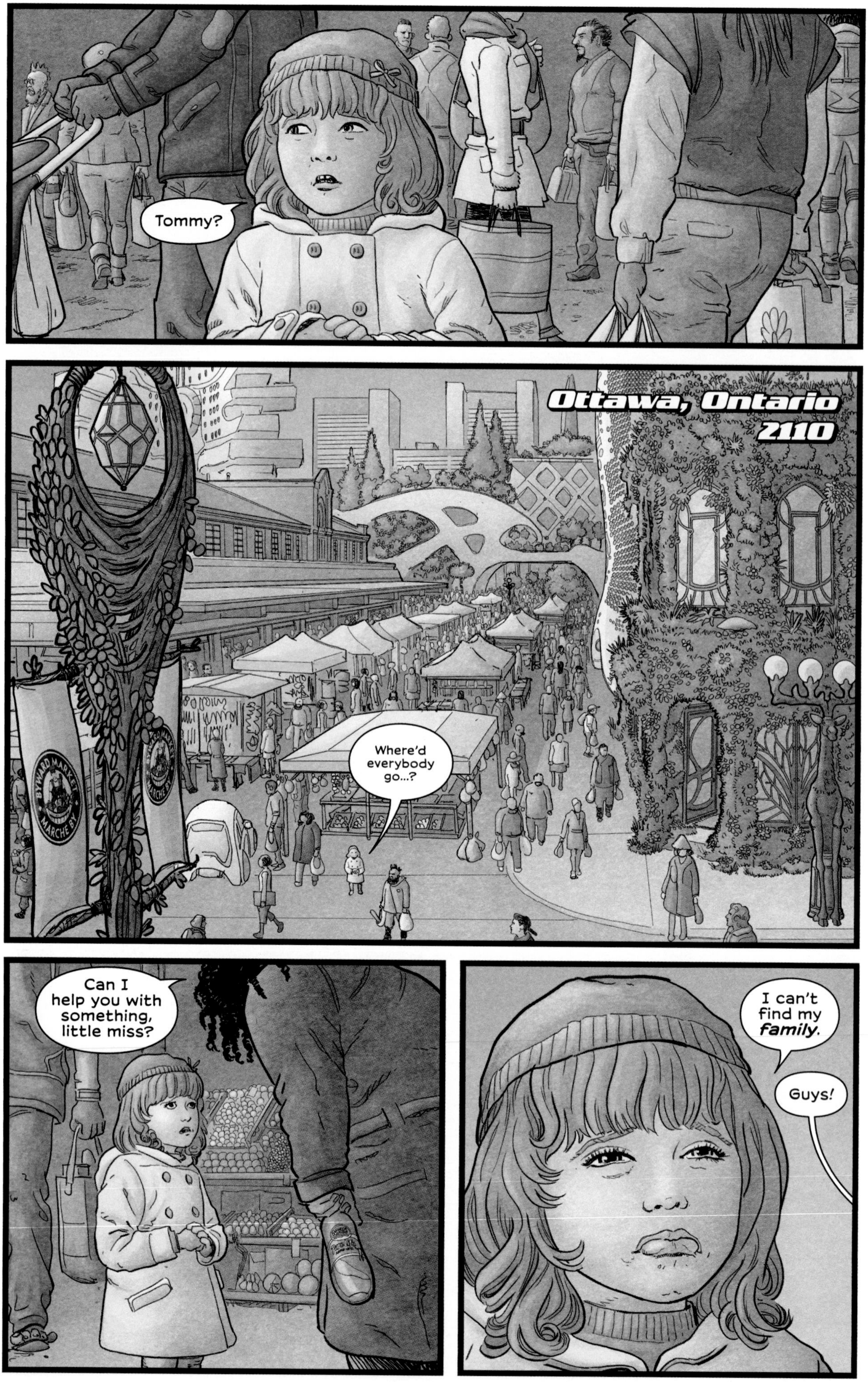
Tommy?
Ottawa, Ontario
2110
Where'd everybody go...?
Can I help you with something, little miss?
I can't find my *family*.
Guys!

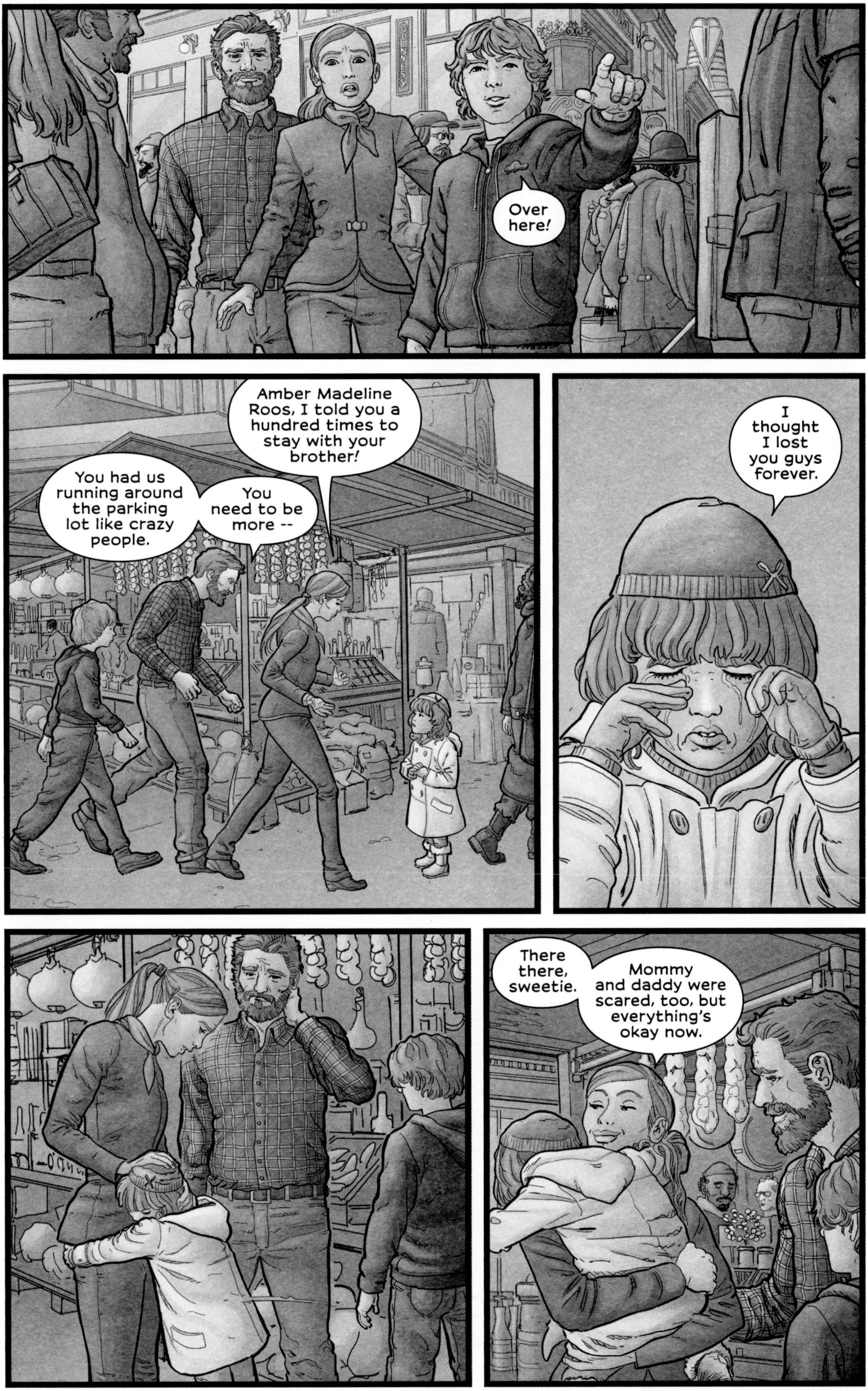

Over here!
Amber Madeline Roos, I told you a hundred times to stay with your brother!
You had us running around the parking lot like crazy people.
You need to be more --
I thought I lost you guys forever.
There there, sweetie.
Mommy and daddy were scared, too, but everything's okay now.

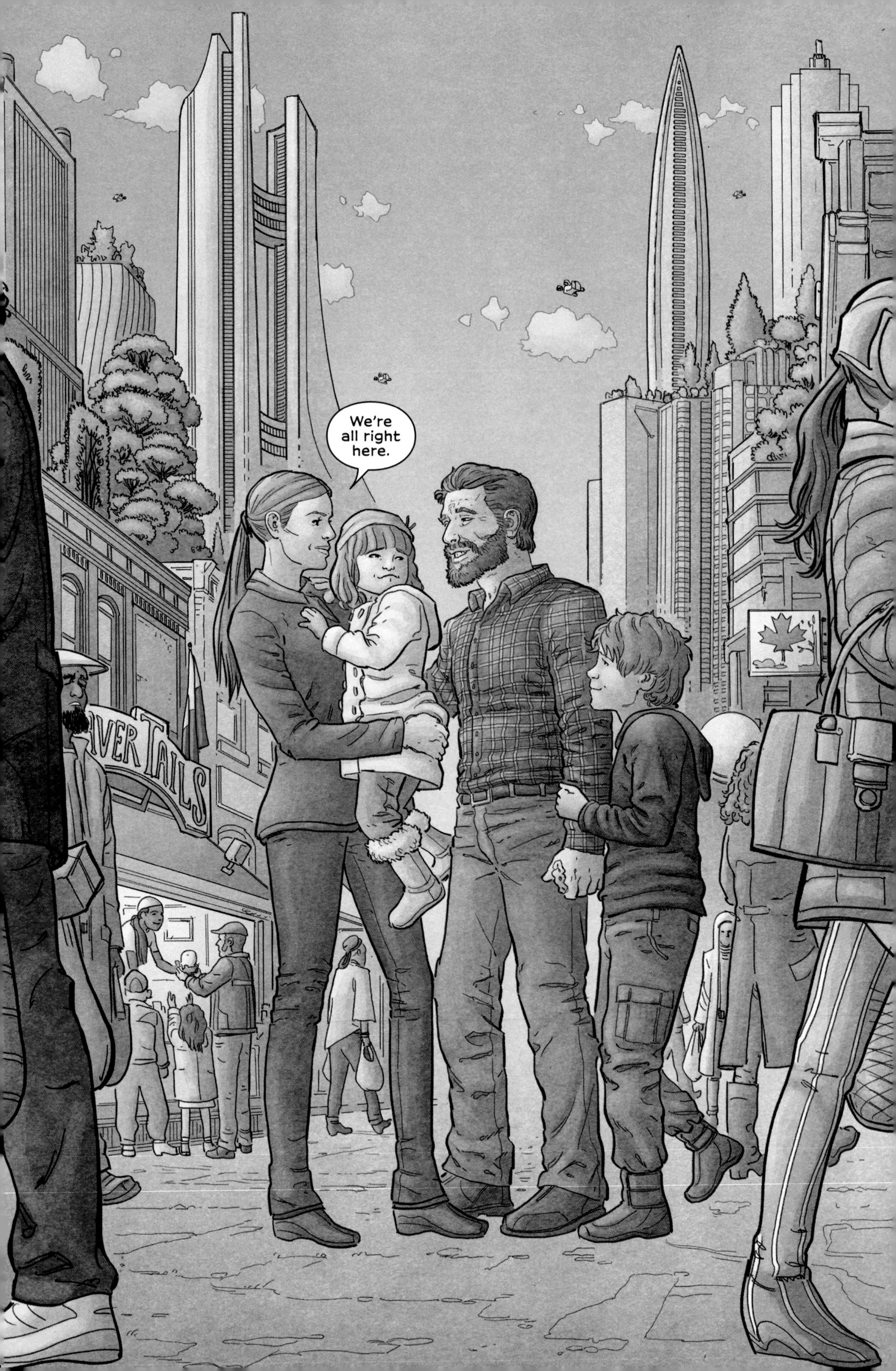
We're all right here.
AVER TAILS

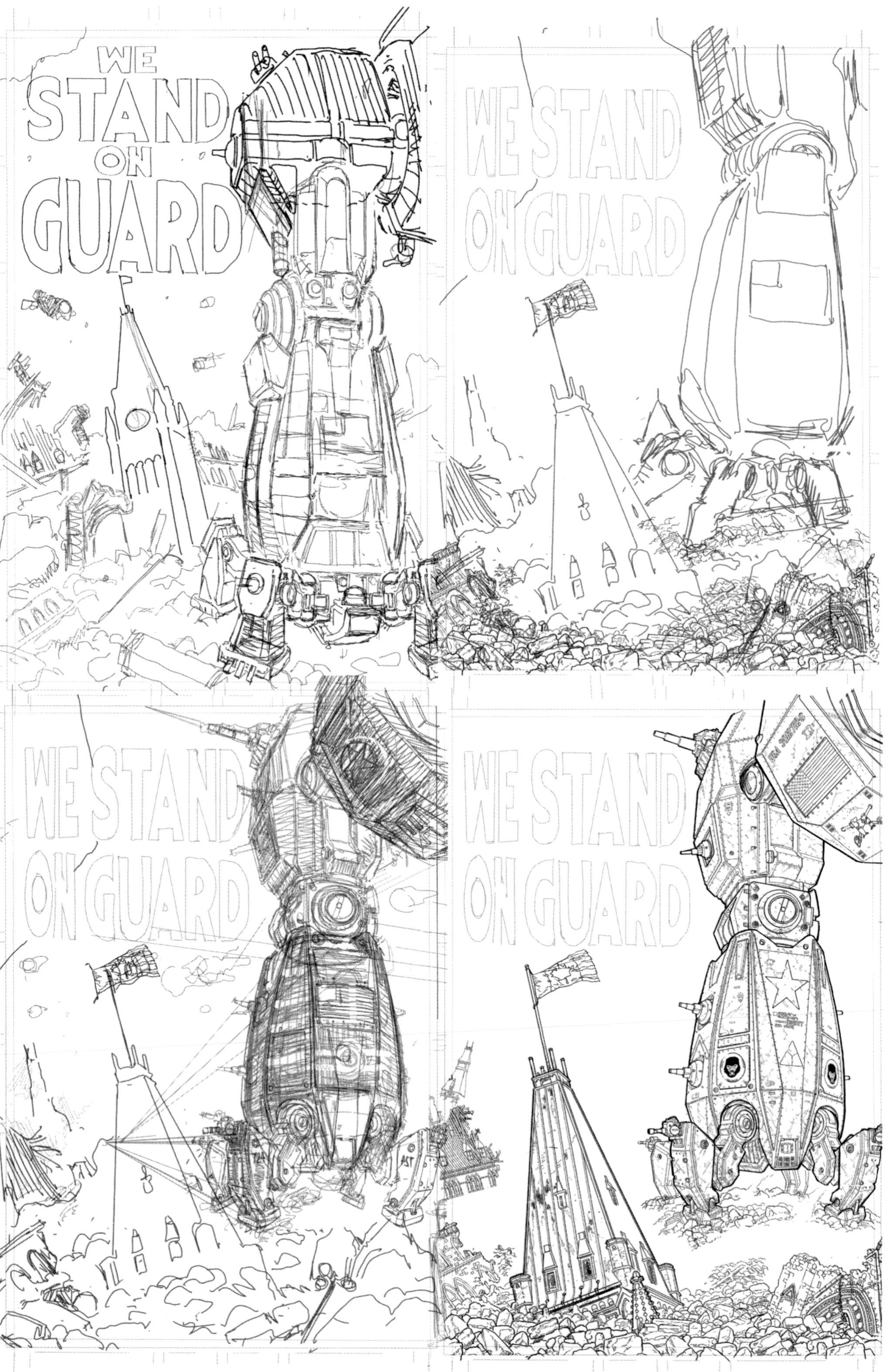
WE STAND ON GUARD
WE STAND ON GUARD
WE STAND ON GUARD
WE STAND ON GUARD

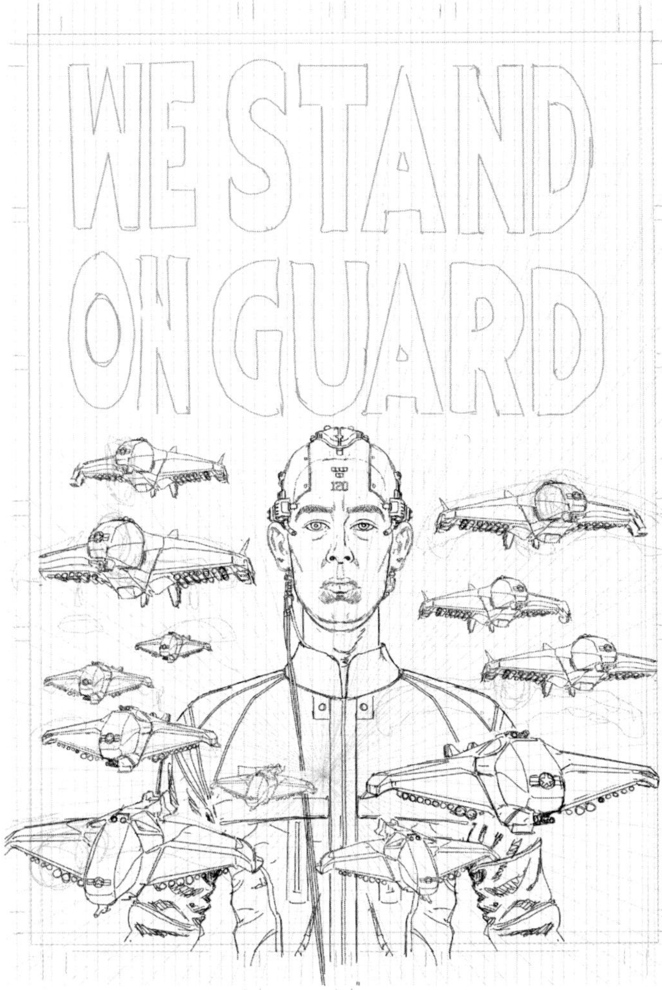
WE STAND
ON GUARD

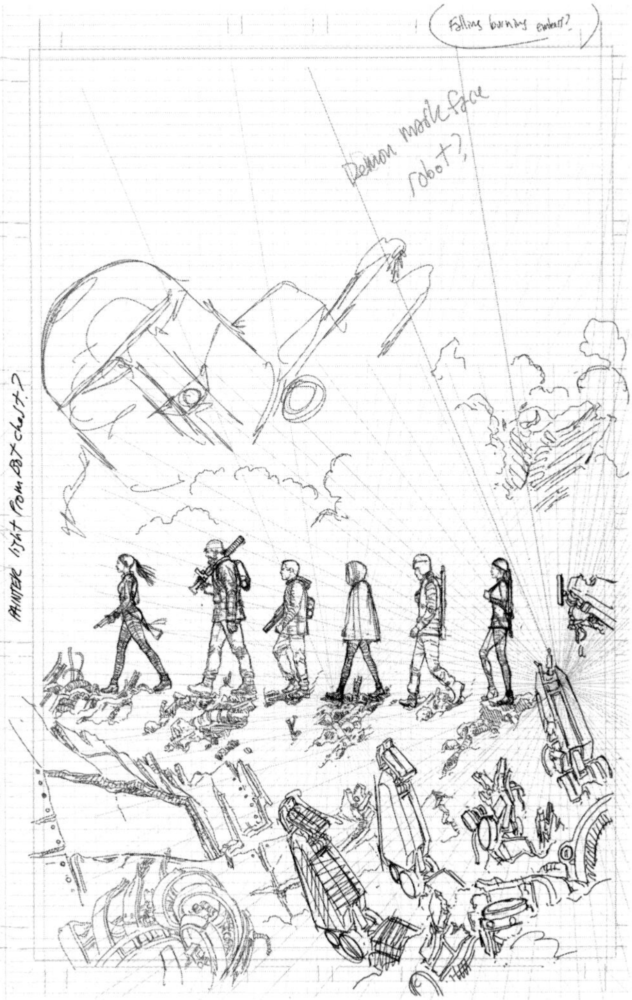
Falling burning embers?
Demon mask face
robot?
PAINTER light from BOT chest?

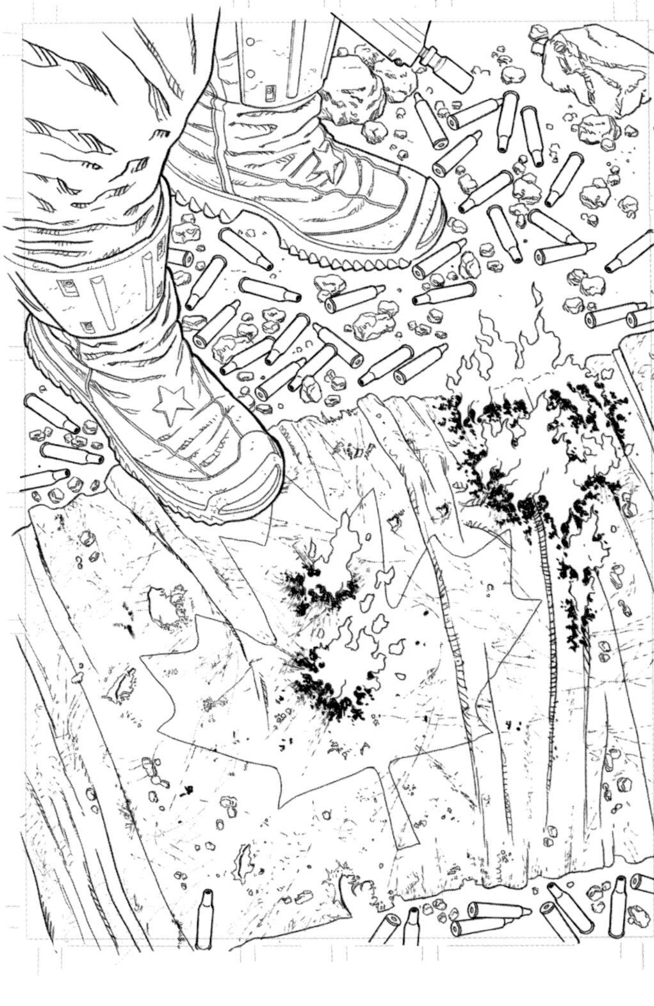

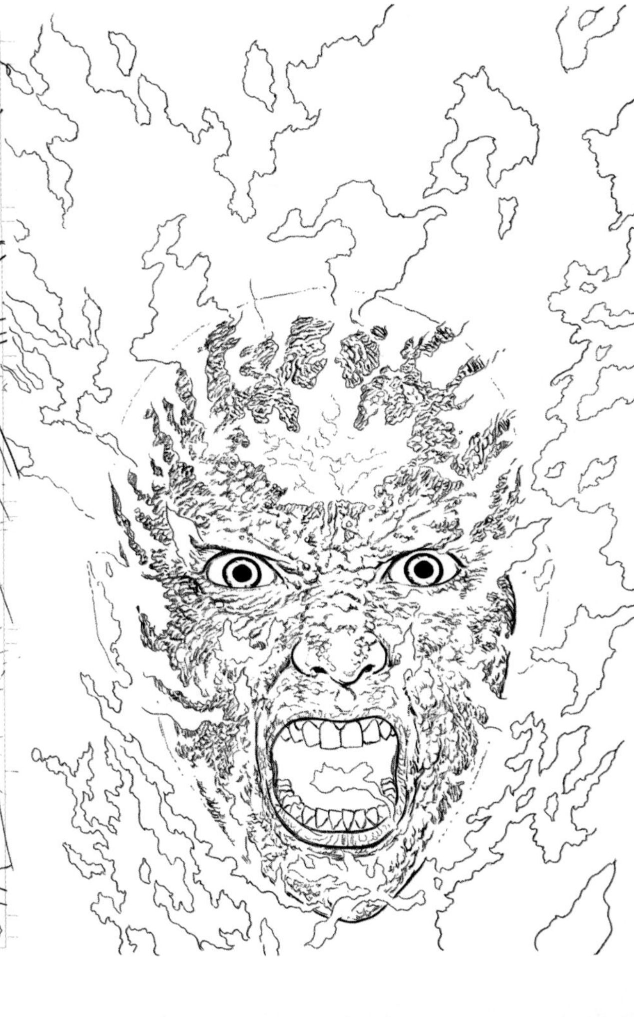

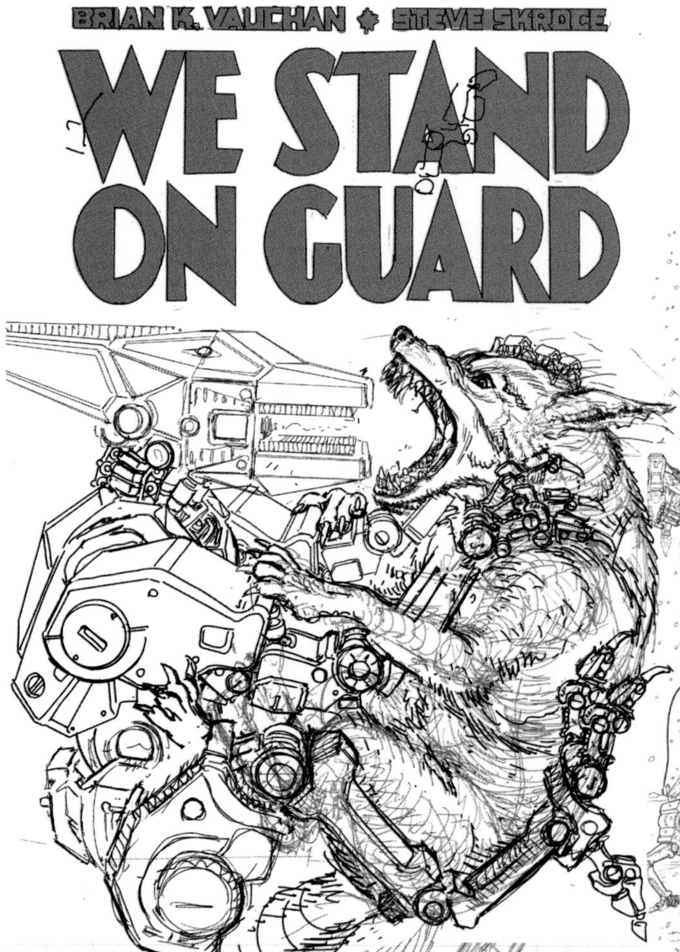
BRIAN K. VAUGHAN ✦ STEVE SKROCE
WE STAND ON GUARD

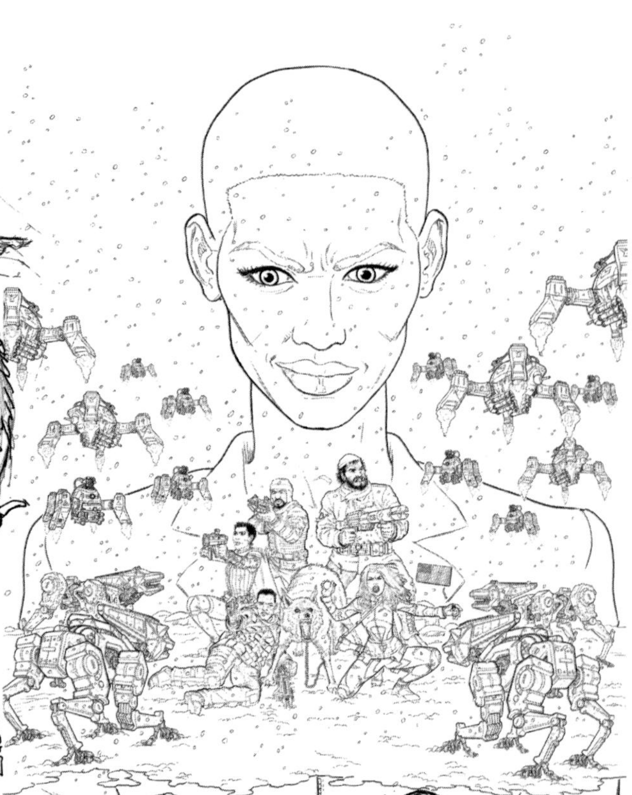

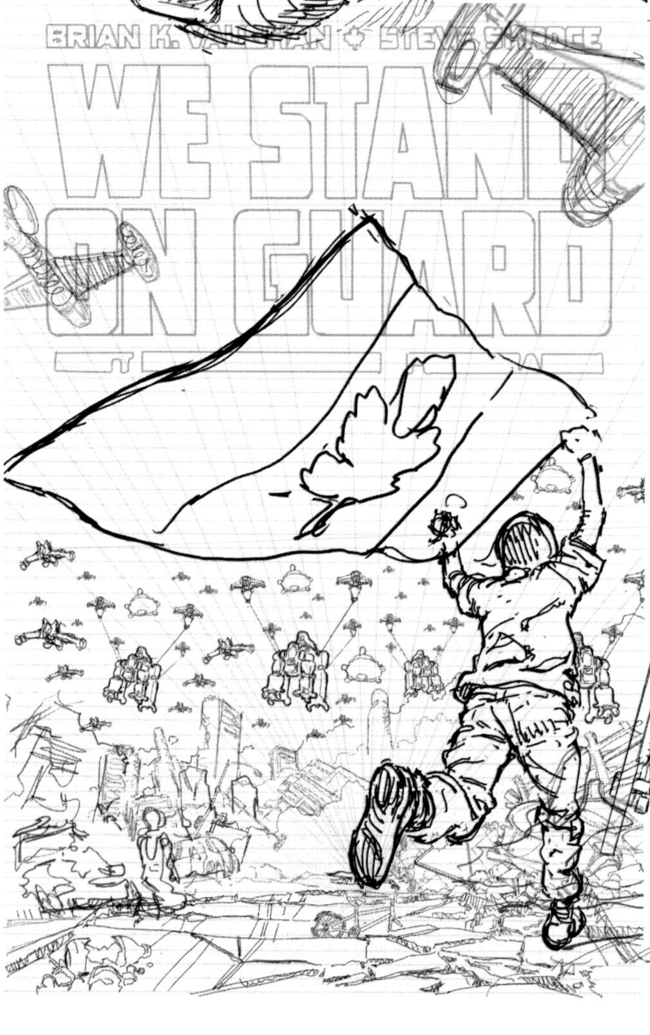
BRIAN K. VAUGHAN
WE STAN
ON GUARD

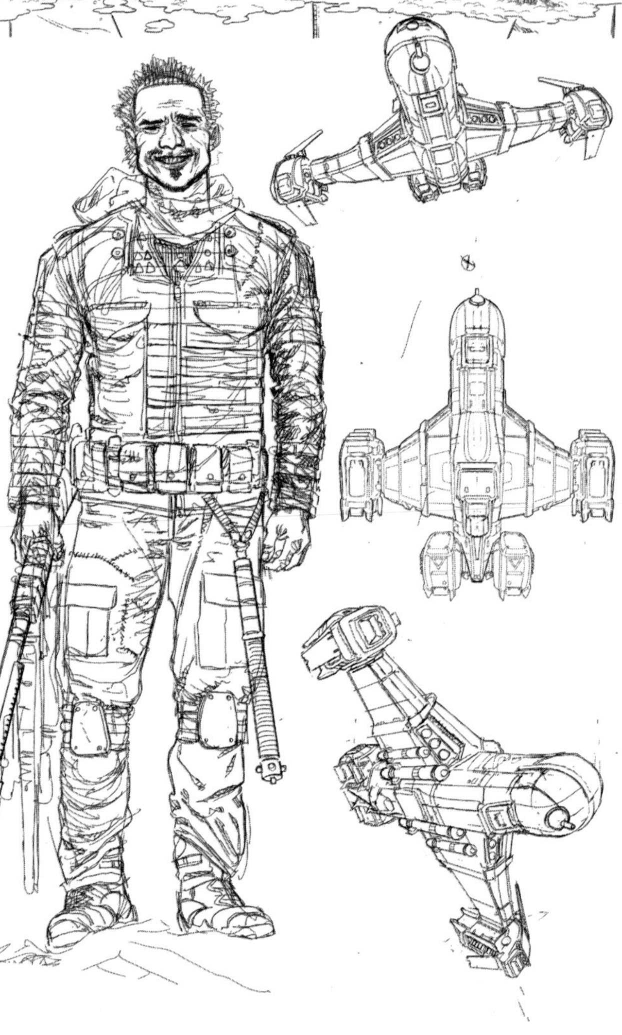

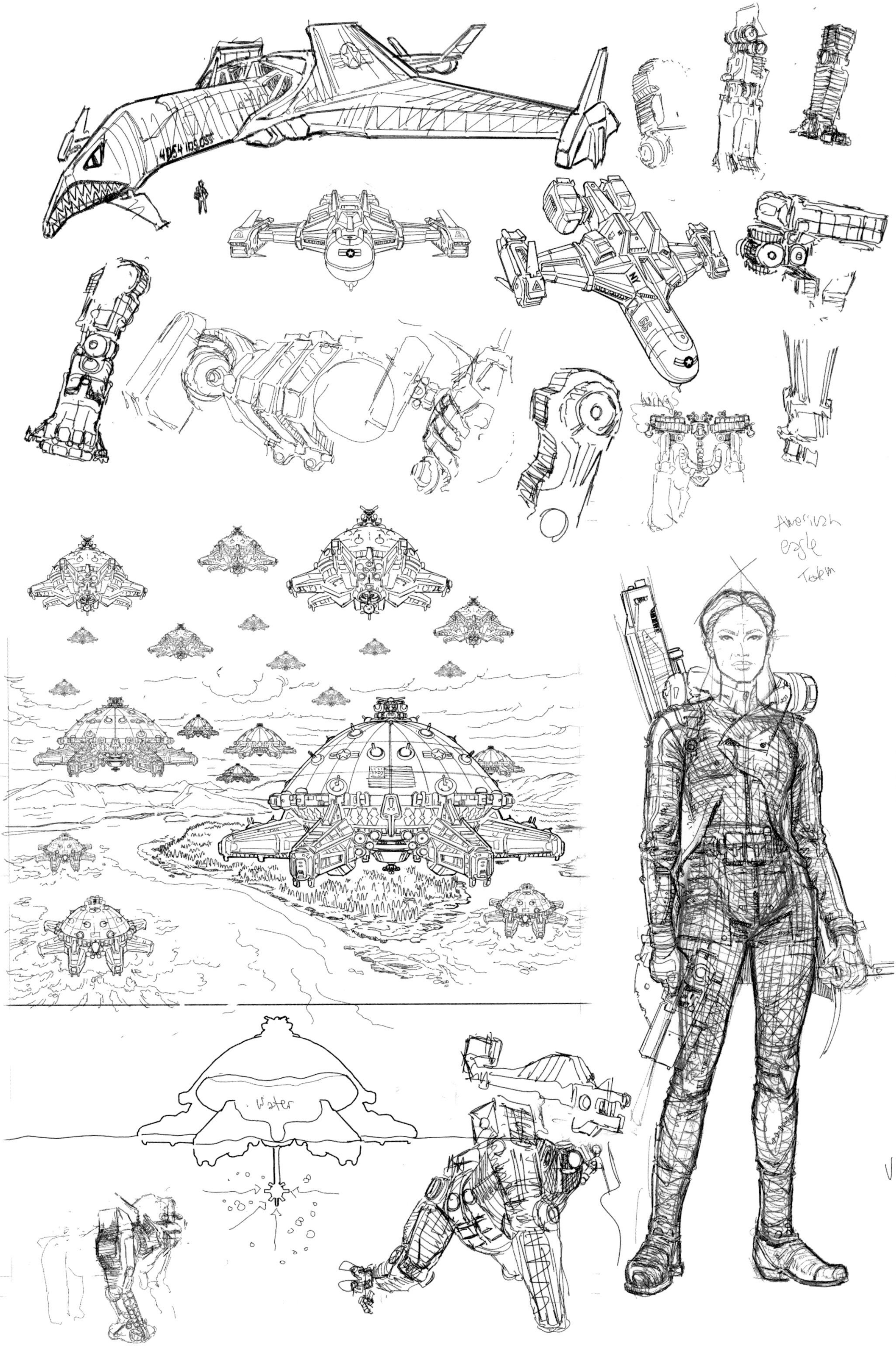
4054 105.OSS
NY
66
wings
American eagle
Water

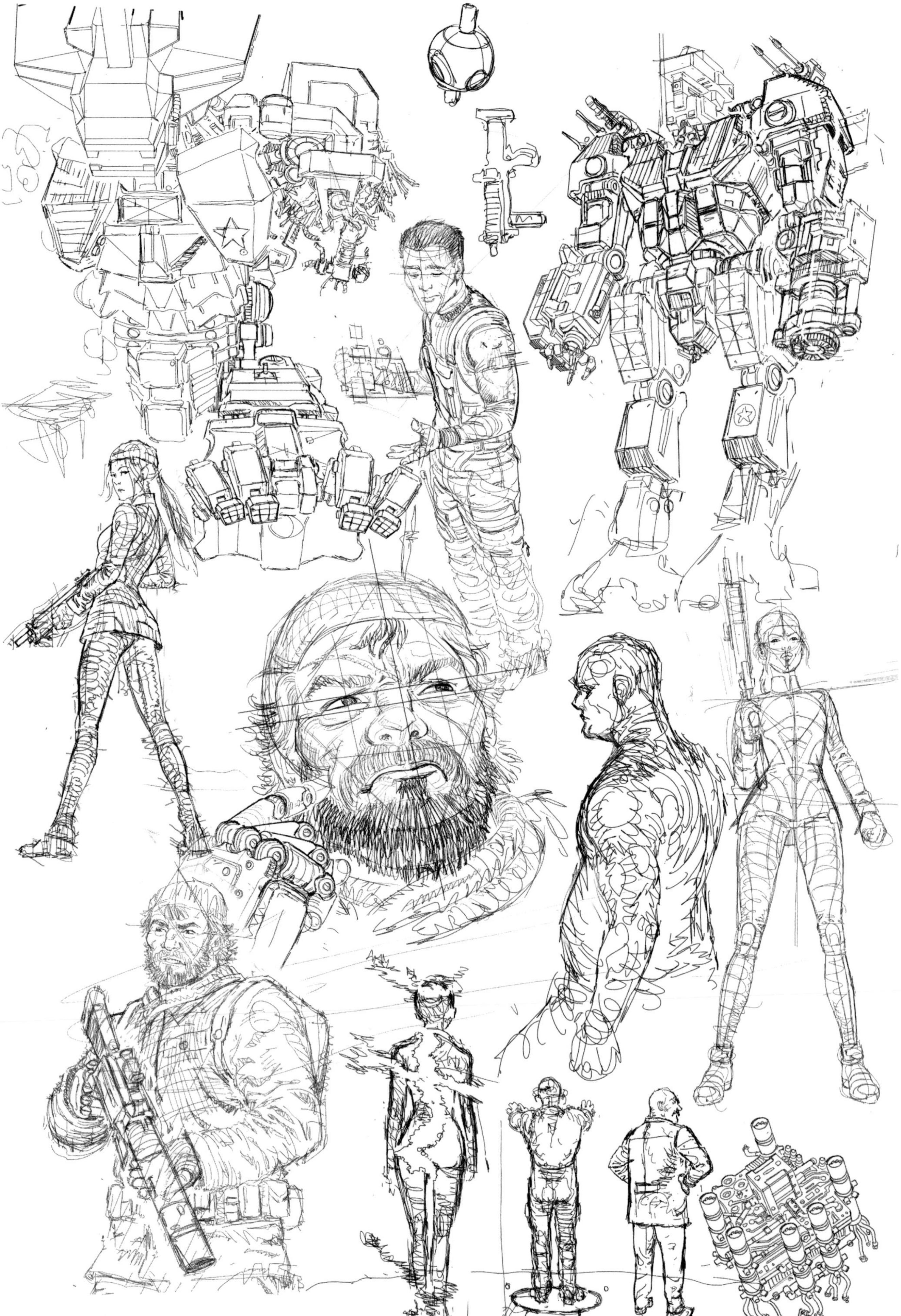

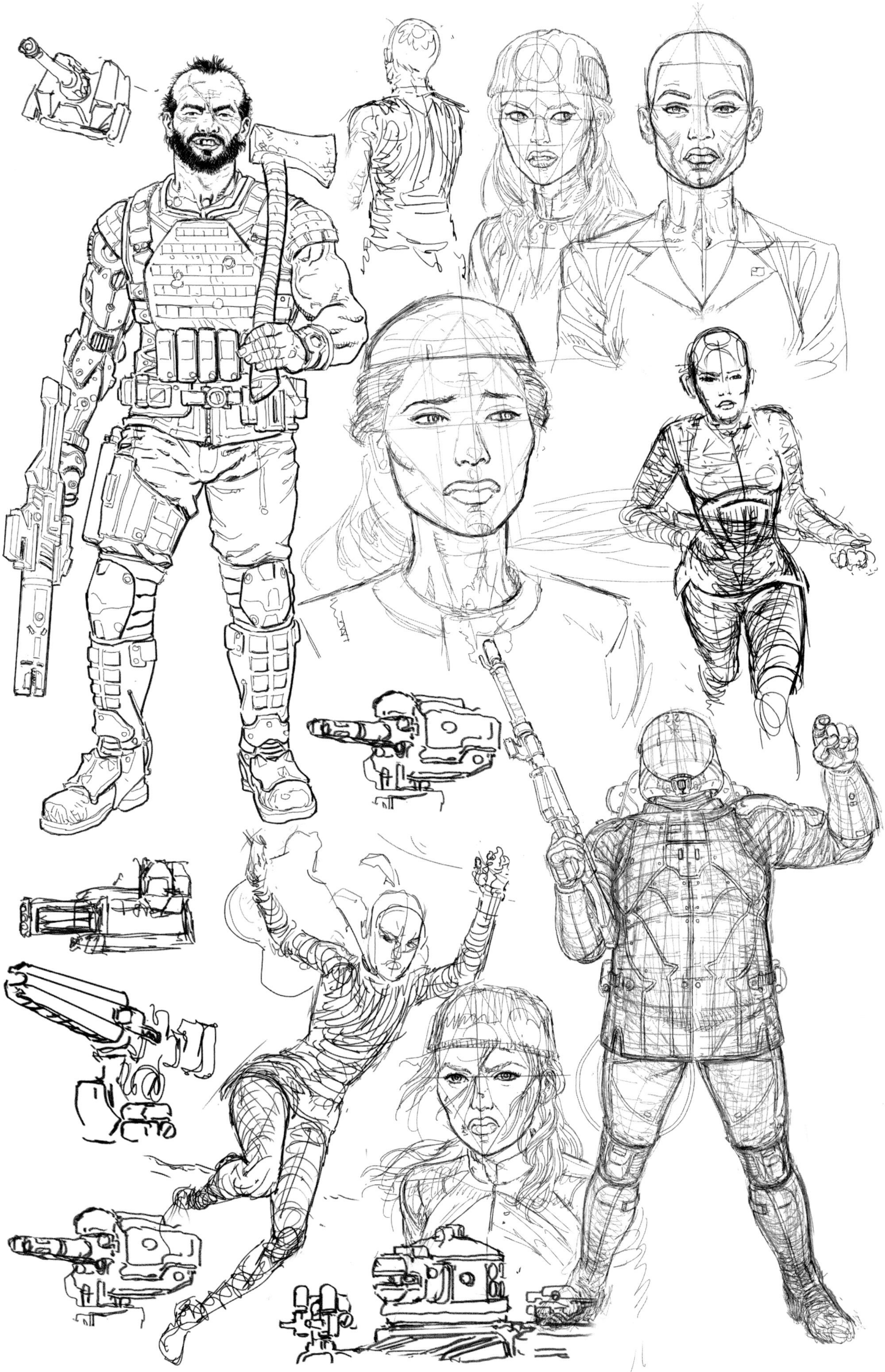

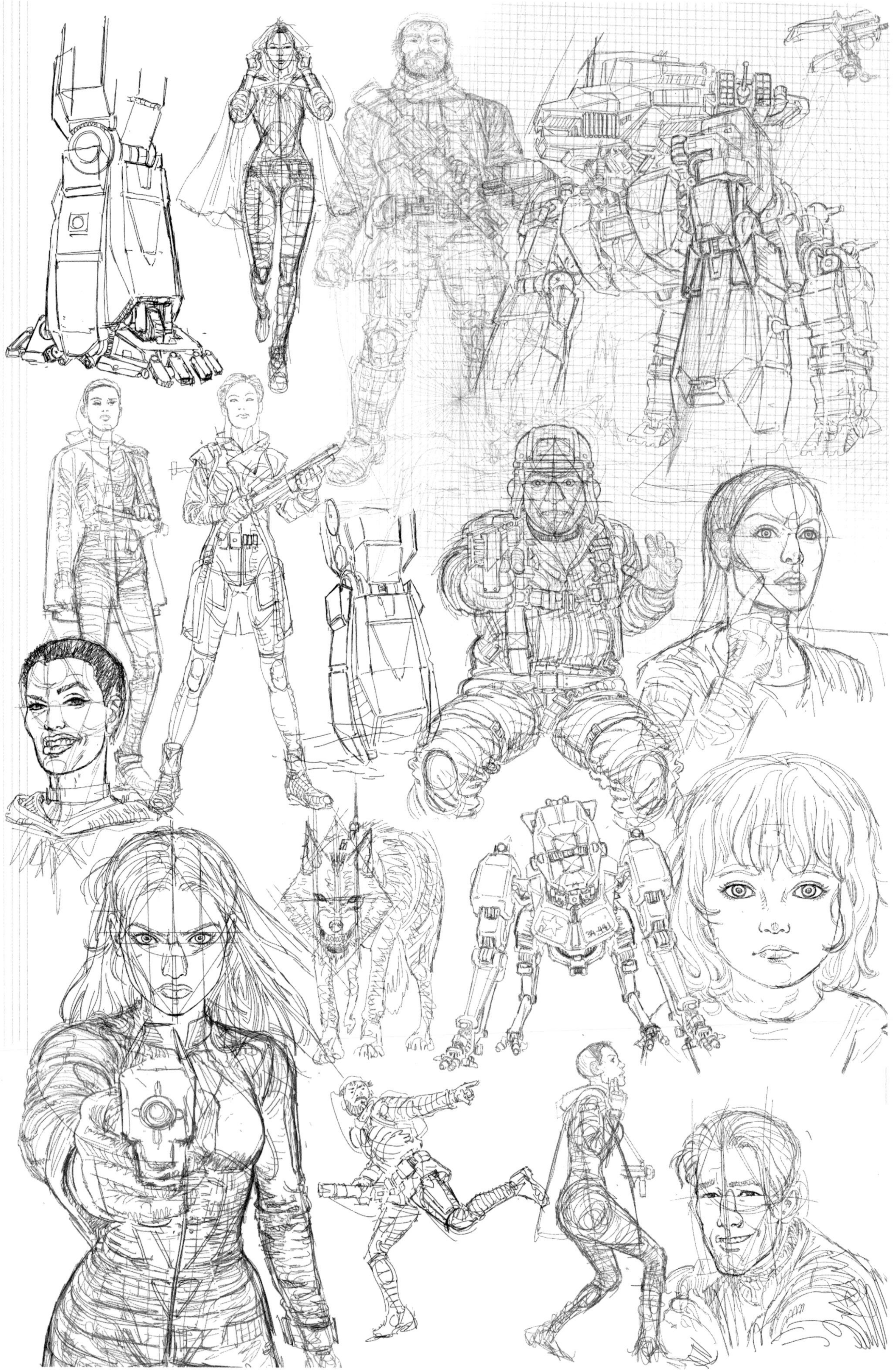

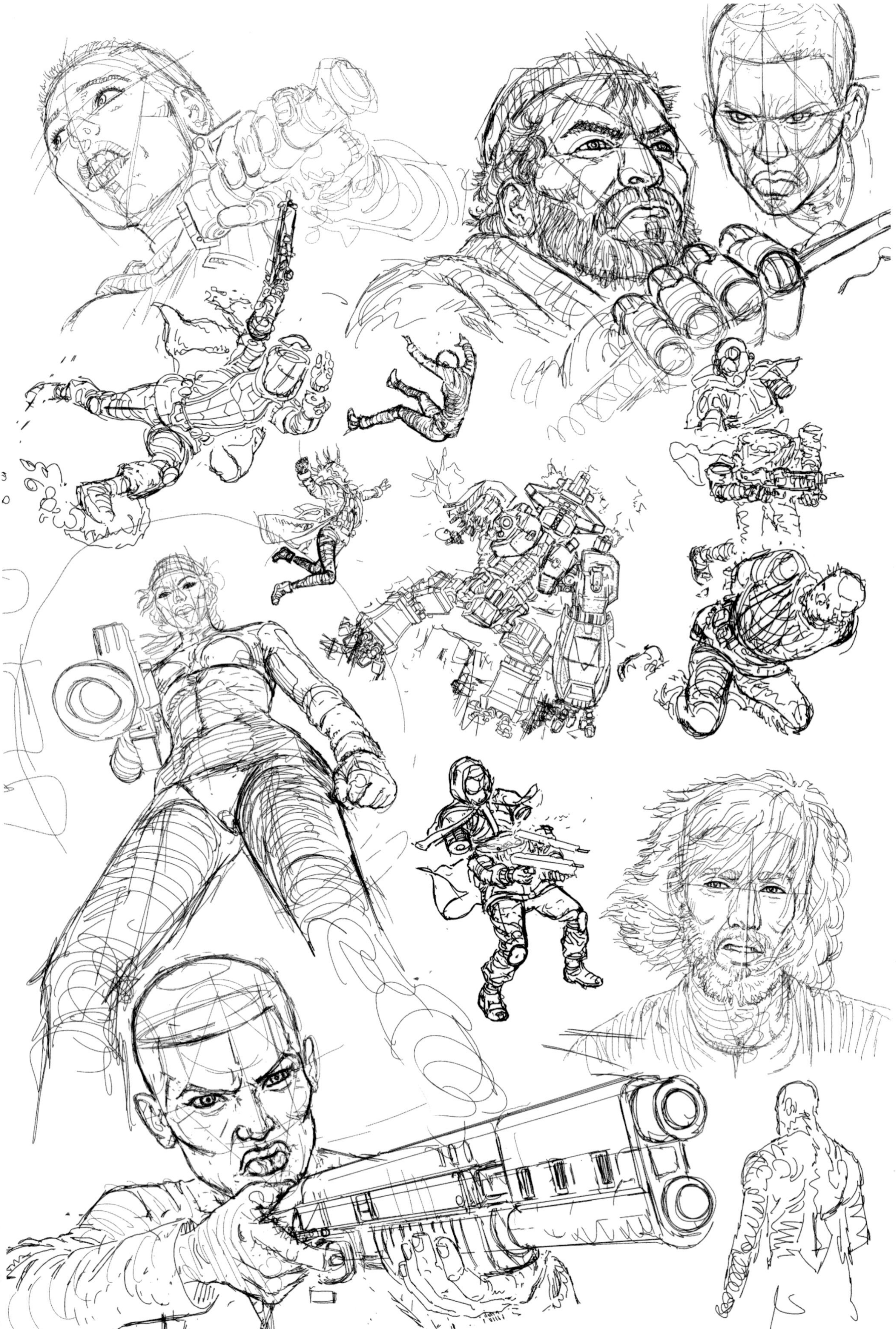

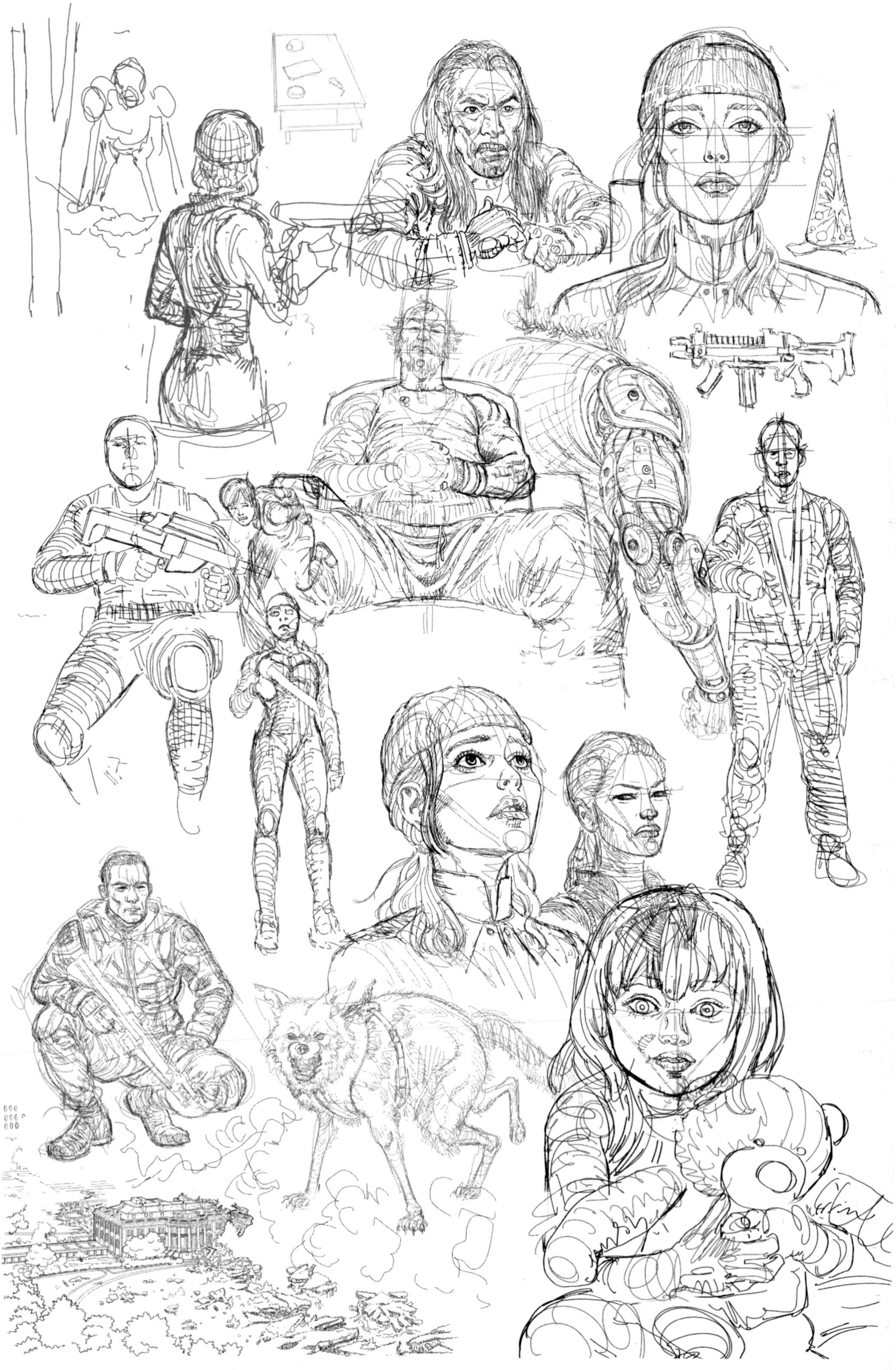